THEODORE ROOSEVELT,

THE PROGRESSIVE PARTY, AND

THE TRANSFORMATION OF

AMERICAN DEMOCRACY

AMERICAN POLITICAL THOUGHT
Wilson Carey McWilliams and Lance Banning
Founding Editors

Theodore Roosevelt, *the* Progressive Party, *and the* Transformation *of* American Democracy

Sidney M. Milkis

University Press of Kansas

Published by the University Press of Kansas (Lawrence, Kansas
66045), which was organized by the Kansas Board of Regents and
is operated and funded by Emporia State University, Fort Hays State
University, Kansas State University, Pittsburg State University, the
University of Kansas, and Wichita State University

Library of Congress Cataloging-in-Publication Data

Milkis, Sidney M.
Theodore Roosevelt, the progressive party, and the transformation
of American democracy / Sidney M. Milkis.
p. cm. — (American political thought)
Includes bibliographical references and index.
ISBN 978-0-7006-1667-1 (cloth : alk. paper)
1. Roosevelt, Theodore, 1858-1919. 2. Progressive Party (1912)
3. National Progressive Convention. 4. United States—Politics and
government—1909-1913. 5. United States—Politics and
government—1913-1921 I. Title.
E757.M65 2009
973.912—dc22   2009018212

British Library Cataloguing-in-Publication Data is available.

Printed in the United States of America

10 9 8 7 6 5 4 3 2

The paper used in this publication is recycled and contains 30
percent postconsumer waste. It is acid free and meets the minimum
requirements of the American National Standard for Permanence of
Paper for Printed Library Materials Z39.48-1992.

*Dedicated, with love and gratitude,
to my long-suffering pal, Carol;
our wonderful recalcitrant children,
Lauren, David, and Jonny;
and my best friend, Stella*

Contents

Preface

The publication of this book marks the latest stage of my ongoing effort to shed light on the progressive tradition in America. For many years, I was preoccupied by the New Deal and the way it transformed party politics in the United States. In the midst of these inquiries, however, I realized that the Progressive era offered important clues to comprehending the broader counters of subsequent reform episodes like the New Deal, the Great Society, and the Reagan "Revolution." Progressives set in motion the central political events of the twentieth century—the rise of mass democracy and the expansion of national administrative power—that continue to shape contemporary developments in American politics. The relationship between state and society has been negotiated in critical ways by the "modern" presidency, a Progressive innovation that has embodied the promise and disappointment of American democracy for the better part of a century.

My interest in reexamining progressivism was piqued by the election of 1912, "the climactic battle of the progressive era."[1] With the help of a brilliant graduate student, Daniel Tichenor, now a chaired professor at Oregon University, I undertook a study of the Progressive Party campaign, an insurgent movement that turned the presidential election of 1912 into a searching and passionate contest for the constitutional soul of the American people. With Theodore Roosevelt, the celebrated former president and most important figure of his age, as its standard-bearer, the Progressives promoted an ambitious, prescient program of economic, social, and political reform that posed profound challenges to constitutional government, at least as it was then practiced in the United States. Dubbed New Nationalism, this program not only commanded a large following but also provoked an extraordinary debate about the future of the country.

The most nutritious fruit of these early labors—a major article that Dan and I coauthored for *Studies in American Political Development*[2]—inspired me to extend these initial inquiries into a book that would attend more carefully to the constitutional debate that the Progressive Party aroused, examine how the other three candidates—William Howard Taft, Woodrow Wilson, and Eugene Debs—reacted to Roosevelt's insurgent campaign, and further mine the very rich archival record that I had begun to uncover. My primary research included an extensive examination of the press's election coverage—both domestic and foreign—that trumpeted the novelty and significance of this presidential contest.

The inspiration to do a more expansive study of the Progressive Party campaign received important and timely support from the director of the University Press of Kansas, Fred Woodward, and my dear late friend Wilson Carey McWilliams, coeditor of Kansas' American Political Thought series. Fred and Carey were as excited as was I at the prospect of a study that would not only examine the most significant developments of this extraordinary campaign but also shed light on the many features of the Progressive Party's political practices and program that would become important ingredients of contemporary politics.

Little did I know at the time that this study would occupy me for more than a decade. Fred Woodward, bless his heart, grew to doubt—if not to regret—the faith he invested in me! Still, he remained exceptionally gracious to the end of a long hard road and helped me realize the full potential of the manuscript. I am also deeply appreciative for the patience and generosity of others at the press, including Michael Briggs, Susan Schott, and Jennifer Dropkin, and freelance copy editor Michelle Asakawa.

Although I am chagrined that it took me so long to complete this book, the delay was felicitous in one respect: it allowed me to end the story with the remarkable campaign of Democratic Senator Barack Obama of Illinois, who has promised to inaugurate a new progressive era. The 2008 election well illustrates how progressivism is best understood as a movement of public opinion that keeps getting brought back to life by the right combination of charismatic leadership and structural change. In fact, both candidates,

Senator Obama and the Republican candidate, Senator John McCain of Arizona, channeled Theodore Roosevelt in their pursuit of the presidency. It was Senator Obama, however, who sounded the loudest trumpet for progressive democracy. The way he won over the country, I would argue, suggests that he was cast perfectly—at a time when America was mired in war and economic crisis—as the leader of the "inspired idealism" that Roosevelt exalted. Obama's successful quest for the presidency, dedicated to so many of the causes that the Progressive Party first celebrated, vividly reminds us that the political principles and practices championed by TR in 1912 have become a powerful, enduring part of our political life.

It is very unlikely that I would have pursued this project so doggedly without the institutional and intellectual support I have gained from my colleagues who share my deep interest in American political development. Along the way, I received helpful comments and encouragement from Walter Dean Burnham, University of Texas; Martha Derthick, University of Virginia; Michael Greve, American Enterprise Institute; Richard Harris, Rutgers University; Mark Hulliung, Brandeis University; Charles Kessler, Claremont McKenna College; Marc Landy, Boston College; Cathie Jo Martin, Boston University; Eileen McDonagh, Northeastern University; Jerome Mileur, University of Massachusetts, Amherst; Michael Nelson, Rhodes College; A. James Reichley, formerly of the Brookings Institution; Jesse Rhodes, University of Massachusetts, Amherst; Bruce Schulman, Boston University; and Jean Yarbrough, Bowdoin College, who offered a generous portion of tough love in reviewing the manuscript for Kansas. The book also benefitted greatly from the research support of Peter Ubertaccio, now a faculty member of Stone Hill College, who worked with me as a graduate student at Brandeis University. Lori Fritz and Emily Charnock gave me indispensable assistance after I joined the faculty of the University of Virginia.

I am especially grateful to Stephen Skowronek of Yale University, who as coeditor of *Studies* provided indispensable support and counsel in launching the project and, as good friend and colleague, gently urged me over the years to complete it. The finished product, I hope, is a good representative of the "APD" field, which owes so much of its prominence to Steve. As a proud member of this multidisciplinary academic movement, I have tried to write a book that combines analytical rigor, careful attention to primary sources, and an appreciation for historical narrative.

After an introduction that places the Progressive Party in the broad stream of American political development, subsequent chapters explore TR's dramatic return to political life; his challenge for the Republican presidential nomination; reformers' plans for a new party; sources of comity and tension within the Progressive Party; the general election; and the meaning of the Bull Moose campaign, as TR famously called it, for American politics and government. In depicting the history of the Progressive Party and the fascinating 1912 election, my particular concern has been to shed light on the intellectual history that shaped it, to uncover the singular debate in American history among those who championed, reluctantly accepted, or abhorred the Progressive Party's conception of democracy.

The story begins with Roosevelt's trip to Europe in 1910, where he began to develop the ideas he would champion in challenging the incumbent president, William Howard Taft, for the Republican nomination and spurring the Progressive Party into existence. A pragmatic reformer as president, who adroitly collaborated with "standpat" conservative Republican leaders in Congress to enact modest progressive legislation, Roosevelt now expressed a serious interest in establishing a more advanced form of social democracy in the United States than he dared contemplate during his nearly two terms in the White House. Once back on American soil, Roosevelt fleshed out a highly ambitious reform program that linked his insurgent campaign to a broader movement that had its origins in political, economic, and social developments at the end of the nineteenth century. These developments formed the backdrop of efforts to bring the various strains of the Progressive movement together as an agent of national reconstruction toward the end of 1911. Encouraged by the cresting of a movement dedicated to fundamental social, economic, and political change, Roosevelt called for measures such as national health insurance, government-led industrial planning, women's suffrage, the direct election of senators, popular referenda on court rulings, and the universal use of the direct primary.

Roosevelt's bold reform proposals were part and parcel of his competition with Senator Robert La Follette of Wisconsin for the mantle of progressive leader. As they jostled to get in front of the progressive parade, La Follette and Roosevelt each played a critical role in giving form to, and amplifying, the principles that would set the tone of the 1912 election. With their speeches and activities, La Follette and TR summoned the forces of reform to oppose President Taft's reelection. These forces, in turn, set in motion a battle for the Republican nomination that challenged the rules and practices that had dominated the presidential selection process in the United States since the early part of the nineteenth century. For the first time in history, the presidential primary, advanced by frantic reform efforts in the states during the election year, became a significant part of a presidential campaign. Just as important, La Follette and Roosevelt formed candidate-centered organizations to circumvent the regular Republican Party apparatus and to appeal directly to voters. In the course of challenging Taft and prevailing political routines, La Follette and TR became bitter rivals. This intramural conflict went deeper than a fight for the right to represent the Republican Party, however; the right to command the emerging forces of reform was also at stake. Although he failed to wrest the nomination away from the incumbent president, Roosevelt's success in the primaries established him, rather than La Follette, as the apostle of progressive democracy and prepared the ground for his campaign as the head of a new party.

The Progressive Party that Roosevelt and his followers created was not just an agent for Roosevelt's ambitions, as most historians and political scientists have claimed, but also a collective enterprise that involved the vital participation of social reformers. The array of activists who gravitated to the Progressive Party looked to a national program of reform dedicated to direct democracy and social justice. Roosevelt gave forceful expression to this collective obligation, in which the new entitlements that the Progressive program promised were to be complemented by a strong sense of duty toward one's family, neighborhood, voluntary associations, and, ultimately, the national political community. With the Progressive program, reformers hoped to create a new concept of citizenship that would fulfill the lofty aspirations for the nation described in the Preamble of the Constitution. But these hopes to engage "We the People" in a quest for a "more perfect Union" were diminished by fierce battles over how to deal with issues like race and business regulation that threatened to fracture the third party.

Hoping to deflect attention from these struggles, Roosevelt emphasized the Progressives' dedication to "pure democracy," which would establish a more personal, unmediated relationship between public officials and public opinion. Although they disagreed about how to deal with the "Negro question" and what measures should be adopted to reform the economy, Progressives tended to agree on the need to recast or create institutions and practices that would nurture a direct system of popular rule on a national scale.

The Progressive commitment to making the American people "masters of their Constitution" provoked considerable controversy during the general election, inspiring Taft and Wilson to attack TR as a demagogue who would undo the founders' statecraft. Yet claiming he was fulfilling the Constitution's bold experiment to provide self-government on a grand scale, TR did not flinch in the face of the controversy that the Progressive program for pure democracy aroused in the country. Realizing that the doctrine of popular rule held together the movement he sought to lead, his defense of it became bolder throughout 1912. Indeed, Roosevelt announced during the general election campaign that "he would go even further than the Progressive platform," for example, subjecting all public officials, including the president, to the recall of voters.[3] Significantly, Roosevelt's unabashed promotion of dramatic electoral and constitutional reform reflected a matter of Progressive Party doctrine, an unwavering devotion to direct democracy. The reforms TR championed made his own candidate-centered campaign, endorsed by the Progressive Party platform, a central issue of the election. Ironically, this doctrinal faith in a more plebiscitary form of democracy would rob the Progressive Party of the organization necessary for surviving the absence of its larger-than-life presidential candidate. In large measure, the demise of the Progressive Party before the 1916 election followed from the almost hopeless task of reconciling loyalty to the progressive idea of democracy with loyalty to a collective organization. Indeed, the challenge of uniting charismatic leadership and progressive causes would continue to plague reformers throughout the twentieth and twenty-first centuries.

The book concludes with an examination of the progressive legacy for American constitutional democracy. The Progressive Party involved an impressive effort, an "experiment" TR called it, to articulate a coherent philosophy and comprehensive program. In undertaking these tasks, its leaders were deeply divided over civil rights and antitrust policy. Moreover, with the approach of World War I, the Progressive movement was further fractured by fundamental disagreements among its leaders over the role of the United States in the world. Arguably, the failure of the 1912 experiment and the party's subsequent decline underscore the incoherence of the Progressive movement. Still, the Progressive Party is appropriately viewed as an effort to define progressivism, temporarily housing a movement of public opinion rather than party, affecting the prestige and fortunes of all political leaders. Beyond the 1912 election the party's program of social reform and "direct democracy" has been an enduring feature of American politics and governance.

Furthermore, the "critical" election of 1912—the fierce, exalted battle waged by the Progressive Party and its critics—marked a fundamental departure in constitutional principles and practices, which progressives and conservatives alike would eventually embrace. Roosevelt and other leaders of the Progressive Party argued with considerable effect that they did not seek to destroy the Constitution but, instead, to revitalize and democratize it. Indeed, without the strengthening of the presidency and the greater national resolve that followed from progressive reform, it is difficult to imagine how the United States would have met the profound challenges posed by economic and racial injustices at home and totalitarian threats abroad. At the same time, in subordinating natural rights to public opinion and limited constitutional government to national administration, Progressives contributed mightily to our current political predicament. Americans strongly support the national government assuming an ever-increasing number of complex domestic and international responsibilities, even as they claim to abhor the national administrative power that follows logically from the expansion of government programs and policies. Meanwhile, "pure democracy," which Progressives prescribed to connect individual men and women to the "modern" state, mocks the Progressive concept of "enlightened administration" and risks exposing citizens to the sort of public figures who exploit their impatience with the difficult tasks of sustaining a healthy representative democracy.

The burden of contemporary reformers who would carry forward the progressive torch is to recapture the understanding of leadership and democracy that has made momentous reconstructions of politics so central to the pursuit of the nation's destiny since the dawn of the twentieth century. Presently at the center of Americans' hopes and discontents, the progressive idea of politics and government is a critical starting point for still another searching look at the meaning and responsibilities of American democracy. This book, I hope, shows how a reconsideration of the extraordinary election of 1912 might contribute to serious and fresh thinking about the future of progressive politics in America.

Sidney M. Milkis
Charlottesville, Virginia
January 2009

ONE

❧

The Critical Year of 1912

The 1912 election was one of the great campaigns in American history. It was the decisive battle of the Progressive era, which witnessed the first comprehensive efforts to come to terms with the fundamental conflicts raised by the industrial revolution. The technological breakthroughs and the frenzied search for new markets and new sources of capital that were associated with rapid industrialization caused unprecedented economic growth. But dynamic growth also generated a wide range of problems that seriously challenged the capacity of the American political system, dominated by highly decentralized party organizations, to respond. Above all, the presidential contenders of 1912 had to grapple with the troubling question of how to curb the excesses of big business—the giant "trusts" that, according to reformers, constituted uncontrolled and irresponsible bastions of power. These combinations of wealth aroused widespread fears that growing corporate influence might jeopardize the equal opportunity of individuals to climb the economic ladder. Reformers excoriated the economic conditions of this period—dubbed the "Gilded Age"—as excessively opulent and holding little promise for industrial workers and small farmers.[1] Moreover, many believed that great business interests had captured and corrupted the men and methods of government for their own profit. Party leaders—both

Democrats and Republicans—were seen as irresponsible "bosses" who did the bidding of "special interests."

Taking place at a defining juncture of American history, the 1912 campaign, as one historian has written, was a "remarkable moment," the rare presidential contest that "verged on political philosophy."[2] The election showcased four impressive candidates who engaged in a remarkable debate about the future of American politics: William Howard Taft, the incumbent Republican president; Woodrow Wilson, the distinguished scholar of American politics, who had been elected governor of New Jersey just two years before; Eugene Debs, the popular labor leader of Indiana who ran on the Socialist Party ticket; and Theodore Roosevelt, the irrepressible former president, who bolted from the GOP and ran as the champion of the Progressive Party. All four candidates recognized that fundamental changes were occurring in the American political landscape, and each attempted to define the Progressive era's "answer to the questions raised by the new industrial order that had grown up within the American constitutional system."[3]

That the 1912 election registered, and inspired, fundamental changes in American politics suggests the historical significance of the Progressive Party.[4] Although Wilson was elected president, the Progressives were the driving force of the election. Indeed, with the exception of the Republican Party of the 1850s, the Progressive Party remains the most important third party to appear on the American political landscape. With the celebrated former President Roosevelt as its candidate, the Bull Moose Party won 27.4 percent of the popular vote and 88 electoral votes from six states. It also elected 13 new members of Congress and 230 state legislators. This was an extraordinary feat. In fact, no third-party candidate for the presidency—before or after 1912—has received so large a percentage of the popular vote or as many electoral votes. More important, as a party that embraced and helped legitimize new social movements and candidate-centered campaigns, the Progressive Party pioneered a plebiscitary form of governance that evolved over the course of the twentieth century and appears to have come into its own in recent elections.[5]

Indeed, many characteristics of contemporary politics, conventionally understood as new (or of very recent history), were born of the Progressive Party campaign of 1912. TR's crusade made universal use of the direct primary a celebrated cause, assaulted traditional partisan loyalties, took advantage of the centrality of the newly emergent mass media, and convened an energetic but uneasy coalition of self-styled public advocacy groups. All these features of the Progressive Party campaign make the election of 1912 look more like that of 2008 than that of 1908.[6] The campaign of 1912 also anticipated an important shift in the conception of the presidency. Previously, the president ran for office and governed as the head of a party. The Progressives saw the party system, grounded in local perspectives, as an obstacle to the expansion of national administrative power essential to economic and social justice. They called for the federal government to assume expansive domestic and international responsibilities that presupposed a strong executive. For Progressives, public opinion would reach its fulfillment with the formation of an independent executive power, freed from the provincial, special, and corrupt influence of political parties.

Roosevelt's very presence at the Progressive Party convention symbolized a new relationship between leaders and those they led. In the past, party nominees had stayed away from the convention, waiting to be officially notified of their nomination; a presidential candidate was expected to demur as a sign of respect for the party's collective purpose. TR's personal appearance at the Progressive convention gave dramatic testimony to his dominance of the proceedings.[7] More significant, it gave evidence of an important historical change of presidential campaigns being conducted less by parties than by individual candidates who appealed directly for the support of the electorate.[8]

Roosevelt's presence in Chicago and the ideals embodied in the "Confession of Faith" he delivered to the assembled delegates posed a fundamental challenge not only to political parties, but also to the very idea of representation that sustained constitutional democracy in the United States. The closing words of his address—"We stand at Armageddon, and we battle for the Lord"—aroused those who were there to such an emotional state that they could only be subdued by a reverential singing of "The Battle Hymn of the Republic."[9] The delegates' reverence went beyond devotion for their candidate, however; it expressed their collective identity. TR's dominant role in the Progressive Party campaign was not simply a matter of his personal popularity. It followed directly from the Progressive animus against mediating institutions—political parties, interest groups, and the constitutional system of checks and balances—that discouraged direct contact between reform leaders and the people. Indeed, the reform-minded delegates who came to Chicago championed the direct rule of the people with a fresh enthusiasm that surprised and impressed the journalists who witnessed the proceedings. After observing an evening of reformist speeches, punctuated by the singing of hymns, "which burst forth at the first flash of every demonstration," a reporter for the *San Francisco Examiner* marveled that the convention "was more like a religious revival than a political gathering."[10]

Roosevelt's appeal to the people was helped considerably by such press reports, which represented a new "nonpartisan" journalism. Before the 1890s, public debate was dominated by the decentralized party press, which had prevailed since the Jacksonian era. The challenge to traditional partisan practices and the development of inexpensive and rapid forms of manufacture had made possible a *"mass* market beyond the confines of one faction, party, or following."[11] Roosevelt was the first president to recognize fully the press's value as a medium to communicate directly with the people, and the first to understand that journalistic support had to be pursued actively and continuously.[12] With his Progressive crusade, he became especially dependent on, and exploited more fully, the mass-circulation newspapers and magazines that presumed to stand apart from existing political practices. The *Examiner,* which was owned by the self-styled progressive publisher William Randolph Hearst, gave voice to Roosevelt's cause, even as it opposed his candidacy. In the religiosity of the delegates, in their repeating singing of "The Battle Hymn of the Republic" and "Onward Christian Soldiers," the *Examiner* detected a political revolution: an unprecedented, comprehensive assault on the partisan practices that had dominated the American political process for nearly a century. "Newspapers that belittle the Roosevelt movement and believe that they can obtain results with insincere criticism and sneers will be disappointed," the *Examiner* predicted. "The People of this country are ready for something new, something different from the old machine routine." The Progressive Party's platform, its support for measures that would establish the right of the people to choose their representatives and influence the councils of government without suffering the interference of political parties, would surely "have the attentive hearing" of the American public.[13]

The results of the election confirmed the *Examiner*'s prescience. Although the Progressive Party did not win the 1912 election, and withered by 1916, its strong showing signaled the significant advance, if not the triumph, of the Progressive idea of democracy. It was neither the Democrats nor the Republicans but the Progressives who set the tone of the 1912 election. The Progressive Party platform proposed the most extensive reforms during the campaign, but, as Eldon Eisenach notes, "all three major parties, in varying degrees and with differing emphasis, urged Progressive measures."[14] The Progressive program of political reform, promising the end of party dominance and the more direct influence of public opinion on politics and government, appeared to be victorious. As "the return to normalcy" of the

1920s showed, however, the 1912 election did not signal the complete triumph of progressive democracy. But with the Progressive Party campaign of 1912, parties were no longer the principal agents of democracy as they had been since the early part of the nineteenth century. Indeed, with the celebration of public opinion spawned by the 1912 election, even so-called conservatives like Calvin Coolidge could hardly resist "going to the public."[15]

TR's Progressive Party campaign would have an especially important influence on his cousin, Franklin D. Roosevelt, who made many of the ingredients of progressive democracy an enduring feature of American political life. Following the example set by TR at the Progressive Party convention, FDR accepted the 1932 Democratic nomination in person. Thereafter, this became settled practice within the two-party system. Like his Progressive forbear, FDR insisted on a direct, unmediated relationship between the president and rank and file. The president, not the party, was to be the center of campaigning as well as governing.[16] TR's crusade also anticipated the New Deal political order in prescribing an expansive welfare and regulatory state, proposing that the United States play a leading role in world affairs, empowering an array of advocacy groups that resisted becoming integrated into a party coalition, celebrating a national "community" in a form that rejected the natural rights tradition that had sustained limited constitutional government since the early part of the nineteenth century, and shifting power from states and localities to the national government, especially to a reconstituted "modern" executive. .

Understood within the Progressive tradition, the New Deal is appropriately viewed as an extension, if not a completion, of the changes in politics and government prefigured by the Bull Moose campaign. After FDR's long tenure, the new understanding of executive responsibilities would lead even conservative Republican presidents to wield the powers of the office in the manner of their progressive predecessors. For all the critical differences between our two most recent presidential candidates—Democrat Barack Obama and Republican John McCain—both proclaimed fealty to presidential leadership in the TR mold: both championed national administrative power, and both claimed that this power must be used in the name of the whole people.

The Progressive Party and American Democracy

The attempt to remake American democracy was not cut from whole cloth; rather, the Progressive Party campaign of 1912 marked a critical way station along a long hard road. Since the late 1880s, reforms in the states had resulted in the advance of the secret or official ballot, the adoption of registration requirements, the growth of civil service reforms, and the introduction of the direct primary in state, local, and congressional elections. Moreover, the enactment of the Pendleton Act in 1883, although of limited application at the start, laid a solid foundation on which to build a federal civil service in succeeding decades.[17] Significantly, Roosevelt's presidency marked the dividing line between the old commitment to party patronage in public affairs and the modern recognition that nonpartisan administration was a principal tool of governance. These measures, combined with the emergence of mass-circulation newspapers and magazines that operated independently of the traditional party press, had begun to weaken the grip of party organizations on candidates, government institutions, and the loyalties of voters.[18]

Hoping to adapt to—indeed, manage—the growing disaffection with traditional partisan practices, party leaders themselves contributed to the advance of these developments. By the early 1890s, the historian Michael McGerr notes, the two parties had almost entirely abandoned "spectacles," featuring torchlight parades and rallies to excite the party faithful, "for the less partisan and less emotional 'campaign of education.'"[19] And yet, in their endeavor to co-opt reforms and exploit new forms of mass communication, party leaders unwittingly participated in changes that undermined the allegiance of candidates and voters to their organizations. The focus of presidential campaigns, especially, shifted from local and state party organizations, which were the foundation of the nineteenth-century party system, to national candidates.[20]

The 1896 election marked the first important change in presidential campaigning. Abandoned by many powerful Democrats because of his defense of "free silver"—that is, the Populist proposal to inflate the currency by basing it on silver as well as gold—and yet confident of his oratorical prowess, William Jennings Bryan became the first presidential candidate to tour the country and appeal directly to the voters. Blessed with a powerful voice and boundless energy, the "Great Commoner" visited twenty-seven states and gave more than 800 speeches. As the historian Gil Troy has described Bryan's groundbreaking campaign, "Consuming up to six meals per day, sleeping in snatches, and taking periodic alcohol rubdowns to preserve his strength—though never imbibing—Bryan sang his silvery song. So many people crowded his train that he spoke from the rear platform of the last car, and a campaign tradition was born"—the "whistle-stop" campaign through strings of small-town railway stations.[21]

Although the Republican candidate, Ohio Governor William McKinley, displayed far more allegiance to conventional party practices, his campaign also revealed the growing importance of candidate-centered campaigns. Building on an approach that Benjamin Harrison had employed on a small scale in 1888, McKinley and his master political strategist, Mark Hanna, mobilized the national Republican Party for a "front porch campaign" in which the candidate greeted delegations of voters to his home in Canton, Ohio. From mid-June through November, McKinley spoke to more than 300 crowds totaling 750,000 visitors from thirty states. Although McKinley's front porch speeches were long on platitudes, each event was carefully planned so as to cultivate a direct, personal bond between the presidential candidate and the voters. Shortly before a delegation arrived, a telegram would reach Canton with information about the group's members, political attachments, and community. By the time the visitors made their way to McKinley's home, the candidate was able to greet some of them by name, mention absent family members, and refer to matters of interest in the visitors' hometowns.[22]

Like Bryan's whistle-stop tour, McKinley's carefully orchestrated front porch campaign foretold the prominence of candidate- rather than party-centered campaigns. Some who visited McKinley's home scavenged souvenirs from Canton, including parts of the famous front porch. Others lavished gifts on the Republican candidate, ranging from inkstands to bathtubs. "These gifts," Troy notes, "attested to the increased centrality of the candidate and the desire of individuals to cement their bond with him."[23]

Subsequent campaigns displayed additional halting steps toward the modern candidate-centered campaign. Not until the 1912 election, however, did the ingredients that were transforming American politics from a party-centered decentralized republic—a "state of courts and parties," as Stephen Skowronek calls it—to a candidate-centered mass democracy come into full view.[24] Although they engaged in practices that departed from traditional partisan norms, neither Bryan nor McKinley had directly attacked party organizations or the critical role these associations played in American elections and government. Nor did Roosevelt, when he was elected in his own right in 1904, publicly challenge traditional party drills. Although TR was very active behind the scenes—appointing the officers of the Republican convention, dictating the platform, and courting funds—he did not attend the convention or actively campaign. Similarly, the 1908 election, pitting Bryan, making his third run for the presidency, against Taft, advanced the form of the candidate-centered campaign—for the first time, both major party candidates stumped actively and openly—but neither campaign challenged the critical function that parties played in nominating and electing candidates.[25] Even the Populist Party, which received 9 percent of the popular vote in 1892, represented an attempt to reform, rather than destroy, the localized democracy that was organized by the two-party system. Like the Republicans of the 1850s, the Populists hoped to form a movement strong enough to break through the existing two-party system. But they had no particular objection to party as a political institution.

In contrast, TR and the Progressive Party elaborated the innovations that had begun to transform the relationship between the presidency and the voters into a comprehensive program of political and constitutional reform. Celebrating a direct relationship between public officials and mass opinion, Roosevelt's Bull Moose campaign gave new meaning to the exalted, elusive idea, stated in the Preamble of the Constitution, that America's sovereign was "We the People." Joined by most of the leading progressive academics, intellectuals, and reform activists in the country, he posed hard challenges to the natural rights tradition and limited constitutional government. The "liberal" tradition, as Louis Hartz called it, and constitutional forms had already been altered in important ways by the rise of localized, highly mobilized parties during the first three decades of the nineteenth century. Foundational principles and institutions also had been redefined by Lincoln and the Civil War Republicans, who championed the idea that the "unalienable rights" of the Declaration should become the lodestar of a more capacious understanding of the national government's responsibility to promote individual freedom.[26] Under TR's auspices, however, the Progressive Party gave effect to a new reform tradition that more fundamentally changed the way Americans thought about the Constitution. It paved the way for the development of a national democracy that presupposed a direct, unmediated connection between public opinion and a "modern executive," memorably ordained by Roosevelt as the "steward of the public welfare."[27]

The old saw of the historical literature on the Progressive era is that the Progressive Party of 1912 was essentially a personal vehicle for Theodore Roosevelt, an organization relegated to serving his own political ambitions. TR's bolt from the Republican convention in 1912, the argument goes, was born of his party's rejection of his designs, after a brief retirement from politics, to return to power. Accordingly, the Progressive Party was not invested with a collective mission and organization that could survive his return to the fold in 1916.[28] Despite its remarkable showing in 1912, the party was forlorn four years later, its fate inseparable from the dynamic leader who embodied its cause. At the end of the day, it had brought neither an ongoing multiparty system nor a fundamental party transformation pitting progressives against conservatives, for which many participants in the Bull Moose campaign had expressed hope.[29]

Consequently, scholars of parties and elections have tended to discount the 1912 election on the grounds that it was, as Paul Allen Beck writes, "the result of a split within the ranks of the majority party over personalities rather than over policies."[30] According to Walter Dean Burnham, it featured a "major-party bolt," but not the kind of protest movement that signals a transformation of American politics.[31] Theodore Roosevelt was a party bolter, and personality conflicts played a big part in fracturing the Republican Party. Just as surely, Roosevelt's disaffection from Taft and Republican Party leaders was the result of his important disagreements with received party wisdom. He led an army of crusading reformers aiming not only for major election reforms but also for measures such as national health insurance, government-led industrial planning, women's suffrage, the direct election of senators, and popular referenda on court rulings. Indeed, TR's bolt was encouraged by the cresting of a movement dedicated to fundamental political, social, and economic change. Roosevelt's insurgency brought to national prominence and bestowed considerable legitimacy on reform developments that had been under way since the beginning of the 1890s.

The Progressive Party thus lies at the very heart of fundamental changes in American politics—changes that were initially, if only partially, negotiated during the Progressive era.[32] The personalistic quality of Roosevelt's campaign was part and parcel of these changes, but they went much deeper than his desire to regain past political mastery. The Progressive Party, with its leadership-centered organization, accommodated and embodied the aspirations of a diverse collection of reformers—insurgent Republican officeholders, disaffected Democrats, crusading journalists, academics, social workers, and other activists—who hoped the new party coalition would realize their common goal of making the federal and state governments more responsive to the economic, social, and political demands of the people. Those who joined the new party had somewhat different and sometimes conflicting reasons for doing so. But according to Benjamin Park Dewitt, the array of reformers who joined the Progressive crusade had a shared sense that the nation confronted a "severe political crisis": "After a period of unprecedented industrial and commercial expansion, during which little or no attention has been given to the problems of government, the people have suddenly realized that government has not been functioning properly and that radical changes are needed. Manifestations of this excitement and unrest are seen on every hand."[33]

By 1912 this widespread excitement and unrest found expression in a national movement. Like the movement it presumed to embody, the Progressive Party encompassed a wide variety of worldviews and reform programs. So large and diverse, in fact, were the organizations and institutions associated with the reformism of the late nineteenth and early twentieth centuries that some scholars have declared the term *progressivism* meaningless and despaired at identifying a coherent movement.[34] As the historian Alonzo Hamby has noted, however, the "meaning of the word 'progressivism' has to begin with respect for the understanding of those who applied the term to themselves."[35] Reformers during the first two decades of the twentieth century, many of whom descended from participants in the Abolitionist movement, saw themselves as participating in a Progressive movement, and although they were more than conscious of the great differences and fractious conflicts that divided them, adhered to the view that they stood for certain common aspirations. "Above all," Hamby observes, "progressives saw themselves as fighters for democracy . . . locked in combat with 'the interests.'" Of course, we should not accept the reformers' view that they were fighting for the public interest uncritically; in important respects, Progressives were elitists and reactionary. Nonetheless, one cannot grasp the strengths and weaknesses of the Progressive movement without recognizing that many of those who identified with it saw themselves as crusaders with a moral mission.[36]

First and foremost, their reform zeal aimed at the concentration of wealth, specifically at giant trusts, which reformers saw as corrupting the foundations of American democracy. In their attempt to come to terms with the challenges of industrialization, Progressives championed three principal causes that would renew the spirit that made America, in the renowned social worker Jane Addams's words, "the most daring experiment in democratic government which the world has ever known."[37] They promoted a new governing philosophy that placed less emphasis on rights, especially when invoked in defense of big business, and stressed collective responsibilities and duties. In conformance with this redefinition of the social contract, Progressives called for the reconstruction of American politics, hitherto dominated by localized parties, so that a more direct link would be formed between government officials and public opinion. Similarly, reformers demanded a revamping of governing institutions, so that the power of state legislatures and Congress would be subordinated to an independent executive power—city managers, governors, and a modern presidency—that could truly represent the national interest and tackle the new tasks of government required by changing social and economic conditions.

Progressive reformers differed dramatically over how the balance among these three somewhat competing objectives should be struck as well as how the new national state they prescribed should address the domestic and international challenges of the new industrial order. But they tended to agree that these were the most important battles that had to be fought in order to bring about a democratic revival. In fact, the Progressive Party campaign is such an important development because it represents a conscious effort on the part of academics, intellectuals, and reform activists to draw disparate organizations and groups together—a test, if you will, of the proposition that there was a Progressive movement dedicated to the common objective of making the national government more accountable to the public good, as they understood it.[38] The Progressive movement, as Roosevelt acknowledged, was "greater than the Progressive Party."[39] But by 1912 the Progressive Party had become the vanguard of reformers who viewed it as their best hope to advance a program of national reconstruction.

Leading social reformers had for many years devoted their energies to a variety of national and local advocacy groups and had recognized kinship among the different policy reforms and causes they represented. Many deliberated at professional gatherings about the need for disparate reform groups to organize into a unified, national movement for progressive government action. Progressives hoped this movement would find common cause in the melding of social reform with "direct democracy," of new collective aims to relieve social and economic distress with energetic popular leadership. In the Progressive Party and the candidacy of Theodore Roosevelt, most militant reformers spied an extraordinary opportunity to transform progressivism into a coherent political force in America.

"More than any single leader," the Progressive editor Herbert Croly wrote, "Theodore Roosevelt contributed decisively to the combination of political and social reform and to the building up of a body of national public opinion behind the combination. Under his leadership as President, reform began to assume the characteristics, if not the name, of progressivism."[40] By bestowing national prominence on progressive objectives, TR's presidency ushered in a new form of statesmanship—one that gave expression and effect to the American people's aspirations for social improvement.[41] Roosevelt greatly admired Abraham Lincoln, who in seeking to purge slavery from the Constitution modified the meaning of national community in the United States.

Lincoln invested the country with a sense of purpose, even a religiosity, that signaled a change in the relationship between the individual and the government. Roosevelt's contribution was to engage the American people in a dialogue about economic problems; not until his time were such problems treated in terms that did not threaten the values of most Americans. "Roosevelt borrowed from [the Populist leader William Jennings] Bryan," the philosopher John Dewey wrote, "but Bryan came from Nazareth in Galilee, and spoke the cruder language of the exhorter and itinerate revivalist. When Roosevelt uttered like sentiments, his utterances had the color and prestige of a respectable cult and an established church."[42] As one progressive leader put it to TR, "You are sort of political father-confessor to whom many of us turn in times of grave doubt and difficulty."[43]

Roosevelt's concept of leadership and his great talent for taking the American people into his confidence made him virtually irresistible to reformers. "Roosevelt bit me and I went mad," Progressive journalist William Allen White wrote about his participation in the Bull Moose campaign.[44] He was not alone. Jane Addams, who seconded Roosevelt's Progressive Party nomination for president, declared that reformers supported TR's candidacy because they viewed him as "one of the few men in public life who has responded to the social appeal, who has caught the significance of the modern movement." He was a leader, she added, "of invincible courage, of open mind, of democratic sympathies, one endowed with power to interpret the common man and to identify himself with the common lot."[45] Indeed, Roosevelt's command of public opinion made him seem indispensable to the progressive cause. As his eventual running mate, Governor Hiram Johnson, of California, wrote TR in urging him to campaign for the presidency in 1912, "I know you have such a hold upon [the people's] imaginations and their affections as no other man within my life has held, and that no amount of politics and no number of politicians could withstand the people if they were aroused by the extraordinary effort on your part."[46]

Not all progressives were so smitten with the "father-confessor" of the movement.[47] Urging reformers to stay away from the new party, Robert La Follette attacked TR for his willingness, as president, to compromise on progressive principles. Dubbing him "the bluffer," La Follette took TR to task for his failure to reject the tariff, which embodied, according to many reformers, the dominance of special interests over the national government; his imperialism and disdain for those who would withdraw from United States commitments abroad; and his long-standing opposition to more advanced progressive policies such as the initiative and referendum.

TR's newfound militant progressivism, displayed in his ardent support for an advanced program of political reform and his bolt from the Republican Party, was but a ploy, La Follette warned, to advance his own personal ambitions. "He will not last," the Republican senator predicted. "In the end the people of this country will get his true measure. No party ever successfully organized about a man. Principles and issues must constitute the basis of this great movement."[48]

La Follette's assault on Roosevelt cannot be dismissed merely as the tendentious observations of a rival for the leadership of the Progressive movement. Many reformers shared La Follette's scorn for TR's charismatic stewardship. Erving Winslow, secretary of the Anti-Imperialist League, wrote a bitter "remonstrance" to Addams for endorsing Roosevelt's candidacy. TR was no friend of social welfare, Winslow insisted. Rather, the former president's positions on economic and foreign policy revealed a wolf in sheep's clothing:

> Mr. Roosevelt's support implies a belief in the infamy of the protective tariff and the beneficent effects of war upon the community, the increase of the navy, the fortification and appropriation of the Panama Canal and the hypocritical support of woman's suffrage: to be decided by the votes of women instead of a natural right. . . . It seems strange that a demagogue with no practical suggestions who has merely embellished every catch-word with vigorous and eloquent language has been able to blind any of the electorate.[49]

Jane Addams also had reservations about Roosevelt. But TR's enthusiastic embrace of causes that Addams and her colleagues long had sought to make part of a national campaign overcame her hesitancy. As Addams informed recalcitrant social workers, the Progressive Party gave her the opportunity to participate meaningfully in the development of an advanced program of reform and the "hope that the coming campaign [would] convince the other parties [to accept] equal suffrage." At the very least, she insisted, "the [Progressive] cause [would] benefit from the education" that the new party would give to the electorate.[50]

The alliance between Roosevelt and social reformers was exemplified in the crafting of the Progressive Party's platform. Its formulation was largely the responsibility of a subcommittee that enlisted the services of a number of individuals at the vanguard of progressive reform. Among these participants was William Allen White, who believed that the platform was emblematic of the party's integrity, proof that the 1912 campaign was led and inspired by Roosevelt but not subservient to him. "I think you fellows overemphasize Roosevelt," he admonished the editor of the *American Mercury:*

> If you had been with me through the four or five days' session of the subcommittee on platform and through the all night session of the General Committee and you had seen the crowd and understood the spirit of the session of the Progressive Party, you would understand that Roosevelt is not the Progressive Party. . . . The Progressive Party is here to stay and I am satisfied it is going to have a place, perhaps not a winning place, but definite in American politics for the next thirty years.[51]

The platform of the Progressive Party, which included most of the causes and programs that reformers had been championing since the end of the nineteenth century, would indeed prove to be of enduring importance, even though the party that gave birth to it would not. The platform called for national regulations and social welfare measures that would not be enacted until the New Deal; indeed, with respect to certain measures, most notably national health insurance, the Progressive Party prescribed core progressive commitments that remain unfulfilled. Moreover, it advocated measures for "pure democracy," including women's suffrage, the direct election of senators, universal use of the direct primary, an easier method to amend the Constitution, the initiative, and referenda on laws that the state courts declared unconstitutional, that have guided reformers who have sought a more direct relationship between government action and public opinion throughout the twentieth and twenty-first centuries.

The Progressive Party's declaration of "pure democracy" was sanctified as a "covenant with the people," as a deep and abiding pledge to make the people the "masters of their constitution." Like the Populist Party of the late nineteenth century, the Progressives invoked the Preamble of the Constitution to assert their purpose of making effective "We the People" in strengthening the federal government's authority to regulate the society and economy. But Progressives sought to hitch the will of the people to a strengthened national administrative power, which was anathema to the Populists. Animated by the radical agrarianism that celebrated the Jeffersonian and Jacksonian assault on monopolistic power, the Populists' concept of national democracy rested in the hope of arousing the states and the Congress for an assault on the centralizing, unholy alliance between the national parties and the trusts. For example, both the Populist Party campaign of 1892 and the populist Democratic crusade of Bryan in 1896 called for limiting executive power, which had been viewed as the keystone of national administration since the nation's founding. In contrast, TR's "respectable" religiosity was allied to a "gospel of efficiency" that could not abide the localized democracy of the nineteenth century.[52] "Progressive democracy demands not merely an increasing employment of the legislative power under representative executive leadership," Croly wrote, "but it also particularly needs an increase of administrative authority and efficiency."[53]

In condemning reformers for lacking a coherent set of principles, contemporary scholars point to the apparent contradiction between Progressives' celebration of direct democracy and their hope to achieve more disinterested government, which seemed to demand a powerful and independent national bureaucracy.[54] The acerbic social critic H. L. Mencken argued that Theodore Roosevelt only thought he believed in democracy. His real creed was enlightened government. Although Roosevelt might have been "carried away by the emotional storms of the moment," by the "quasi-religious monkey shines" that marked the Progressive Party's creation, Mencken noted, TR's "remedy for all the great pangs and longings of existence was not a dispersion of authority, but a hard concentration of authority."[55]

Without question, the Progressive Party's commitment to strengthening popular rule was diminished by its desire to cope with economic problems and inequalities by expanding national administration.[56] But those who joined the Progressive Party argued, not without reason, that the expansion of social welfare provisions and "pure democracy," as they understood it, were inextricably linked. Reforms such as the direct primary, as well as the initiative and referendum, were designed to overthrow the localized two-party system in the United States, built on Jeffersonian and Jacksonian principles, which bestowed on the separated institutions of the federal government a certain unity of control while at the same time it restrained programmatic ambition and prevented the development of a stable and energetic administration of social policy. By the same token, the triumph of "progressive" over "pioneer" democracy, as Croly framed it, would put the American people directly in touch with the councils of power, thus strengthening the demand for government support, and allow — indeed, require — administrative agencies to play their proper role in the realization of progressive social welfare policy.[57]

Still, the profound shift in the political principles and practices that Progressives championed did not entail a straightforward evolution from localized to centralized government.[58] Indeed, the Progressive Party crusade was seriously hampered by fundamental disagreements among its supporters over issues that betrayed an acute sensitivity, if not attachment, to the commitment in the country to local self-government. The party was deeply divided over civil rights, leading to bitter struggles at the Progressive Party convention over delegate selection rules and the platform that turned on whether the party should confront the shame of Jim Crow. In the end, it did not, and it accepted the right of the states and localities to resolve the matter of race relations. Moreover, Progressive delegates waged an enervating struggle at the party convention over whether an interstate trade commission with considerable administrative discretion or militant antitrust policy was the appropriate method to tame the trusts. New Nationalists, led by Roosevelt, prevailed, pledging the party to regulate, rather than attempt to dismantle, corporate power; however, this disagreement carried over to the general election. The Democratic Party, under the tutelage of their candidate for president, Woodrow Wilson, and his advisor Louis Brandeis, embraced a New Freedom version of progressivism, which prescribed antitrust measures and state regulations as an alternative to the expansion of national administrative power.

The split between New Nationalism and New Freedom Progressives cut to the very core of the "modern" state that the programmatic initiatives touted by Progressives anticipated. As Croly acknowledged, the Progressive Party's program presupposed national standards and regulatory powers that "foreshadowed administrative aggrandizement." And yet Progressives could not agree on how administrative power should be used. Indeed, the conflict between New Nationalism and New Freedom Progressives revealed that many reformers shared the profound uneasiness of their Populist forbears about the very prospect of expanding national administrative power. This anxiety was not merely a hastily contrived reaction to the administrative ambitions of New Nationalism. Rather, it was allied to a celebration of local self-government that was deeply rooted in American political culture. Woodrow Wilson expressed reverence for provincial liberties in a series of lectures that he delivered at Columbia University in 1908:

> Moral and social questions originally left to the several states for
> settlement can be drawn into the field of federal authority only
> at the expense of the self-dependence and efficiency of the several
> communities of which our complex body politic is made up. Paternal
> morals, morals enforced by judgment and choices of central authority

at Washington, do not and cannot create vital moral habits or methods of life unless sustained by local opinion and purpose, local prejudice and convenience, — unless supported by local convenience and interest; and only communities capable of taking care of themselves will, taken together, constitute a nation capable of vital action and control.[59]

Wilson's concern for "local opinion and prejudice," which was allied to a sympathetic, although not uncritical, view of party politics, has led historians like George Mowry and Richard Hofstadter to charge that so-called Progressives were, in truth, backward looking, if not reactionary, middle-class Protestants who sought reforms to restore individualism and to restrain the forces of collectivism wrought by the industrial revolution.[60] It is true that most Progressives were middle-class, and many scorned not only big business but also labor unions. Moreover, some influential Progressives and the policies they championed denigrated the rights of African Americans and immigrants. Nonetheless, even most New Freedom Progressives came primarily from the ranks of a new, professional middle class that accepted "modernization." Indeed, their reluctance to embrace centralized administration did not represent a commitment to local self-government as traditionally understood and practiced. The "compound republic," as James Madison called it, was shaped in the nineteenth century by party organizations and legal doctrines that formed a wall of separation between the national government and society. No less than New Nationalists, New Freedom Progressives wanted to breach that wall. They wanted to expand the responsibilities of the national government but hoped to find nonbureaucratic and noncentralized solutions to the ills that plagued the political economy.

Reconciling government centralization and administrative decentralization involved, in part, building on measures such as the Sherman Act, enacted in 1890, that would rely on competition and law rather than administrative tribunals to curb the abuses of big business. New Freedom Progressives also hoped to cultivate local forums of public discussion and debate that would "buttress the foundations of democracy." For example, Woodrow Wilson and Louis Brandeis were active in the social centers movement that sought to make use of school buildings for neighborhood forums on the leading issues of the day. This movement, which began early in the twentieth century with local experiments in cities such as Rochester, New York, emerged as a national association by the eve of the 1912 election. Its ambition, as George M. Forbes, the president of Rochester's Board of Education, announced at the National Conference on Civic and Social Center Development, was to form local institutions through which the people in the community could gain an understanding of civic obligation:

> We are now intensely occupied in forging the tools of democracy, the direct primary, the initiative, the referendum, the recall, the short ballot, commission government. But in our enthusiasm we do not seem to be aware that these tools will be worthless unless they are used by those who are aflame with the sense of brotherhood. If action of a democracy is to be but the resultant of a clash of selfish interests, it is hardly worth battling for. . . . The idea [of the social centers movement is] to establish in each community an institution having a direct and vital relation to the welfare of the neighborhood, ward, or district, and also to the city as a whole. . . . [This] means that our public school buildings, consecrated to education, may become the instruments of that deepest and most fundamental education upon which the very existence of democracy depends.[61]

The movement for neighborhood organization was not entirely new, of course. The tradition of local self-government in the United States went well beyond the legal division between the national and state governments and left considerable discretion to counties and townships. As Alexis de Tocqueville observed in the 1830s, the vitality of townships and counties depended on the well-founded idea in the United States that "each man [was] the best judge of his own interest and best able to satisfy his private needs." The practice of leaving townships and counties in charge of their "special interests," in turn, cultivated civic attachments by giving each individual "the same feeling for his country as one has for one's family." Happily, Tocqueville concluded, "a sort of selfishness makes [the individual] care for the state."[62]

The more populist Progressives hoped to extend the "municipal spirit" that Tocqueville so admired into twentieth-century urban America. At the same time, they hoped to reconstruct the primary unit of political life as a more cosmopolitan civic sphere, as a place that could more easily dovetail with the nation and, indeed, the international community. As the prominent progressive intellectual Mary Parker Follett put it, "The relation of neighbors one to another must be integrated into the substance of the [national] state. Politics must take democracy from its external expression of representation to the expression of that inner meaning hidden in the intermingling of all men."[63] This rather cryptic, idealistic aspiration found more concrete expression in the progressive hope for the neighborhood school, which according to social centers activists was the only "non-exclusive institution" in the United States.[64] Moreover, Progressives defended institutions, such as labor unions, moral and political reform associations, settlement houses, and universities, that they deemed would prepare individual men and women to have a direct effect on government. Combined with the advent of new forms of political communication, such as independent magazines and newspapers, Herbert Croly argued, these institutions would enable "the mass of people to assume some immediate control of their political destinies."[65]

Ultimately, the progressive hope of strengthening self-government in the United States depended on transmuting local self-government into direct rule of the people, who would not have to suffer the interference of decentralizing associations and institutions. Only then could individuals participate in a national movement of public opinion that might cultivate a "more perfect union." "Truly, the voice of the people is the voice of God," wrote a progressive journalist in the early part of the twentieth century; "but that means the voice of the *whole* people."[66]

Just as surely as the progressive schism over the appropriate methods to reform the political economy betrayed fundamental disagreements in its ranks, so its program of direct government elicited a shared sense of endeavor. New Freedom Progressives and New Nationalist reformers alike championed institutions and practices that they hoped would nurture a well-digested, direct system of popular rule. As one leading reformer wrote, "the people must be made supreme in government. . . . The things that hinder must be removed, and, where needed, new instruments must be provided whereby the sovereignty of the people may be effectively and directly exercised."[67]

During the 1912 election campaign, in fact, TR joined Wilson in celebrating the use of schoolhouses as neighborhood headquarters for political discussion. Declaring his enthusiastic approval for the maxim "Public buildings for public uses," Roosevelt proposed that neighborhood schools be turned into a "senate of the people," where they could discuss the issues of the hour.[68]

Indeed, TR's bolt from the Republican Party freed him to make a bolder, more consistent defense of "pure democracy" than Wilson, who, as the nominee of the Democrats, was necessarily more constrained by the structure and organizational practices of the traditional two-party system. Moreover, Wilson's respect for provincial liberties made him reluctant to join the progressive assault on political parties. "Students of our politics," he warned, "have not always sufficiently recognized the extraordinary part political parties have played in making national life which might otherwise have been loose and diverse almost to the point of being inorganic a thing of definite coherence." National parties had played a critical part in forging a country out of America's local communities and sectional interests, Wilson enthused, even as those organizations recognized the legitimacy of provincial concerns: "It has been nothing less than a marvel how the network of parties has taken up and broken the restless strain of contest and jealousy, like an invisible network of kindly oil upon the disordered waters of the sea. It is in this vital sense that our national parties have been our veritable body politics."[69] Respectful of the role traditional partisan organizations and practices had played in gathering the great diversity of local and regional interests into a nation, Wilson hoped, as the Democratic standard-bearer, to reform rather than dismantle political parties.

The Progressive Party, as the historian Morton Keller has written, stood for "something new under the American political sun."[70] Denying that a great nation could arise from the provinces, Progressives reinterpreted the meaning of American democracy. They challenged the local freedoms championed by decentralized parties, as well as the ethnocultural and regional divisions so central to nineteenth-century political culture. In disdaining localized party politics, TR gave voice to Progressives' faith in the American people's aspiration for social justice, and to the responsibility of leaders to give effect to these aspirations. The one doctrine that unified the disparate strands of the Progressive Party, he sensed, was its advocacy of a new understanding of popular rule. Just as his followers believed that parties were the linchpin of corruption and injustice, so they championed, as one reformer put it, "government at first-hand; government of the People; directly *by* the People."[71] Roosevelt thus made the cause of "pure democracy" the centerpiece of his frantic run for the White House. Above all, the measures of direct popular rule championed by TR—especially the initiative, referendum, recall, and an easier method to amend the Constitution—marked the Progressive Party campaign as militantly reformist. As Dewitt observed after TR's dramatic quest for the presidency, "These measures have been more widely discussed, more bitterly condemned, and more loyally praised than almost any other measures connected with the whole progressive movement."[72] Dedicated to such a radical reconstruction of self-rule, the Progressive campaign made the election of 1912 an event of extraordinary intellectual ferment. "The American Democracy," Croly enthused in the aftermath of the national campaign, "is becoming aroused to take a searching look at its own meaning and responsibilities."[73]

Beyond mere order, then, as the political theorist Wilson Carey McWilliams has written, "Progressives were engaged in a quest for a democracy on the grand scale, informed by the believe that the human spirit or conscience, guided by [enlightened administration], could eventually create a vast and brotherly republic of public spirited citizens."[74] This high ambition moved Progressives to propose reforms that would have humanized American life in a number of ways. At the same time, it also led them to endanger valued principles and institutions, such as individual rights, federalism, and limited government. Consequently, the Progressive Party campaign engendered not just an important debate over economic and political reforms—a struggle between Wilson and Roosevelt for the meaning of progressivism—but also a four-cornered contest for the soul of the American Constitution.

The Progressive Party and the American Constitution

As Mowry has written, Roosevelt's defense of progressive democracy, in the election of 1912, "was one of the most radical ever made by a major American political figure."[75] The Progressive program seemed to challenge the very foundation of republican government: the idea, underlying the U.S. Constitution, that space created by institutional devices such as the separation of powers and federalism allowed representatives to govern competently and fairly. Likewise, the Progressive idea of democracy rejected party politics, at least as they had traditionally worked in the United States. Forged on the anvil of Jeffersonian democracy, political parties in the United States were welded to constitutional principles that impeded the expansion of national administrative power. The origins and organizing principles of the American party system established it as a force against the creation of the "modern state." The Progressive reformers' commitment to building such a state—that is, to the creation of a national political power with expansive programmatic responsibilities—meant that the party system had to be either weakened or reconstructed. As Barry Karl notes, the Progressive campaign of 1912 "was as much an attack on the whole concept of political parties as it was an effort to create a single party whose doctrinal clarity and moral purity would represent the true interest of the nation as a whole."[76]

Roosevelt's bold support of direct government "impaired considerably [his] chance of securing the Republican nomination," Mowry has written. For by attacking the party organization and the courts he "alienated the conservative wing of his party, which might have supported him for the sake of possible victory." Standpat Republicans and large industrial interests who long had appreciated TR's disdain for radical economic and political remedies rapidly abandoned the former president.[77]

In fact, the opposition to Roosevelt's program went far beyond the embattled "stand-patters." All but the most radical of his supporters considered the defense of pure democracy, especially the proposal for the popular recall of judicial decisions, a violation of the keystone of individual freedom. Amid TR's challenge to representative institutions, moderate Progressives sought to fashion a new understanding of Republican conservatism, one rooted less in a militant defense of property rights and business, one that harked back to the Whigs' defense of ordered liberty. Taft and like-minded moderates in the Republican Party, such as Elihu Root, characterized their battle against insurgency as a struggle for the future of constitutional democracy in the United States. During the 1912 election, the burden of this fight fell most heavily on Taft. The incumbent president had supported the pragmatic progressive program TR had pursued while in office, when he worked for moderate reforms, such as the Hepburn Act, which strengthened the Interstate Commerce Committee's authority to regulate the railroads, with the cooperation of Republican Party regulars. But in the wake of TR's championing of "pure democracy," Taft resolved to "stand pat" in defense of the Constitution, which the Progressive idea of democracy threatened to destroy. As Taft told an audience in Boston, Massachusetts, TR's defense of direct democracy "sent a thrill of alarm through all the members of the community who understood our constitutional principles and who feared the effect of the proposed changes upon the permanence of government."[78] It was unthinkable to the great majority of leaders in Congress and the states, and to the great mass of people as well, Taft argued, that Roosevelt should seriously propose to have a plebiscite on questions involving the construction of the Constitution.[79]

In response to such criticisms, Progressives insisted that the political reforms championed by the new party's platform were not a radical rejection of the American constitutional tradition, but an effort to fulfill it. State and local machines, they argued, had perverted the original design of the Constitution, which was dedicated to the emancipation of the American people from provincial and special interests, embodied by the Articles of Confederation. Whereas the Articles of Confederation read, "We the undersigned delegates of the States," the Preamble to the Constitution of 1787 was declared by "We the People." The change to "We the People," claimed

Theodore Gilman at a Progressive Party rally in Yonkers, New York, "was made at the Federal Convention with the full understanding of the meaning and effect of the new form of words," signifying that the new Constitution represented the aspirations of one sovereign people to create a "more perfect Union."[80] Political parties had preempted this original design, shifting power to states and localities in the service of "local self-government." Jeffersonian and Jacksonian reforms were necessary in the nineteenth century to thwart the "aristocratic" pretensions of the Federalists, but the problems thrown up by the industrial revolution demanded that Progressives revisit the potential for national democracy in the original Constitution. As Croly put it, "The nationalism of Hamilton with all its aristocratic leaning, was more democratic, because more constructively social, than the indiscriminate individualism of Jefferson."[81] Just as the original theory of the Electoral College had been abandoned after the "Revolution of 1800," closing the space between presidential politics and popular choice, so Gilman claimed, "the people now propose to come into closer touch with their representatives by the abolition of the machine, and the substitution thereafter of the direct primary, the initiative, referendum, and recall. This is all one logical and irresistible movement in one direction, having as its object the restoration of our form of government to its original purity and ideal perfection, as a government under the control of 'We, the people,' who formed it."[82]

Gilman's defense of the Progressive Party's program of political reform against the charge of radicalism received indirect support from social democrats, who were hardly less hostile to the progressive idea of democracy than were conservatives. Eugene Debs attacked the Progressive Party as "a reactionary protest of the middle classes, built largely upon the personality of one man and not destined for permanence."[83] The Progressives' fragility stemmed not just from TR's notoriety, Debs argued, but also from the flimsy doctrine that underlay it. Although supportive of political reform, Debs had long considered devices such as the referendum a very small part of the Socialist Party program. Debs was thus chagrined that TR "stole the red flag of socialism" to symbolize his so-called fight for the "right of the people to rule." That Roosevelt selected the crimson bandanna handkerchief as the symbol for the Progressive Party did not make socialism, which he had long denounced as anarchy, respectable. Rather, this fight for the rule of the people deflected attention from the injustices of capitalism, Debs complained, which were truly the cause of the people's discontent.[84]

TR stole not only the red flag of socialism but also the Socialists' thunder, just when they seemed to be emerging as an important influence in the country. Doubling the support they gained in 1908, Debs and the Socialist Party won 6 percent of the popular vote, the best showing of a socialist party in American history. By all accounts, however, the Socialist support would have been greater save for the preemption of the Progressive Party, which very deliberately presented itself as a substitute for socialism in America. The Progressive Party campaign thus sheds important light on the enduring complex question of why no socialist party emerged as an important influence on American politics and government.

The Progressive Party's millennial celebration of direct rule of the people was not reactionary, as Debs and other social democrats alleged. Yet it beheld a program of reform that sought to preserve the dignity of the democratic individual. Emphasizing the candidate instead of the party, the Progressives deflected attention from class conflict. Seeking to build a welfare state that was sustained by public opinion rather than through a social democratic party, it emphasized individual political action. The primary, referendum, and recall, after all, were devices that asked citizens to vote their individual consciences. Progressives were disdainful of collective organizations, such as the Democratic and Republican parties, formed on personal, family, or community attachments. Similarly, they found repugnant the idea of sectarian partisanship where "enlightened" voting decisions were submerged in class or racial conflicts. To the extent that progressive democracy was radical, it represented a sui generis American form of radicalism—one conceived to rescue American individualism from a blind attachment to the Constitution, especially from fealty to "high priests" of the Constitution. In the final analysis, however, the Progressive faith in public opinion represented a compromise with the widespread fear of a centralized state in America, a willingness on the part of even the most nationalist of reformers to accommodate these fears even as they sought to strengthen national administrative power. As the militant New Nationalist Croly wrote, "An authoritative representative government, particularly one which is associated with inherited leadership and a strong party system, carries with it an enormous prestige. It is frequently in a position either to ignore, to circumvent or wear down popular opposition. But a social program purchased at such a price is not worth what it costs."[85]

Like many leading intellectuals who joined the Progressive Party crusade, Croly was influenced by the philosophy of pragmatism, which made a strong contribution to twentieth-century reform in the United States. They owed a great deal to William James, who, as the intellectual historian James Kloppenberg has written, "broke down the dualisms that had undergirded empiricist as well as rationalist philosophy, dualisms that had already contributed indirectly to the abstract and dogmatic theorizing characteristic of laissez-faire and revolutionary socialism."[86] This search for a middle way, however, meant more than the practical accommodation of reform aspirations to the American way of life. Pragmatism, as it gained expression in the Progressive Party campaign, entailed "a conscious commitment to incremental reform and democratically guided experimentation in public policy," one that rejected revered American traditions such as natural rights, an independent judiciary, and constitutional forms that restrained majority rule.[87] As Croly put it, the idea of reconciling "American nationalism and American democracy is in truth equivalent to a new Declaration of Independence. It affirms the American people as free to organize their political, economic, and social life in the service of a comprehensive, a lofty, and far-reaching democratic purpose."[88]

A study of the 1912 Progressive campaign thus illuminates a vital debate about the future course of American constitutional democracy. This debate sheds light on roads not taken as well as those that were. In setting the tone of the 1912 election, the Progressive Party established a path of reform that left both conservatism, as Taft understood it, and social democracy behind. Similarly, the importance of TR's leadership in advancing progressive doctrine and practices tended to subordinate the movement's support for "grassroots" democracy to the plebiscitary schemes in the platform, such as the initiative, referendum, and recall, that exalted mass opinion. Indeed, in the wake of the excitement aroused by the Progressive Party, Wilson, whose New Freedom campaign was far more sympathetic to the decentralized state of courts and parties than TR's, felt compelled—or saw the opportunity—as president, to govern as a New Nationalist Progressive. As such, the Progressive Party's brief existence helps us better understand historical forces—most notably, a joining of social reform, "direct democracy," and the cult of a leader—that weakened political parties and advanced a distinct form of "modern" politics in the United States.

The Progressive Party's vision of politics and government rested uneasily in the soil of a nation that paid homage to individual rights and local self-government. Nonetheless, the epic of reform at the dawn of the twentieth century forced Americans to grapple with the central question of the founding: is it possible to achieve self-rule on a grand scale?[89] This was the question that had divided the Federalists and Anti-Federalists as the nation took form. As the Anti-Federalist Cato warned, "Enlarge the circle of political life as far as conceived by the Constitution and we lose the ties of acquaintance, habits, and fortune, and thus, by degrees, we lessen the attachments, till, at length, we no more than acknowledge a sameness of species."[90] The persistence of local self-government and decentralized political associations through the end of the nineteenth century postponed the question of whether the framers' concept of "We the People" was viable. But with the rise of industrial capitalism, constitutional government entered a new phase. It fell to Progressives to confront the question of whether it was possible to reconcile democracy with an economy of greatly enlarged institutions and a society of growing diversity.

This question was at the epicenter of the momentous contest of 1912, and it confronts any scholar attempting to come to terms with the legacy of the Progressive Party campaign. To a point, the wayward path of progressivism validated the Anti-Federalists' fears. Despite the Progressives' championing of mass democracy, the mix of attack on political parties and commitment to administrative management conspired to make American politics and government seem more removed from the everyday life of citizens. Yet progressive reformers invented institutions and associations that enabled citizens to confront, if not resolve, the new problems thrown up by the industrial revolution. Indeed, many of the political organizations that are central to contemporary American democracy—labor unions, trade groups, civic and religious associations—were founded during the Progressive era. Moreover, as the history of the Progressive Party illustrates, reformers have sought to ameliorate the tension between administrative aggrandizement and self-government by resting their reform faith in charismatic leaders and a restituted executive office, a modern presidency, which displaced Congress and political parties as the principal agent of popular rule. As Croly expressed this faith in celebrating a New Nationalism, "At present our administration is organized chiefly upon the principle that the executive shall not be permitted to do much good for fear that he will do harm. It ought to be organized on the principle that he shall have full power to do either well or ill, but that if he does ill, he shall have no defense against punishment."[91] The achievements and disappointments of the modern presidency, currently embraced by liberals and conservatives alike, hold the most important lessons for understanding the Progressive era's legacy for American government. In this sense, the Progressive Party campaign of 1912 and the extraordinary constitutional debate it engendered offer important lessons on the strengths and weaknesses of American democracy at the dawn of the twenty-first century.

TWO

༄

Roosevelt, Progressive Democracy, and the Progressive Movement

Theodore Roosevelt's quixotic race for the White House began in 1910. This campaign for past mastery was not launched in the United States; rather, it began in Europe, on a tour that took him to France, England, and Germany. During this tour, TR gave a series of lectures that displayed serious reflection about the state of the industrialized world. Although these lectures were ostensibly cosmopolitan and delivered before audiences that honored Roosevelt as a world historical figure, they showed the former president to be preoccupied with American democracy and his ambition to reform it. The significance of these speeches soon became clear to the American press, which gave extensive front-page coverage to TR's European tour and speculated that Roosevelt was in the midst of formulating a platform that might return him to the White House.

Indeed, no sooner did he set foot in the United States than TR was embroiled in politics: first in New York, where he was implicated in nomination contests and a campaign for the enactment of a direct primary law, then in national politics, where a movement was emerging to dethrone his chosen successor, William Howard Taft. By the end of the summer of 1910, Roosevelt was maneuvering to regain what he believed was rightfully his. To be sure, he disavowed any interest in the 1912 election, but his public denials barely disguised deep disappointment in Taft and churning ambition to challenge the incumbent president. Roosevelt's objective was not merely a desire to return to the White House; his ample personal ambition was tied to a larger desire to place himself at the head of the Progressive movement, fueled by economic, social, and political conditions, which posed fundamental challenges to the political order that had dominated nineteenth-century America. As the head of this movement, TR hoped to shape a political realignment that would not only bring an end to the decentralized polity that had endured for over a century but also bring about a change in the nation's constitutional principles and institutional arrangements. TR characterized his objectives as conservative reform that would inoculate the Constitution against socialism; in truth, he championed a sui generis American form of radicalism, which promised to transform fundamentally the concept and practice of representation in the United States.

TR was not alone in his desire to define progressivism and master progressive forces. In order to fulfill his reform ambition he had to wage a struggle with Robert La Follette for the leadership of the Progressive movement. This bitter struggle for the soul of progressivism aroused a great contest of principle over the very meaning of representative democracy in the United States. Although steeped in personal animosity, the conflict between TR and La Follette exposed fault lines in the Progressive movement—fundamental differences in philosophy and political practice that would hobble the forward march of national reform throughout the twentieth century. For all their differences, however, TR and La Follette shared a commitment to progressive democracy; in their struggle for leadership of the Progressive movement both gave voice to a new understanding of popular sovereignty that framed the 1912 election and established candidate-centered campaigns as a core feature of American politics.

Progressivism Abroad: America and the Modern Idea of Democracy

There was no sign that Theodore Roosevelt would force a searching debate about the Constitution and popular government when he left the White House in 1909. To the contrary, TR's decision to leave the presidency seemed to belie his burning ambition and to buttress constitutional government. Had he decided to stand for another term in 1908, he almost certainly would have been renominated and most likely would have been reelected. But he had promised in November 1904 that he would not run again. The three and a half years he had already served, Roosevelt stated at the time, constituted his first term. Because he considered the custom that limited presidents to two terms a wise one, he issued a statement on election night declaring that he would not be "a candidate for or accept another nomination."[1]

Although Roosevelt was sorely tempted to go back on his promise in 1908, the fact that he did not do so revealed his commitment to the traditions and institutions of constitutional government. Roosevelt believed strongly that the powers of the president needed to be expanded for the good—indeed the survival—of the nation. But just as he felt compelled to obey conventional party practices in 1904, which proscribed incumbent presidents from actively campaigning, so he deferred to the two-term tradition. "I believe in a strong executive; I believe in power," he admitted to the British historian George Trevelyan; "but I believe that responsibility should go with power, and that it is not well that the strong executive should be a perpetual executive."[2] When Roosevelt went off to hunt big game in Africa, it was widely believed that he did so to leave his successor, William Howard Taft, absolutely free to make his own mark on the presidency.

Toward the end of his trip to Africa, however, Roosevelt began to receive news that suggested Taft was not a worthy successor. A tariff fight in Congress had split the Republican Party between its conservative and insurgent wings. Roosevelt had managed to straddle these factions, in no small part because he had been willing to forego a fight on the tariff, which his conservative party brethren viewed as the core policy of the GOP's pro-business philosophy. Because the 1908 Republican campaign platform called for a downward revision of protectionist measures, Taft had no choice but to face up to the demands of progressives in his party that tariff policy, which in their eyes embodied the domination of special interests over the councils of government, be reformed. In the end, he sided with the "Old Guard" Republicans and signed the Payne-Aldrich tariff, claiming dubiously that it did not betray his campaign pledge to fight for downward revision of tariff rates. Taft's willingness to cooperate with Old Guard Republicans—the likes of Joseph Cannon of Illinois, in the House, and Nelson Aldrich of Rhode Island, in the Senate—even as they were losing influence to a bipartisan progressive coalition in Congress, gave the impression that his administration had no intention of protecting, let along advancing, Roosevelt's legacy.

That impression was confirmed when Taft dismissed Gifford Pinchot, head of the Forest Service, who was a leading advisor to TR on conservation matters, which were very close to the ex-president's heart, and an intimate

White House advisor during the Roosevelt years. A week prior to his dismissal, Pinchot wrote TR a letter that warned of a growing rift between Taft and progressives. Taft's betrayal was not attributable to the president's "deliberate bad faith," Pinchot observed, but, rather, to "his surprising weakness and indecision." An article of faith of progressive democracy, confirmed in important ways by Roosevelt's time in office, Pinchot claimed, was that the president must be "the advocate and active guardian of the general welfare." Taft, in contrast, Pinchot revealed, followed "the advice of the last man who talk[ed] to him," thus forfeiting power to reactionary party leaders and the interests that controlled them. "Unless Mr. Taft turns squarely about and promptly abandons his present direction and tendencies," Pinchot warned, "I foresee a clear cut division between the administration and the reactionaries on the one side, and the progressives and the great mass of people on the other."[3]

Rather than turning "squarely about," Taft sided with the conservatives. He supported Cannon when progressive insurgents in the House, led by Republican George Norris of Nebraska and Democrat Champ Clark of Missouri, instigated a revolt that weakened substantially the Speaker's and the party organizations' institutional powers; dismissed Pinchot, who had challenged Secretary of the Interior Richard Achilles Ballinger's efforts to weaken conservation measures; and collaborated with Cannon and Aldrich in their campaign to purge the progressives from the Republican Party in the 1910 congressional nomination contests. As Taft slouched toward an alliance with the Old Guard, a "back from Elba" movement formed to return Roosevelt to the White House.[4]

The end of Roosevelt's self-imposed exile was delayed for a time by a triumphant tour of Europe, in which he was greeted by dignitaries and covered by the press as though he were a reigning rather than an ex-president. TR's European tour was not merely ceremonial, however. He delivered five major speeches, which bespoke his views on America and its relationship with the rest of the world. Two of these addresses, in particular—one delivered at the Sorbonne, another at Oxford University—suggested that Roosevelt's ambition still churned, not just for power but also for the opportunity to transform political life in the United States and to make its presence felt in international affairs. Indeed, the trip to Europe appeared to encourage TR to think seriously about the possibility of establishing a more advanced form of social democracy in the United States than he dared contemplate during his nearly two terms as president.

The subject of TR's speech at the University of Paris was "Citizenship in a Republic."[5] Elaborating on a theme that seemed more appropriate for America than France, Roosevelt warned that a country faced a moral crisis as "its pioneer days" passed. The maturing of a commercial republic created conditions that accentuated "vices and virtues, energy and restlessness, all the good qualities and all the defects of an intense individualism, self reliant, self-centered, far more conscious of its rights than its duties, and blind to its shortcomings."[6] The softening of morality in democratic republics such as France and the United States, TR observed, posed an especially dangerous risk. In a polity ruled by one or a few, "the quality of rulers is all important." A government "by, of, and for the people," in contrast, would be conditioned "upon the way in which the average man, the average woman, does his or her duty, first in the ordinary, every-day affairs of life, and next in those great occasional crises which call for heroic virtues." In praising the "commonplace, every-day qualities and virtues," TR stressed "the will and power to work, to fight at need, and to have plenty of children." The most important of these, the ex-president claimed, in phrases that sent "an audible titter" through the large and distinguished audience, was bearing offspring, the eternal "crown of blessings," for the "first essential in any civilization is that the man and the woman shall be father and mother of healthy children, so that the race shall increase and not decrease."[7] In highlighting the blessing of fertility Roosevelt touched a nerve—the French had long worried about their country's birthrate, to the point that it was a national obsession. Either TR was blind to these sensibilities or he was determined to speak the truth to his audience, as he understood it, regardless of the discomfort it stirred.

Roosevelt's sermon on private virtues was joined to a celebration of public responsibility. In elaborating on the latter, he championed the doctrine, first promoted during his presidency, that individual men and women were born for action, for the "strenuous life." Roosevelt urged his predominantly studious audience to resist the temptation of "intellectual aloofness":

It is not the critic who counts; not the man who points out how the strong man stumbles, or where the doer of deeds could have done better. The credit belongs to the man who is actually in the arena, whose face is marred by dust and sweat and blood; who strives valiantly; who errs, and comes short again and again, because there is not effort without error and shortcoming; but who does actually strive to do the deeds; who knows the great enthusiasms, the great devotions; who spends himself in a worthy cause; who at best knows in the end the triumph of high achievement, and who at the worst, if he fails, at least fails while daring greatly, so that his place shall never be with those cold and timid souls who know neither victory nor defeat.[8]

The translation of moral principles into action was critical, TR believed, because there were hard battles to fight at home and in the world. The crux of his message at the Sorbonne was the tendency, more pronounced in the United States than in France, to "admire a false standard of success," the most egregious being the "deification of material well-being in and for itself." Roosevelt delivered most of his speech in English, but he pronounced the following words, stating his position on the "moneyed interests," in French, so as to give them special emphasis: "In every civilized society property rights must be carefully safeguarded. . . . But when it clearly appears that there is a real conflict between [property rights and human rights], human rights must have the upper hand, for property belongs to men and not men to property."[9]

According to the press and other observers, TR's address at the Sorbonne aroused to enthusiasm his effete audience and a "blasé" city. One member of the audience, the president of the Academy of Moral and Political Sciences, praised Roosevelt for enunciating principles that aimed to develop "an American soul, one and inseparable, regardless of the differences of politics and religion." It was France's duty, he continued, to "consider whether we cannot learn a lesson from contemporaneous America." The newspaper *Le Temps* (the forerunner of *Le Monde*) declared that the speech should be taught to students in France as the epitome of national republican duty; it printed 57,000 copies of the Sorbonne address and distributed them free to every schoolteacher in France.[10]

Roosevelt's address was no less acclaimed, albeit more controversial, in the United States. Conservative Republicans, such as Henry Cabot Lodge, fretted that TR's oration presupposed his return to the rough-and-tumble arena of American politics, this time armed with a bolder, more radical program of reform. Roosevelt's prescription for economic reform, which scorned both laissez-faire and socialist remedies for the economic dislocations resulting from the industrial revolution, did not sound especially militant to European ears. Noting the conservative nature of American democracy, the newspaper *Liberté* sniffed, "Ah! Mr. Roosevelt is lucky to be an American. Is he aware that if he were French he would be looked upon as a terrible reactionary?"[11] Not only was TR's advocacy of social reforms modest when compared to the prescription of European social democrats, but his reformist ambition was joined to strong executive power, which French republicans were determined to avoid. On October 1, 1911, looking back on his Sorbonne speech, Roosevelt scorned the French who "unlike the English and Americans . . . do not dare trust any one man with temporary exercise of large power for fear they will be weak enough to let him assume it permanently."[12]

And yet, constitutional principles, buttressed by the decentralized party system, had constrained executive power in the United States since the early part of the nineteenth century. As Roosevelt learned during his time as president, life was not easy for even the most conservative of reformers in early twentieth-century America. TR's challenge to the right of property, especially, touched a nerve in his own country. "'Capital' and 'combinations' or 'aggregations of capital' and 'corporations' are all understood and have certain limits," Lodge acknowledged. But TR's use of the term *property* could apply to anyone; it "ranged from a Vanderbilt down to . . . the small property owner . . . the backbone of the country." Everyone thought his speech in Paris "remarkably fine," Lodge wrote to Roosevelt, "but I discover that talking about the property of Frenchmen and talking about our own property are two different things."[13]

Roosevelt's Romanes lecture at Oxford University, delivered a few months later, was less controversial and caused less of a stir in both the host country and his own than did the Sorbonne address. Nonetheless, this lecture, the longest and most ambitious of his European addresses, gave further confirmation of his desire to regain the highest office in a troubled but potentially great nation. At Oxford, TR took as his subject the "strange analogies" between "those physical groups of animal life which we designate as species, forms, races, and the highly complex and composite entities which rise before our minds when we speak of nations and civilizations." Just as some species became extinct, TR pointed out, so did certain civilizations. More to the point, some civilizations, such as Mesopotamia, disappeared without leaving their mark on future peoples, whereas others, such as Rome, lived on through the "veins of modern" nations.[14]

TR's long exposition of the rough parallel between biological and social history shed light, he claimed, on the futures of Great Britain and the United States. There was much that should give the British and American people concern; just as surely, TR insisted, one could find hope in their refusal to yield "to the craven fear of being great." The Anglo-Saxon sense of international responsibility caused TR to wax optimistically about the prospects for the British and American peoples to leave a lasting legacy for world civilization. "You belong to a nation which possesses the greatest empire upon which the sun has ever shone," TR told his listeners; "I belong to a nation which is trying, on a scale hitherto unexampled, to work out the problems of government for, of and by the people, while at the same time doing the international duty of a great power."[15]

Whether Great Britain would remain a great nation or the United States would become one depended on "national character." Once more, TR preached the "homely commonplace virtues"; once more, he decried "the ominous sign" of the "diminution of the birth rate." Just as "Rome fell by attack from without . . . because the ills within her borders had grown incurable," so also modern nations that aspired to greatness must attend to the slackening of moral character that threatened them: "The really high civilizations must themselves supply the antidote to the self-indulgence and love of ease which they tend to produce." Speaking in more general—his critics said platitudinous—language than he had in France, Roosevelt warned that modern civilized nations had many and terrible problems to solve within their own borders, the most important of which stemmed from the development of industrial capitalism. These problems arose partly from the juxtaposition of poverty and riches; even more troublesome was "the self-consciousness of both poverty and riches." Each nation had to deal with these matters "in its own fashion," TR admitted, but the "spirit" of the approach should be the same everywhere. "It must be a spirit of broad humanity; of brotherly kindness; of acceptance of responsibility, one for each and each for all; and at the same time a spirit as remote as the poles from every form of weakness and sentimentality."[16]

TR's earnest analogy between natural and social history, as well as his vague prescription for the enlightened management of the ills that threatened the survival of modern nations, was not considered an impressive intellectual contribution. His audience sensed, however, that he possessed the necessary leadership qualities to navigate a middle path between wealth and deprivation. "In the way of grading we have at Oxford," said the Archbishop of York, "we agreed to mark the lecture 'Beta Minus,' but the lecturer 'Alpha Plus.' While we felt the lecture was not a very great contribution to science, we were sure that the lecturer was a very great man."[17]

No less than economic conditions, race relations tested the greatness of leaders in the United States and Great Britain. Many contemporary scholars consider TR's talk of biology and races mischievous, an understanding that in the hands of one so ambitious could result in vicious prejudice at home and abroad. Like many progressives, Roosevelt's understanding of reform was influenced by the science of evolution, which was "inseparably connected with the great name of Darwin." He argued in *The Winning of the West,* which was published in 1894, that "the conquest and settlement by the whites of the Indian lands was necessary to the greatness of the race and to the well being of civilized mankind."[18] To his credit, however, Roosevelt freed himself from the most noxious views of an Aryan race and eventually took some care to note the dangers of "biological analogies of history."[19] By the time of the Oxford address, he no longer subscribed to a perverse understanding of evolution, common in the United States at the time, that championed white supremacy. Although hardly a vanguard of enlightened race relations, TR lectured his Oxford audience on tolerance. "True liberality [in domestic affairs]," he stated, "shows itself to best advantage in protecting the rights of others, and especially of minorities." Similarly, in foreign policy "there can be no justification for one race managing or controlling another unless the management and control are exercised in the interest and for the benefit of that other race."[20]

If there was a danger lurking in TR's Oxford homily, it was the expectation that leaders like himself could manage politics at home and abroad benignly. TR posed as a "radical democrat," a self-characterization that anticipated the platform of his Progressive Party campaign. But the responsibilities with which he charged the national government—the duty to serve "humanity" in domestic and foreign affairs—presupposed expanding national administrative power so far as to risk making self-rule impractical. Exalting enlightened administration risked a plebiscitary democracy in which citizens would invest their faith and power in a leader who might govern for, but would hardly be of, the people. From this perspective, it is not surprising that the conservative London *Times* saw TR as imparting useful lessons to republican countries like France and the United States on the necessity of strong leadership: "The inhabitants of purely democratic countries have difficulty in realizing the nature of the limited monarchies which exist in Europe. [We] believe that [Roosevelt's] journey has opened the eyes of the cultivated Americans who have made it to a new conception of the modern monarchical regime."[21]

TR's ambition to play the "modern monarch" was no less apparent to his Oxford hosts, who alluded to it playfully in conferring an honorary degree on him. Lord Curzon, chancellor of the university, proclaimed Roosevelt the first of America's world leaders, destined to return to the seat of power that, it seemed, he now regretted leaving: "Most strenuous of men, most distinguished of citizens today playing a part on the stage of the world, you who have twice administered with purity the first magistracy of the Great Republic (and may perhaps administer it a third time), peer of most august kings, queller of men, destroyer of monsters wherever found, yet the most human of mankind, deeming nothing indifferent to you, not even the blackest of the black."[22]

Such playful banter must have amused TR and, more seriously, intensified the temptation he felt to betray his promise that he would not run again for president. Taft's defection to the Old Guard sent Roosevelt back to the United States with renewed purpose and a rekindled thirst for power. He sailed home determined to rededicate the modern executive office he had created and to restore—indeed, strengthen—its connection to the American people. The social democratically inclined *Manchester Guardian*, although very skeptical of his reform credentials, acknowledged that Roosevelt's return to America was likely to have important political consequences. The *Guardian* objected to the "sentimentality" of TR's Romanes Lecture, especially to its inattention to the heroic work done in "fighting down carbonic acid and tubercle, sweating and alcohol, in New York, London, and Manchester." Nonetheless, it admitted that "Mr. Roosevelt's hold on his countrymen is worth thinking over. It is probably greater than any man before him has ever exercised." Roosevelt, the *Guardian* predicted, would probably attach himself to the "reform" label in order to run for the presidency again.[23]

Roosevelt's European tour, in fact, revealed that he thought the United States must give up its exceptional faith in "unalienable rights" and join the great European powers in protecting individual men and women from the destructive forces of industrialization. As he made clear in his Oxford lecture, Roosevelt shared with many intellectuals and social activists of this period in the United States the view that America must assume a civilizing and redemptive mission at home and abroad. But to assume their true greatness, Americans must join "a world movement of civilization," with the potential "to bind the nations of the world together while yet leaving unimpaired that love of country in the individual citizens which in the present stage of the world's progress is essential to the world's well being."[24]

As the international press observed, there had been a long-standing "habit" for Americans to view Europe as a "wayback," effete, and decadent civilization. But Roosevelt, echoing a number of progressives, frequently expressed in public and private during his tour that he found the contrary to be the case.[25] Fittingly, he expressed his greatest faith in world progress in Germany, where a number of his country's leading reformers had attended universities. Many progressives adopted a Hegelian view that "humankind was lifted ever closer to the achievement of universal ideals through the victories and defeats among peoples and states that defined each historical period."[26] Although American intellectuals were repelled by Germany's authoritarian government—and most could not abide Hegel's position that war was the highest ethical moment for the state—they appreciated its leading place among nations in developing a state insurance system to protect men, women, and children from the harsh realities of industrialization.[27] "When in America we study labor problems and attempt to deal with subjects such as life insurance for wage-workers," Roosevelt noted in his address at the University of Berlin, "we turn to see what you do here in Germany." Anticipating the uneasy, fervent alliance that he would seek to form with those in America who shared the European ambition to build a "modern" state, Roosevelt concluded his Berlin lecture on the sort of idealistic note that he had rarely expressed before in discussing reform possibilities:

> Never has philanthropy, humanitarianism, seen such development as now; and though we must all beware of the folly, and the viciousness no worse than folly, which marks the believer in the perfectibility of man when his heart runs away with his head, or when vanity usurps the place of conscience, yet we must remember also that it is only by working along the lines laid down by the philanthropists, by the lovers of mankind, that we can be sure of lifting our civilization to a higher and more permanent plane of well being than was ever attained by any preceding civilization.[28]

New Nationalism and the Steward of the American People

Roosevelt's intention to spur his country to join the "world movement of civilization" became clear as soon as he set foot on American soil. No sooner had he arrived in New York than the former president found himself embroiled in New York state politics, battling at the behest of Governor Charles E. Hughes for a direct primary bill. Having just been feted in Europe as a highly acclaimed world statesman, and still at the height of his popularity in America, Roosevelt sent a message to the New York legislature urging passage of the reform bill, only to watch state lawmakers decisively defeat the proposal. "The first skirmish has served to throw Mr. Roosevelt back into public life," wrote his cousin Philip in a firsthand account of the

Bull Moose campaign.[29] This "skirmish" was telling, for it revealed the true purpose of Roosevelt's effort to regain the White House: a battle to close the space between the people and their representatives—one that required an assault on the two-party system that anchored the decentralized organizational politics that progressives abhorred. Roosevelt's feeling, confirmed by progressive allies like Gifford Pinchot, that Taft had all too readily made peace with this politics focused his attention on national events. The ambition that Roosevelt expressed in France, Great Britain, and Germany for his country to emerge as a Great Republic would be quixotic, he believed, so long as its politics remained wedded to provincial loyalties. Shortly after the New York battle revealed the resilience of "pioneer democracy," TR used the occasion of a speech in Osawatomie, Kansas, to return to the national political stage with a bold statement of his progressive program.

The Osawatomie speech was delivered on August 31 at the dedication of the John Brown battlefield, commemorating the radical abolitionist's fight for a free constitution in "Bloody Kansas," a struggle that pushed the country to the brink of civil war. Warning that dire times can turn political dramas over to individuals of John Brown's temperament, TR linked his own commitment to reform with Lincoln's desire to cleanse and strengthen the nation. Just as Lincoln struggled with the proponents of slavery to save the Union, so Roosevelt declared himself the leader of a movement poised to do battle with the special interests and privileges, born of industrial capitalism, that preyed on the decentralized republic.

The Osawatomie speech introduced the theme of New Nationalism, derived from Herbert Croly's celebrated book, *The Promise of American Life,* published in 1909, which the distinguished progressive jurist Learned Hand recommended to TR while the former president was still traveling in Europe. "I hope that you will find in it as comprehensive and progressive a statement of American political ideas and ideals as I have found," Hand wrote.[30]

Croly's book was bound to attract TR's attention. Although not uncritical of Roosevelt's leadership, *The Promise of American Life* depicted his presidency as marking a critical stage of American political development—one that promised to rescue the country once and for all from its infatuation with local self-government. Croly criticized Roosevelt's presidential program—the Square Deal—as little more than an effort to extend the Jeffersonian-Jacksonian creed of "equal rights for all, special privileges for none" into the twentieth century. Nonetheless, he insisted that the real meaning of TR's reform was "more novel and radical than the [president had cared] to admit." By linking the executive more directly to public opinion and preparing the federal government to play an important role in domestic and world affairs, Roosevelt gave birth to "a new national democracy" that "tended to emancipate the American idea of [popular rule] from its Jeffersonian bondage."[31]

As Hand put it to Roosevelt, "I think that Croly has succeeded in stating more adequately than anyone else,—certainly of those writers whom I know,—the bases and perspective growth of the set of political ideas which can be fairly described as Neo-Hamiltonian, and whose promise is due more to you, as I believe, than anyone else."[32] Hand knew that Roosevelt had long been interested in resurrecting Hamiltonian principles. "I have never hesitated to criticize Jefferson," TR wrote in 1906; "he was infinitely below Hamilton: I think the worship of Jefferson a discredit to my country; and I have . . . small use for the ordinary Jeffersonian."[33] A self-styled "radical democrat," TR shunned Hamilton's distrust of democracy. At the same time, like many progressive reformers, he considered Hamiltonian nationalism and its faith in strong government as essential prerequisites for reforming American politics.

Lincoln's leadership, TR claimed, provided an essential lesson on how to resuscitate the Hamiltonian tradition. "Men who understand and practice the deep underlying philosophy of the Lincoln school of American political thought," Roosevelt wrote in his *Autobiography,* "are necessarily Hamiltonian in their belief in a strong and efficient National Government and Jeffersonian in their belief in the people as the ultimate authority, and in the welfare of the people as the end of government."[34] TR was thus no doubt flattered by Croly's claim in *The Promise of American Life* that the whole tendency of his presidential program was "to give a democratic meaning and purpose to the Hamiltonian tradition and method."[35]

His reverence for Lincoln notwithstanding, Roosevelt viewed himself as a national leader with an opportunity to transcend the limitations Lincoln faced, and perhaps accepted, in his battle with slavocracy. Lincoln was a dedicated partisan who sought to reform rather than overcome the tradition of local self-government in the United States. Even though some of his Republican brethren did not share his appreciation for localized party politics, the abolition of slavery and the preservation of the Union left the country chronically divided. The Civil War and the constitutional amendments that followed had ostensibly shifted the terms of nation-state relations to the national government; but the potential centralizing effects, even though embodied in the Fourteenth and Fifteenth Amendments to the Constitution, were compromised by the ensuing failure of Reconstruction in the South.

Indeed, although the states were the core polities and played the principal role in regulating business during the first century of the nation's history, it was their local subdivisions—counties, municipalities, townships—that in the nineteenth century performed the bedrock public functions of road-building, poor relief, criminal justice, and schooling.[36]

Roosevelt, Croly claimed, "was the first political leader of the American people to identify the national principle with an ideal of reform."[37] TR hoped that his progressive vision of industrial democracy would bury the issue of race, that it would reunify the nation in a war against privilege. As he put it in the Osawatomie address:

> The New Nationalism puts the national need before sectional or personal advantage. It is impatient of the utter confusion that results from local legislatures attempting to treat national issues as local issues. It is still more impatient of the impotence which springs from overdivision of governmental powers, the impotence which makes it possible for local selfishness or for legal cunning, hired by wealthy special interests, to bring national activities to deadlock. The New Nationalism regards the executive as the steward of the public welfare. It demands of the judiciary that it shall be interested primarily in human welfare rather than in property, just as it demands that the representative body shall represent all the people rather than any one class or section.[38]

Roosevelt's privileging of "human welfare" over "property" echoed his pronouncement at the Sorbonne that "human rights" must take precedence over "property rights." Attempting to insulate himself from the criticisms of Lodge and the Old Guard that he threatened to shake the foundation of a free enterprise system, TR quoted Lincoln, who said, "Labor is prior to, and independent of capital. Capital is only the fruit of labor, and could never have existed if labor had not first existed. Labor is the superior of capital, and deserves much higher consideration." Lincoln spoke these words in his first State of the Union Address in defense of the middle class, noting that a large majority of Americans were neither laborers nor capitalists—"neither work for others nor have others working for them." TR's New Nationalism speech, in contrast, was delivered in a social atmosphere in which economic lines were hardening. "We cannot afford weakly to blind ourselves," TR warned, "to the actual conflict which faces us today."[39]

Although Roosevelt stood for a Square Deal during his presidency, he had long insisted, and now emphasized, that his attempt to navigate between laissez-faire and socialism did not mean he stood "for fair play under the present rules of the game." Rather, he stood for "equality of opportunity and of reward for equally good service." More to the point, TR asserted that the absence of an "effective State, and, especially, national restraint upon unfair money-getting" had "tended to create a small class of enormously wealthy and economically powerful men, whose chief object is to hold and increase their power." This ruthless pursuit of power and fortune had to be regulated. The time had come, Roosevelt argued, for a "policy of a far more active governmental interference with social and economic conditions in this country than we have yet had." Calling for reforms such as the enactment of graduated income and inheritance taxes, Roosevelt argued that a national state had to be formed that could push back against jealous advocates of property rights. "The man who wrongly holds that every human right is secondary to his profit must now give way to the advocate of human welfare, who rightly maintains that every man holds his property subject to the general right of the community to regulate its use to whatever degree the public welfare may require it." Long an advocate of conservation, which he made a popular cause during his presidency, TR now insisted that "the health and vitality of our people are at least as well worth conserving as their forests, waters, lands and minerals, and in this great work the national government must bear a most important part."[40]

Roosevelt exalted the executive—"the steward of the public welfare"—as the principal advocate for the national community. This implied that the president must become the center of a revamped executive branch empowered to regulate social and economic conditions in the public interest. Roosevelt's New Nationalism thus foreshadowed, as Croly recognized, centralized administration and threatened the nation's deep and abiding commitment to democratic individualism. The emancipation of the national government from parties and interests threatened to create a form of statism that Americans long had been taught to shun and fear. Indeed, many progressives rejected Roosevelt's view that the American romance with localism was emblematic of an outdated "pioneer" form of democracy. The prominent Wisconsin reformer Robert La Follette, elected to the Senate in 1906, and the "attorney for the whole people," Louis Brandeis, emphatically opposed TR's emphasis on national regulation, looking, instead, to vigorous reform in the states and militant antitrust policy in Washington to transfer power from the few to the many.[41]

La Follette and key supporters such as Brandeis would give birth to the

National Progressive Republican League in January 1911 with the purpose of elevating the Wisconsin senator and his neo-Jeffersonian form of progressive politics to the White House. Anticipating his own campaign, animated by a less compromising challenge to the Jeffersonian tradition, Roosevelt criticized reformers' dedication to competition and decentralization as unrealistic. "Combinations in industry are the result of an imperative economic law which cannot be repealed by political legislation," he said in the New Nationalism speech. "The effort at prohibiting all combination has substantially failed. The way out lies, not in attempting to prevent such combinations, but in completely controlling them in the interest of the public welfare."[42]

The former president was equally troubled by La Follette's program of political reform. The National Progressive Republican League, believing that "popular government is fundamental to all other questions," advocated extensive reforms of the political process that would weaken political parties and establish a stronger connection between representatives and the public. To that end, it championed "first, the election of the United States Senators by direct vote of the people; second, direct primaries, for the nomination of all elected officials; third, the direct election of delegates to National Conventions with opportunity for the voter to express his choice for President and Vice President; fourth, amendment to state constitutions providing for the initiative, referendum and recall; fifth, a thorough-going corrupt practices act."[43]

Roosevelt acknowledged the practical value of such mechanisms of direct government to the progressive cause. Indeed, he praised the Wisconsin legislature for its circumspect consideration of the initiative, referendum, and recall. However, TR contrasted the legislators' practical approach to political reform, their interest in "practical results," with La Follette's "abstract talk about 'the rights of the people' or 'the wisdom of the multitude,' or any appeals of the type made by the men of 1789 in France."[44] Roosevelt declined to join La Follette's league, arguing that the political reform the Wisconsin senator championed in the service of popular rights would undermine the competent and energetic administration of national and state policies. Like Hand, TR believed that populist insurgents in the Midwest and West had little understanding of the New Nationalism, which required the sort of resolve he had demonstrated as president to both reconstitute the executive and expand administrative power. As Hand wrote Croly:

They have about as much sense of what you are after and the few individuals here in the East who sympathize with you, as they have [of]

CHAPTER TWO

Neo-Cart[es]ianism. Their damned nostrums [of] popular government are all well enough, in their way, but I doubt whether they have even understanding of these, and I can't see that their plans go any further or contemplate any administrative program.[45]

Although initially skeptical of direct government measures such as the initiative, referendum, and recall, Roosevelt did embrace the league's support of electoral reform, especially the direct primary. The direct election of representatives, he argued, was an essential ingredient of national reconstruction. In Osawatomie, TR celebrated public opinion as a force that might ensure popular control of the national state that New Nationalists proposed to build. "We need to make our political representatives more quickly and sensitively responsive to the people whose servants they are," TR declared. "More direct action by the people in their own affairs under proper safeguards is vitally necessary. The direct primary is a step in this direction."[46]

Roosevelt's temperate support for direct democracy was joined to his refrain, central to his speeches in Europe, about the importance of good character. The involvement of individual men in politics—he was not yet prepared to champion women's suffrage—was not an entitlement, as such, but an opportunity to develop "the right kind of character." Good character, however, TR stated declaratively in Osawatomie—character that made for a good father, husband, and neighbor—required a "genuine and permanent moral awakening," a new sense of public obligation that would not occur without "the kind of law and the kind of administration of the law which will give to those qualities in the private citizen the best possible chance of improvement."[47] Progressivism, properly understood, meant that Americans had to overcome the limitations of their past, TR believed, and he intended to play a principal part in the transformation of the nation's character.

Roosevelt's speech at the John Brown celebration, Lodge wrote, "startled people [in Washington]." Even some moderate Republicans feared the implications of his critique of property and political parties.[48] Indeed, it occurred to some observers in government and the press that TR's celebration of stewardship in the service of the public welfare transcended the differences between Democrats and Republicans. It portended, they feared, a novel and mischievous relationship between leaders and those they led. The speech was not cut from whole cloth, of course. It covered ground that TR touched on as president and echoed some of the words he spoke at the

Sorbonne and Oxford. But, as a *New York Times* editorial opined, the New Nationalism speech "was more comprehensive" than any other of his previous addresses.

> The tone is that of the leader, of a man defining his programme before the public, defending it, arguing it, assailing his opponents. . . . A striking feature of it is that the cause does not appear to be the cause of the speaker's party, and the rivals pressed are not Democrats. The campaign is that of Mr. Roosevelt against whosoever does not agree with him, and these are Republicans, not Democrats. It presents itself as a personal campaign. No distinct objective is formulated, but the central figure is the orator himself.[49]

The Progressive Cause and Candidate-Centered Politics

Despite his cautious approach to political reform, Roosevelt's New Nationalism was fraught with constitutional implications. To the extent that the government became committed to a reform program that was essentially national in character, he recognized the American people, deeply suspicious of centralized power, would become increasingly impatient with institutional arrangements that separated the cup of power from their lips. Yet the advocacy of direct democracy threatened to undermine the foundations of constitutional government, to exploit the tendency of individuals living in a democracy to reject the need for space between government and people.

For a time, however, it was La Follette, not TR, who seemed destined to champion the new idea of democracy in the coming presidential election. A number of people, recognizing that his New Nationalism speech anticipated another run for the presidency, were prepared to join the "back from Elba" movement and wrote TR to suggest that an organization be formed to promote a Roosevelt candidacy for the 1912 election. But Roosevelt held back throughout most of 1911, conceding that a progressive was unlikely to deny Taft the nomination. The best thing for the reform wing of the party, he believed, was "to do what we can with Taft, face probable defeat in 1912, and then endeavor to reorganize under really capable and sanely progressive leadership." Without saying so directly, TR seemed resigned to bide his time—to become leader of the progressive forces after 1912 and, ultimately, the candidate of a remade Republican Party in 1916.[50]

Seizing the opportunity to command the growing insurgent wing of his party, La Follette announced his candidacy on June 17, 1911. He did so after securing pledges of financial support from, among others, Gifford Pinchot and his brother Amos. Roosevelt must have viewed the growing support for La Follette, which now included one of his closest and most important political allies, with more than a little uneasiness. Nonetheless, he continued to have real doubts, not only about the progressives' chance to deny an incumbent president the nomination of his party, but also concerning the dominant message of the National Progressive Republican League. TR believed direct democracy was at best a means to a thorough national reconstruction—the sort of transformation of moral principles he called for in his speeches at the Sorbonne and Oxford. "It is half amusing and half pathetic to see so many good people convinced that the world can be reformed without difficulty merely by reforming the machinery of government," he wrote La Follette in September 1911. Although Roosevelt supported the direct primary, he cautioned that the reform of nomination contests "can only give the chance to the majority to have good government if they choose to take the trouble to get it; and if they do not take the trouble, the boss will run the . . . primary exactly as he ran politics before the . . . primary was adopted." "Good machinery," he continued, "is indispensable in order to produce the best results, but the best machinery will be of no use unless . . . men have the right attitude on public questions—and of course the right attitude must include not merely understanding what is needed by the people, but the right spirit and the necessary courage and capacity to make this spirit effective."[51]

"Of all the figures in American history," the political theorist Mark Hulliung has written, "Teddy Roosevelt was one of the most 'republican,' one of the few who was even in some sense classically republican, a Roman in the modern age, who could not too often extol the 'virile virtues,' the manly, heroic, masterful code of the Roman warrior and statesman."[52] TR wanted the United States to transcend itself: to escape its natural rights tradition, to acknowledge duty and responsibility, and to realize its potential as a great republic. Celebrating the "rights of the people," he feared, risked conceding too much to an idea of equality that would render strong leadership in the service of national community a chimera. Commenting on the Jacksonians' celebration of the president as the "tribune of the people," Alexis de Tocqueville warned that democratic leaders in America were sorely tempted to flatter the people as "too superior to the weakness of human nature to lose the command of their temper for an instant." In treating people as their masters, in assuring them that "they have all the virtues without having acquired them," democratic leaders inevitably deprived themselves of honor; "by sacrificing their opinions, they prostitute themselves."[53]

Roosevelt styled himself a friend of popular rule but insisted that a sincere and effective democratic leader had to lead, and not slavishly follow, public opinion. When Charles Dwight Willard, a militant California progressive, took TR to task in February 1911 for his tepid support of direct democracy—especially for his unwillingness to promote measures such as the initiative, referendum, and recall—Roosevelt warned of the dangerous tendency "to speak of democracy . . . as if it were a goddess, as if the mere name had a fetishistic or superstitious value." In the first instance, TR denied that the elimination of institutions like legislatures would strengthen popular accountability. The people, properly understood, would lose influence to a "small and alert minority" when left to their own devices in a mass society. Self-rule might be served by direct government in a small community, as evidenced by the town-meeting style of government in New England. But public opinion would lose its harmony and effectiveness when methods of direct democracy were introduced in a large city like Los Angeles, let alone the mass society that composed America's national "community." More fundamentally, TR argued, as he had repeatedly since his return to public life, that machinery abetting majority rule itself counted for nothing when compared to "the spirit of the people": "In our government the question of the *rights* of the people is not nearly as important as the question of the *duties* of the people. Here the people is sovereign. Let the sovereign beware of flatterers!"[54]

The architects of the Constitution, especially James Madison, claimed that prudent institutional arrangements could buttress, if not substitute for, "republican responsibility." Given TR's neo-Hamiltonian orientation to reform, it is not surprising that he emphasized leadership rather than constitutional forms as a way to "refine and enlarge the public views." The Constitution, at least as it was interpreted at the beginning of the twentieth century, valued local self-government and individual rights, not duties and responsibilities. What's more, extant constitutional arrangements, which privileged Congress and state legislators, acted as a powerful gravitational pull against statesmanship as Roosevelt understood it. Only true republican statesmen, those who might elevate the conversation of American democracy and cultivate a vital sense of national community, could work against this pull.

The rule of the majority is good only if the majority has the will and the morality and the intelligence to do right; and the majority of the peoples of mankind are not yet in such shape that they can prosper under the very kind of rule which is essential for us here in America to have, and under which alone *we* can prosper and bring ourselves to the highest point of developed usefulness.[55]

America's great leaders, not "slavish" followers of public opinion, had been critical agents of national development in America's past. TR hoped to join that distinguished fraternity, even if it meant resisting the vanguard of the Progressive movement. "You say that I can never be admitted into your lodge by the use of words such as I have used," he wrote at the end of his letter to Willard: "Friend, friend, in my lodge the masters of the past are Washington and Lincoln, and admission to it is not by words or fine, futile phrases, but by service and achievement; and it is only by membership in this lodge that good can really be done by the lovers of mankind."[56]

During his presidency, Roosevelt sought to adhere to the compromise that Washington and Lincoln struck between national leadership and constitutional propriety. As Croly appreciated, TR styled himself as a new kind of popular leader. He was the first president, for example, to secure reform legislation by appealing directly for popular support, thus overcoming the resistance of Congress and even the leaders of his own party. As Roosevelt reflected on his efforts to overcome the opposition of the Republican Old Guard in enacting the Hepburn Act (1906), which enhanced the power of the Interstate Commerce Commission to regulate railroad shipping rates and to enforce its regulations, "Gradually I was forced to abandon the effort to persuade them to come my way and then I achieved results only by appealing over the heads of the Senate and House leaders to the people, who were the masters of both of us."[57] Nonetheless, Roosevelt also believed that a balance must exist between presidential initiative and congressional deliberation in order to maintain the constitutional system of government. Accordingly, even as he insisted that the modern president had to assume a more prominent place in public affairs than his nineteenth-century predecessors, even as he made unprecedented efforts to form a direct personal tie with the public, TR worked assiduously to win support in Congress by cooperating with Republican leaders in the House and Senate. In fighting for the Hepburn Act, for example, Roosevelt directed his energies not just to the podium but also, more craftily, to the halls of Congress.[58]

Even as he sought to return to power, Roosevelt hoped to work within, rather than fully confront, his party and the constitutional order it supported. But his determination to stay out of the 1912 contest and to resist progressive leaders' infatuation with "the People" was sorely tested by La Follette's candidacy, which appeared to be gaining momentum toward the end of 1911. Three hundred Progressives, representing thirty states, gathered in Chicago on October 16 at a National Progressive Republican Conference to endorse the Wisconsin senator as "the logical candidate" for the 1912 GOP nomination. The keynote of the conference was a call for justice that could be traced back to the earliest awakenings of American democracy: wrest power from "the representatives of special privilege." But the league's program for industrial reform presupposed a departure from the decentralized republic born of Jeffersonian and Jacksonian democracy. Moreover, the Chicago gathering celebrated a political program that did not envision remaking the Republican Party as much as it championed a politics without parties. The conference endorsed a resolution championing a *candidate*-centered presidential selection process, in which the party convention would rubber-stamp the verdict of popular state contests: "We favor the ascertainment of the choice of Republican voters as to candidates for president by direct primary vote held in each state, pursuant to statute, and where no such statute exists we urge that the Republican state committees provide that the people be given the right to express their choice for president."[59]

TR's supporters at the conference, such as James Garfield of Ohio, who had served as the Secretary of the Interior in his administration, were startled to see that the vanguard of the Progressive movement was quickly evolving into a new form of candidate-centered campaign organization, which rested near-complete faith in a single leader. The "great need of the hour," the conference participants believed, "was a recognized leader under whom the progressive forces in every state could be united." So long as TR demurred, the logical candidate to forge unity out of the disparate progressive forces was La Follette, who had an impressive record of accomplishment as governor of Wisconsin and U.S. senator. Senator Moses Clapp of Minnesota gave dramatic testimony of the progressives' commitment to create a new, more direct connection between national leaders and the American people: "I believe . . . that this great uprising, this force that is making itself felt from ocean to ocean, will waste itself in internal discord unless we take a symbol around which to rally. Senator La Follette in himself is a platform that represents the progressive spirit."[60]

TR, of course, intended himself to represent the national reform spirit. It was becoming clear, however, that it would be difficult for him to do so on his own terms. The burgeoning support for La Follette suggested that the Progressive movement was cresting more rapidly than he had expected. Moreover, with the ascendance of La Follette, Roosevelt was no longer the natural leader of the progressive reformers. To gain its support, he would have to participate in a battle for the mantle of reform leader, in a contest that would require the sort of appeal to public opinion he had stubbornly proscribed. Garfield, who had come to the Chicago meeting straight from New York, where he had conferred with TR, testified to the difficulty of stalling the La Follette bandwagon. He had hoped to prevent the conference from endorsing La Follette, but, as he conceded to TR, "I fully recognized the great value of a definite leadership at this particular time, and as there was no other man who has as strong a following as La Follette, I deemed it expedient to consent to the endorsement which was afterward adopted."[61]

La Follette and his political allies could not have been comforted, however, by the letter Garfield wrote to the Wisconsin senator the following day. "Although he was willing to yield" his "individual opinion on the subject and agree to the final resolution as drawn," Garfield explained, he viewed the conference action as "a recommendation, not a pledge." Moreover, he urged the senator and his political friends to accept the possibility that "Republicans in the different states" might find it advisable "to select unpledged delegations or delegations for other progressive candidates." Expressing the vain hope that progressive reform ambitions would trump personal rivalry, Garfield concluded, "I know that you feel the cause is of far greater importance than the fortunes of any of its adherents, and that we must all be free to adopt the course that will be the most effective in our own localities."[62]

In fact, the contest between La Follette and Roosevelt would reveal that grand idealism and candidate-centered ambition were inextricably joined in the emerging reform movement. In part, the tension between movement politics and the quest for personal command was attributable to the inherent nature of electoral politics. Equally important, however, was the progressive reform program, which celebrated a direct personal connection between leaders and citizens that could all too easily degenerate into a contest of naked ambition and mutual recrimination. Hoping to avoid such a contest, La Follette dispatched two of his supporters to New York: Chicago newspaperman Gilson Gardner and the muckraking journalist Ray Stannard Baker.

As TR reported to Lodge, Gardner and Baker asked him "to make an announcement that he would refuse the nomination if offered it." Roosevelt "refused them point blank." Insisting that he "emphatically did not want the nomination," TR added, nevertheless, "that I should certainly not definitely state that if it did come in the form of a duty I would refuse to perform that duty." Offering Lodge a refrain he would repeat thereafter in much of his correspondence about his candidacy, Roosevelt wrote, "in other words, as Abraham Lincoln used to say, no man can justly ask me to cross such a bridge until I come to it."[63]

The tone of the letter must have persuaded Lodge that his friend was rapidly approaching this bridge—and that he was about to cross it not as a classical republican but, rather, as a champion of progressive democracy. Taking Lodge to task for his attack on reforms such as the initiative and referendum, TR more than hinted that he was preparing to endorse such measures: "I do wish that you would not imitate ultra-Progressives by treating machinery which may be quite right in one place and quite wrong in another as supremely important," he wrote. But then TR hastened to add, "There are many States in which the people are groping for a remedy, and I believe it is idle in such States to try to persuade them not to adapt the remedy because under totally different conditions a couple of thousand years ago, a totally different people in Rome or Athens failed in endeavoring to work out a system that was only remotely analogous to the present system." Once intent on distinguishing old New England remedies and contemporary progressive ones, Roosevelt now viewed progressive democracy as the contemporary equivalent of the town meeting, which, he reminded Lodge, was "regarded as . . . ultraradical a hundred and twenty-five years ago."[64]

As the presidential election year approached, TR's political rivals feared that an effective Roosevelt organization had been formed to serve progressive democracy. Just as he had spurned La Follette's importunity that he definitively renounce his candidacy, so Roosevelt refused to reassure Taft at the start of the presidential election year that "under no circumstances" would he accept another nomination for presidency. TR's refusal to close the door on another race for the White House confirmed the fears of the Taft administration that a "Roosevelt movement" was now operating openly and stood in the "path of the president to certain and easy renomination."[65]

La Follette had witnessed more tangible evidence of the growing influence of a Roosevelt movement at a convention of the Ohio Progressive League that met at the end of December 1911. Hoping to solidify his position as the candidate of the growing insurgency in a key state, the La Follette forces had traversed Ohio and selected delegates thought to be pledged to their candidate. Their plans were thwarted, however, when Garfield and Gifford Pinchot spoke out against giving any candidate the progressives' endorsement. After a heated debate, the convention voted 52–32 to pass a resolution, proposed by Pinchot, leaving open the preference for president.[66] "The Progressive Conference at Columbus yesterday was thoroughly satisfactory," Garfield reported to Roosevelt. "After a hard fight we adapted the resolutions theretofore agreed to." More than hinting that TR had decided to enter the fray, he continued, "The extreme La Follette men would have made a very bad blunder had La Follette been endorsed. As it is, we will be able to bring together practically all the Progressives in the State."[67]

Although he continued to demur in public, Roosevelt now was only waiting for the right opportunity to announce his candidacy. Agitated by this inevitability and fearful that some of his most intimate and important supporters, such as the Pinchot brothers, were preparing to join the Roosevelt campaign, La Follette took a series of missteps that gave Roosevelt the opening for which he was looking. In late January 1912, La Follette wrote a supporter in Illinois asking for help in circumventing his own state organization for fear that some of its key members had left the reservation. Asking for the names of leading Illinois progressives he might rely on, La Follette wrote, "There are those in the [La Follette] Headquarters at Chicago who are giving more attention to encouraging sentiment for another candidate than they are to organizing the sentiment for the candidate for whom the headquarters were opened."[68] He wanted the list of reliable supporters to preserve his own personal organization, La Follette stated angrily, "because I do not propose to have anyone play me for a stalking horse for anybody."[69]

This state of agitation, which tended to repel rather than renew the loyalty of his wavering supporters, must have affected La Follette when he attended the annual banquet of the Periodical Publishers' Association, held in Philadelphia, a few days later. Exhausted by his strenuous campaign, upset by the news that his young daughter must have an operation, and discouraged by knowledge of "the studied undermining of his candidacy by his own supporters," La Follette considered canceling the talk to the publishers. But having been told repeatedly that the Roosevelt movement was encouraged by opposition to his candidacy in the Northeast, he probably felt great pressure not only to show up but also to give an address that would burnish his reform credentials.

By his own admission, La Follette "flunked" the test of his Progressive candidacy in Philadelphia.[70] Following New Jersey governor and Democratic hopeful Woodrow Wilson, who gave a crisp rendition of the need for liberalizing trade, La Follette proceeded to lecture his audience about the destructive influence of money in American political life. Unfortunately, he strayed from his text, a well-reasoned address on the emergence of the corporation and the threat it posed to American democracy, to launch an attack on journalists. This diatribe in the midst of newspaper publishers might have exalted La Follette as a courageous reformer, willing to call powerful interests to account. But the attack was so poorly executed, at such length, that the result was a complete disaster. The senator rambled on for two and a half hours, and when he finished, well after midnight, few remained in the room but the deeply embarrassed guests at the head table. As the *Philadelphia Evening Bulletin* reported:

> Respectful attention gave way at the end of an hour to confusion and at the end of two hours the confusion took on the proportions of an uproar, composed largely of demands from various parts of the big banquet hall that the Senator from Wisconsin "sit down. . . ." When the Senator from the Middle West resumed his seat, after vehemently asserting that he would take his own time to conclude, it was the consensus of opinion that the La Follette Presidential boom had received a mortal hurt, if indeed, it was not dead.[71]

In part, the collapse of La Follette's campaign followed from a disastrous event, influenced by the stress of personal circumstances; more deeply, the senator was the victim of political reform that his candidacy presumed to champion. La Follette was "a revelation of a new type of politics," one of his supporters wrote. He "threatens to leaven our political selfishness and party rot with a sincere, simple loving manhood."[72] La Follette soon learned, however, that the candidate-centered campaign this new politics required imposed personal challenges that he was not especially well suited to master. Like W. Jennings Bryan, he was a superb stump speaker, but the mass democracy that Progressives prescribed called for a more artful approach to public opinion leadership. Much of the press's criticism of La Follette focused not on the substance of his address but, rather, on his speaking style and personal qualities. The senator's ability as a public speaker was compared unfavorably with that of Governor Wilson, "who was suave, urbane, polished and did not forget that 'brevity is the soul of wit.'"[73] La Follette's style may have been effective in the Senate, where his emotional attacks on special interests had made him a leading figure in the Progressive movement. But his Philadelphia performance more than hinted that his slashing, polarizing rhetoric would not work as well in the emerging national media, especially when it was directed at those who published newspapers.

La Follette's speech did praise the weekly and monthly magazine publishers, less partisan than newspaper editors and a critical lifeline to mass opinion. But his distinction between newspapers and popular magazines . was lost amid the rambling protracted attack on the press. Even muckraking journals, he warned toward the end of his excruciating address, were vulnerable to the control of special interests. No less than newspaper publishers, the owners of these periodicals were in danger of becoming dependent on advertising, a "new peril" that in time would seek to "gag" national magazines. La Follette's unstinting populism and his unwillingness to pay court to the emerging mass media on which progressive reformers depended suggested that he would be left behind as more sophisticated practitioners of the new politics like Wilson and TR eagerly embraced the methods of mass appeal.[74]

Viewing La Follette's Philadelphia debacle as the opportunity for which they had been waiting, TR and his allies put an end to the ex-president's restless political exile. Seven governors—the chief executives of West Virginia, Nebraska, New Hampshire, Wyoming, Michigan, Kansas, and Missouri—sent a "somewhat cooked letter," as Roosevelt's daughter called it, urging Roosevelt to become a candidate for the 1912 Republican nomination for president. The letter, dated February 10, insisted, rather disingenuously, that their request for Roosevelt to accept the nomination if it was offered him was "unsolicited and unsought," but if he declined to accept the nomination, he would be "unresponsive to a plain public duty."[75] Roosevelt demurred no longer: his brief response, dated Saturday, February 24, was published in the Monday newspapers. The governors' letter, he acknowledged, "put a heavy responsibility" on him, expressing as it did "the carefully considered convictions of the men elected by popular vote to stand as the heads of government in their several States." At the same time, Roosevelt concluded, the decision was not his or the governors' to make but the American people's. Giving notice that his republican resistance to militant progressives' notion of direct democracy had weakened, TR stated his commitment to "the genuine rule of the people" and expressed his hope that the people would be given the opportunity, "through direct primaries, to express their preferences as to who shall be the nominee of the Republican presidential convention."[76]

So eager was he to jump into the fray that Roosevelt did not wait until his letter to the governors was published to announce his candidacy. On February 21, arriving in Ohio to give a speech before the state's constitutional convention, Roosevelt made a brief stop in Cleveland, where he was met by an admiring crowd and a local politician, W. F. Eldrick. "I want a direct answer, Colonel," said Eldrick. "All your friends want to know now, whether you are to be a candidate." TR's response added a colorful and enduring phrase to the vocabulary of American politics: "My hat is in the ring!"[77] This phrase, used by cowboys to signal they were ready to fight, would become the mantra of a new politics in which candidates, rather than parties, dominated campaigns. Earlier that day, addressing the constitutional convention in Columbus, TR detailed his platform of "pure democracy" that went well beyond his previous defense of the direct primary and championed the rights of the people with the same fervor he had only a few months earlier condemned in his criticism of the National Progressive Republican League's platform.

A Charter of Democracy

Roosevelt's Columbus speech, the *Nation* observed, was "the Osawatomie speech all over again, only sharpened. So direct an appeal to radicalism and to disturbing agitation Mr. Roosevelt never made before."[78] An independent but constitutionally conservative journal, the *Nation* took exception to Roosevelt's growing militancy with respect to economic and political reform. "The ends of government are to secure a high average of moral and material well being among our citizens," he proclaimed. "It has been well said in the past that we have paid attention only to the accumulation of prosperity, and that from henceforth we must pay equal attention to the proper distribution of prosperity." "Our aim," Roosevelt added solemnly, "should be to make this as far as may be not merely a political, but an industrial democracy."

Industrial democracy did not require an attack on property. Roosevelt denied, as the *Nation* charged, that "prosperity" was "property misspelled." To be sure, true progressives were "bound to prevent any unfair and improper distribution [of wealth]"; but "it behooves us to remember," Roosevelt continued, "that there is no use in advising methods for the proper distribution of prosperity unless the prosperity is there to distribute." Nonetheless, TR insisted, "human rights" should be held "supreme over all other rights."

"We stand for the rights of property," Roosevelt further elaborated, "but we stand even more for the rights of man." This meant, as Roosevelt had indicated in his Kansas address, that business practices had to be squared with the public interest: "We have only praise for the business man whose business success comes as an incident to doing good work for his fellows, but we should so shape conditions that a fortune shall be obtained only in honorable fashion, in such fashion that its gaining represents benefit to the community." Granting that the wealthy individual had rights, TR still insisted that "he [held] his wealth subject to the general right of the community to regulate its use as the public welfare require[d]."

In truth, Roosevelt's "industrial democracy" merely stated more pointedly what he had been saying since his European tour. What gave the Columbus speech its "intensely radical nature," as the press characterized it, was his constitutional program, his defense of "pure democracy," which championed institutional arrangements that would be "a means of . . . securing rather than thwarting the absolute right of the people to rule themselves and to provide for their social and industrial well being." Prior to the Columbus speech, TR was widely viewed as a pragmatic Republican who might reconcile regular and insurgent members of the party. But now he embraced a "Charter for Democracy" that established him, rather than La Follette, as the radical alternative to the staid politics of Taft. "The only safe course to follow in this great American democracy," he argued, "is to provide for making the popular feeling effective." In this spirit, Roosevelt urged that "weapons" be placed in the hands of the people that "would make the representatives more easily and certainly responsive to the people's will." These initiatives included not just the direct primary, which TR endorsed in his Osawatomie speech, but also the methods of direct government that he had hitherto refused to embrace: the initiative, referendum, and recall; the direct election of U.S. senators; and, most controversial of all, the recall of judicial decisions. When state courts invalidated state laws on the grounds that these statutes were in conflict with the state or national constitution, TR asserted, such opinions should be subjected to the court of public opinion:

> If any considerable number of people feel that the decision is in defiance
> of justice, they should be given the right by petition to bring before
> the people at some subsequent election, special or otherwise, as might
> be decided, and after opportunity for debate has been allowed, the
> question whether or not judges' interpretation of the Constitution is to

be sustained. If it is sustained, well and good. If not, then the popular verdict is to be accepted as final; the decision is to be allowed to be reversed, and the construction of the Constitution definitely decided; subject only to action by the Supreme Court of the United States.[79]

"Roosevelt's speech struck home," Garfield wrote in his diary after observing the "splendid reception" it received in his home state. "A great day," he continued; "TR's hold on the people is marvelous."[80] The Columbus address reverberated far beyond the enthusiastic crowd that heard it. Given great play in the press, it stirred the country and aroused intense reaction in the nation's capital. "Since your Columbus speech and especially since your announcement, the air in Washington has been electric — charged as it was during the days of your administration," a supporter wrote TR a few weeks later: "There is gloom at the White House and the Taft headquarters because they realize now it is a fight to the finish. They appreciate, moreover, that your Columbus speech has made the issues of the campaign, has forced Taft on the defensive, and finally has made the President leader of the reactionary forces."[81]

The radical ground that TR staked out in his Columbus address was anything but terra firma, however. "That bold statement impaired considerably Roosevelt's chance of securing the [Republican] nomination," the historian George Mowry has written. "For by attacking American judicial institutions he alienated the conservative wing of his party, which might have supported him for the sake of a possible victory."[82] Standpat Republicans and large industrial interests who had long appreciated TR's disdain for radical antitrust policy rapidly abandoned the former president. No one jumped from the Roosevelt bandwagon more quickly than Lodge, who had been watching the ex-president's growing reform ambition with apprehension since the New Nationalism speech. Lodge owed much to his lifelong friend; indeed, without TR's steadfast support, it is unlikely that he would have been reelected to the Senate in 1910. But TR's Columbus speech so offended Lodge that he could no longer support him for president: "I found myself confronted with the fact that I was opposed to your policies declared at Columbus with great force in regard to changes on our Constitution and principles of government. . . . I knew, of course, that you and I differed on some of these points but I had not realized that the differences were so wide."[83]

The opposition to Roosevelt's program went far beyond the embattled stand-patters. Hand was a strong supporter of TR's New Nationalism, but he grew alarmed at Roosevelt's growing enthusiasm for direct democracy, fearing, as his biographer Gerald Gunther has written, the "populist, sometimes demagogic qualities" of Roosevelt's leadership. "The marvelous child is almost always right," Hand wrote to a mutual friend; "I think he does not have to pick out the path of reason, but is drawn on by the goal." Nonetheless, he continued, "I wish you or someone else could have side-tracked the appeal by referendum, which is really a stupid make-shift."[84]

Roosevelt's attack on the courts was not as crudely expedient as Hand suggested. In fact, he and TR had been debating the proposal for holding popular referenda on court decisions since the previous November. Roosevelt sent Hand proofs of an address he had given at New York City's Carnegie Hall on October 20, 1911, entitled "The Conservation of Womanhood and Childhood," which first issued his call to subordinate decisions of the courts to public opinion: "The people should be enabled with reasonable speed and in effective fashion themselves to determine by popular vote whether or not they will permit the judges' interpretation of the Constitution to stand."[85] As a sitting judge on the federal district court, Hand regretted that he "could not object more" to TR's attack on the judiciary. But he had to admit that cases like *Lochner v. New York,* decided in 1905, in which the Supreme Court held unconstitutional a New York law that prohibited the employment of bakery workers for more than ten hours a day or sixty hours a week, badly distorted the meaning of the due process clause of the Fourteenth Amendment.[86]

The decision that prompted Roosevelt's Carnegie Hall address and the more specific call to reform the judiciary in Columbus was an opinion pronounced by the highest court in New York, *Ives v. South Buffalo Ry. Co.,* handed down in March 1911, which held that the state's recently enacted workmen's compensation law was unconstitutional.[87] The *Ives* decision was so disturbing to progressives like Hand and TR because it confirmed the enduring importance of "Lochnerism," which interpreted the Fourteenth Amendment as a bulwark of property that forbade the sort of basic protections against corporate power that had gained currency in most other industrial countries. Hand especially regretted how this "substantive due process" empowered judges to trump legislatures — the "kind of interpretation of such vague clauses as 'due process of law' [that] takes away from the legislature the power to do those things which are recognized as within the legislative power in every civilized country of the world." Nonetheless, he "could not quite swallow the necessity of having public pressure put on judges for any purpose," for to do so would "utterly pervert" the duty of judges to interpret the law. To transmute judges into the servants of public opinion, he lectured Roosevelt, would be no less evil than to bestow legal power on them. For Hand, the remedy for judicial impropriety was not to eliminate judicial independence but, instead, to rest the power of judicial review in a more sensible understanding of the law, even if that meant excising vague clauses from the Constitution:

> Really we [judges] have got ourselves in the mess we are now in here in America, by failing to remember how strictly our duties should be interpretive. . . . In construing the vague clauses of the Bill of Rights we have done the most damage, and something must be done to change it, but I really think that I had rather take them out of the Constitution altogether than make the judges respond to any popular pressure.[88]

Hand's reaction to Roosevelt's proposal confirmed the ex-president's belief that his plan to curb judicial imperialism was not radical. Rather, it was an alternative to more extreme solutions, like Hand's, which contemplated purging the Bill of Rights from the Constitution. "Evidently I must try to make my expressions more clear," his reply to Hand stated. He did not propose to allow the voters to recall judges, as La Follette prescribed, "but in Constitutional cases [as egregious as the *Ives* decision] the alternative must be to secure the right of appeal from judges." Anticipating his Columbus speech, TR made clear that his "idea would be to have a Constitutional Convention provide that the people shall have the right as to whether or not the judges' interpretation of the law in such a case is correct, and that their vote shall be decisive."[89] In actuality, Roosevelt claimed, he sought to avoid the delegation of policy to an unchecked legislature that might embody the sort of factionalism that plagued France and England and worried the architects of the Constitution. As he wrote to Henry Stimson,

> I am keenly aware that there are not a few among the men who claim to be leaders in the progressive movement who bear an unpleasant resemblance to the lamented Robespierre and his fellow progressives of 1791 and 1792. What I am earnestly trying, as far as my abilities permit, is to prevent this country from sinking into a condition of political oscillation between the progressive of the Robespierre type and the conservative of the Bourbon type.[90]

Roosevelt gave public testimony that his remedy for mischievous judicial activism was not "revolutionary" but, rather, "the highest and wisest kind of conservatism" in a second widely publicized speech at Carnegie Hall on March 20, 1912. Responding to a proposal that Hand had sent him a few days before this address—proposing that state legislatures and Congress, not the courts, should have the power to determine "due process of law"—TR acknowledged that judicial imperialism would be aborted by amending state constitutions so that judges would be denied power "to review the legislature's determination of a policy of social justice." As Hand had suggested, this could be accomplished either by providing that any act of the legislature would be "due process of law" or by defining "due process of law in such strict terms that no court [could] have [an] excuse for substituting its own view of public policy for the legislature's." But TR rejected this remedy, claiming that his own was both more democratic and less radical: "For under the method I suggest the people may sustain the court as against the legislature, whereas, if due process were defined in the Constitution, the decision of the legislature would be final."[91]

Roosevelt's claim that popular referenda on judicial rulings would buttress, rather than weaken, constitutional forms did not persuade self-styled guardians of judicial independence. As will be discussed in Chapter 3, once TR threw his hat in the ring the burden of defending constitutional sobriety fell most heavily on William Howard Taft. Taft had repeatedly denied that he was an enemy of progressive reform; however, the opposition aroused by TR's plan for popular recall of judicial decisions allowed the incumbent president to find honor in the charge of conservatism leveled against him. As he declared in an address to the Massachusetts Legislature, the suggestion that judges should be subject to the discipline of popular elections exalted "popular will . . . above the written Constitution."[92] Such proposals, Taft warned in an address given in observation of Lincoln's birthday, "undermine existing governments, and are directed toward depriving the judiciary of the independence without which they must be an instrument of either one man or majority tyranny."[93]

In response to the firestorm caused by the Columbus speech, TR reminded his critics that he had not called for the recall of decisions issued by the federal courts. He only meant the procedure of judicial recall to be available in certain states, where the courts had embraced a doctrine of substantive due process that weakened severely the legislature's police power—that is, in cases like *Ives*, where the courts construed the due process clause as if "property rights, to the exclusion of human rights, had a first mortgage on the Constitution."[94] In his Carnegie Hall address of March 20, Roosevelt stated his determination "to stand on the Columbus speech," declaring, "I am proposing merely that in a certain class of cases involving the police power, when a State court has set aside as unconstitutional a law passed by the legislature for the general welfare, the question of the validity of the law . . . be submitted for final determination to a vote of the people, taken after due time for consideration." It was absurd, Roosevelt insisted, for several state courts to deny elected representatives the right to enact policies, such as workers' compensation and minimum wage and hour laws, that were intended only to ameliorate the worst abuses of industrialization. Taft's criticism of his proposal, TR insisted, was less a defense of judicial review, properly understood, than it was "a criticism of all popular government."[95]

TR was far from certain, however, that such circumspect constitutional reform would be adequate. Like it or not, he wrote Hand, the state and national courts would have to restrain their defense of property, lest they lose the confidence of the people. "I would much prefer that the judges should themselves change their attitude. . . . I hope that criticism such as mine will tend to bring about this result. If it does not, then there will have to be a change in the fundamental form of the law of the land."[96] Indeed, the overwhelming theme of TR's second Carnegie Hall speech was, as its title announced, "The Right of the People to Rule." Reiterating his position that voters should be given sufficient time to reflect on the constitutional issues they were asked to resolve, TR stated his conviction that any constitutional remedy "express the sober and well thought-out judgment, and not the whim, of the people"; but, he insisted, "when that has been ascertained, I am not willing that the will of the people shall be frustrated."[97]

Since his New Nationalism speech, Roosevelt had argued that the Progressive movement's purpose was to strive for social and industrial justice: "genuine rule of the people was the means to that end." Yet with the second Carnegie address, "pure democracy" began to take on a life of its own. National leadership, he now claimed, should reside in public servants who "answer[ed] and obey[ed]," not the commands of the special interests but those of the whole people":

In order to succeed we need leaders of inspired idealism, leaders to whom are granted great visions, who dream greatly and strive to make their dreams come true; who can kindle the people with the fire from their own burning souls. The leader for the time being, whoever he may be, is but an instrument, to be used until broken and then to be cast aside; and if he is worth his salt he will care no more when he is broken than a soldier cares when he is sent where his life is forfeit in order that victory may be won. In the long fight for righteousness the watchword for all of us is, spend and be spent. It is of little matter whether any one man fails or succeeds; but the cause shall not fail, for it is the cause of mankind.[98]

Determined to grasp the scepter of reform leadership, TR appeared to sacrifice the possibility of republican leadership on the altar of direct rule of the people. Ostensibly, the "cause" of progressivism—the allegiance reformers pledged to direct democracy and social and industrial justice—gave reform leadership its dignity, indeed its heroic quality. But the celebration of public opinion appeared to leave leaders to the beck and call of the people. The "right of the people to rule" demanded more than writing into laws measures such as the direct primary, recall, and referendum. It also required rooting firmly in custom the unwritten law that the representatives derived their authority "directly" from the people.

Despite the controversy his plan for direct government stirred, Roosevelt refused to discard it. Indeed, he made it the center of his campaign for president, and his commitment to the principles of his Columbus speech deepened throughout the election year. Received wisdom has it that Roosevelt's celebration of direct democracy was a serious political error. "Much ink has been spilled over the question why Roosevelt, usually the skilled politician, made such an egregious mistake," Mowry has written.[99] Similarly, the *New York Times* reported a tendency among pundits "to think that Colonel Roosevelt had chosen this method of taking himself out of the contest for the Republican nomination this year." TR did not really want to make another campaign, the thinking went, and "had deliberately constructed for himself a platform which he knows the country will not accept."

In fact, Roosevelt's objective transcended rather than fell short of the GOP nomination. He intended to go directly to the people to challenge the very foundation on which both the Democratic and Republican parties rested. Another explanation of TR's behavior, dismissed as "fantastic" by the *Times*, probably came closer to the truth: "Roosevelt has deliberately attempted the great realignment of parties that has been so much discussed in recent years."[100]

That this was neither fantastic nor idle speculation is revealed by the correspondence TR had with the reformers to whom he had sent drafts of the Columbus speech. Roosevelt's exchange with Amos Pinchot a week prior to his trip to Ohio is especially revealing. Pinchot complained that the address was too modest in its approach to the political economy, that it needed to offer straightforward positions on policy issues such as the tariff that had long been central to party conflict. That kind of advice, TR retorted, "seemed to embody the kind of statement I am most anxious to avoid, the kind of statement that would make the people at large tend to regard the Insurgents as merely an ordinary political party." To settle for a plank on the tariff "would make me seem to be uttering a conventional and insincere platitude."[101]

As the correspondent Charles Washburn wrote of the 1912 election, "Roosevelt entered this campaign without, as the main purpose, a desire to gratify a personal ambition but as the *leader of a cause*."[102] Put another way, TR had the rare ambition that yearned for unusual recognition and achievement. "Theodore is absolutely sincere," his personal friend and political opponent Lodge wrote. "He feels that he has a *mission*. The presidency to him is merely incidental and he believes that he is heading a great movement in behalf of popular rights and popular freedom."[103] With his Columbus and Carnegie Hall speeches, then, Roosevelt intended to seize the leadership of a moral crusade: taking command of the Republican Party might, under the right conditions, contribute to that mission. But party struggles per se were almost beside the point. Roosevelt benefited from, and helped to advance, political changes, calling for a direct, personal relationship with the American people that relegated parties to a position of secondary importance in American democracy. "Probably nothing in Roosevelt's career so won the attachment of the American people as the fact that he had the courage to take them into his confidence," John Dewey wrote. Those who pronounced Roosevelt's defense of the recall of judicial decisions a colossal blunder failed to appreciate fully that the Progressive movement embodied powerful sentiments to erode the constitutional barriers between public officials and ordinary citizens. "What they never understood," Dewey observed, "was the admirable affection and unbounded faith with which the American people repaid one who never spoke save to make them sharers in his ideas and to appeal to them as final judges."[104]

The Political Awakening of Social Reformers

Roosevelt's Columbus and New York speeches solidified his position as the leading spokesman for insurgents who hoped a combination of charisma and organization could draw together the disparate strands of progressive reform. Just as surely, TR's embrace of such a bold reform program signaled his recognition that a new form of politics had emerged that was shattering the usual categories of parties and interests in the United States. Indeed, TR's commitment to militant reform and his decision to reenter the fray of American presidential politics were encouraged by many progressives, who assured him that his attack on traditional institutions was not impractical but, instead, a logical response to the emergence of developments that signaled the birth of a new political order. The spread of the official ballot, the increase of direct primaries in the states, and the expansion of civil service reforms had been weakening the two-party system and encouraging candidate-centered campaigns since the 1890s (see Chapter 1). As the progressive Republican governor of California, Hiram Johnson, wrote in a letter of October 1911, urging TR to challenge the incumbent president, "the rules of today are vastly different and the method of playing . . . the game has changed, and even in those rock-ribbed places where this is not apparent . . . politics is entirely different."[105]

La Follette, too, had a strong claim to lead the movement that championed this new politics. Even after his "flunk" in Philadelphia, he remained in the contest for the Republican nomination. Roosevelt had moved considerably in La Follette's direction; indeed, once he resolved to toss his hat in the ring, he became an ardent apologist for populist reforms that he had strongly condemned until the end of 1911. Having viewed TR as the more likely candidate to take them to the promised land even before La Follette's Philadelphia implosion, most progressive leaders welcomed his sudden conversion to "pure democracy." Reformers like Gifford Pinchot were thus frustrated at La Follette's stubborn refusal to withdraw from the race as the insurgent tide shifted to TR. La Follette's recalcitrance, Pinchot feared, would subject the Progressive movement to a fractious, enervating contest of personal ambition. As he wrote to Johnson, who also had defected from the La Follette camp,

For La Follette to persist in his candidacy . . . once the Roosevelt leadership had become a fact . . . could have but one result, namely, to divide the Progressive strength. There could be but one reason for persisting — personal resentment against Col. Roosevelt. For the first time in his life Senator La Follette, if he pushed the campaign in a way to divide the Progressive strength, would be placing personal ambition above principle; personal resentment above the general welfare and the advancement of the people's cause.[106]

Understandably, La Follette insisted that he, not Roosevelt, whom he scorned as "the Bluffer," stood for the "well defined principles" of the Progressive movement. As William E. Smythe, one of La Follette's loyal California supporters, noted in an address, Roosevelt's defense of "pure democracy" was not only of recent vintage but also half-baked. Even the Columbus and Carnegie Hall speeches, Smythe insisted, failed to approach the "frontier of progressivism." TR still opposed important causes such as the recall of judges and the expeditious resolution of constitutional controversies by the people:

> In California we may, and frequently do, amend our constitution in eight or ten months. The legislature submits an amendment in March and we vote it up or down in November. Mr. Roosevelt explained . . . at Carnegie Hall . . . that under his plan it would take at least two years for the people to get action, possibly longer. . . . I concede that he uses language that sounds radical, but I am sorry to say that upon analysis his radicalism promises no relief from the arbitrary rule of the courts.[107]

In the view of La Follette and his supporters, Roosevelt's limited support for popular rule went hand in hand with his tolerance of large corporations. Rejecting La Follette's steadfast opposition to big business, TR viewed the concentration of commercial power as inevitable in a modern economy. The only practical solution to corporate abuse was to establish a strong government commission, under the supervision of a reconstituted executive office, to control large businesses. Such a proposal was folly to La Follette and his political ally, Louis Brandeis, who praised the Wisconsin senator's longstanding battle against commercial power. In a speech that foreshadowed the leading issue that would divide Roosevelt and Wilson during the general election, Brandeis warned of the social costs of corporate America, which exploited workers and resisted with all its might their attempt to bargain collectively: "You find that . . . profits extracted from the American people have been used not to improve the condition of the hundreds of thousands of American citizens who are gathered together in the organization as workers to make the wealth of our people, but are used to crush them and fasten upon these employees the power of the huge corporation."[108]

Roosevelt's proposal to expand national administrative power as a countervailing force against corporate abuse would backfire, La Follette and his supporters insisted. As Smythe claimed in rejecting TR's call for the creation of a strong national regulatory commission, "Can you imagine any more

CHAPTER TWO

dangerous or sinister power to give to the President of the United States than the power to fix the price of almost everything you consume, remembering the vast financial interests involved in the result? If the trusts have a reason for going into politics now, what sort of a reason would they have in trying to elect and control a president then?"[109]

That TR and La Follette offered such fundamentally different approaches to reforming the abuse of commercial power exalted their personal contest for the Republican nomination into a struggle for the soul of the Progressive movement. Significantly, the transformation of American politics that the candidate-centered campaigns of La Follette and TR embodied took place just as this movement was cresting. It was no mere coincidence that at the same time Roosevelt began to align himself with a more radical form of progressive politics, a large and significant array of social workers came to recognize that their reform aspirations required more decisive political advocacy. Social work in 1912 was not a profession; rather, it was a cause championed by reformers who had a strong commitment to social justice. Although some of these reformers were paid full-time executives in social work agencies, foremost champions of the "cause" also included academics, clergymen, settlement house workers, members of charity organizations, public officials, journalists, various professionals, and other activists. These leaders, representing the vanguard of social and economic reform during the Progressive era, served together as organizers, advisors, or board members of various local and national social organizations. Moreover, those associated with social work met and discussed a range of social and economic issues at the National Conference of Charities and Correction, sessions of the American Sociological Society and American Economic Association, gatherings of settlement house reformers, and meetings of the social service commissions of the Men and Religion Forward Movement and Federated Council of Churches.[110]

These social workers observed with considerable interest the struggle between Roosevelt and La Follette for the mantle of reform leader. Nonetheless, from their perspective, progressivism represented more than a personal or philosophical contest between two political statesmen vying for the presidency. To many social workers, the 1912 campaign seemed to be the climax of a twenty-year struggle for reform. They had been deliberating for two decades on the "prevailing method of private philanthropy" and on "how to alleviate suffering to cure the ills that, by common belief, many of our fellow citizens [were] inevitably doomed to bear."[111] Yet many engaged in social work discovered, as Jane Addams had in her service at Hull House in Chicago, that the "wretched mode of life" experienced by the poor of urban industrial centers was "too far-reaching to be cared for by any private philanthropy."[112] At the state level they struggled for shorter working hours and safer conditions for industrial workers, for a minimum wage for women laborers, old age insurance, better housing laws, consumer protection, and other reforms.

Although social reformers celebrated La Follette's and his political allies' achievements in Wisconsin, they found that their reform proposals foundered in most other states. Frustrated by reactionary courts, legislators, and administrators, most reformers blamed the traditional two-party system and a constitutional structure of decentralized and fragmented power for inaction. In addition, they became convinced that their political goals of economic and social improvement could only be achieved by organizing disparate reform groups behind a unified *national* program of energetic government.[113]

Reformers with strong ties to social work helped organize at the national level such groups as the National Child Labor Committee, the National Women's Trade Union League, and the National Association for the Advancement of Colored People (NAACP). As a prominent member of the Child Labor Committee, the NAACP, the National American Woman Suffrage Association (NAWSA), and many other national advocacy groups, Jane Addams observed that "what was needed was a great cause which should pull together the detached groups."[114] More precisely, she believed that an unprecedented political effort committed to wide-ranging social justice reforms—one that might bring together the disparate strands of progressivism—was absolutely essential. Significantly, she also argued, as political leaders such as La Follette and Roosevelt did, that such an agenda would require a more "direct" democracy, one that made government at once more centralized and more responsive to public opinion. Even as Roosevelt and La Follette competed for the nomination of the Republican Party, Addams and other social workers recognized that the cause of social work might require a new party—a novel form of party organization that championed a more direct link between representatives and public opinion. Explaining how she and other reformers became actively engaged in national politics and the election of 1912, Addams wrote:

More and more, social workers, with thousands of other persons throughout the nation, had increasingly felt the need for a new party which should represent "the action and passion of the times," which should inaugurate an educational campaign with leaders advocating its measures to the remotest parts of the country, which should send representatives to Congress and to the state legislatures who had been publicly committed to social reform and who were responsible to constituents for specific measures.

Only such a party could crystallize the advanced public sentiment to be found in various localities, and make of it a force for national progress. . . . There was already a vast array of specific proposals in process of realization in various states, and there was earnest agitation in others for reforms dependent upon legislation, but it all lacked unity and coherence.[115]

The idea for a new party, then, did not emerge merely from TR's desire to regain command of the nation. It had been percolating among civic groups that gradually developed into a movement of national insurgency. A year before Roosevelt found himself embroiled in the New York direct primary battle, several prominent members of the National Conference of Charities and Correction (NCCC) deliberated on how social workers might influence national politics. The NCCC began as a subcommittee of the American Social Science Association in 1874. Four years later it became independent and was composed almost entirely of state boards of charities. By the end of the first decade of the twentieth century, the NCCC had come to play a leading part in transforming thought and practice devoted to ameliorating poverty. Initiating changes that shifted reformers' attention from individual to social responsibility, the NCCC led the way in linking economic deprivation to the progressive ideal of government action. In 1909 its leaders set out to use the new Occupational Standards Committee to formulate a national program of social justice that might unite various reform organizations. This committee was charged by the conference's newly elected president, none other than Jane Addams, to undertake an intense three-year study. If all went well, they expected the study to culminate in a thoroughgoing blueprint for social reform that would be unveiled to members in 1912. More important, they hoped the report would galvanize social reformers as a decisive and unified political force in that year's presidential election.

The first chair of the Occupational Standards Committee, Paul Kellogg, was a settlement house resident in New York City as well as a skilled writer, editor, and social researcher for the New York Charity Organization Society. A year later, he would become the editor-in-chief of the *Survey*, a journal devoted to social work and political reform. In a preliminary report to the NCCC in 1910, his committee called on every conference member "to contribute courageously from his experience toward the formulation of [industrial] standards in public opinion and law."[116] His successor in 1911 was Florence Kelley, a Hull House resident, champion of child labor protection, and general secretary of the National Consumers League.

The concern to affect public opinion and law spoke to the NCCC's support for direct democracy. Just as the Occupational Standards Committee developed a program of industrial reform, so the *Survey* lent support to political reforms such as the recall. Acknowledging that the recall would rarely remove any particular judge or administrator who disregarded social and economic reform, the *Survey* insisted that such skepticism missed the larger objective of measures such as the initiative, referendum, and recall, which was to remake American democracy. As a March 1912 *Survey* editorial counseled:

> The individual official may be truculent and spurn instruction . . . but the educational process goes on. A public opinion is slowly created in the atmosphere of which the decisions which subvert social justice and the administrative abuses simply cannot survive. This is what we mean in this connection by the education of judges and of public officials. Its one indispensable element is public understanding and fair-minded but frank criticism of such decisions and public acts as affect the public welfare.[117]

By the time the NCCC gathered for its annual session in June 1912, the Occupational Standards Committee—now led by Owen Lovejoy, secretary of the National Child Labor Committee, and Margaret Dreier Robins, president of the National Women's Trade Union League—had issued a remarkably comprehensive "platform of social standards." This platform advocated an adequate living wage, an eight-hour workday, occupational safety and health, "the right to a decent home," the abolition of sweatshops and child labor, workmen's compensation for victims of industrial accidents and "trade diseases," old age insurance, and even insurance against unemployment. "The responsibility rests upon this group of citizens representing the advance guard of those who love and labor for their fellowmen," Lovejoy implored conference members, "to see that these or better standards are embodied in the laws of our country." Significantly, the committee expressed its hope that its platform of social reform "may be promulgated by political parties" so as to "direct public thought and secure official action."[118]

The NCCC's president in 1912, Judge Julian Mack, expressed similar themes in his opening address to the social workers, ministers, academics, physicians, public officials, and others attending its annual meeting. Sounding a far more distinctly political trumpet than past presidential addresses, Mack declared that the purpose of the gathering was to produce "a stronger and more unified effort of all of the forces working for good in the community." He charged reformers to toil "not for alms, not for charity" but for "those measures which, in dealings between the individual and the State, will accord to each man that justice which he is due."[119] Important differences separated participants at the national conference, much as they did within the vast constellation of progressive advocacy groups. Moreover, the NCCC maintained a policy of not endorsing particular parties or candidates. Yet supporters of the Occupational Standards Committee's social reform platform, Kellogg recounts, met shortly after the conference adjourned to plot a course of action for the upcoming election.[120] While La Follette and Roosevelt were declaring their intention to wage a decidedly modern presidential campaign, then, key social reformers like Addams, Kellogg, Kelley, Lovejoy, and Robins, as well as many of their supporters and colleagues, sought to make social justice and direct democracy reforms the centerpiece of the 1912 election. The active participation of these leading social reformers in the election, in turn, helped to ensure that progressive insurgency and the creation of the Progressive Party would represent a collective endeavor, a deliberate attempt to tighten the buckle around the disparate streams of reform—and forge a coherent Progressive movement.

Conclusion: Progressive Democracy—The Men and the Movement

The question reformers faced in the 1912 election, Gifford Pinchot wrote to Robert La Follette as the campaign maneuvers between Roosevelt and the Wisconsin senator intensified, was whether "the Progressive groups would disintegrate, or draw closer together." "Was the movement which was conquering the minds of the people so rapidly to have a leader," he asked, "or was it to be too scattered for the lack of a man to follow?" Given progressive reformers' commitment to transforming American democracy, this question was a very troubling one, indeed. Believing that the two-party system impeded the forward march of social and economic justice, insurgent candidates like Roosevelt and La Follette formed candidate-centered campaigns that could appeal over the heads of party leaders directly to public opinion. Shut out of party councils, social workers formed civic organizations that could not easily abide the negotiations and compromises that were required to build a partisan coalition capable of governing in a large and diverse society. The celebration of a progressive democracy thus made difficult the formation of a recognizable organization with common goals. By 1911 "it became very plain" to Pinchot and other progressive leaders that "what was needed was a rallying point, and that the Progressive movement could not be kept in efficient fighting condition without a candidate for the Republican Presidential nomination."[121]

Given that both Roosevelt and La Follette styled themselves as insurgent candidates with little chance to win the GOP nomination, they claimed to be fighting for a cause, not to advance their own political fortunes. But the new politics made personal ambition and programmatic achievement hard to distinguish. Their attack on political parties resonated in the United States, where the celebration of the democratic individual had always made political parties suspect. But interested observers abroad viewed the awakening of a "new style" of politics in the United States with great skepticism. The notion that a leader might embody the aspirations of "the People" seemed an especially mischievous formula for reform. In Great Britain, the reformist *Manchester Guardian* was more critical of TR's insurgency than was the conservative *Times*. Both English newspapers noted with disapproval, however, that Roosevelt's campaign was a "combination of restless, emotional and ephemeral elements." To foreign observers, it seemed, Old Guard Republicans celebrated property, regular Democrats touted local issues, and Progressives built their campaign around their "psychological candidate." In the end, the nomination contest among Taft, Roosevelt, and La Follette was less a principled contest than it was a quarrel full of "personal invective."[122]

Nonetheless, the combat for the Republican nomination eventually led to the formation of a new party, which suggested that a collective purpose existed beyond the personal invective that injected itself so dramatically into the early days of the 1912 election. That purpose ultimately rested in the hope of remaking American democracy. Only by freeing the citizenry from the decentralizing associations and institutions that dominated the nineteenth-century polity could individual men and women participate in a national movement of public opinion. Some progressives, such as Woodrow Wilson and Louis Brandeis, would eventually invest hope in the possibility that a reformed party politics would abet the creation of a national community. But most reformers viewed parties as "the worst obstacle to the advance of practical democratic participation."[123] Reformers indulged in the hope that once emancipated from the provincialism of partisanship, the people would display their potential for broadmindedness. Roosevelt expressed this hopefulness in a 1911 address entitled "Nationalism and Democracy": "Our aim, the aim of those of us who stand for true progress, for true Nationalism, for true democracy, is not only to give the people power, but, ourselves as part of the people, to try to see that the power is used aright, that it is used with wisdom, with courage, with self-restraint, and in a spirit of the broadest kindliness and charity toward all men."[124]

The progressive assault on party politics, at least as traditionally practiced in the United States, went hand in hand with the view of reformers that religious conviction was critical to the development of a national community. The most exalted purpose of the insurgency that crested in 1912 was to transform the rights-based culture that had long shaped American political life into a society awakened by sentiments of duty and obligation. This objective, the principal theme of TR's addresses in France and Great Britain, animated the religious conviction of the Progressive movement, especially the Social Gospel movement, which gave concrete expression and practical organization to the moral imperatives of reformers' aspirations. Leading social gospelers, such as Raymond Robbins of the Men and Religion Forward Movement and Lyman Abbott, editor of the *Outlook,* which published many editorials that TR wrote after leaving the presidency, viewed progressive insurgency as a political expression of their objective to promote Christian social action. Just as reformers praised the *whole* people, social gospelers proclaimed a religious devotion that downplayed, if it did not scorn, particular theological doctrines and denominations. As Julian Mack noted at the 1912 gathering of the National Conference of Charities and Correction, Social Christianity gave progressive democracy its moral calling:

> No event of the past year has been so full of promise for the future as the great Men and Religion Forward Movement. . . . However strong may be the emphasis that has heretofore been laid upon social service as a religious duty, surely the bonds of human brotherhood would be strengthened and the cause of social justice advanced if a broader Forward Movement, limited not to men, and not to the followers of a single religion were, by the united action of such representatives of all faiths as are gathered here tonight, carried into every city, village, and hamlet of our land.[125]

The Social Gospel had a profound influence on the progressive insurgency of 1912. It injected religious fervor into the candidate-centered campaigns of Roosevelt and La Follette and helped enlarge the personal invective of the contest they waged into a crusade for a new form of politics that promised to transmute the religion of America into a national democracy. But this practical idealism was not unique to social gospelers. It was shared by the academic reformers, social workers, professionals, and journalists who enlisted in the cause of progressive democracy. "However formulated," Eldon Eisenach has written, "Progressives insisted that democracy and democratic reform required a national will strong enough to generate bonds of sufficient strength to encourage sacrifice for social justice and the common good."[126]

As James Morone has shown, since the beginning of the republic Americans had expressed a "democratic wish" that lived uneasily with their obsession with rights.[127] Nonetheless, prior to the Progressive era, the idea of democracy had grown out of local communities, religious institutions, voluntary associations, and localized parties. In this sense, American democracy was an institutional elaboration of the Anti-Federalists' critique of the Constitution, which emphasized that vital political participation was only possible in small places. As democracy emerged during the nineteenth century, it thrived in small towns that were the political centers of early American life, encouraging citizens to become attached to their local government, which they saw as close to their concerns and accessible to their influence. In this way, Tocqueville marveled, democracy in America was strongly allied with individualism, with a sort of "selfishness" that made individuals "care for the state."[128]

Those who rallied around the candidacies of La Follette and Roosevelt viewed this sort of provincial liberty as an obstacle to a true sense of national community, a denigration of America's destiny to achieve economic and social justice at home and to spread the idea of popular rule abroad. As the prominent Social Gospel editor, and close ally of Roosevelt, Lyman Abbott, expressed this idea, America was truly a "city on a hill," but had not always been "conscious of the spirit which has possessed her." Now, however, Abbott wrote hopefully, Americans had come to realize that "democracy is more than a scheme of government . . . a theory of economics . . . a plan of education . . . a form of religious institutions. Democracy is a great religious faith: a superstitious faith, if you will, but a great religious faith. It is faith in man."[129]

Above all, the "Forward Movement" intended to sanctify a new civic faith that rested not in the Declaration of Independence and the Constitution but, rather, in the emancipation of popular rule from natural rights, political parties, and the law. Progressive intellectuals like Croly tended to express this elusive, exalted vision in mystical terms. "Faith in things unseen and unknown is indispensable to a progressive democracy as it is to an individual Christian," he wrote. "In the absence of such a faith, a democracy must lean, as the American democracy has leaned in the past, upon some specific formulation of a supposedly or temporarily righteous Law; but just in proportion as it has attained faith it can dispense with any such support." Invoking St. Paul, Croly concluded that Americans' belief in the Declaration and the Constitution was akin to Christians' belief in the scriptures. A more mature faith would come from seeking salvation in "the person and mission of Jesus." By logical extension, Americans would better seek salvation in the person and mission of leaders like Theodore Roosevelt.[130]

It remained to be seen, of course, whether such a mystical form of democracy could take hold in the United States. "Telling Americans to improve democracy by sinking comfortably into a community, by losing themselves in a collective life, is calling into the wind," the historian Robert Wiebe has written. "There has never been an American democracy without its powerful strand of individualism, and nothing suggests there ever will be."[131] Of greater concern, expressed not just by Roosevelt's opponents but also by skeptical allies such as Hand, was whether such an abstract notion of democratic faith, which scorned the particulars of social and political life, would give rise to a cult of personality in American political life. "I am sick of the whole lot," Hand fumed. "Either they are full of sound and fury signifying nothing, or they twist around a whirligig with prayers written on it, like the Grand Lhama [sic] of Tibet, and think that they can exorcise all the devils within the four seas."[132] Freed from the rule of law, aroused by the call for "a new millennium," critics of progressivism's "faith" wondered, what would protect Americans from popular leaders who would, as Alexander Hamilton warned in *The Federalist Papers*, "flatter their prejudices to betray their interests"?[133]

The tension between candidate-centered politics and national community would come into full relief during the contest for the Republican nomination. That contest would be joined by President Taft—the first time an incumbent actively sought to be renominated—who reluctantly answered the call of regular Republicans demanding that he had the duty to defend inherited political practices and institutional arrangements against the hard challenges posed by the insurgent campaigns of Roosevelt and La Follette. This highly personal yet deeply principled intramural scrum marked the first time that popular primaries were a significant factor in a presidential campaign. Those contests, moreover, resulted in a full-throated debate on progressive democracy and the fundamental challenge it posed not only to the existing political order but also to foundational constitutional principles and institutions.

⋙

THREE

The First Primary Campaign: Candidate-Centered Politics and the Battle for the Republican Presidential Nomination

By the end of 1911, as La Follette's campaign stalled, Gifford Pinchot and many other progressive leaders came to believe that only Roosevelt's presence in the campaign could serve as "a rallying point for the Progressive movement."[1] La Follette remained an active candidate until the Republican convention; indeed, his stubborn persistence may have deprived Roosevelt of the opportunity to seize the nomination from an incumbent president. By the middle of April 1912, however, it was clear that TR had become the most effective voice of progressivism. With his "Charter of Democracy" speech, followed by the dramatic declaration of "The Right of the People to Rule" in Carnegie Hall, Roosevelt answered the call of most insurgents who believed that he was the only progressive who could be nominated for president. At the same time, his celebration of "pure democracy" in those speeches alienated the Republican leaders who controlled the nomination of his own party.

With his embrace of progressive democracy, however, Roosevelt's campaign transcended party politics, at least as traditionally practiced in the United States. Taft controlled federal patronage and enjoyed support from most GOP machines, thereby ensuring his control of state conventions, which still dominated the presidential nomination process. Roosevelt's only chance for the nomination lay in challenging the convention system that had dominated the presidential selection process since the early part of the nineteenth century. Roosevelt thus made the direct primary the cause of his nomination fight. "The great fundamental issue now before the Republican party and before our people can be stated simply," he declared to the Carnegie Hall audience. "It is, Are the American people fit to govern themselves, to rule themselves, to control themselves? I believe they are. My opponents do not."[2] Opposed by the Republican machinery for the first time, TR hoped that an unprecedented candidate-centered campaign, which embodied a broader commitment to direct democracy, might wrest the electorate free from the stranglehold of party bosses.

With Roosevelt's campaign for "the right of the people to rule themselves," the 1912 presidential election became the first in United States history in which direct primaries were a significant factor. Political reforms had established the popular selection of party candidates as a fixture of local, state, and congressional elections during the first decade of the twentieth century; however, the 1912 election was the first in which this reform affected a presidential election.[3]

Prior to TR's campaign, the direct primary was used to select delegates in only six states: North Dakota, California, New Jersey, Wisconsin, Minnesota, and Nebraska. All of these states, save New Jersey—which enacted a direct primary law as part of Governor Woodrow Wilson's reform program—were in the Midwest and West, where progressive reforms had to this point made the greatest impact. Roosevelt and his political allies were determined to make the direct primary a national issue. Indeed, the Roosevelt headquarters publicly challenged the Taft forces to contest the nomination by means of a direct primary in every state of the Union. The Taft organization, led by the ruthlessly efficient William McKinley (no relation to the former president), rejected the challenge. "I do not favor changes in the rules of the game while the game is in progress," McKinley wrote in a letter to Senator Joseph Dixon of Montana, the manager of TR's insurgent forces. Another Taft man, Congressman Phillip P. Campbell of Kansas, added that "the Republican Party does not believe in an appeal from the umpire to the bleachers."[4]

Such a denial played right into Roosevelt's hands. This was no game, he claimed, and the interest of the regular Republicans in confining the people to the bleachers was an "astounding indictment of the convention system." The convention system was founded during the Jacksonian era to link presidential contests, hitherto dominated by the congressional caucus, to the "grass roots," to the state and local party organizations that were truly

CHAPTER THREE

representative and accountable to public concerns. Implicit in the idea of the national convention was that delegates who nominated presidential candidates derived their authority directly from the rank and file; that they came, as Andrew Jackson put it, "fresh from the people."[5] Most progressives held that this system had become decrepit, that it was the linchpin of corruption and injustice. Disassociated from the reformist zeal present at its founding, TR contended, the convention system had been transformed into an instrument of privilege, of "minority tyranny." As he noted in a letter widely distributed by the Roosevelt organization to promote the direct primary:

> Our opponents take the view that this contest is merely a game, that the object of the contest is to win prizes for the contestants, and that public office is a reward that goes to the winners of the game and that, therefore, it is a piece of allowable (although rather tricky) smartness to refuse to make changes in the laws during the progress of the contest, if these changes would deprive the lead captains of the political world of advantage they now hold over the plain people. . . .
>
> The issue may be stated as follows: Should election laws be framed with a view to the interests of politicians or should election laws be framed with a view to carrying out the popular will? . . . We regard the present contest not as a contest between individuals—for we are not concerned with the welfare of a particular individual, neither with mine nor with any other man—but as a contest between these two radically different views of the function of politics in a great democracy.[6]

As a consequence of Roosevelt making the direct primary a *cause célèbre,* many northern state legislatures fought fiercely over the adoption of electoral reform. In the end, Massachusetts, Pennsylvania, Illinois, Maryland, Ohio, and South Dakota adopted the device. "With the six states in which the system was already in operation," George Mowry wrote, "this made a sizable block of normal Republican states from which a popular referendum could be obtained."[7] Yet these victories could not obscure the fact that the direct primary had great shortcomings. The *New York Times,* then a defender of constitutional sobriety, thought the spectacle of "aspirants for the Presidential nomination madly racing over the country, haranguing their fellow-citizens night and day, abusing each other or intriguing against each other, and appealing for votes, to all intents and purposes begging for votes," threatened to weaken the fabric of "a well ordered Government of laws." "This is our first Presidential campaign under the preference primary plan," the *Times* sniffed. "We hope it may be our last."[8]

Some champions of "direct action of the people" were no less distrustful of the primary system. Success in a series of primary contests required candidates to put together personal organizations, a costly venture. This made TR's candidacy dependent on "financial angels," such as George Perkins, who had made his fortune on Wall Street, and the millionaire publisher Frank Muncy. As La Follette, whose enthusiasm for the presidential primary ebbed considerably over the course of his battle with the Roosevelt forces, complained of his opponent's organizational heft, "Headquarters were opened in New York, Washington, Chicago, and states east and west. Newspaper writers were engaged at large prices to boom his candidacy. Special trains were hired, and the 'receptive candidate' started in frantic pursuit of the nomination. In the history of American politics, there has never been in a primary campaign for the presidential nomination, an approach to the extravagant expenditures made in this campaign."[9] Adding to the expense of the campaign was the need of the Roosevelt organization to recruit its own foot soldiers to root out votes in the primary states. The *New York World* reported that 1,200 paid workers were in the field in the Illinois, Pennsylvania, Massachusetts, Maryland, Nebraska, and Missouri campaigns.[10] Fairly or unfairly, the elaborate and expensive campaign TR mounted subjected him to the charge of selling out progressive principles to special interests.

Just as problematic for La Follette, as his "flunk" in Philadelphia showed, was that candidates like Roosevelt, and, on the Democratic side, Woodrow Wilson, were more gifted at the art of direct democracy. Roosevelt displayed these gifts during his presidency, when he began to redefine the executive office's relationship to popular opinion. As the *Washington Evening Star,* which supported Taft, acknowledged with grudging admiration and deep concern, "Mr. Roosevelt knew the value of advertising. . . . He managed to let his light shine before men so constantly they could not forget him for a day. All he said and did found its way around in readable, and sometimes sensational, form. The deaf read and blind heard about him and all his works. He reached all classes and conditions."[11] Experiencing firsthand Roosevelt's gifts as a political advertiser in the Republican primaries, La Follette shared the alarm sounded by the conservative press that the primary campaigns subordinated principles to popular infatuation with charisma. He complained bitterly that Roosevelt's name and effervescent campaign style exalted a cult of personality that cheapened the fight for the right to lead the Progressive movement. The Roosevelt campaign, he charged, "substituted vulgar personalities and the coarse epithets of the prize ring for the serious discussion of great economic problems and for the time being brought ridicule and contempt upon a great cause."[12]

La Follette's contempt cannot simply be dismissed as the sour grapes of a scorned candidate. The salvos he fired at Roosevelt would become a common refrain, a standard critique of presidential primaries once they became a staple of American politics. But, as TR's eventual bolt from the Republican convention and extraordinary third-party campaign revealed, the battle for the Republican nomination was not consumed by Roosevelt's ambition and personal invective. Roosevelt based his primary and Progressive Party campaigns on neither administrative competence nor leadership ability but, rather, on the program he heralded in his Columbus and Carnegie Hall speeches. Indeed, a critical feature of Roosevelt's "grass roots up" campaign involved mailing these addresses directly to hundreds of thousands of voters.[13] Early on, the *New York Times* predicted that Roosevelt's attack on the party organization would hardly leave a mark, "that the great majority of [primary] voters . . . would go their accustomed party way," and the "disturbers of the political peace," such as Roosevelt, "would be quieted."[14] But such skepticism underestimated the powerful spell that the progressive idea of democracy cast over the American people. William Randolph Hearst, no admirer of Roosevelt, admitted that the ex-president's campaign proved effective because it represented progressive policies that had a great deal of popular support. Voters who supported him in primaries were not expressing an endorsement of TR "but rather a condemnation" of the longstanding but badly weakened politics that Taft, as well as Democratic and Republican Party leaders, endorsed. "Colonel Roosevelt had the good sense and political shrewdness to see Mr. Taft's mistakes, and to profit by them. He had the discretion to plant himself upon positions that were plainly in the line of people's wishes, and to keep steadily and persistently hammering away at them."[15]

Roosevelt's principled campaign, culminating in the birth of the Progressive Party, had so aroused the country that the election of 1912 became an event of extraordinary intellectual ferment. Even the British press, which frequently lampooned the whirligig of American politics, conceded the importance of this campaign. Although it abhorred the "personal invective" of the primary contests, the *Manchester Guardian* acknowledged that Roosevelt's campaign "infused a seriousness and earnestness into American politics that have been lacking for two generations, during which American politics have seldom amounted to much more than struggles for office or agitations of the tariff which were rendered of no avail by the adroitness of professional politicians."[16]

In the face of TR's challenge to accepted party practices, indeed to the very foundation of the localized polity on which the two-party system rested, the Old Guard was militantly determined not to nominate him, no matter how popular his candidacy proved to be. But the Republican leaders' rejection of Roosevelt's insurgency backfired badly. The GOP, of course, championed a national policy of industrial capitalism, including protective tariffs, a gold standard, and the development of a national network of railroads. Since 1896, moreover, the Republican Party organization, influenced especially by Mark Hanna's savvy leadership, had adapted to—indeed, abetted in important respects—the growing importance of candidate-centered campaigns. Nevertheless, as the phrase *stand pat,* which Hanna introduced into American politics, suggested, regular Republicans stood resolutely for the party organization's authority to dictate candidates, an independent judiciary, and, apart from pro-business policies, restraining the power of the national government to regulate the society and economy. And yet, their snub of Roosevelt's insurgency only ensured a national hearing for his Progressive Party campaign. Indeed, TR's success in the primaries, combined with his steadfast defense of pure democracy, extending even to popular referenda on judicial rulings, animated an election of deep constitutional significance. His battle for the nomination of the Republican Party—framed as a fight for "the right of the people to rule"—launched a campaign that raised the deepest constitutional questions and instigated a debate about the future of constitutional government in the United States. "So our nascent, insurgent, still unfolded democracy, which unites many men in a common hostility to certain broad economic and political developments, is now passing over to a definite program," the progressive thinker Walter Weyl wrote hopefully in 1912. "It is becoming positive . . . and seeks to test its motives and ideals in relation to American history and conditions."[17]

Marching to the Coliseum: The Fight for the Republican Nomination

Once Roosevelt "threw his hat in the ring" in early February, his campaign for the nomination of the Republican Party stirred a dramatic contest that the press readily identified as "absolutely distinctive"—a "wholly novel" experience in American politics. TR professed at first to have no intention of bolting the Republican Party and pledged to support any candidate the GOP nominated at its national convention, to be held in the Chicago Coliseum later that summer. He would "be entirely happy" to support President Taft should the latter win the nomination, TR insisted. Because he was "fighting for principle," the issue was in "no sense a personal one." Since his entry into national politics, in fact, Roosevelt had supported the right of the national convention to select presidential candidates.[18] At the same time, Roosevelt acknowledged that the campaign platform he announced in his Columbus speech—emphasizing the direct primary, judicial recall, and other "pure" democracy initiatives—portended a fundamental challenge to existing party practices. His celebration of the direct primary as a principal part of this program gave prominence to a novel candidate-centered campaign. Indeed, no sooner had he entered the fray than Roosevelt implied he would not abide by the custom that major presidential candidates should not actively seek the nomination of their parties. TR made clear that if it became necessary, he would take command of the Roosevelt movement, indeed, even break historical precedent by attending the Republican convention. With this promise, or threat, TR highlighted his support for forging a direct relationship between candidates and voters.[19]

Such a militant challenge to long-standing party practices belied Roosevelt's pledge of loyalty to the Republican Party. This challenge went beyond those states that had adopted the direct primary; TR and his political allies also sought to influence the choice of delegates in states in which they were selected by party machinery rather than popular vote. Roosevelt could not afford to ignore these contests: there were 1,078 delegates to the Republican national convention, with 540 needed to nominate; roughly 360 delegates were to be chosen in the states with direct primaries while the rest of the delegates were chosen by district conventions, caucuses, state conventions, or some combination of methods that privileged party regulars. The party drills that proved the most difficult to influence were located in the South, where federal patronage controlled Republican organizations that sent many delegates to the national convention but commanded few votes in the general election. Roosevelt made noises about revitalizing these "rotten boroughs" and challenging the one-party South, but McKinley, the leader of the Taft forces, had been busy since early February building up a political organization below the Mason-Dixon Line that would be impervious to insurgent appeals. Applying machine tactics mercilessly, McKinley dismissed any declared, or suspected, Roosevelt supporters from patronage positions. Moreover, local postmasters were told in no uncertain terms that their reappointments depended on bringing Taft delegations to state conventions.[20]

The Taft administration's strategy paid early dividends. The first southern state convention to select delegates met in Florida on February 6 and organized a solid Taft delegation. Nonetheless, in a pattern that would be repeated throughout the region, Roosevelt supporters bolted from the state conclave, held a second convention, and nominated a contesting delegation of Roosevelt men. Ormsby McHarg, an experienced political organizer who had secured southern delegates for Taft in 1908, headed the Roosevelt drive. Although most Taft delegates were selected legally, they were contested in almost every southern state by Roosevelt bolters. The contest between TR and Taft thus cast aspersions on traditional party drills, throwing many conventions into intense and sometimes violent confrontations. Some of the wildest scenes took place not in the South but in border and northern states, where Roosevelt forces, hopeful of dominating their states' partisan drills, were more reluctant than their southern brethren to organize a parallel organization. In Oklahoma, a Roosevelt delegate toting a revolver menacingly approached the pro-Taft presiding officer. One man died of a heart attack in the ensuing melee, and three others were injured by fistfights before Roosevelt won the state's ten delegates at large. Perhaps the most riotous conditions occurred in Michigan. Despite the presence of state troops, a mass fight broke out on the platform. Indiana Senator Albert Beveridge, a Roosevelt supporter, refused to give his keynote address amid the uproar. Unable to agree on anything, the convention split in half and elected two chairmen. As state troopers tried in vain to restore order, both conventions, occupying the same platform, simultaneously selected two sets of delegates.[21]

In the end, 254 delegate seats to the convention were contested. These contests were to be decided by the Republican National Committee, dominated by Taft supporters, who were hopeful that the president would win the nomination hands down, that the raucous conventions were but a lot of sound and fury signifying nothing. In contrast, Roosevelt supporters anticipated that the primary contests, many of which would take place in rockribbed Republic states, would weaken allegiance to the incumbent president. Although domestic pundits were skeptical that the direct primaries would turn the tide, interested foreign observers believed that TR had a chance. As the London *Times* observed, those who dismissed Roosevelt's insurgency as chimerical handicapped the Republican contest by rules that might have been rendered "obsolete." Noting how TR's challenge had left the regular

Republican machinery unsettled, the *Times* averred that the primaries were the most "important positive creation of American radicalism."[22]

Still, Roosevelt's campaign, bogged down in bitter state convention skirmishes, got off to a slow start. In late March and early April, his own state of New York selected an overwhelming Taft delegation. Even more troubling for Roosevelt were the results of the preferential primaries in New York County, where the strong Republican machine engineered a decisive triumph for the incumbent president. TR claimed, not without reason, that these results were marred by ballot irregularities within the New York metropolitan area and rules that gave the state party complete control over the selection of delegates outside of it.[23]

Roosevelt could not voice similar objections, however, in the first true popular primary, held in North Dakota, where La Follette bested the ex-president by a two-to-one margin. The results of the North Dakota primary were especially disappointing to the Roosevelt forces, for it took place in the Midwest, thought to be a stronghold of the ex-president. The North Dakota results appeared to turn on Roosevelt's passive stance toward the tariff, which many progressives, especially those in agricultural regions, viewed as the embodiment of a perilous concentration of commercial power.[24] As La Follette wrote to supporters in Wisconsin who were going to North Dakota to campaign on his behalf, "this power . . . is one of the great issues that [will confront] the next administration. It will be decided whether the people's money shall be held centralized in the grip of a few hands for purposes of speculation and destruction or whether it shall be kept and controlled in local centers for the encouragement of legitimate prosperity and growth."[25] The enthusiasm with which La Follette's antimonopoly message was received did not clearly indicate, as the Wisconsin senator's supporters hoped, that TR's candidacy was in serious jeopardy. Many North Dakota voters expressed a favorable view of Roosevelt. Nonetheless, La Follette's decisive victory threatened to expose a schism between reformers who championed a strong executive as the "steward of the public welfare" and those who celebrated antitrust initiatives and other decentralizing measures as remedies for the ills thrown up by the industrial revolution. If not healed, this split would undermine TR's claim that he fought for "the right of the people to rule."

With Taft able to hold his own in the Northeast and the prospect of La Follette denying TR decisive gains in the Midwest, the progressive Republican Charles J. Bonaparte lamented that a Roosevelt victory was scarcely more than a "forlorn hope."[26] Those who condemned Roosevelt to failure, however, received a shock when he won the Illinois primary, a contest that signaled a significant changing of the tide. Illinois was the first large state to hold a popular primary, which the state legislature enacted into law only ten days before. Pressured by the *Chicago Tribune,* which was owned by Medill McCormick, one of TR's most important supporters, the Illinois governor called a special session of the state legislature to consider a change in the state's delegate selection rules. A primary bill was quickly enacted on March 30, and the election was held on April 9. The haste with which the direct primary was put in place only seemed to enhance the drama of Roosevelt's triumph. Turning out in large numbers, Republican voters favored Roosevelt by a two-to-one margin over Taft, a decisive victory that appeared to guarantee the former president all but two of the fifty-eight Illinois delegates. Equally important, La Follette fared poorly in the state, diminishing fears among progressives that personal factionalism would hobble their movement throughout the course of the primary contests.

The Illinois victory kept Roosevelt in the running for the Republican nomination. Most Republican Party leaders still insisted that TR could not get the nomination, but they worried about his "power of appealing to the masses" and began to question seriously whether the time had not come to consider a substitute for the incumbent president as a GOP standard-bearer.[27] More important, as one astute reporter who was covering the campaign wrote, Roosevelt's victory "doubled the chances for a third party." Roosevelt's impressive vote in Illinois gave authority to "his claim that the people [were] behind him." Should TR do well in the preferential primaries that followed and still be denied the Republican nomination, he would have the moral authority to bolt and become the head of a strong third-party ticket.[28]

Roosevelt's triumph in the Illinois primary was followed by another important victory four days later in Pennsylvania. Helped by the organization of William Flinn, a fierce rival of the state GOP boss, Boies Penrose, TR utterly routed Taft in the popular vote, winning the state's sixty-four district delegates, and later, at the state convention, all twelve of Pennsylvania's delegates at large. With La Follette all but eliminated from the race, the contest for the Republican nomination now focused on a bitter struggle between the incumbent president, who controlled most of the regular party organizations and pledged delegates, and his progressive challenger, who represented a fundamental threat to partisan drills that had prevailed since the early part of the nineteenth century. Conservatives abroad viewed the Illinois and Pennsylvania primaries as proof of the fragile state of the American party system and the need of GOP leaders to take TR's insurgency seriously. TR's campaign for pure democracy, they warned their American brethren, had aroused anger and distrust "among what in England would be the upper and upper middle classes" but "could not safely be taken to reflect the opinions and aspirations of the less vocal but numerically more powerful ranks of the 'plain people.'"[29] Indigenous conservatives, viewing TR and his progressive democratic platform as a profound threat to constitutional forms, were less measured in their reaction to the Illinois and Pennsylvania contests. As the *New York Times* editorialized after the Pennsylvania primary, Roosevelt's victories were a "misfortune not alone for William H. Taft, not alone for his party, but for the Nation . . . another proof that this greatest democracy of all time, a democracy now approaching the middle of the second century of its existence, is not yet secure against the chief peril that besets democracies—the ambitious, plausible, selfish, and even conscientious demagogue."[30]

Joining the chorus of indignation at Roosevelt's disregard for constitutional democracy, the *Nation* scorned the "new political maxim" he enjoined when urging the enthusiastic Pennsylvania crowds that greeted him: "Vote as You Shout." In the past, the *Nation*'s editors claimed, even America's most dangerous demagogues had the "grace to say they wanted the people . . . to register at the polls the free and mature opinion of thoughtful citizens." Roosevelt's insurgency, they warned, was "the modern substitute for the deliberate expression of the will of freemen. Fortunately, the American people have not been given to that sort of thing, and there is no reason to fear that they now will be."[31]

Roosevelt's success in the string of primaries that took place during the next several weeks, however, began to shake conservatives' faith in Americans' constitutional sobriety. From early April until the middle of May, Roosevelt won primaries in California, Minnesota, Nebraska, Maryland, and South Dakota. Roosevelt's winning streak was interrupted in Massachusetts, where Taft won a very close victory. Yet, because, as one editorial put it, the Bay State "should have been Taft territory," the press tended to view the divided Massachusetts results as a "Roosevelt victory."[32] Indeed, although Taft won the state's preferential primary and, consequently, a slight majority of the delegates selected in congressional districts, the eight delegates-at-large pledged to TR won a narrow victory over the Taft slate. Roosevelt "magnanimously" instructed these at-large delegates to support Taft, thus ingeniously displaying his "impartial" support for the direct primary. In all likelihood, TR acknowledged, the preference primary, in which voters expressed direct support for Taft or Roosevelt for president, better represented the will of rank-and-file Republicans than did the vote for at-large delegates, even though these delegates, too, were pledged to support one or the other candidate. Giving up all claim to the at-large delegates thus highlighted the foremost principle of his campaign: "the right of the people to rule." Exalting the fight for the Republican nomination into a struggle for the cause of self-rule, Roosevelt issued a statement that concluded: "I should desire to get at the polls the genuine expression of the majority of the whole people; because my only purpose in being elected President would be to put into effect certain principles and policies which I ardently believe and which I could not possibly put into effect unless I had behind me the hearty support of the majority of our citizens."[33]

Whose Constitution Is It?

With his nomination no longer assured, Taft believed that he had no recourse but to wage an open fight against Roosevelt. In departing from the tradition that presidents did not actively seek their party's nomination for reelection, Taft made clear that only the extraordinary character of the primary campaign caused him to do so. "I regret the necessity which brings me out," he said repeatedly. "I feel humiliated that I, as President of the United States, am the first one that has had to depart from the tradition that keeps the President at home during political controversy."[34]

This was not the first time that Taft had broken precedent. In 1908, following the importunities of TR and Republican strategists, Taft agreed to campaign actively against William Jennings Bryan. He thus became the first Republican to undertake a "rear platform" campaign and the first victorious presidential candidate to have engaged in a full-scale speaking tour. But Taft's precedent-shattering 1912 campaign, marking him as the first president to stump for his own renomination, was a more dramatic and, by all accounts, painful bow to the transformation of American politics. The drumbeat of Republican newspapers contributed significantly to Taft's reluctant decision to participate actively in the nomination battle. Most newspapers, many of which had been wedded to the Republican Party since the Civil War, strongly opposed Roosevelt's insurgent campaign and scorned the primary contests. Yet in the face of TR's success in the primaries, they urged Taft to take up the gauntlet—it was his "duty," the New York World lectured in a typical editorial. The primary contest was not a personal one, as the incumbent president at first appeared to believe. Rather, Roosevelt fought for a "new system of government": "This [was] no ordinary political rivalry for the presidency, but a rivalry that [involved] the conflict of fundamental principles."[35]

By late April, amid the heated Massachusetts primary, Taft finally accepted the challenge of openly fighting for his office. Although he had been criticizing progressive principles and policies since Roosevelt issued his "Charter of Democracy" in February, the president had avoided attacking TR, or appealing for votes, directly until the Massachusetts primary campaign. "If in this contest there were at stake only my own reputation or satisfaction of my own ambition," Taft declared in Boston, "I would, without the slightest qualm and without care as to the result, continue my silence under [Roosevelt's] unjust attacks. . . . But . . . I represent a cause." That cause, Taft announced, was the commitment of the Republican Party to "wise progress," "to the progress of the people in pursuit of happiness under constitutional government and of the maintenance of such a government against threatened innovations, calculated to undermine our cherished institutions of civil liberty regulated by law and preserved by an independent judiciary."[36]

Taft's reluctant decision to enter the fray opened a new phase of the 1912 presidential campaign. In part, the incumbent president's active participation accentuated the candidate-centered nature of the contest, heightening the personal acrimony that the primary contest engendered. At the same time, by breaking precedent and going on the stump, Taft confirmed the constitutional significance of the presidential campaign. In fact, there is a real sense in which the most important exchange in the constitutional debate of 1912 was the one between TR and Taft.

Viewing himself as Roosevelt's heir apparent, President Taft had supported and extended the pragmatic progressive program that was the legacy of TR's presidency, working for moderate industrial reform with the cooperation of Republican Party regulars. And yet, as noted in Chapter 2, by 1910 Taft had begun to suffer the slings and arrows of insurgency. These assaults were greatly abetted by the rise of muckraking journalists, who wrote mainly for low-priced mass-circulation magazines such as *McClure's Magazine* and the *Outlook*, weekly and monthly publications whose influence on public opinion was hardly less important than that of Roosevelt himself. In 1911 Taft had sought to raise the postal rates on popular magazines, indignant that the government was subsidizing journalists who presumed "to be controllers of public opinion and occupy a disinterested position."[37] But the president failed to dent the image of these magazines as "the agents of Heaven in establishing virtue." Unable to persuade Congress to challenge the special political position of independent journalists, he consoled himself with the hope that there soon would "be a sickening of the popular stomach with this assumption of pure disinterestedness and of attack on indefinite persons scheming against the public weal without specification or proof."[38] By 1912, however, the power of the "disinterested" press had grown, and the alliance of muckrakers and insurgent politicians had weakened his presidency and undermined popular support for regular partisan practices.

In the aftermath of the Illinois and Pennsylvania primaries, Taft found his efforts to carry on the pragmatic tradition of reform the object of scorn and derision, the victim of TR's celebration of "pure democracy." "The initiative, the referendum, and the recall, together with a complete adoption of the direct primary as a means of selecting nominees and an entire destruction of the convention system are now all made the *sine qua non* of a real reformer," Taft lamented. "Everyone who hesitates to follow all of these or any of them is regarded with suspicion and is denounced as an enemy of popular government and of the people."[39]

Yet his very "hesitation" allowed Taft to find honor in the charge of conservatism leveled against him. Attempting to ward off TR's indictment, first leveled in the Carnegie Hall speech, that he was a champion of oligarchy, Taft insisted that he was a progressive. Indeed, he insisted that only "conservative progressive government," buttressed by constitutional forms, made lasting reform possible. In a practical sense, Taft argued, upholding constitutional limitations on majority rule protected representative government. He claimed that popular elections—even expressions of so-called direct democracy—did not represent the "whole" people. The voters, Taft argued, "did not include the women and children, that in number the voters were less than one-fourth of all the people . . . ; so that the Government was controlled not by all the people but by a representative part of the people, to wit, a majority of the adult males." Taft thus insisted that his resistance to progressive measures that would weaken constitutional restrictions on majority rule, which TR attacked as proof that the president was a reactionary, really showed that he, not his opponent, was the true guardian of the people's rights. "I [have] pointed out the fact that this popular Government of ours is a Government by the adult voting males in order to show the necessity for constitutional restrictions to protect the nonvoters among the people against possible injustice and aggression of a majority of the voters."[40]

In truth, Taft fretted less about the protection of nonvoters, such as women and African Americans, whose disenfranchisement his speeches ignored, than he did about the necessity of protecting property.[41] Taft's sober assessment of human nature betrayed the depth of his conservatism. Without the right of property and constitutional protection of minority rights, he believed, an excited and untrammeled majority, aroused by a demagogue, would ride roughshod over the "unalienable" freedoms championed by the Declaration of Independence. The dangers he saw in TR's Charter of Democracy was a constant source of strife in the cyclical life of the ancient republics; the same threat, Taft claimed, that motivated the founders toward a properly checked and balanced republican government:

> With the effort to make the selection of candidates, the enactment of legislation, and the decision of the courts depend on the momentary passions of the people necessarily indifferently informed as to the issues presented, and without the opportunity to them for time and study and that deliberation that gives security and common sense to the government of the people, such extremists would hurry us into a condition which would find no parallel except in the French revolution, or in that bubbling anarchy that once characterized the South American Republics. Such extremists are not progressives—they are political emotionalists or neurotics—who have lost that sense of proportion, that clear and candid consideration of their own weaknesses as a whole, and that clear perception of the necessity for checks upon hasty popular action which made our people who fought the Revolution and who drafted the Federal Constitution, the greatest self-governing people that the world ever knew.[42]

Support for "pure democracy," Taft charged, found its "mainspring" in the very same "factional spirit" that James Madison warned against in his famous discussion of republican government in *Federalist* 10, an unruly majority that would "sacrifice to its ruling passion or interest both the public good and the rights of other citizens."[43]

In resisting this temptation to flatter the whims and passions of the majority, the most sacred duty of true conservatives was to uphold the courts. As Taft told an audience in Boston, TR's defense of direct democracy embraced "a tendency in modern politics to exalt above the written law and above the written constitution what is called 'popular will,' as if it were a higher law to which we must all admit allegiance and, by obeying it, ignore or transgress statutory and constitutional limitation." Roosevelt's support for the recall of judicial decisions did not propose to denigrate constitutionalism per se, to assert that "judges . . . ignore statutes and constitutions because of a conflicting popular will." Rather, Taft argued, TR's Charter of Democracy put forward the "more insidious proposition that plain construction of the statute or constitution is to be defeated and a strained and otherwise impossible construction put upon the language of the statute or constitution in deference to what is supposed to be the popular will." In the end, there was no rule for interpreting the people's view of the Constitution, except "the observation and imagination of the person who is appealing to it."[44] TR's claim to embody constitutionalism, Taft observed, drew most clearly the fundamental issue that was at stake in the primary contest for the Republican nomination:

> The Republican party . . . respecting as it does the constitution . . . the care with which the judicial clauses of that fundamental instrument were drawn to secure the independence of the judiciary, will never consent to an abatement of that independence in the slightest degree, and will stand with its face like flint against any constitutional changes in it to take away from the high priests upon which to administer to justice the independence that they must enjoy of influence of powerful individuals or of powerful majorities.[45]

Roosevelt's threat to constitutional forms, Taft alleged, was confirmed by the ex-president's willingness to break the third-term tradition—America's "most useful and necessary government tradition." TR denied that his 1912 campaign violated the pledge he made soon after the 1904 election to uphold "the wise custom which limits the President to two terms": the three and one-half years he had served after McKinley's assassination constituted his first term, Roosevelt acknowledged, and "under no circumstances" would he "be a candidate for or accept another nomination." He meant, TR clarified, that he would not accept a nomination for a "*consecutive* third term." As the progressive magazine he wrote for, the *Outlook*, put it: "When a man says at breakfast in the morning, 'No, thank you, I will not take any more coffee,' it does not mean that he will not take any more coffee tomorrow morning, or next week, or next month, or next year." That Roosevelt and his political allies took his pledge and the hallowed two-term tradition so lightly, Taft argued, gave dramatic testimony to TR's disdain for constitutional principles. TR and his followers, the president insisted, meant to displace constitutional forms with executive aggrandizement—a political recipe that threatened to exalt this self-styled champion of the people to near-imperial status. "I need hardly say that such an ambitious plan could not be carried out in one short four years," Taft said of Roosevelt's Columbus platform. "We are left to infer, therefore, that 'the job' which Mr. Roosevelt is to perform is one that may take a long time, perhaps the rest of his natural life. There is not the slightest reason why, if he secures a third term, and the limitation of the Washington, Jefferson, and Jackson tradition is broken down, he should not have as many terms as his natural life will permit. If he is necessary now to the Government, why not later?"[46]

Roosevelt never retreated in the face of this controversy. He insisted, as he had in his Carnegie Hall address, that Taft exaggerated the challenge his Columbus manifesto posed to the courts. "Remember that my proposal for a referendum to the people of certain decisions has nothing to do with the Federal Courts, with which at the moment I am not dealing," he reiterated in a campaign stop at Omaha, Nebraska. TR's immediate objective was to impugn state supreme court rulings declaring laws unconstitutional that legislatures enacted "in the interest of social and industrial justice under the police power or general welfare clause of the Constitution." In such cases where state courts had overruled legislative decisions to pass worker compensation or hours and wages legislation, which seemed, in the face of the harsh conditions loosed by the industrial revolution, rather moderate, it was eminently reasonable "for the people to have the matter referred to them for decision, so that they shall decide between their servant, the Legislature, and their servant, the court, and themselves interpret the meaning of the constitution which they themselves adopted for their own guidance."[47]

As noted in Chapter 2, Roosevelt linked this carefully calibrated proposal to a larger critique of the courts and existing constitutional forms. Indeed, once he bolted from the Republican Party and took up the cause of the Progressive Party, TR would express support for modifying the federal constitution to forge more direct ties among the president, the courts, and mass opinion. Although his critique of constitutional forms was more circumspect during the primary contests, Roosevelt held "absolutely to [his] conviction that some basis of accommodation must be found between the declared policy of the States on matters of social regulation in the interests of health, of decent living and working conditions, and of morals, and the attempt of the courts to substitute their own ideas on these subjects for the declarations of the people, made through their elected representatives in the several states."[48] Redressing state court decisions that declared and enforced "nothing but the will of judges against the will of the people" was of great urgency, TR insisted, for such cases were "turning large classes of people against the 'life, liberty, and property clauses'" and inclining "them toward Socialism."[49]

Returning to, and making public, the argument he had made to Learned Hand after his Columbus speech (see Chapter 2), TR insisted that his proposal to allow voters to restore modest progressive legislation overturned by state courts was conservative reform. He did not propose to substitute legislative supremacy for constitutionalism, as was the case in England, Canada, France, and Germany. Rather, he asked that "the power of the people in every State be made practically, and not merely as a matter of empty theory, supreme over all the servants of the people, and that their sober judgment, deliberately arrived at, be made binding alike on both the State courts and state legislatures as equal co-ordinate authorities in dealing with the interpretation of the constitution as regards the police power clause."[50] As TR wrote a friend abroad, "It is difficult for an Englishman to understand the extreme conservatism of my proposition as to the referendum to the people of certain judicial questions, and this difficulty arises from the fact that in England no human being dreams of permitting the court to decide such questions!" In actuality, TR claimed, he sought to avoid the delegation of policy to an unchecked legislature that might embody the sort of factionalism that plagued England and other representative democracies and worried the architects of the Constitution. Invoking the framers' view that the people required the institutional power of a supreme parliamentary power to make their oppressive designs effective, he wrote: "I do not propose to make the legislature supreme over the court; I propose *merely* to allow the people . . . to decide whether to follow the legislature or the court."[51]

Of course, TR also feared that the average American citizen might have a difficult time recognizing his judicial reform initiative as conservative. With Taft's encouragement, they could easily interpret progressive democracy as a *sui generis* American form of radicalism—one conceived to diminish American individuals' emotive attachment to the Constitution, especially the designated "guardians of the Constitution." In defending themselves against this charge, TR and his progressive allies often sought refuge in Lincoln and the revered president's defense of public opinion. Taft was quick to point out, however, that the progressives' assault on the Republican Party overlooked Lincoln's strong support for the American party system. More particularly, Taft argued, such insurgents were "altogether forgetful of the fact that in Lincoln's life the man and the party were so closely united in aim and accomplishment, that the history of the one is the history of the other."[52] By the same token, Taft also appealed to Lincoln's Whiggish and Republican devotion to natural rights, which rested in the people's "reverence for the constitution and laws."[53] Lincoln's understanding of equality, the president insisted, was thus bounded by an understanding of the Declaration and Constitution that championed private property, limited government, and, outside of a severe crisis like the Civil War, administrative decentralization.

Taft was on solid ground when pointing out that Lincoln's Republican Party did not sanction a constant national government presence in society and economy. The failure of Reconstruction confirmed that Republicans were not committed to expanding national administrative power to remake the economy and society. At the same time, TR had a legitimate claim that Lincoln's defense of property was more capacious than was Taft's characterization of it. TR rightfully argued that Lincoln did not make a fetish of the Court, that his response to the *Dred Scott* case, especially, showed a commitment to the right of elected representatives and public opinion to render constitutional judgments. Indeed, Lincoln refused to accept *Dred Scott* as a binding precedent. The great issues that the case raised had to be resolved by the American people. Chief Justice Roger Taney had denied African Americans citizenship on the grounds that the grand words of the Declaration of Independence—"all men are created equal"—did not include "the enslaved African race." But Lincoln insisted that the Declaration's meaning, and its relationship to the Constitution, was not a narrow legal issue. It raised the most basic questions about the nature of American rights and responsibilities. Lincoln granted that the *Dred Scott* decision was binding on the parties to the suit, but he would not allow it to determine the future course of slavery policy. Rather, slavery was an issue to be settled in the court of public opinion, through the regular course of elections. Otherwise, as Lincoln put it in his first inaugural address, "the people will have ceased to be their own rulers, having to that extent practically resigned their government into the hands of an eminent tribunal."[54] Lincoln and the Union's triumph in the 1860 election and the Civil War that followed ensured that *Dred Scott* would not stand and that the Court would not rule the nation.

Roosevelt insisted that his call for popular referenda on state court decisions was offered in the same spirit as Lincoln's challenge to the Taney Court. He took special pleasure in responding to Taft's criticism of what TR first proclaimed in his New Nationalism speech at Osawatomie, Kansas, as the "Progressive creed": "We stand for the man and the dollar, but if we had to choose between them, we stand for the man rather than the dollar." Taft pounced on this slogan. He told a New York audience, which gathered to honor Lincoln on his birthday, that private property was not established in order "to gratify love of some material wealth or capital"; rather, "it was established as an instrument in the progress of civilization and the uplifting of man." It promoted, Taft continued, equality of opportunity by "assuring man the results of his own labor, thrift and self-restraint." The president thus condemned Roosevelt's celebration of "human rights over property rights" as dangerous demagogy. Anyone who mounted the platform and announced he preferred the man above the dollar, Taft insisted, "ought to be interrogated as to what he means thereby—whether he is in favor of abolishing the right of the institution of private property and taking away from the poor man the opportunity to become wealthy by the use of the abilities that God has given him, the cultivation of the virtues with which practice of self-restraint and the exercise of moral courage will fortify him."[55]

Taft's interrogation of TR's challenge to the conventional understanding of property rights exposed him to a lampooning. "The humorous side of this," Roosevelt told his Omaha audience, "comes in the fact that Mr. Taft was evidently ignorant that I was merely quoting Lincoln's letter, which he wrote to some Boston correspondent in 1859. The 'demagogue on the platform' of whom he spoke was Abraham Lincoln!"[56] Lincoln had, in fact, made such a statement in a letter he wrote declining an invitation to speak in Boston at a birthday celebration honoring Thomas Jefferson. The tone of the letter, however, suggested that he intended it to be read at the event. With respect to the view of leading Democrats such as his archrival Stephen Douglas that *Dred Scott* must be upheld, Lincoln wrote: "The democracy of today holds the *liberty* of one man to be absolutely nothing, when in conflict with another man's right of *property*. Republicans, on the contrary, are for both the *man* and the *dollar*; but in cases of conflict, the man *before* the dollar."[57]

TR likened his own defense of social and economic reform to Lincoln's defense of the slave's right to the fruits of his or her own labor:

> In the same way I am for the human right of the overworked girl or the crippled working man or working woman against the so-called property right of the employer; I am for the right of the workmen against the factory owner or mine owner who runs the company stores; I am for the right of the legislature to prohibit men, women, and children being huddled like pigs in a tenement house room as against the property right of the owner of the tenement house.[58]

Roosevelt insisted, then, that his defense of progressive democracy, not Taft's, invoked Lincoln's understanding of the "unalienable rights" that the Declaration sanctified. A proper defense of natural rights did not presuppose that men and women were "born free"; rather, their rights depended on an honored past and a collective will to fight for those rights. As historian Daniel Walker Howe has observed, Lincoln reinterpreted Jefferson to make " 'the proposition that all men are created equal' . . . a positive goal of political action, not simply a pre-political"—*natural*—"state that government should preserve by inaction."[59] The Union's struggle, Lincoln told the special session of Congress in July 1861, was to maintain that "form and substance of government, whose leading object is, to elevate the condition of men—to lift artificial weights from all shoulders—to clear paths of laudable pursuit for all—to afford all, an unfettered start, and a fair chance, in the race of life."[60]

The contest between TR and Taft for ownership of Lincoln points to important differences between their understanding of constitutionalism; these constitutional disputes, moreover, mark the Republican primary contests as a critical episode in the development of American political ideas and institutions. Although he did not recognize Lincoln's quote that put the "man before the dollar," Taft cannot be accused of falsely attributing to Lincoln a commitment to party politics, natural rights, and constitutional forms. Lincoln acknowledged that "public opinion in the country is everything." But to him, public opinion meant more than the sum of individual preferences. It was a body of beliefs that instilled national identity. His characterization of a government "of the people, by the people, for the people" presupposed a moral fabric woven of the country's best possibilities. As Lincoln's son, Robert, argued in a letter written to endorse Taft's candidacy, by these words, "he could only mean that Government under which he lived, a representative Government of balanced executive, legislative and judicial parts, and not something entirely different—an unchecked democracy."[61] Lincoln's Gettysburg Address thus expressed his faith not only in the people's decency but in their constitutional heritage, rooted in the Declaration of Independence, and to their political parties that allied democratic passions to the social contract and engaged them in a continual debate about the meaning of their rights.

In the end, TR and his political allies proposed to emancipate public opinion from the restraining influence of the Declaration and Constitution. Lincoln proposed to join the Declaration of Independence and the Constitution through formal amendment; the progressives proposed a new understanding of freedom that subordinated formal constitutional procedures to public opinion. As Croly wrote in *The Promise of American Life*:

> The idea of a constructive relation between American nationality and American democracy is in truth equivalent to a new Declaration of Independence. It affirms the American people as free to organize their political, economic, and social life in the service of a comprehensive, a lofty and far-reaching democratic purpose. At the present time there is a strong, almost dominant tendency to regard the existing Constitution with superstitious awe, and to shrink with horror from modifying it even within the smallest detail; and it is superstitious fear of changing the most trivial parts of the fundamental legal fabric which brings to pass the great bondage of the American spirit. If such an abject worship of legal precedent for its own sake should continue, the American people will have to be fitted to rigid and narrow lines of a few legal formulas; and the ruler of the American spirit, like the ruler of the Jewish spirit of old, will become a lawyer. But it will not continue, in case Americans can be brought to understand and believe that the American national political organization should be constructively related to their democratic purpose.[62]

TR sought to bring Americans to this understanding and belief during the remarkable primary contests of 1912. Taft's defense of the old order helped clarify the fundamental issues in play. Did TR and his political allies merely seek, as they argued, to apply "to the issues of the present day the principles for which Abraham Lincoln stood"? Or, as Taft insisted, and Croly acknowledged, did the Progressives propose to "adopt" a "new Declaration" that presupposed replacing constitutional government with a plebiscitary form of democracy—or, as the Illinois reformer Charles Merriam put it, a "democratic Caesarism"?[63] In truth, both TR and Taft made reasonable arguments. Just as Taft upheld the hallowed commitment to individual rights in American democracy, so TR argued that true self-reliance required a due sense of responsibility for one's community and country. As he declared in his Sorbonne speech, discussed in the previous chapter,

> We can just as little afford to follow the doctrines of an extreme individualism as the doctrines of an extreme socialism. Individual initiative, so far from being discouraged, should be stimulated; and yet we should remember that, as a society develops and grows more

complex, we continually find that things which once it was desirable to leave to individual initiative can, under the changed conditions, be performed with better results by common effort.[64]

The Excitement and "Menace" of the Primaries

The constitutional debate between Taft and Roosevelt culminated in May with important primaries in California and Ohio. These primaries seemed to confirm, as Taft feared, "the hold which Roosevelt still [had] over the plain people."[65] With the help of Governor Hiram Johnson, who had constructed one of the most effective progressive state organizations in the country, TR easily captured California, winning more popular votes than Taft and La Follette combined. La Follette's failure to effectively challenge TR for the support of California progressives showed conclusively that he would not be able to revitalize his candidacy before the Republican National Convention. La Follette had the support of the Scripps newspapers and spent a month campaigning in the state. But, even though he did well in San Diego County, where there had recently been considerable labor unrest, he failed to seriously dent the popular perception that TR represented the cause of progressive democracy.

TR's dramatic California triumph in the service of that cause dealt another serious blow to the incumbent president and the party organization that supported him. Taft did especially poorly in the southern part of the state, a Republican stronghold, where Roosevelt outpolled him by almost a two-to-one margin.[66] "The lesson of the campaign so far," the *Manchester Guardian* reported after the California contest, was "the Insurgency movement, the revolt against the 'bosses,' the 'machine,' and the 'big interests' is as vigorous as ever," so much so that a "new style" of politics seemed to have emerged triumphant in the United States.[67]

Indeed, the incumbent president had reluctantly agreed to deploy new methods in defending the old order; he sought to match TR's highly effective personal organization and campaign with a direct appeal to the voters of his own. Unlike Roosevelt, who depended on his own organization for support, Taft relied on the regular GOP organization. In general, however, the plan and methods that the Roosevelt and Republican organizations used in appealing to the voters were the same. William McKinley, who was the manager of both the Republican Congressional Committee and the Taft campaign, had managed by the time of the Massachusetts primary to tie "the two campaigns closely into one." No less than TR's progressive organization, the Republican machine employed methods of publicity that emphasized the personal contest between Taft and Roosevelt. House Republican staff set up a shipping room in the capitol on "standpat row"—the nearby offices of conservative Republican congressmen—that served virtually as a Taft "mail order house": "the cords and tons of [Taft campaign material] were stacked in rooms and corridors; trucked out and carried down elevators; and dumped into the second class mail."[68]

Taft chose to make a last-ditch fight for the "old style" of politics and the constitutional sobriety he claimed it represented in his home state. By the time of the Ohio primary, the personal duel between Taft and Roosevelt had become so central to the nomination contest that its principal thrust was a contest between their respective publicity bureaus in Washington. Oscar King Davis, a well-known Washington correspondent for the *New York Times,* resigned his position to head the Roosevelt publicity campaign. Taft was immediately driven to set up a large publicity bureau of his own under the supervision of Leroy T. Vernon, an enterprising young correspondent of the Chicago *News.* Both the Roosevelt and Taft headquarters emphasized direct appeals from the individual candidates to the voters. Bulletins and ads were distributed to daily newspapers and weekly magazines; nationally prominent figures and local notables crossed the state to campaign for one or the other of the candidates; and speeches or pamphlets were mailed to thousands of voters.

As the personal "duel of the presidents" heated up, however, there was no substitute for the candidates to meet the voters in person: mobilized by the Taft and Roosevelt machines, "towns and cities that had not greeted a President or ex-President for half a century came out and listened in audiences of thousands and tens of thousands."[69] Both Roosevelt and Taft hired special trains to traverse the state: they spoke in nearly all of Ohio's eighty-eight counties, traveled 1,500–2,000 miles delivering their messages to the voters, and gave about ninety scheduled talks during the campaign. Just as the contemporary candidate-centered campaign takes its toll on the health of the candidates, so it was true at the birth of the presidential primary system. Both TR and Taft put so much strain on their vocal cords during the Ohio contest that both required medical treatment for their throats during the course of the final intense week of campaigning.

Although the two candidates and their followers declared this heated contest to be a war of principles, the *Manchester Guardian,* even as it was fascinated and impressed by the emergence of a new form of politics in the United States, confessed during the Ohio campaign that "at the present rate the principles threaten to be submerged beneath personal invective."[70] Roosevelt publicly refused to make personal attacks on the president, believing that it would be bad form to hurl insults at Taft in his own state. Still, reports surfaced of his dismissing the president in private as a "Puzzlewit" and "man of flabby intellect." Claiming that it was too late for TR to decry personal attacks, Taft showed less restraint, publicly condemning his challenger as a "honeyfugler," "demagogue," and "hypocrite." The personal animosity between Roosevelt and Taft was such that when their two private cars came to rest next to one another for a few hours in Steubenville, "there was no exchange of amenities which under ordinary circumstances might have been expected between the present and former president of the United States, both of the same party and only a short time ago the best of friends." Instead, the two candidates and their entourages studiously avoided each other, thus disappointing a "hopeful crowd gathered to see if the candidates—or at least their supporters—might engage in a knock-down brawl on the spot."[71]

In truth, given the doctrine of progressive democracy, the cult of personality and principled debate were unavoidably intertwined. Roosevelt's campaign widely distributed his Carnegie Hall address, which ended in a dramatic peroration claiming that a successful battle for "social and industrial justice, achieved through the genuine rule of the people," depended on "leaders of inspired idealism" who could "kindle the people with the fire from their own burning souls." Indeed, the direct primary—the *cause célèbre* of TR's insurgent campaign—subordinated the party and the principles it stood for to the leadership qualities of the individual candidates. As the New York Republican Party chairman, William Barnes, declared in a speech during the Ohio contest, the progressive platform necessarily exalted the personal over the collective responsibility of the Republican Party:

It is absurd to have preferential Presidential primaries and then hold a [party] convention. The direct nomination of candidates for office with a party label is illogical because such candidates for office do not emanate as the result of conciliation, consultation and grouping of those holding similar ideas, but stand upon their own personal platform. Such nominees should appeal to the electorate as independents. The logical sequence of the direct nominations idea is the abolition of the official primary altogether. The exigencies of this abnormal situation have compelled the President of the United States, for the preservation of his party, to make a personal campaign in order to undo the damage done by a mendacious opponent.[72]

From this perspective, Taft's attack on Roosevelt as a "demagogue" was not merely personal invective but partly a principled attack on his celebration of "pure democracy." As the *Outlook,* with which TR had a very close relationship, acknowledged, "personal references" with regard to "motive" were indefensible, but those of "another kind (involving questions of competence, equipment, and public record)" were not only justified but also "absolutely essential to that free discussion on which popular self-government depends":

> If Mr. Taft believes that Mr. Roosevelt during his Administration committed acts that were injurious to the country, he not only has a right, he has a duty, to point them out and to specify them and to give them as reason why Mr. Roosevelt should not be put in office again. If he believes that Mr. Roosevelt is not equipped for the Presidency, Mr. Taft has not only a right, he has a duty, to point out those particulars in which his equipment is defective, giving instances and specification. If he believes that Mr. Roosevelt has shown by the proposals he makes for changes in forms of government or in law that he is a dangerous man, Mr. Taft has not only the right, he has the duty, to say so.[73]

Taft did believe strongly that it was his duty to decry TR's defense of "pure democracy," to state his position that it portended a plebiscitary politics that would destroy representative constitutional government. Taft's Ohio speeches echoed many of the attacks he had made on TR and progressive democracy in previous primary campaigns. But the Ohio contest saw Taft make a greater effort to market his message, to infuse it with humorous and personal attacks on his opponent, which, according to the press, seldom failed to elicit laughter and applause. Claiming that TR's challenge to his incumbency ought to be denied because of the "wild constitutional principles" it championed, Taft caricatured his opponent's presentation of self as indispensable reform leader:

> He says the reason the American people are going to elect him is because he is necessary for the job. . . . Well, I hope the American people will not think that he is necessary for the job. I want to call your

attention to what the job is which he proposes. It is the millennium that he is going to bring about when he gets into office. All bosses are going to disappear, politicians are going to be fewer, and he is going to have a finger in every community, in every State, in every county, and everything is going to heaven.[74]

Taft's satirical reference to TR's assault on "bosses" and "politics" directly linked the progressives' defense of popular primaries and their attack on the party system. Roosevelt had more than hinted since April that if Republican Party leaders refused to accept the verdict of the people as expressed in the presidential primaries, he might bolt the party and run as a third-party candidate.[75] Paradoxically, Taft chose the occasion of the Ohio primary contest to defend the Republican Party organization and its right to make decisions independently of the verdict rendered by primary voters. Knowing that this defense had to resonate with a popular audience, Taft again made fun of TR's political ambition, comparing him to Louis XIV, the "Grand Monarch of France," who declared, "I am the State." This, the president argued, was TR's position toward the Republican Party and the country. "I venture to think that the Republican Party will get along and live long after him, and that he is not indispensable either to the party or to the country. It will be a sad day in the history of the country when a man becomes indispensable to it. We shall have to change the form from a republic to some other form if that be the case."[76]

Taft's defense of political parties during the Ohio primary campaign was not always fervent or perfectly consistent. Warming to the personal nature of the primary contest, he alleged that Roosevelt too associated with bosses, citing William Flinn, who provided critical organizational support in Pennsylvania, and Walter Brown, the chairman of the Ohio Republican State Central Committee, who gave TR indispensable organizational support in the Ohio primary contest. Yet, unlike TR, who celebrated presidential party leadership, Taft defended the local nature of party organizations, as well as the prerogative of "bosses" to make important political decisions in local affairs. Citing Roosevelt's failure to mount an attack on party regulars during his own presidency, Taft argued that such forbearance was understandable; indeed, he insisted that chief executives neither could nor should control party organizations. "The President has nothing to do with upholding or destroying bosses," he insisted. "Bosses are made by local conditions. . . . I am not engaged in going about cutting off the heads of bosses. I cannot do it. . . . It is the function of the people at home to reform matters."[77]

Moreover, hedging his bets against a defeat in the Ohio contest, Taft and his supporters claimed that he deserved to win the nomination regardless of what happened in the primaries. TR's celebration of the direct primaries and denigration of state caucuses, they insisted, were a desperate and contemptuous assault on valued institutions. Taft admitted that many local party leaders were corrupt, and he acknowledged that he had no objection to establishing direct primaries in local elections "with certain limitations." This would be "a practical step to oust the boss and destroy the machine built on patronage and corruption." But he defended the state party—the "unit of the national party"—as part and parcel of responsible collective responsibility that buttressed constitutional government. The president was confident that he would win the Republican nomination, he stated during the Ohio contest, because the national convention would be "organized by the friends of constitutional government."[78] This was not to claim that the state caucuses and the national convention were free of political manipulation. But Taft insisted that the great majority of party leaders at the state and national levels were "honest and anxious for the party to succeed by serving the people well in the government with which the party may be entrusted." The convocation of such leaders in state caucuses and the national convention added a critical measure of deliberation to the selection of candidates for office and the statement of party policies. "Conference and discussion lead to wise results," Taft averred, "and conference and discussion and deliberation with reference to party politics was not possible at the polls." Such responsible deliberation would be especially impracticable at the national level "when the electors numbered into the millions."[79]

Against Taft's proposition that party leaders played a critical role in protecting republican government, TR and his supporters gave a forceful defense of a more populist version of party and constitutional government. Toward the end of the Ohio campaign, TR lambasted Taft's understanding of the party convention. Calling out the GOP leaders who stood by Taft's side, he asserted in a speech at Columbus, the site where he had delivered his Charter of Democracy three months earlier, that a "government administered by Messers Lorimer, Guggenheim, Barnes, Gallagher, and their like, in defiance of the will of the people," would not uphold constitutional forms but, rather, "[defraud] the people of their rights." Any individual who voted against him in the Ohio primary, Roosevelt asserted, would be strengthening this "reactionary cause." A vote for the progressive cause, TR and his supporters also insisted, was a vote not to destroy but to save the Republican Party. As an *Outlook* missive that targeted the battle in Ohio claimed, "It is only under the assumption that the party consists of the party workers and leaders and bosses that the old-time convention system can be reconciled with the belief in self-government." In contrast to this traditional convention system, progressives argued that parties consisted of those who believed in party principles and voted the party ticket. The presidential primaries launched in the 1912 campaign supplied to the "party voters" — "the rank and file of the party army" — an opportunity "to record their will and their judgment with regard to party candidates." Such primaries were thus "based on the theory that the party is not composed exclusively of party leaders, or party bosses, or party workers, but consists of all those who may fairly be termed the party voters."[80] That virtually every Republican state that had conducted a primary had voted against Taft strengthened the progressive theory of the "party voter" and highlighted the great importance of the Ohio primary, which took place in arguably the most important site of GOP support.

Roosevelt won a sweeping victory, capturing thirty of the forty-two district delegates selected by the Ohio primary voters. The final popular vote was La Follette 15,570, Taft 118,362, and TR 165,809. Roosevelt's stunning triumph over Taft in the president's home state was magnified by the national interest in the contest. The *New York Times,* a strong supporter of Taft, reported that large throngs, resembling general election gatherings in size and enthusiasm, crowded in front of the Times Building to view the Ohio returns. The *Times'* disappointed observation that "a sort of sophomoric enthusiasm took the place of . . . quiet dignity" as mounting returns sealed the president's electoral fate signified not just a national repudiation of Taft, but a crisis of the "old political order" that he championed.[81] "For the President this is [not merely] a reverse, it is unquestionably a disaster," the newspaper editorialized.[82] Just as gloom settled over Taft's campaign quarters, so jubilation pervaded the Roosevelt organization. "This ends Taft and nominates Theodore," James Garfield, Roosevelt's leading progressive supporter in Ohio, wrote in his diary.[83] Before the Ohio primary, Roosevelt had been very guarded about his chances of capturing the nomination; now, TR admitted with surprise, he was "reasonably sure" of controlling the Republican convention.[84]

Still, neither the decisive Roosevelt triumph in Ohio nor those that followed in New Jersey and South Dakota, the final primary contest of 1912, ended the debate about TR's right to the Republican nomination. The *New York Times* editorials and coverage of the campaign played a principal part in mobilizing most daily newspapers against the Roosevelt candidacy. The

Times was, TR's political supporters admitted, the "patron saint of respectability and old style civic virtue."[85] Even as it acknowledged the Ohio contest as a terrible defeat for Taft, this journalistic agent of respectability urged
GOP party leaders not to abandon the incumbent president. First, the primaries polled only a small percentage of GOP rank-and-file voters. Most
delegates were selected in state party caucuses—which, the *Times* urged,
should ignore the verdicts rendered in the twelve primary states. Noting
correctly that Roosevelt's candidacy targeted not only Taft but also the Republican Party and, indeed, the critical role that party conventions played
in nurturing responsible constitutional government, as conservatives understood it, the *Times* also insisted that the nomination of TR would mark a
fatal self-inflicted wound. Similarly, delegates should not seek a compromise
choice, for to do so would be to ignore the nature of the contest between
Roosevelt and Taft, which was "as a matter of principle incompatible, ir-
reconcilable": "Mr. Roosevelt has attacked the integrity of the Republican
Administration, and the countercharge has been made, only too plainly
true, that the third term Roosevelt movement is an attempt to bring about
revolutionary changes in our laws and our institutions." Should the GOP
hold the line, the *Times* editorialized, the prospects for the party system to
survive the progressive insurgency would be much improved.

The Democratic candidates also had engaged in primary contests. But
these campaigns were sideshows to the war between TR and Taft: the Democratic primaries occurred in predominantly Republican states and tended
to be much less heated than the struggle waged by Roosevelt and Taft. "The
Democratic party [convention] will be held under conditions seemingly favorable to deliberation and wise decision," the *Times* opined hopefully. Republican steadfastness combined with Democratic sobriety would yield a
"balance of forces" and "incentives to prudent and enlightened action" that
could lead to the survival of the two-party system and the preservation of
constitutional forms.[86]

In the face of the conservative press's onslaught, Roosevelt's closest journalistic ally, the *Outlook,* took the lead in defending progressive democracy.
The campaign between Roosevelt and Taft, it claimed, "had been a School
of the People," providing a critical object lesson on what was at stake in the
primary contests. Those who believed that self-government was, at best, a
necessary evil, the *Outlook* editorialized, would see in such a series of popular contests for the Republican nomination "an intensification of that evil."
In contrast, those who viewed primary campaigns as an opportunity to learn
about the heft of the candidates and the legitimacy of the principles and

issues they championed—those who believed that "democracy is a school in which are learned the results of self-control and self-direction"—would see in these "primaries a new sign of the progress of the Nation in self-education."

Roosevelt's allies admitted that the "judgment of the many" was not always better than "the judgment of the few." They expressed sympathy with *Life* magazine's position that the primary contests denigrated the presidency, the popular journal's objection to "the cries and echoes of accusation and recrimination, the bemiring of reputations that once were fair, and the neglect of public business for a long period while public officials [had] been campaigning." But such disadvantages of progressive reforms revealed the "painful process of education." The miring of President Taft in a disconcerting "rough and tumble match for renomination" was but evidence of "the lesson that in America at least the many are willing to accept the responsibility and make their own decisions." The ugliness of the primaries, the *Outlook* insisted, was the cost of democracy:

> It may be that other forms of government are more efficient and produce better immediate results than that form of government which we call democracy. It is possible that oligarchical Germany carries on more effectively than democratic America the business of ruling a state. But democracy is more than a form of government; it is a form of education; and it is clear from this campaign that the American people are ready for that process of education that comes through the choice of Presidential candidates and the determining of National party policies.[87]

Of course, as noted in Chapter 2, many progressives were deeply interested in "state-building." Learned Hand's colloquy with TR over the judicial recall proposal expressed his hope that progressive democracy would buttress American constitutional government with a full-blown welfare state. "I am weary to death of the Rule of the People and a millennium created by constant elections and never-ending suspicion of authority," Hand wrote in the midst of the primary contests. "When will the day come that some courageous men will stand sponsors for a real programme of 'social justice' in the words of our leader?" Gazing enviously across the Atlantic, not at Germany but at the precocious experiments in social democracy going on in Great Britain, Hand asked Felix Frankfurter plaintively, "Can you see a single man who would really dare to commit himself to any plan like the Fabians? Why have we nowhere any Fabians? Why aren't all of us Fabians?"[88]

Even some progressives who supported TR's celebration of "pure democracy" expressed doubts that its innovations would strengthen self-government. The muckraking journal *McClure's Magazine* ran an exposé, written by George Kibbe Turner, that characterized the candidate-centered primary contests as an exercise in "manufacturing" rather than educating public opinion. Echoing many of the concerns that La Follette expressed about Roosevelt's personal organization at the outset of the nomination contest, Turner revealed how the TR-Taft campaign for the Republican nomination brought to fruition a contest of personalities and dueling candidate organizations that appeared to subordinate principles and issues to what amounted to huge marketing campaigns. Most problematic, the "duel of the presidents" cost an enormous amount of money. Although unable to estimate the costs precisely, Turner concluded that three factors, all potentially damning, were clear about the primary campaigns: the cost of the campaign could not possibly have been under $1 million; because these costs were incurred by individual candidates rather than parties, they had to be paid for by individual backers; and these backers tended not to be small contributors but, rather, rich individuals or interests.[89] Without elaborate campaign finance reform, therefore, *McClure's* feared that the presidential primary would become a "menace," a "great new danger to the republic." Indeed, it insisted that candidate-centered organizations posed a much greater danger to democracy than did party organizations; the latter, at least, had the potential for collective responsibility. "The national primary resolves itself into a huge advertising campaign," a *McClure's* editorial concluded; "and in advertising—political as well as commercial—Napoleon's cynical belief that 'God is on the side of the heaviest battalions' is too apt to be true to make for comfortable reflections in a democracy."[90]

The end of the primary campaign thus left the campaign of 1912 in a swirl of personal acrimony, party maneuvers, and fundamental conflict over the rules by which presidential candidates were selected. The struggle between the old and the new political order—what one commentator, invoking the tensions between North and South that led to the Civil War, dubbed "the new irrepressible conflict"—was clouded by the clash of personalities and ambitions as well as serious disagreement among progressives about how to translate the ideal of pure democracy into political and governmental practice. Yet, as an article in the moderate progressive journal the *Independent* insisted, "The unpleasant personalities that have marked the presidential campaigns this year must not be confounded with the real issues at stake."[91] Taft's beleaguered supporters were united in the belief that "America [had] progressed in the direction of popular government as far as is safe, that facing the danger to the Republic [lay] in preserving, and perhaps increasing, the checks and restraints upon their power." In contrast, most progressive reformers, for all their disagreements, seemed united in the proposition "that the danger to the Republic is from too great power in the hands of the few; that safety lies in developing, if not increasing, the power of the people; that the remedy for the evils of democracy is more democracy."[92]

In championing "the power of the people," insurgents, whether they supported TR or La Follette, had come to demand a Progressive Party. That aspiration now focused on the Republican convention in Chicago, which would begin on June 18. The Democratic convention would follow soon thereafter in Baltimore, but most reformers had grave doubts that the delegates who gathered there, representing a party so dependent on the "solid South," could be "transformed into a steady constructive instrument of progressive government." Of course, TR and his political allies also were deeply skeptical that the bosses who would control the majority of delegates in Chicago could be won over to their cause. All that was certain was that a hard fight lay ahead, for "a great old party" could "not be transformed or a new party of power organized without discomforts and bitterness." By hell or high water, reformers believed, there had to be a realignment of parties, lest the progressive movement "end in talk." As the *Independent* admonished on the eve of the Grand Old Party's national convention, "The Progressives must either capture the Republican Party or else organize a new one."[93]

The Road to Armageddon: The 1912 National Republican Convention

The approach of the Republican convention led to a hardening of the lines between Roosevelt and the party regulars. Most observers speculated that Taft survived the brutal preconvention battles with a slim majority, but there was great uncertainty about whether he could hold that lead at the Chicago Coliseum. Roosevelt hoped, and Taft supporters feared, that his success in the primaries, which took place in states that ordinarily had voted Republican in presidential elections, might shake loose enough delegates who were chosen in state caucuses to give him the nomination.

In the face of TR's challenge to accepted party practices, however, the

Old Guard much preferred defeat with Taft to a Republican victory with Roosevelt. As Taft himself summed up the party leaders' position in a letter to New York Republican boss William Barnes,

> I quite agree with you that the victory in November is by no means the most important purpose before us. It should be to retain the party and the principles of the party, so as to keep it in a condition of activity and discipline a united force to strike when the blow will become effective for the retention of conservative government and conservative institutions. . . . It is the Republican Party with its old principles that we must labor to maintain and keep vitalized and active. If victory comes in November well and good; if it does not we shall know that in June we accomplished a great victory and that we are merely holding our forces in line for victory in the future.[94]

Taft's position on the GOP's political fortunes should not be dismissed as entirely self-serving. Roosevelt's celebration of a direct appeal to the electorate, and the severe challenge it represented to the very legitimacy of the party organization, made a *Republican* victory as such chimerical. Regular party leaders, therefore, were determined to use their control of the party councils to nominate Taft on the first ballot. The first test of their will would come in the resolution of the 254 contested delegate seats. Although Taft was able to count on the support of the great majority of the nonprimary delegates, Roosevelt's organization claimed that many of these contests were illegitimate. If Roosevelt could win only a quarter of these disputes, the nomination would be his.

The Republican National Committee, dominated by Taft supporters, convened in Chicago on June 6, two days after the last primary and twelve before the start of the convention, to hear allegations that the president had acquired a majority of the delegates by patronage and fraud. Most of the challenges came from the South, the result of the rump conventions, organized by Ormsby McHarg, which sent rival delegations to Chicago. Roosevelt supporters first attempted to discount the South, arguing that most of the delegates selected below the Mason-Dixon Line represented "rotten borough states which never cast a Republican electoral vote."[95] But the committee, by a 39–14 margin, defeated a Roosevelt proposal to reduce the number of delegates representing southern states.[96] Taft's majority support held steady in subsequent committee decisions. Proving to be a reliable

and forceful "steamroller," the Taft faction not only rejected the rival southern delegations, which even many Roosevelt supporters admitted rested on
tenuous legal grounds, but also showed ruthless disregard for more credible
insurgent grievances.

Roosevelt and his followers were especially incensed by the committee's
disqualification of their delegates from California and Texas. According
to state law, California awarded all its delegates to TR, who won a large
majority of votes in that state's primary contest. But as a sign of the Taft
steamroller's determination to squash any prospect of Roosevelt controlling
the convention, it replaced two of the colonel's supporters with those of
the president on the grounds that party rules prescribed not statewide but,
rather, county selection of convention delegates. On the basis of questionable evidence, the committee claimed that one of California's counties, which
sent two delegates to Chicago, had cast its votes for the president. "Other
contests may involve assaults on single delegations," Governor Hiram Johnson protested. *"This case is an assault on the whole primary system."*[97]

And yet the dispute over the Texas delegation, which appeared to contra-
dict the logic of the committee's decisions regarding southern conventions,
was cited by Roosevelt forces as perhaps the most telling sign of the Taft
steamroller's disregard for fair play.[98] Texas was the only southern state
where the head of the Republican organization, Cecil Lyon, was a Roosevelt
supporter; indeed, Lyon was a close personal and political friend of TR. In
a reversal of fortune, the regular state organization supported Roosevelt's
insurgent campaign, sending a delegation in which 32 of the 40 members
supported TR, whereas the Taft people, headed by Henry F. MacGregor,
convened a rump convention and, alleging fraudulent practices, challenged
nearly all the Roosevelt delegates before the national Republican gathering.
Although admitting these delegates were legally selected, the national committee proceeded to unseat most of Roosevelt's Texas supporters, claiming
the rival Taft delegation had more public support.[99]

Through such work, which appeared to uphold party or state laws arbi-
trarily, the Republican National Committee awarded 235 disputed votes to
Taft and only 19 to Roosevelt. The committee's staunch support of President Taft encouraged Roosevelt to break an important party precedent, thus
adding to the drama of the convention. Unsettled by the Taft steamroller, he
decided to attend the convention and take command of his supporters' preparation for what would be, according to the press, "the death struggle of
one wing of the party against the other."[100] Traditionally, serious candidates

for their party's nomination had stayed away from the convention, a custom reaching back to the origins of the two-party system that protected
the Democrats and Republicans from candidates diminishing their status
as collective organizations with pasts and futures. Taft had no intention of
going to the convention; Roosevelt paced the floor of his study awaiting
a credible excuse for doing so. Once he received a dire message from his
leading supporters in Chicago—C.Q.D., standing for "Come Quickly, Disaster"—Roosevelt immediately gathered his family and set out for the site
of the battle on June 14. Before boarding the train, he launched a fusillade
at the Republican National Committee from the *Outlook* offices, claiming
that "the contest for the Republican nomination has now narrowed down
to a naked issue of right and wrong; for the issue is simply whether or not
we shall permit a system of naked fraud, of naked theft from the people to
triumph."[101] Warming to the excitement aroused by TR's decision to attend
the convention, Medill McCormick's *Chicago Tribune* welcomed TR to the
battlefront with a banner across every page of its issue of June 18, the day
the convention was to open: "The Eighth Commandment: Thou Shall not
Steal." The Chicago Coliseum, the large hall in which the proceedings were
to be held, became in the dramatic words of a *Tribune* editorial "the temple
at Gaza and Samson is between the pillars."[102]

Roosevelt's precedent-shattering visit to Chicago thus confirmed that
his battle for control of the Republican nomination was part of a larger
war, a political crusade to transform American politics. "This vain, wrong
headed, impetuous man in his mood of shameless self-glorification has gone
to the convention city to browbeat his opponents," the *New York Times*
fumed. "Nothing like it, nothing so destructive to the dignity of our institutions, was ever dreamed of in the uncouth early days of our Republic."[103]
This was not the way most of the public viewed TR's assault on traditional
party practices, however. The debate over the recall of judicial decisions
itself might have been too abstract to arouse the public. But the Republican
steamroller, publicized in great detail by magazines and newspapers, enabled Roosevelt to frame the struggle for the Constitution as one between
the people and the "boss," which everybody, whether a citizen of Maine or
California, understood. As the conservative London *Times* appreciated, the
stolid Taft was the "antithesis of all ordinary conceptions of the American
'boss.'" Nonetheless, the president had "stood in" with the party organizations in Washington, and the authority of these associations rested in the
power of state and local politicians who effectively plied a far-flung spoils
system. "Paradoxically," the *Times* observed, because it was so familiar to

voters in the States, "the people versus 'boss' issue . . . made an excellent platform for a national campaign."

Roosevelt's assault on the regular Republican machinery, therefore, departed from recent reform movements that appealed to certain regions and party factions. According to his conservative critics, TR was auditioning for the leadership of a radically transformed democracy that would resemble the class-based politics of Great Britain and Western Europe. As the *Times* put it, "One looks . . . in vain for the old division between the Radical West and the Conservative East, so conspicuous in the days of the bimetallism agitation and later. In the sense that Mr. Roosevelt is trying to use the 'plain people' to break down 'government of a privileged minority' he cannot be acquitted of trying to substitute a national movement of class for geographical prejudice and party lines."[104]

But as the Socialist Eugene Debs alleged, and lamented, Roosevelt's candidate-centered campaign transcended an appeal to class. TR's arrival in Chicago on Thursday, June 15, elicited an enthusiasm reserved for a great national hero. As his young cousin Nicholas observed, "Everyone was howling with delight, and cries of 'Teddy!' filled the air. At the cross streets, as far as we could see to either side, or back or forward, people were wedged in like pins. Everyone cheered. Everyone screamed. Everyone was hurled along in the irresistible force of the delighted mob."[105] Newspapers estimated the welcoming crowd at 50,000 people. The progressive journalist William Allen White, a loyal member of TR's inner circle, averred that "if ever an American was a hero of a hot and crowded hour, it was Theodore Roosevelt that day in Chicago." A more detached and humorous Roosevelt ally had ten thousand handbills printed and distributed, announcing that TR would "walk on the waters of Lake Michigan at 7:30 Monday evening."[106]

Historian Patricia O'Toole has written that Roosevelt's performance on Monday evening, June 17, the eve of the Republican National Convention, "would far surpass the advertised walk on the water."[107] TR had agreed to deliver the major address at a meeting of the Chicago Auditorium to rally his supporters. "By speaking before a word was uttered in the official Republican forum," she observes, Roosevelt "could upstage the party and by planting the idea that the convention was about to perpetuate a swindle, he could pave the first mile for his bolt."[108] TR told the nearly six thousand wildly enthusiastic supporters who came to the Coliseum to hear him that between sixty and eighty delegates had been stolen by the party bosses who controlled the convention. It did not matter to Roosevelt and his supporters that he had used the very same tactics in 1908 to designate Taft as his rightful heir or that the weight of tradition was on the side of regular Republicans. TR claimed to champion the cause of a new form of politics, justified by the primary contests, that required party leaders to worship at the shrine of public opinion. Thus Roosevelt not only condemned practices that appeared to involve obvious fraud; he also scorned the actions of party leaders that were perfectly legal but resisted the sentiment of public opinion. TR excoriated the Ohio Republican convention, for example, for awarding six at-large delegates, who were not selected by the state's primary, to Taft, even though Roosevelt beat the president in the popular contest by 47,000 votes. This action, done with the approval of Taft, made perfectly clear, Roosevelt insisted, what the president meant by "government of the people by a 'representative part' of the people." TR had acknowledged that the at-large delegates in Massachusetts should go to the president, because that is what the people appeared to sanction; in contrast, Taft's unwillingness to grant that the at-large delegates in Ohio belonged to his opponent showed that his understanding of representative government meant "government of the people by politicians who shall misrepresent them in the selfish interest of someone else."

Since April, Roosevelt had warned of a walkout should the Old Guard defy the clear intention of the Republican primaries. The peroration of his June 17 speech did more than encourage his political followers to bolt the convention. It contained the famous words that reached beyond his Republican supporters and summoned a new party to battle:

> It would be far better to fall honorably for the cause we champion than
> it would be to win by foul methods, the foul victory for which our
> opponents hope. But the victory shall be ours, and it shall be won as
> we have already won so many victories, by clean and honest fighting
> for the loftiest of causes. We fight in honorable fashion for the good of
> mankind; fearless of the future; unheeding of our individual fates; with
> unflinching hearts and undimmed eyes; we stand at Armageddon, and
> we battle for the Lord.[109]

Roosevelt's final words, expressing the evangelical fervor of the Social Gospel movement, revealed his view, and that of his most devoted followers, that they were engaged in a political battle with supremely high stakes. Noting how Roosevelt's exodus from the Republican convention helped arouse a crusade to remake American democracy, Walter Rauschenbusch, the great theorist of Social Gospel, wrote:

The entire upheaval in the political alignment of 1912, the demand for direct primaries, for direct legislation, for the recall of judges, for the popular election of senators, are an expression of the profound and durable conviction of the nation, drawn from a fearfully costly process of education, that our whole political organization, as it stood ten years ago, had been turned into an instrument to victimize the people on behalf of private interests. Really, nothing more damning can be said than this tremendous verdict of a whole nation.[110]

The most steadfast resistance to Roosevelt's apocalyptic assault on the Republican convention came not from Taft, who scrupulously adhered to the traditional practice that prevented presidential candidates from intruding on party councils, but from New York Senator Elihu Root. Taft's supporters had selected Root to serve as temporary chairman and keynote speaker of the convention. Their hope was that the distinguished senator, who had served the Roosevelt administration as secretary of war and secretary of state, possessed the "strength of character" that would "give weight to his [parliamentary] decisions and thus add undaunted resolution to the regulars' determination to fend off the heated contests that Roosevelt supporters were sure to bring to the convention floor."[111]

Root's gravitas put TR in a difficult situation. He had great respect for Root—once calling him "the ablest man that has appeared in the public life of the country"—yet believed that his old friend, by accepting the Taft forces' invitation to preside over the convention, had "ranged himself against the men who stand for progressive principles" and represented "the men and policies of reaction."[112] Roosevelt's opposition to Root was no doubt influenced by the knowledge that William Barnes, the New York State boss who organized against TR in the April primary, had telegraphed appeals to the New York delegates-elect to support Root as temporary chairman.[113]

Roosevelt's reluctant but firm decision to oppose the Republican National Committee's designation of Root set the stage for one last decisive battle in the dramatic struggle for control of the Grand Old Party. Like the primary contests, the convention fight melded personal animosities and a deeply principled struggle over how democratic the Constitution should be. As an alternative to Root, Roosevelt and his supporters settled on Governor Francis E. McGovern of Wisconsin, in the hope that he would draw support from the small, determined, and potentially pivotal La Follette bloc of delegates. TR had made an overture to La Follette and his supporters in his June 17 address, asking "his fellow progressives who have supported other candidates to remember that one of the cardinal principles of the doctrines which we hold in common is our duty normally, loyally and in good faith to abide by the well-thought-out and honestly expressed action of the majority."

Governor McGovern, who was selected as a La Follette delegate, enthusiastically answered this call. As one of his aides wrote to a disgruntled constituent who considered McGovern's collaboration with Roosevelt a betrayal of the governor's pledged allegiance to La Follette, "Never in the history of the country has there been such a clean-cut issue between the Progressives and Reactionaries. On the one hand the National Committee offered Senator Root. Opposed to him was Governor McGovern. There was no middle course."[114] La Follette and most of his supporters, however, did not see things this way. Viewing the fight between TR and the Wisconsin senator for the mantle of leader of the Progressive movement as more fundamental than the contest for Republican convention delegates, they refused to join a united front against President Taft's steamroller. No sooner was McGovern's name placed in nomination than La Follette's campaign manager, Walter L. Houser, sprinted to the platform to make a statement. "This nomination is not with Senator La Follette's consent," he declared. "We make no deals with Roosevelt. We make no trades with Taft." Houser's denunciation sealed the Roosevelt forces' fate.[115] According to McGovern, it also destroyed the last bastion of progressive Republicanism. As he conveyed to a La Follette stalwart in a bitter postmortem, "Mr. Houser connived at the organization of the convention by the political bosses who were managing the Taft campaign. The organization of the convention upon this basis, as subsequent events showed, defeated La Follette, disorganized the Progressives and renominated Taft."[116]

When the roll call of states for vote on temporary chairman was completed, Root was elected by a count of 558 to 501. If the 39 delegates pledged to La Follette had voted for McGovern, he would have been elected chairman. If McGovern had taken the chair, he might very well have influenced the resolution of the Roosevelt camp's delegate challenges on the convention floor, thereby denying Taft some 70 votes and, perhaps, the nomination. As La Follette would write after the convention, "If I had not had an 'iron brigade' (though a small one) at Chicago . . . the Bull Moose would have had his way."[117] Instead, the progressive forces, badly divided by the contest that TR and La Follette had waged, lost this first decisive convention skirmish.

When Root took the gavel, Taft's nomination and the adoption of a conservative platform became virtually a foregone conclusion.

Still, Root performed his duty as captain of the Taft steamroller with panache, helping to frame the general election campaign that would follow. Like Taft, Root was neither a pliant tool of party bosses nor a champion of laissez-faire. Like Taft, too, he had been a trusted advisor and close friend of Roosevelt and a valued ally of the Square Deal. Indeed, Root was far less troubled than Taft had been by Roosevelt's New Nationalism, as pronounced in 1910. Supportive of measures that would extend the federal government's authority to regulate the economy and society in the service of social welfare, he wondered only what was so "new" about it.[118] Nonetheless, Root was no less appalled than Taft by Roosevelt's program of pure democracy. After Roosevelt came out for judicial recall in his Columbus speech, Root was "absolutely opposed to that proposal," fearing that "it would change the whole constitutional basis" of American government. "I could not have been for Roosevelt in the face of that," he said many years later in defense of his split with a dear personal and highly valued political friend.[119]

In spite of his staunch opposition to Roosevelt's Charter of Democracy, however, Root refused Taft's request that he campaign for him and denounce TR's insurgency in the critical Ohio primary contest. To participate actively in a candidate-centered campaign, Root believed, in which presidential hopefuls traipsed about the country appealing directly for popular support, would confound any effective effort to resist "pure democracy." He could not "discuss [Roosevelt] personally nor contrast [Taft] with him in public discussions," Root explained to the president, "without being subject . . . to the charge of betraying confidence and loyalty."[120] Indeed, Taft's unprecedented personal campaign for renomination had badly compromised his attempt to champion party deliberations and restrained popular sovereignty. Nonetheless, Root assured Taft that he supported his renomination and would help it by attacking Roosevelt's program for reform and defending the Constitution:

> So far as concerns exposition and argument against the constitutional views announced in the Columbus speech and insistence upon the vital and destructive nature of these views, and so far as opinions and public declaration that I consider you to be entitled to a renomination to the Presidency and that I am in all my influence as Senator or

otherwise to secure the adherence of my State to that view, I have no doubt or difficulty, because in all those matters I had a duty to perform and no one would justly condemn me for performing it honestly and sincerely.[121]

Root's sense of duty was inextricably linked to his "almost religious and fanatical devotion to . . . the party cause."[122] Taft accepted Root's refusal to campaign for him gracefully, but privately he was deeply disappointed and expressed puzzlement that the New York senator hesitated to "cut his bridges behind him and go as far as he can for the cause he really believes in." Yet Root decided that the most important contribution he could make was to fight for constitutional democracy within the party arena; he thus took a resolute stand at the Republican convention, where he artfully combined exalted principle and relentless partisan maneuvers. Eschewing the custom to deliver a bland keynote address that would placate all party factions and foster unity for the general election, Root attacked the Roosevelt faction and called on the party to unite behind the principles of constitutional government.

His speech, praised by the conservative *New York World* as a brilliant defense of the American constitutional system, echoed—indeed, surpassed—Taft's credible efforts to recast the Republican Party from the champion of business to the guardian of constitutional forms.[123] Warning against the attack on partisanship of the progressive insurgents, Root began with a defense of party. Without the qualities of "coherence and loyalty" that parties added to a "free popular government," Root argued, the polity would become "a confused and continual conflict between a vast multitude of individual opinions, individual interests, individual attractions and repulsions." The Republican Party, he continued, owed its past success to its "confident and just assertion that [it] was not a mere fortuitous collection of individuals, but . . . a coherent and living force as an organization."[124]

Recounting the accomplishments of the McKinley, Roosevelt, and Taft administrations, Root praised the Republican organization, not for defending property, but for promoting a strong national government: "Throughout that wide field in which the conditions of modern industrial life require that government shall intervene in the name of social justice for the protection of the wage earner, the Republican national administrations . . . have done their full, enlightened and progressive duty to the limit of the national power under the Constitution."[125] Nonetheless, Root insisted toward the end of the speech that the party's progressivism—its liberal interpretation of the national government's powers—must not carry over into an attack on constitutional forms, such as "local self government," the "boundaries of official power" between the branches of government, and the "declarations and prohibitions of the Bill of Rights." "We shall not apologize for American institutions," Root lectured the jeering Roosevelt supporters. "We cherish with gratitude and reverence the memory of the great men who devised the American constitutional system . . . their lofty conception of human rights, their deep insight into the strength and weakness of human nature, their wise avoidance of dangers which had wrecked all preceding attempts at popular government."[126]

Root's peroration thus made clear his strong belief that standpatters should enlist as soldiers in the battle for the "solemn covenant that between the weak individual and all the power of the people . . . shall forever stand the eternal principles of justice declared, defined, and made practically effective by . . . the limitations of the Constitution."[127] The Republicans' constitutional sobriety must include unyielding support for an independent judiciary, Root added, "for in no other way can our country keep itself within the straight and narrow path prescribed by the principles of right conduct embodied in the Constitution."[128]

Root's partisan defense of the Constitution rejoined the battle between conservatives and progressives for the idealism of Lincoln. The Grand Old Party had a special responsibility to revere the framers and their work, he told the delegates, because it was "born in protest against the extension of a system of human slavery approved and maintained by majorities." The Republican Party, then, could only claim Lincoln as its patron saint if it dedicated itself to the hard but necessary task of obviating social and economic evils within a framework of a constitutionally constrained democracy. Quoting Lincoln's first inaugural, Root lectured the Roosevelt forces that the "only true sovereign of a free people . . . is a majority held in restraint by constitutional checks and limitations." The way to honor Lincoln was not to weaken constitutional forms but, instead, to "humbly and reverently seek for strength and wisdom to abide by the principles of the constitution against the days of our temptation and weakness."[129]

Root's skillful handling of the convention also invoked Lincoln, who joined exalted rhetoric to a mastery of partisan maneuvers. Philip Jessup's sometimes critical biography notes that Root was the "dominant force in the convention": he firmly handed down rulings that secured Taft's nomination, withstanding blistering abuse by the Roosevelt forces.[130] Most important, Root decided to allow the seventy-two Taft delegates whose seats were challenged on the convention floor to cast a vote on the disputes in question, insuring that the Taft forces would prevail in these contests. Root's control of the proceedings went beyond such critical matters, however. Determined to thoroughly crush the insurgent challengers, he resisted their attempt, made at Roosevelt's request, to refuse to cast a vote in the final ballot on the nominee. Where Roosevelt delegates did not respond and in some cases where they replied, "present but not voting," Root called the alternates, even if they happened to be Taft supporters. Although Root's recalcitrance did not affect the final vote, which Taft would have won without the tainted alternates' support, the ruling, which preempted the Roosevelt supporters' protest against what they viewed as a fraudulent convention, "raised a great storm."[131]

Through it all, Root managed to infuse the Taft steamroller and standard partisan operating procedures with a certain dignity.[132] Even most Roosevelt supporters admitted that Root gave a "superlative performance," albeit in the service of a "bad cause."[133] The account of Root's performance by William Allen White, a staunch champion of Roosevelt's insurgency, expresses especially well how the New York senator was such a worthy conservative opponent, indeed, embodied the conservative virtues that he and Taft sought to champion:

> The gaunt thin line features of this man so conspicuously the intellectual leader of a convention which had been melted into a rabble, stood there calm, serene, and sure in his domination of the scene. Root's hands did not tremble, his face did not flicker. He was master. . . . He knew . . . that hundreds of his outraged fellow Republicans, men who had once been his friends, were glaring at him with eyes distraught with hate. I have never seen mass passion sway men before or since as that great multitude was moved those first hours after Root took command. Root seemed to us like a diabolical sphinx. He pushed the program through steadily, and as swiftly as possible.[134]

Root's dignified efficiency did provide one light moment among the bitter fractious nomination contest. It was near the middle of the convention, when P. W. Howard of Mississippi rose to a point of order. Recognized by Root, Howard cried out, "The point of order is that the steam roller is exceeding the speed limit." Amid great laughter, Root, showing a rare hint of amusement, answered: "The point of order is sustained. The justification is that we have some hope of getting home Sunday."[135]

Conclusion: The Conservative Victory and the Birth of a New Party

To the satisfaction of Root and Taft, when the delegates left Chicago that Sunday, they were a very different, far more conservative party. "President Taft is overjoyed at the result at Chicago," the *New York Times*, the president's most loyal press ally, reported. "He did not want the nomination for himself but for what it meant to the Nation—a return of the Republican Party to its attitude of chief conservator in the Nation of constitutional representative government."[136]

The fierce fight over the Constitution would continue, however. No sooner had Taft been nominated than the bulk of Roosevelt delegates marched to Orchestra Hall, where in the very early hours of the morning a new party was born. Having received his supporters' offer of an independent nomination, TR expressed a willingness to run as a Progressive, but not before plans were carried out to link his candidacy with a collective enterprise. Roosevelt's financial angels, the publisher Frank Munsey and the financier George W. Perkins, had dramatically pledged their fortunes to the cause, proclaiming, "Colonel, we will see you through."[137] So dependent on these forward-looking millionaires, Roosevelt was anxious to allay criticism that those who bolted the Chicago convention composed only a Roosevelt faction bent on redeeming his personal ambition. TR thus deferred formal acceptance of the new party's nomination until the collective mission and grassroots support of the new movement could be demonstrated. "This is now a contest that cannot be settled along the old party lines," he insisted. At stake were principles as "broad and deep" as the foundation of American democracy, and he urged delegates "to find out the sentiments of the people at home, and then again to come together, I suggest by mass convention, to nominate for the Presidency a progressive candidate on a progressive platform, a candidate and platform that will enable us to appeal to Northeasterner and Southerner, Easterner and Westerner, Republican and Democrat alike, in the name of common American citizenship." At that time, Roosevelt demurred, should the delegates choose to nominate another candidate, if they deemed it better for the movement, he would "give his heartiest support."[138]

Root and Taft were neither surprised nor disappointed that the Roosevelt supporters bolted; indeed, they saw this exodus as confirmation that they had purged dangerous radical elements from their midst. They did not believe, as the London *Times* warned, that the thwarting of progressives at the

Republican convention "might be overshadowed in history by what happened after it adjourned."[139] Root clearly expressed his view that the selection of Taft was a critical victory in the speech notifying the president of his renomination, delivered at the White House on August 1. Taking advantage of the custom at the time that the presidential nominee stay away from the convention and await a party delegation bearing the official notification of the delegates' decision, Root gave a short address that acknowledged the deep split in the party, but urged Americans to understand that the split involved not merely personalities and policies but also a fundamental conflict over the future of constitutional government in the United States. Root claimed that the GOP schism transcended parties; therein he agreed with Roosevelt. As he put it, Taft's renomination had a "broader basis than mere expression of choice between different party leaders representing the same ideas." Taft had been nominated, Root continued, because he stood "preeminently for certain fixed and essential principles which the Republican Party maintains." The president believed "in preserving the constitutional government of the United States," and he was "in sympathy with the great practical rules of right conduct that the American people have set up for their own guidance and self-restraint in the limitations of the Constitution — the limitations upon governmental and official power essential to the preservation of liberty and justice." "To sweep away those rules of self-restraint would not be progress but decadence," Root concluded.[140]

Taft accepted the nomination with remarks that confirmed his dedication to constitutional forms and his determination to stand by them in the campaign. "The Republican party stands for the Constitution as it is," he stated, "with such amendments adopted according to its provisions as new conditions thoroughly understood may require. We believe that it has stood the test of time and that there have been disclosed really no serious defects in its operation." Taft agreed with Root that the future of constitutional government was "the supreme issue in the campaign." Neither the Democratic Party nor Roosevelt's followers could be trusted to resolve this issue responsibly, so that the American people would retain their "popular constitutional representative form of government." Among the contenders for the presidency in 1912, Taft proclaimed, only the Republican Party stood for "the nucleus of that public opinion which favors constant progress and development along safe and sane lines under the Constitution as we have had it for more than 100 years" and believed "in the maintenance of an independent judiciary as the keystone of our liberties and the balance wheel by which the whole governmental machinery is kept within the original plan."[141]

Amid the personal animosities and fractious maneuvers, then, a clear fundamental issue seemed to frame the coming battle. As the astute progressive thinker and Roosevelt supporter Herbert Croly put it:

> The progressives found themselves obliged to carry their inquisition to its logical conclusion—to challenge the old system, root and branch, and to derive their own medium and power of united action from a new conception of the purpose and methods of democracy. The conservatives, on their side, could claim without hypocrisy or exaggeration that essential parts of the traditional system were being threatened, and they could ask prudent men to rally to its defense. A sharp issue was created between radical progressivism and its opponents, which could not be evaded or compromised.[142]

At the same time, however, the birth of a new party signaled the arrival of a novel form of politics, which progressives championed and conservatives found hard to resist, that emphasized individual candidates, personal organizations, and self-styled platforms that could deflect attention from parties and issues that transcended the moment. Soon the battle between Taft and Roosevelt would be joined by the Democratic nominee Woodrow Wilson and the Socialist candidate Eugene Debs, who had their own answers for the profound issues aroused by the political and economic developments of the early twentieth century. The contest among these four individuals was both fascinating and important, but their efforts to appeal directly to the people sometimes left voters confused as to what they stood for besides their own ambition. Moreover, muckraking journalists aroused suspicion that the contenders for the presidency, especially Taft, Roosevelt, and Wilson, were all too beholden to the financial supporters and interests who bankrolled their expensive candidate-centered campaigns. "Out of the tumult and shouting of the presidential campaign one thing can be understood clearly," *McClure's Magazine* editorialized in the wake of the stirring and disturbing nomination contests. "We must have restraining laws on the new procedures of democracy which are now so rapidly being introduced in the United States."[143]

The warning that candidate-centered politics would reduce to an obscenely expensive cult of personality reverberated throughout the 1912 election and would become a common refrain when progressive democracy came into its own after World War II. For a time, however, this dark prophecy was drowned out by the excitement of the birth of a new party. Observing that so many prominent reformers responded to Roosevelt's stand for the "eternal principles of righteousness," the *Kansas City Star* enthused that "a convention so representative of the forward movement in the United States probably never has assembled since the first convention of the Republican party in 1856." Warming to the possibility that their third party, like the Republicans of the 1850s, might become the "first party," other Progressive dailies scoffed at the critics who dismissed their leader as an insincere opportunist or dangerous demagogue. To his followers, as the next chapter reveals, TR was "incontestably the Lincoln of his time."[144] Such a comparison may have bestowed undeserved praise on Roosevelt; but without question, it was his insurgent campaign and the formation of the Progressive Party that made the election of 1912 a critical contest, resulting in an enduring change in the way Americans selected and related to their representatives.

✴

FOUR

"Enthroned on the Seat of Righteousness": The Formation of the National Progressive Party of 1912

Plans to take the Progressive Party beyond the Orchestra Hall rump convention began at once. Roosevelt's supporters met the next day, on June 23, to sanctify their new political creation. As TR's cousin Nicholas Roosevelt wrote in his account of the proceedings, the bolters were sobered by the loss of some key supporters, such as Governor Herbert S. Hadley of Missouri, who had led the progressive forces in their fight over the disputed delegates on the floor of the national convention. That Hadley and most other leading progressive Republican officeholders stayed with the GOP confirmed that the insurgents "faced a terrible fight against Republicans, Democrats, Bosses, Interests, and Newspapers."[1] As they contemplated that battle, the press reported, "there was no cheering or handclapping," "no cry of 'eat em alive Teddy,'" as there had been during the convention disputes. The solemnity of the occasion that signaled the birth of a new party, one that promised to inject a new sense of idealism and religiosity into American politics, instead elicited a call for prayer. In response, Dr. W. H. Mixon, of Selma, Alabama, an African American clergyman and a Roosevelt delegate who was excluded from the Republican convention, began to recite the Twenty-third Psalm. No sooner had Reverend Mixon uttered the first line—"The Lord is my shepherd"—than the delegates rose and repeated it with him.

Following the prayer, another Roosevelt delegate began to sing "America, the Beautiful," and in a moment the others were singing.[2]

The reverent progressive voices persuaded a skeptical press, even those who remained adamantly opposed to TR and the third-party movement, that the insurgent forces were resolute, that "no freakish whim" controlled the "sternly serious" men and women who had aligned themselves with the former president: they were determined to "wage a progressive fight . . . to the finish."[3] Roosevelt voiced what he took to be the sentiments of his followers in a speech delivered soon after the convention, at Point of Pines, Massachusetts. "And ever before their eyes," he said of those pledged to fight with him, "turns the vision of a giant republic enthroned on the seat of righteousness and with the voice of the sovereign striving to utter the biddings of divine right."[4]

Braced by this exalted calling, Roosevelt and his key political allies set out to build a strong organization for the new party, one they hoped would begin a "new era of politics," an era, as one observer insisted, "whose ideals" were "reliably accorded their true weight."[5] Senator Joseph M. Dixon of Montana, who directed Roosevelt's primary campaign, was named party chair, and national headquarters were established in New York City. Dixon released the "call" for a new party in early July, signed by sixty-three leaders representing forty states. The "mass convention" that TR prescribed in his Orchestra Hall address was set to open in Chicago on August 5. In the interim, feverish efforts were made to form organizations throughout the country, including the South, where no candidate for president had campaigned against the Democratic Party since before the Civil War.

Most significant, Roosevelt and the national headquarters worked with progressive reformers in the states to form a separate slate of Progressive electors, as well as candidates for the Senate, House, and other local offices. Those few professional politicians who walked out of the Republican convention with TR were unenthusiastic about running a Progressive campaign for offices at all levels of government. Among the most important of the pragmatic voices was that of William Flinn, the former Republican boss of Pittsburgh, who had provided TR with critical organizational support in the Pennsylvania primary. Flinn was more interested in seizing the Pennsylvania Republican organization from Senator Boies Penrose than he was in setting up a third party. He frankly admitted to TR that he had little faith in the permanent existence of the Progressive third party, and he proposed a plan to support Roosevelt nationally and the Republican ticket locally.[6] Flinn's concerns were shared by most other professional organizers and officeholders, who feared that a third-party organization would leave them in the political wilderness.

Yet hoping to form a collective and purposeful organization, Roosevelt and most of his insurgent allies opposed such a coalition scheme. They feared that if the Progressives ran only presidential and vice-presidential candidates, the new party would be accused, as many conservatives and some reformers charged, with being nothing more than "a personal party, a Roosevelt party."[7] With the exception of those states where the progressives had captured the Republican Party and some of the southern states where the Democrats were invincible, the new party fielded a full slate of candidates, including a complete ticket for the state legislatures. TR himself took a hand in recruiting candidates. "Roosevelt's wide network of friends, acquaintances and associates served him well and helped the new party greatly," the historian John Gable noted.[8] Perhaps the most important members of this Roosevelt network were the individuals who had served during his presidency and now assumed critical positions of leadership in the new party. Former cabinet members, such as James R. Garfield of Ohio; those who had been federal attorneys, such as Francis J. Heney of California; former diplomats, such as Paxton Hibben of Indiana; and those who had been key policy advisors, such as Gifford Pinchot of Pennsylvania, all "looked for a restoration and the completion of the unfinished business of the Roosevelt administration."[9]

The importance of such figures in the councils of the Progressives might have confirmed, despite the broad slate of candidates mounted, that the third party was little more than a personal vehicle for TR's ambition. But social reformers with little or no previous contact with Roosevelt answered his call for a crusade of righteousness and devoted their energies—indeed, their zealous idealism—to the new party movement. Paul Kellogg, the editor of the *Survey,* a journal dedicated to social reform, recalled that he and other supporters of the National Conference of Charities and Correction's social reform platform (see Chapter 2) decided in 1912 that delegations of social workers should go to each party's convention to urge adoption of their proposals as platform planks. As Kellogg described the key planks of this platform, it

> held that the human waste which modern large-scale production throws back upon the community in the shape of trade injuries, occupational diseases, overwork and overstrain, orphanage and depleted households gives the public a stake in the human side of industry; that because of

this public element, the public is entitled to complete facts as to the terms of work—hours, wages, accidents, etc.; that with these facts and with the advances made by physician and neurologist, economist and engineer, the public can formulate certain minimum standards below which it can be scientifically demonstrated that work can be carried on only at a social deficit; and, finally, that all industrial conditions falling below such standards should come within the sphere of governmental supervision and control, in the same way that subnormal sanitary conditions because they threaten the general welfare are subject to regulation.[10]

Along with John Kingsbury of the New York Association for Improving the Conditions of the Poor, Homer Folks of the New York State Charities Aid Association, and several other leaders, Kellogg went to Chicago to present the social reform plan to the Republican platform committee. Not surprisingly, given the Taft forces' control of the convention, after a short hearing, their proposals were summarily rejected.[11] A plank on equal suffrage brought by a delegation of the National American Woman Suffrage Association led by Jane Addams was similarly dispatched.

When Roosevelt and his supporters walked out of the Republican National Convention of 1912 and formed a new party, it signaled to Addams, Kellogg, Lovejoy, and other social reformers an opportunity to bring various social causes under one reform tent. They saw in the new Progressive Party the possibility of transforming many political movements into one. Whereas Republican stand-patters swiftly rejected the political overtures of these social reformers, there was good reason to believe Roosevelt and his new party movement would be hospitable to their aspirations. Indeed, soon after the GOP convention, Roosevelt assured Ben Lindsey, an independent Democrat with close ties to social reformers, that he would take a "strong affirmative stand" on their platform, including women's suffrage, for which TR had previously expressed only lukewarm support.[12]

Social reformers had good reason to accept Roosevelt's testimony that he would back their causes. During his presidency, Roosevelt had called for an investigation of the labor conditions of children and women and subsequently for stringent regulations of both.[13] Perhaps most important, his address in Columbus, Ohio, the charter for TR's insurgent campaign, indicated Roosevelt's growing commitment to social reform. Indeed, his celebration of democracy was sometimes described merely as a "means" to the "end" of "social and industrial justice."[14] TR reiterated this theme in a New Orleans speech of April 1912 that was later reprinted in an essay in the *Outlook,* just a month before the National Conference of Charities and Correction held its annual meeting in Cleveland. Roosevelt assailed judges, legislators, and other stand-patters who "beat back the forces that strive for social and industrial justice, and frustrate the will of the people."[15] In his view, direct democracy reforms and social justice reforms went hand in hand. "The object must be the same everywhere," he declared: "that is, to give the people real control . . . in a spirit of the broadest sympathy and broadest desire to secure social and industrial justice for every man and woman, so that the lives of all of us may be lived . . . under conditions that will tend to increase the dignity, the worth, and the efficiency of each individual."[16]

That Roosevelt persuaded many social workers to join the new party added an important dimension of collective identity to his strong personal popularity. This collectivism was reinforced by the social workers' strong ties to the Social Gospel movement, which helped invest the new party with a religious fervor that seemed absent from the party drills that consumed the Democratic and Republican organizations. As a *Survey* editorial enthused hopefully, "The gospel of social reform preached by the present-day social worker has been made orthodox in the Protestant churches of America, has become at last a dogma of Christian faith." This was the theme of a speech that the celebrated Social Gospel minister Walter C. Rauschenbusch gave at a National Conservation Congress that met toward the end of April, a gathering that sought to solidify the connection between Christian faith and social reform. Jane Addams delivered another key address at the "Conference on the Church and Social Evil," in which she emphasized the "boundlessness of human obligation." John Mitchell, former president of the United Mine Workers of America, echoed Addams's message. Invoking those who perished on the *Titanic,* which sank a few weeks before the National Conservation Congress convened, Mitchell "recalled that a thousand men had stood back so that women and children might be saved. This, he said, was the rule of the sea! Would that it were the rule of land also! Then the movements to protect women and children from exploitation in industry would not be checked and thwarted before the legislatures of America."[17]

Many preachers of the Social Gospel viewed Roosevelt and other progressive leaders as "only the mouths, the tongues of a movement already in the hearts of men." Such was the view expressed by James A. McDonald at an international Bible conference that gathered in Winona, Illinois, during the heat of the 1912 presidential campaign to proclaim the religious significance of the third party. Leading social reformers, McDonald declared, "caught the voices of the common people. When they let out their sails for a breeze beyond that a gale was blowing. It was a cry . . . of the toilers, the underprivileged, and even the cry of the rebellious." Roosevelt and the Progressives thus did not represent, as their detractors claimed, "the death knell of democracy," he preached, "but the birth cry of a democracy yet to be."[18]

Even as many social reformers saw in Roosevelt a potential savior, a number of progressive leaders warned them to ignore his call to join the new party. They insisted, as Taft had throughout the primary campaigns, that TR was a flawed leader whose personal ambition would overwhelm their collective aims. TR's progressive rival, Senator Robert La Follette, whose refusal to support Roosevelt in Chicago likely doomed his effort to get the Republican nomination for president, insisted that the Progressive Party was but an extension of the plebiscite TR had conducted in the Republican primary contests. As he wrote in his widely distributed progressive journal, "Roosevelt's whole record demonstrates that he has no constructive power; that he is a progressive only in words; that he is ever ready to compromise in order to win, regardless of platform promises or progressive principles."[19]

La Follette's warning was dismissed by many progressives as the ranting of a bitter and disappointed rival. But his concern was echoed by more impartial observers, some of whom did not doubt, but rather feared, Roosevelt's resoluteness. As the progressive journalist Ray Stannard Baker expressed in a lengthy evaluation of the leading progressive contenders of 1912, "No one has a greater admiration for many of [Roosevelt's] . . . qualities than the present writer, but what a pity that he should have been drawn into this campaign! There are thousands of people in the country who are for Roosevelt—but not for President. We admire him, but we don't want him to own us or own the country." Appealing to Ralph Waldo Emerson's characterization of genius, Baker concluded, "He thinks we wish to belong to him, as he wishes to occupy us. He greatly mistakes us!"[20]

The charge that Roosevelt would smother the reformist potential of the Progressive Party took on greater urgency when the Democrats nominated Woodrow Wilson for president. Although Wilson long had been an opponent of the Bryan wing of the party, he had been identified as a progressive since his election as governor of New Jersey in 1910. Moreover, unlike the leadership qualities and campaign practices of other contenders for the Democratic nomination, Wilson's "seemed entirely modern."[21] Like Roosevelt, he did not stand firmly on a party platform but claimed to run on "his own definition of his own principles."[22] Unlike TR, however, Wilson sought to work within, rather than attack, the two-party system. Similarly, he proposed a reform program that did not so obviously pose a fundamental challenge to constitutional forms or the courts' role in upholding them. Compared to Roosevelt, then, some progressives viewed Wilson as a safer ally.

Nonetheless, most social reformers viewed a powerful, charismatic leader as indispensable to the task of remaking American democracy. They subscribed to the principles of Roosevelt's Charter of Democracy, which emphasized the critical link between heroic leadership and social reform. Indeed, this connection followed logically from the Progressives' celebration of public opinion. Social reformers like Lovejoy, Kellogg, and Addams believed that the marriage of public opinion and programmatic change, of direct democracy and social justice, required a magnetic candidate who could give expression and effective leadership to their causes. Accordingly, they and many other progressives saw the celebrity and power of Roosevelt as indispensable to their reform agenda. As Herbert Croly wrote in *American Magazine*, "[Mr. Roosevelt's] leadership is indispensable just at the present, because his extraordinary personal popularity with the American people endows the new party at once with volume and momentum."[23] In short, these reformers, adhering to the tenets of progressivism, viewed direct democracy and candidate-centered campaigns as essential instruments for securing the goals of social and economic reform. It remained to be seen, however, whether the new party could reconcile its members' faith in heroic leadership with their dedication to a collective program of social and industrial justice.

The Consecration at Baltimore: Woodrow Wilson, the Democratic Party, and the Progressive Movement

The prospect of the Progressive reformers forging a collective identity would be affected dramatically by the Democratic National Convention that convened in Baltimore on June 25. Roosevelt's speech at Orchestra Hall had called for the new party to select a candidate and write a platform that would "appeal to Republican and Democrat alike, in the name of common American citizenship." The appeal to progressive Democrats, of course, was most likely to resonate if the Baltimore convention nominated a conservative to run on a states' rights platform. "Should this happen," the London *Times* observed, "a long step would have been taken towards the logical Conservative and Liberal division of parties, the lack of which has sapped the vitality of the American party system."[24] The view that a fundamental realignment might transform American politics so that it resembled party politics in Great Britain and Western Europe was not limited to the foreign press. The progressive journalist Samuel G. Blythe wrote a story in *McClure's Magazine* at the end of the primary season that foretold, albeit in a fictional narrative, of a "political revolution in America," brought on by an agreement of leading Democrats and Republicans to reconfigure as Progressive and Conservative parties. A "committee of citizens," the story fantasized, released a call to the American people to join them in remaking American politics:

> The condition is here. The time is here. The men are here. This is the hour. We have seen conservatives and radicals in the Republican party and conservatives and radicals in the Democratic party striving to secure a nomination, in the fatuous belief that, whichever is successful, the conservatives of their party will support the radical or the radical support the conservative merely because of party allegiance. The situation is impossible. What the people of this country want is an opportunity to vote as they think, not a command to vote as self-constituted party leaders think.[25]

The "big split" that foreign observers and progressive leaders anticipated was foiled by the Democratic convention. William Jennings Bryan, whose influence on the Democrats during the Progressive era was no less than, and arguably surpassed, TR's effect on the Republicans, led his party to embrace many features of progressive democracy. Indeed, the Democratic Party's nomination of Woodrow Wilson and the delegates' inclusion of many progressive measures in the platform on which he ran followed largely from Bryan's dramatic intervention at the Democratic National Convention in Baltimore.

The Democratic convention did not begin auspiciously for progressives. Just as the Republican National Committee had selected Elihu Root for convention chair so that he might uphold conservative principles and traditional party practices, so the Democratic National Committee chose Judge Alton Parker, the failed presidential candidate of 1904, to preside over the Baltimore convocation. Like Root, Parker, a conservative with close ties to Wall Street, was elected over the protest of his party's progressive delegates; they nominated Bryan for the convention chair. Although he lost to Parker in a vote of 579 to 510, Bryan would not concede control of the convention to conservative Democrats. As the convention was about to put candidates in nomination for the presidency, the Great Commoner appeared on the platform and delivered a speech, whose drama might only have been surpassed by his famous Cross of Gold address at the 1896 Democratic National Convention. He urged the delegates to adopt a resolution that condemned "members of the privilege hunting and favor seeking class."[26] Taking more specific aim at his target, Bryan called on the delegates to adopt a resolution that opposed "the nomination of any candidate for President who is the representative of or under any obligation to J. Pierpont Morgan, Thomas F. Ryan, August Belmont or any other representative" who had close ties to big business. The Wall Street financier, Morgan, was a Republican. But Ryan was a delegate from Virginia, and Belmont represented New York at the convention. For good measure, Bryan's "electrifying resolution," as it was characterized by the press, also called "for the withdrawal from this convention of any delegate or delegates constituting or representing [the money power]."[27]

Roosevelt and his supporters followed the proceedings in Baltimore with considerable satisfaction. Hearing of Parker's selection as temporary chairman, Roosevelt asked the press rhetorically, "Doesn't that remind you of something?" This test vote appeared to vindicate the Progressives' attack not just on Republicans but also on Democrats and what they took to be the incorrigible conservatism of the two-party system. It was not unreasonable for insurgents to expect that opponents of the progressive reform would control events in Baltimore as they did in Chicago, and that Bryan's resolution, like TR's address at the Chicago Auditorium, portended his leading a bolt from the convention. Progressive Democrats and Republicans proposed an alliance between TR and Bryan, even broaching the possibility of second spot on the ticket for the Great Commoner. Francis Heney, an important Republican progressive from California and one of TR's chief lieutenants at Chicago, was sent to Baltimore to confer with Bryan about developments and, as the press intimated, to encourage him to leave the Democratic Party and form a progressive alliance with Roosevelt.

In the wake of Bryan's diatribe against them, and hearing of his consultation with Roosevelt's emissary, conservative Democrats resigned themselves to, and even began to hope for, a bolt. They answered his resolution speech with shouts of "go over to Roosevelt where you belong." An editorial in the conservative *New York Times* charged that Bryan's progressivism, like Roosevelt's, thinly veiled disappointed personal ambition: "It is not unlikely that his secondary purpose in offering the resolution was to prepare the way for deserting Democracy and going over to Roosevelt's third party. . . . His performance last night showed him to be openly a traitor to his party and a traitor without the slightest pretense of principle."[28]

In the end, however, Bryan and conservative Democrats reached a modus vivendi in the candidacy of Woodrow Wilson. Bryan, himself, was not a candidate. Although he still had considerable support in the party, especially among southern and western Democrats, the Great Commoner had lost three presidential elections, and party regulars, even those who greatly admired him, believed that they should invest their faith in a new, less polarizing leader. Still, as Wilson acknowledged in April 1911, "No Democrat [could] win whom Mr. Bryan does not approve."[29] The excitement that Bryan's resolution stirred—the condemnation of the "privilege hunting and favor seeking class" passed overwhelmingly, albeit without the provision that required the purging of delegates—made it very unlikely that a conservative Democrat would be nominated.

Four contenders vied for the Democratic nomination: Governor Judson Harmon of Ohio; Congressman Oscar W. Underwood of Alabama, the majority leader in the House; Congressman Champ Clark, the Speaker of the House and the highest-ranking Democratic officeholder in the country; and Wilson. Harmon and Underwood were conservatives, which for all intents and purposes left the delegates with a choice between Wilson and Clark. Clark, who commanded the loyalties of the regular Democratic organization and, as a longtime political ally of Bryan, the support of many progressives in the party, outpolled Wilson in most of the primaries and conventions outside the South. Although the primary contests were more important to and aroused more passion among progressive Republicans, progressive Democrats, too, considered them an important barometer of the candidates' strength. With the support of William Randolph Hearst's newspapers, which depicted Wilson as an unreliable reformer, and local machines, which damned Wilson as anti-immigration, Clark won especially impressive victories in Illinois, Massachusetts, and California during April and May.[30]

Like their Republican counterparts, however, the Democratic delegates refused to slavishly follow the verdict of the popular primary contests. But Clark's failure to get the nomination did not follow from the party regulars' fear that he was too radical; rather, his candidacy collapsed in the wake of Bryan's charge that the Speaker had sacrificed progressivism in order to accommodate the conservative wing of the party. In truth, Bryan had been disappointed in Clark's record as Speaker, believing that he had not fought the Taft administration with enough resolve in matters such as tariff reform.[31] That Clark and his followers supported Judge Parker, rather than Bryan, for chair of the convention confirmed the Nebraska populist's concern that Clark could not be trusted. That mistrust turned to outrage when Tammany Hall boss Charles Murphy delivered New York's ninety delegates to Clark on the tenth ballot, which gave the Speaker a clear majority for the first time. Although the Democrats adhered to a two-thirds rule, a hallowed—some claimed antiquated—device that embodied the party's commitment to states' rights, every candidate since 1844 who received a majority of delegates had gone on to win the nomination. But Bryan sought to defy history. Making his second dramatic appearance on the platform, Bryan warned that he would not take part in the selection of any candidate whose nomination was obtained through the machinations of Tammany Hall. Bryan, who had come to the convention as a pledged delegate for Clark, now proclaimed his support for Wilson and, more ominously, as the press reported, "virtually announc[ed] his intention to bolt the Democratic ticket" and join Roosevelt's new party if a "Wall Street–controlled candidate for the Presidency were nominated by this convention."[32]

In contrast to the conservatives' response to his anti–Wall Street resolution, there were no cries for Bryan to join Roosevelt after the assault on Tammany Hall. Instead, conservative Democrats and party regulars engaged in quiet negotiations with Wilson's lieutenants, who persuaded Illinois's boss-led delegation to abandon Clark and the Underwood forces to shift their support from the southern congressman to the New Jersey governor. This agreement between the Wilson leaders and Democratic regulars proved to be the turning point in the convention, which ended with Wilson getting the nomination on the forty-sixth ballot.

Faced as they were by the choice between two progressive candidates, conservative Democrats and party regulars ultimately came to the conclusion that Wilson was an attractive and safe progressive who gave their party the best chance to withstand Roosevelt's insurgency. "Clark's dour demeanor and vapid oratory," the historian John Milton Cooper has written, "gave him a reputation of a party hack that made him easy to underestimate."[33] Even many of those Democratic leaders who did not underestimate Clark feared that the voters would, and that he would be no match for Roosevelt's popular attack on the "bosses." As the *New York Times* editorialized, "What folly with such a progressive as THEODORE ROOSEVELT in the field, to present CHAMP CLARK! Will the Democrats oppose ursus horribilis with a chipmunk? With Mr. ROOSEVELT bestriding the whole landscape, voters of a progressive turn of mind would never find the Speaker." Wilson could not be so easily dismissed. "As a student of the world affairs, as the President of a University, as a historian, and Governor of his State," the *Times* opined, "he has become versed in political knowledge, he has become familiar with the transaction of public business."[34]

A relative newcomer to politics—he was elected governor of New Jersey in 1910—Wilson's views were a complex amalgamation of "radical reaction and robust reform."[35] His scholarly writing expressed a critical view of the founders and a deep interest in thinkers such as Georg Hegel and Edmund Burke, who prescribed an organic view of political life. When applied to America, this infatuation with "organicist conservatism" took the form of a progressive commitment to reconstituting the idea of citizenship, taming corporate power, and recasting the executive as the steward of the people.[36] Wilson's record as governor, moreover, revealed his explicit commitment to deploying executive power in the service of social, economic, and political reform.

Even as he championed reform, however, Wilson, a native of Virginia, called for a cautious approach to progressive democracy. Arguing that the failure of Reconstruction offered a powerful lesson on the dangers of national democracy, he was reluctant to abandon the Democrats' long-standing support for states' rights. Indeed, his support for local self-government was marred by a racism that would rear its ugly head during Wilson's presidency. Wilson's embrace of racial segregation did not so clearly distinguish him from more militant progressives, whose subordination of natural rights to national community could lead to indifference, if not avowed hostility, to civil rights. Nonetheless, Wilson's progressive principles, eventually embodied in his New Freedom platform, were more deliberately, if uneasily, joined to individualism, support of the two-party system, and limited constitutional government.[37]

Wilson's gravitas, allied to a sober progressivism, made him an especially attractive alternative to the more militant reformism that TR represented. As the *New York Times* reflected in an editorial stance that was common among conservative newspapers, "A sound Democrat, progressive in every sense, but a conservative in respect to the foundation principles of the Constitution of this Government, would, if nominated by the Democrats," have the best chance to defeat "a Republican party rent in twain by the selfish ambition of MR. ROOSEVELT and the frightful ravages of the preference primary."[38] Wilson seemed to fit this bill. His confrontation with machine politicians in New Jersey and his skillful maneuvering of a reform program through the state legislature burnished his progressive credentials. In a glowing tribute to Wilson, *McClure's Magazine* regaled its readers with the story of the governor's defiant, successful opposition to the powerful New Jersey boss James Smith and his machinations to win a Senate seat for himself. *McClure's* also praised Wilson's effective sponsorship of a legislative program that included such progressive measures as the direct primary law and the creation of a public service commission to regulate transportation and public utility companies. "As a result of the assertion of real leadership by a governor of great intelligence and force," Burton Hendrick, the progressive author of the piece, enthused, "there must be recorded a real miracle in politics: New Jersey is a 'progressive' State. Its legislation is as far 'advanced' as that of Oregon, California, and other Western commonwealths."[39]

Yet Wilson's progressivism was carefully calibrated to conform to the Jeffersonian traditions of the Democratic Party. Whereas TR praised heroic leadership and prescribed that the president become the "steward" of a powerful central government, Wilson called for a reform program that rested in ordinary interests, that would emancipate such interests from special privilege as embodied in the giant trusts. Rather than empowering the national government to regulate big business, as TR's New Nationalism recommended, Wilson proposed to destroy "the process of monopoly." "The men who understand the life of the country are the men who are on the make," he claimed,

> and not the men who are already made; because the men who are on the make are in contact with the actual conditions of the struggle, and those are the conditions of the nation; whereas, the man who has achieved, who is the head of a great body of capital, has passed the period of struggle. He may sympathize with the struggling men, but he is not one of them, and only those who struggle can comprehend what the struggle is.[40]

Moreover, Wilson justified his reform positions with assurances that he would pursue them within the framework of constitutional government. Speaking to a Boston audience in April, he invoked British conservatism, not to criticize American constitutional arrangements but, rather, to scorn radical assaults on them. Wilson proclaimed himself "a disciple of Edmund Burke, who was opposed to all ambitious programs on the principle that no man, no group of men can take a piece of paper and reconstruct society."

The governor's progressivism thus foreswore an attack on constitutional forms and prescribed an incremental approach to reform. "I believe that politics, wise statesmanship, consist in dealing with one problem at a time and the circumstances of each particular case," Wilson assured the conservatives of his party. As he further characterized this understanding of pragmatism, "Progressiveism [*sic*] is the adaptation of the business of each day to the circumstances of that day as they differ from the circumstances of the day that went before."[41] Although Wilson's incremental approach to reform resembled superficially William James's principle of experimentation, his celebration of the "man on the make" and competition appeared to disavow the sort of bold reform that Roosevelt and his followers embraced. As John Dewey insisted, pragmatism, properly understood—the "experimental method"—"was not just messing around nor doing a little of this and a little of that in the hope that things will improve."[42]

The Democratic platform was tailored to Wilson's moderate reform. It included several progressive proposals that presumed to answer the question, expressed in the form of a toast, that was frequently asked at Democratic banquets during this election season: "What Would Jefferson Do?" The platform called for tariff reform, strengthening antitrust laws, the creation of a Department of Labor, the ratification of recently proposed constitutional amendments to establish a federal income tax and the direct election of senators, and presidential primaries. As impressive as these reform planks were, just as notable was the platform's silence on most of the more "radical" constitutional measures championed by Roosevelt and his followers. Indeed, expressing the fear of executive power of populist progressives such as Bryan, especially its use in foreign affairs, the platform, disavowing TR's ideal of stewardship, called for a constitutional amendment that would limit presidents to single terms. As the London *Times* noted with relief and appreciation, "The sanctity of the bench is upheld, the initiative, referendum and recall are ignored, and there are important declarations of a single Presidential term. Perhaps it [the Democratic platform] may be most fairly described as constitutionally conservative, and socially and economically progressive."[43]

In part, the Democratic Party's nomination of Wilson and the pledge of his rivals to support him shored up the party organizations and the traditional practices that sustained them. From the perspective of party regulars, the Republican and Democratic conventions, although roiled by radical insurgency, prevailed against the folly of the primary contests and provided the voters with a meaningful choice between responsible progressivism and conservatism. "Neither candidate won on the expressions of the primaries," the *New York Times* instructed. "Both [Taft and Wilson] won as a result of the conferences of the delegates assembled in convention in the honored method of representative government." Just as the primary contests aroused personal animosities and encouraged popular demagogy, so the conventions elicited "the calm preference of the people."[44]

Some progressives, too, as Chapter 3 discussed, viewed the primary as a menace: these contests, they feared, threatened to denigrate collective responsibility and make candidates, whose personal campaign organizations were extremely expensive, beholden to wealthy individuals. Although he supported the direct primary, Wilson expressed more faith in political parties than did Roosevelt and his Progressive brethren. Implicitly criticizing TR, Wilson stated in his gubernatorial campaign that he did not get into politics to "break up parties." Political machines, he insisted, were "useful pieces of furniture," which had a "legitimate sphere" in nominating candidates, mobilizing voters, and providing organizational muscle in translating platform proposals into government programs. The great danger in progressives' attack on "bosses," Wilson warned, was that parties might be destroyed, thus reducing politics to craven individualism. "We don't want to break parties," he concluded in stating his determination to work within the Democratic organization; "we want to save and moralize parties — save them by a sense of responsibility and teach them that right conduct is service of the community and what is right."[45]

As governor, Wilson managed to practice what he preached. Rather than attempt to go over the heads of the legislators and forge a direct relationship with public opinion, he established himself as leader of the New Jersey Democratic Party. Working closely with the legislative caucus, he used his popularity to exercise leadership over the party councils, thus gaining the support not just of reformers but also of many party regulars for his program. Hendrick's celebratory piece in *McClure's Magazine* reserved special praise for Wilson's party leadership, which he viewed as a method to reconcile partisanship and progressivism:

> Governor Wilson's real service is that he has dissipated a great
> American governmental superstition: the idea that political parties
> should work under a divided leadership; that a governor, elected by
> public opinion on certain definite issues, should divorce himself from
> public opinion and those issues immediately upon assuming office.
> He has shown the necessity of uniting under centralized party control,

both the executive and legislative branches, and has proved that, once such centralization is established, the power of the boss disappears. That is Mr. Wilson's great contribution to the solution of our political problems.[46]

During the primary campaign and Democratic National Convention, Wilson sought to apply this solution to presidential politics. Just as the candidate-centered contest between Taft and Roosevelt came to a head in the Massachusetts primary, Wilson gave a speech in Boston in which he urged Democrats to avoid personal rivalry and fractious politics. Although the Hearst papers championed Clark and attacked Wilson, the New Jersey governor refused to take the bait and urged his party to avoid the recriminations from which the Republicans suffered. "The United States is greater than one man," Wilson stated as a preface to his critique of the acrimonious contest between Roosevelt and Taft. "One of the distressing circumstances of our time," he continued, "is that the Republican party is now rent asunder because, not of a contest of principle, but of a contest with regard to the individual merit of two persons." Of course, as a Democrat, he would like to see the Republicans "utterly defeated," Wilson admitted. At the same time, he insisted the Republican primary contests beheld an important lesson for the Democrats on the limits of progressive democracy. "What difference does it make to us which of these men is the honest man?" he asked as his audience laughed and applauded. "When Mr. Taft and Mr. Roosevelt are dead and unexpectedly quiescent," Wilson teased, "we shall look to this time as a time when we excited ourselves about nothing." In the wake of Republican self-destructiveness, Wilson counseled, the responsibility of the Democrats was clear: to select a progressive leader behind whom the party could unite. "Our first duty is to see that the country has a united party to depend upon; and I believe this is the time when the country is looking as it never looked before to the Democratic party as the instrument of success and rehabilitation."[47]

The protracted and heated contest in Baltimore severely tested Democratic unity. But the primary contests had not embittered Democratic contenders as it had Republican rivals. Moreover, Bryan, not Wilson, led the attack on "the bosses" at the convention. Although Wilson's supporters urged him to follow Roosevelt's example and attend the convention to command his troops in person, Wilson refused to do so.[48] Instead, it was the party regular, Speaker Clark, who rushed to Baltimore to steady his supporters, who were wavering under Bryan's relentless attack and the importunities of even the most conservative newspapers that the delegates embrace the more attractive candidacy of Wilson.[49] Moreover, ignoring William Randolph Hearst's advice that he reject the Democratic platform and enunciate his own less compromising program for the general election, Wilson delivered a speech accepting the Democratic nomination in early August at Sea Girt, New Jersey, that adhered to and sought to flesh out the broad themes agreed to in Baltimore. Focusing on the ways that Republican tariff policy led to an unsavory partnership between the national government and large corporations, Wilson sounded the Democratic trumpet against the ancient enemy of the American promise of opportunity: government-protected monopoly. Echoing sentiments he expressed during the primary contests, his principal theme was adopting Jeffersonian truths to the novel conditions of an industrial age:

> Power in the hands of great business men does not make me apprehensive, unless it springs out of advantages which they have not created for themselves. Big business is not dangerous because it is big, but because its bigness is an unwholesome inflation created by privileges and exemptions which it ought not to enjoy. While competition cannot be created by statutory enactment, it can in large measure be revived by changing the laws and forbidding the practices that killed it, and by exacting laws that will give it heart and occasion again. We can arrest and prevent monopoly. It has assumed new shapes and adopted new processes in our time, but these are now being disclosed and can be dealt with.[50]

Many progressives feared that Wilson's nomination would deflect the hammer blows that the new party hoped to land upon traditional party organizations and practices. In certain important respects, however, Wilson's "conservative progressive" program confirmed the birth of a new political age. Wilson's nomination would have been much less likely had Roosevelt and those who enlisted in his political crusade not, so to speak, backed the Democratic delegates into a corner. Bryan's effective intervention was abetted greatly by the party regulars' understanding that it behooved them to nominate a candidate who could keep progressive Democrats in the fold. Nonetheless, once they invested their hopes in Wilson, Democratic regulars conceded that progressive politics would dominate the campaign. As a Democratic senator confided to Wilson, La Follette believed "the real fight would be between you and Roosevelt in November . . . a view very generally shared by the shrewdest of Washington correspondents and many well-informed members of Congress."[51] Louis Brandeis, hitherto a strong proponent of La Follette's candidacy, agreed with the Wisconsin senator's assessment and began to turn his attention to the Democratic Party. "Mr. Bryan has certainly handled the Convention in a masterful way," he wrote soon after the Democratic gathering, "and has made an admirable beginning in his effort to purify the Democratic party and drive the money lenders from the temple."[52]

Wilson's nomination, therefore, preempted the possibility of a campaign that would offer a clear choice between progressivism and conservatism. It portended, instead, a battle between rival reform candidates who would vie for leadership of the Progressive movement. The carefully calibrated Democratic platform "was not apt to be of great practical importance in the campaign," the London *Times* predicted the day after Wilson was nominated. "The really interesting thing about the coming contest promises to be the test it affords, first, of the real strength of American radicalism, and, secondly, of Mr. Roosevelt's position. Is Mr. Roosevelt strong on account of his personality, or because heretofore he has almost alone represented the vague and apparently widespread longing for a change which since yesterday Democracy has also promised to satisfy."[53]

In truth, the difference between Wilson's executive-centered party leadership and the candidate-centered campaign championed by Roosevelt was sometimes difficult to discern. The governor's campaign methods made it especially hard to determine whether he was the representative of a collective organization with a past and a future or, as Herbert Croly suggested, hiding "behind the fiction of partisan responsibility" to reach the White House and carry out his own reform program.[54] Wilson, in fact, was among the first contenders in the 1912 presidential field to set up his own organization. William F. McCombs, a New York lawyer, who ran an association of Princeton alumni that worked to find employment for forthcoming graduates of the university, took advantage of the nationwide network this position afforded him to raise the necessary funds to finance a Wilson campaign organization. By August 1911, Wilson publicity—in the form of pamphlets, magazine articles, and speeches—was distributed from McCombs's office in New York. Seeking to expand the campaign's reach to newspapers, McCombs in early 1912 set up an office in the capital under the direction of Washington newspaperman Tom Pence. Pence and his staff fed Wilson news to Washington correspondents, a long list of daily papers, and some six thousand weekly magazines. McCombs's organization combined with Wilson's campaign tours to establish the New Jersey governor, who had not run for office until 1910, as a serious candidate for the Democratic nomination.[55]

Even though Wilson and his "amateur" organization did not do that well in the primary contests, his campaign drew glowing reviews from progressive commentators, who contrasted his style favorably with the "old-fashioned" strategies employed by the other Democratic contenders. Whereas Harmon and Clark ran as party brokers, an April 1912 piece in *McClure's Magazine* reported, "Wilson's methods have been entirely modern; he has taken a definite stand upon practically every important question of the day. Whatever we may think of the man's ideas and character, we at least know what his ideas and his character are. Like Roosevelt, he wears his political heart upon his sleeve."[56]

As noted, Wilson tacked toward more moderate positions as the convention approached. But he did so not merely as a party broker but, rather, as the oracle of a conservative reform program that Democratic partisans could embrace, that they found to be far more palatable than the form of progressivism represented by Roosevelt. In the end it was Wilson, not the party leaders, who defined the terms of the 1912 Democratic campaign. Wilson answered the question of "what Jefferson would do" by making the curse of monopoly his principal campaign theme. At the same time, in accepting his party's nomination he ignored the "Jeffersonian" issues of limiting the president to one term and states' rights.[57] As Wilson characterized his relationship to the party in the Sea Girt address,

> We are not about to ask the people of the United States to adopt our platform; we are about to ask them to entrust us with office and power and the guidance of their affairs. They will wish to know what sort of men we are and of what definite purpose; what translation of action and of policy we intend to give to the general terms of the platform which the Convention at Baltimore put forth, should we be elected. . . . The platform is not a program. A program must consist of measures, administrative acts, and acts of legislation. The proof of the pudding is the eating thereof. How do we intend to make it edible and digestible?[58]

Even as he showed respect for the Democratic organization and embraced his party's platform, then, Wilson supplemented his partisan loyalty with a plea for administrative discretion. He thus left open the possibility that he might put his own progressive stamp on the general election campaign and, if elected, the presidency. As a result, no less than TR, Wilson was faced with the complex task of reconciling collective identity and progressive leadership. That he chose to attempt this merger within the framework of the traditional party system did not resolve the tension between collective responsibility and "modern" leadership. Wilson himself, Croly predicted, in spite of his adept strategy in gaining his party's nomination, would not be able to "permanently reconcile progressivism with Democracy."[59]

The Collective beyond the Candidate: Forging a Progressive Party

Roosevelt quickly dispelled any doubt that Wilson's nomination would curtail his commitment to the new party. "I'll stick in this fight even if I don't get one electoral vote," he told a group of leading supporters the day after the Democratic convention adjourned. As the press reported, "Roosevelt disabused his stalwarts of any idea that he was afraid to go on with the battle." He reminded them that he had started the third party before the Baltimore convention met and his effort to establish it as the vanguard of the progressive movement "was not to be influenced by the candidacy of Woodrow Wilson any more than that of President Taft." Among the loyal band that joined TR at his Sagamore Hill home for this pronouncement were George Perkins and Frank Munsey, Roosevelt's chief financial backers during the primary contests. Perkins and Munsey had pledged their fortunes to Roosevelt's insurgent candidacy at the time he decided to bolt the Republican Party (see Chapter 3). With their steadfast support once again confirmed, Roosevelt was assured that the funds he had during his preconvention war would not be withdrawn.[60]

Although Roosevelt and many of his followers had respect for Wilson, most of them agreed that his candidacy was seriously compromised by its association with the Democratic Party. As Everett Colby, a New Jersey Progressive, wrote to Roosevelt, "There are some superficial people who will think that we should support Wilson, but that is a short-sighted view to take of the situation. Wilson will be checkmated by his party at every move. Within one moment after his election, if he is elected, he would find it necessary to begin a fight in the Democratic Party such as you fought in the Republican Party and found to be futile."[61]

Roosevelt took a similar line in trying to head off defections of his loyalists to the Wilson camp. The most notable supporter who threatened to leave the new party was Governor Chase S. Osborn of Michigan, one of the seven Republican governors who signed the public letter in February that urged Roosevelt to "throw his hat in the ring" (see Chapter 2). On July 3, Osborn issued a letter to the press that urged progressives to support the Democratic candidate for president. "The issue is clearly joined for the people," he claimed. "It is Wall Street v. Wilson."[62] Osborn also wrote three private letters to TR that urged him not to run because "Woodrow Wilson represents in public life and among the people what you represent."[63] Roosevelt's response echoed Colby's contention that Wilson would not be able to bridge the chasm between progressive democracy and traditional party politics. "I do not believe that it would be right for us, excellent man though Wilson is individually, to support him. It would mean restoring to power the Democratic bosses in Congress and in the several States," he wrote, "and I don't think we can excuse ourselves for such action." Referring to the Democrats' effort to weld progressivism to their party's traditional commitment to states' rights, TR added, "The platform enunciated at Baltimore was one of the worst I have ever seen."[64] Similarly, Judge Learned Hand, although he had serious reservations about Roosevelt's constitutional views, urged reformers to stick with the Progressive Party, lest they forfeit the opportunity to found a "real national democracy." "[The Democrats] are just as heterodox on the subject of States Rights as they ever were before," he wrote the young progressive, Felix Frankfurter. "In the end Wilson will either have to compromise his principles that at present have significance or he will split open his party."[65]

Although Osborn and most leaders of the new party movement were kept in the fold, Wilson's candidacy and his attack on the scourge of monopoly resonated with certain reformers in a way that portended trouble for Roosevelt's New Nationalism platform. Roosevelt and other reformers who championed a strong regulatory state dismissed Wilson's attack on the tariff, which the Democratic platform denounced as "the principal cause of the unequal distribution of wealth," as a diversionary tactic that failed to recognize the need "to enlarge or magnify . . . the powers of the federal government." Just as TR proposed to regulate, rather than break up, the trusts, so he prescribed a tariff commission of experts to set or abolish rates on a "scientific basis." Yet some of Roosevelt's most ardent progressive supporters, such as Amos Pinchot, viewed the tariff as a root cause of the unsavory connection between government and big business. Even as they abandoned La Follette's candidacy after the Philadelphia debacle (see Chapter 2), many progressive leaders favored the Wisconsin senator's approach to economic reform, which emphasized reducing tariffs and strengthening the antitrust laws. The expansion of national administration, they feared, would necessarily compromise not only the prospects of taming commercial power but also of fulfilling the promise of progressive democracy. How, they asked, could a vast modern nation-state truly be the direct representative of the people? "The question of the regulation of trusts is perhaps the most important one which confronts the American people both in State and Nation," Pinchot wrote to Roosevelt, in proposing language for the Columbus speech. "It is plain that under our constitution and under our state and federal laws our systems, which were not designed to meet this industrial development, are suffering from a concentration of power that has worked great injustice to the individual."[66]

As noted in Chapter 2, Roosevelt was not receptive to Pinchot's suggestion. Anticipating a criticism he would make of Wilson, TR argued that a tariff plank was a conventional nostrum that failed to get at the root of economic injustice. Given Roosevelt's disinterest in disentangling the connection between government and business, Wilson's nomination and the Democratic Party's platform caused Pinchot and other Progressives of his stripe much anxiety. "Wilson's nomination has certainly dealt a terrific blow to our new party," Pinchot wrote the Progressive owner of the *Chicago Daily Tribune,* Medill McCormick. "In fighting the Democratic party under Wilson we lose a great deal of our moral issue—the issue that a party has when fighting another party owned, operated, and led by the servants of the big interests." Pinchot's concerns were magnified by TR's close alliance with the publisher Muncy and the financier Perkins, both millionaires, whose fortunes would be critical to mounting the Progressive Party campaign. Pinchot acknowledged that the intentions of such individuals had been unassailable; nonetheless, he warned, "the public, even in [their home state of New York], would never accept them as real progressives who have gone into the fight without any ulterior motive." Their association with the party could only muddle the choice between Wilson and TR—indeed, highlight the advantages of the Democratic candidate's pledge to sever the unsavory partnership between corporations and government.[67]

Pinchot decided to stick with Roosevelt in spite of his respect for Wilson, because he believed that it was "as desirable as ever that a party which is purely a progressive institution should be established in this country."[68] His misgivings about Roosevelt's platform and the financial angels who would bankroll the former president's candidacy portended serious intramural battles that would hamper the birth and development of the Progressive

Party. Nonetheless, Roosevelt's strong defense of "the right of the people to rule" and "social and industrial justice" transcended, for the time being, disputes over particular policy positions and ameliorated skepticism about the motives of his financial backers. Indeed, TR's fervent embrace of reform enlisted the support, as he put it, of many individuals of "the crusading temperament" who were eager to stay the course, even though the "probabilities [were] against success."[69] Social reformers such as Jane Addams and Raymond Robins, of the Men and Religious Forward Movement, having been rejected by the Republicans and finding many of their most important causes, such as women's suffrage, ignored by Wilson and the Democratic platform, were not only welcomed by but also given prominent leadership positions in the new party. In July, shortly after Roosevelt's bolt from the Republican fold, the prominent social worker John Kingsbury, who had organized the reformers' visits to the national party conventions, now initiated a meeting at Oyster Bay with Roosevelt that also included Henry Moskowitz, a young settlement worker who was the head resident at Madison House in New York, and Paul Kellogg, the editor of *Survey*. With a memo on the National Conference of Charities and Correction's platform in tow, social workers urged Roosevelt to make their social reforms the cornerstone of his Progressive campaign. In a letter to Addams, Kellogg wrote that "this report was all grist to T.R.'s mill in launching the Progressive party. . . . Roosevelt took over the Cleveland program of standards of life and labor practically bodily."[70] Social workers would be well represented at the Progressive Party convention a few weeks later in Chicago, where a number of these reformers served as delegates, played an important part in the writing of the platform, and gave critical addresses.

The participation of social reformers in the new party movement promised to infuse a collective Progressive identity that might endure beyond the 1912 election. As Kellogg wrote,

It is a truism of political history that minority parties ultimately write the platforms for all the parties. In time, the causes which they have the temerity to espouse are taken up by the established organizations when direct appeal to the latter may have proven fruitless. Doubtless this feeling has played a part in leading . . . social workers to throw themselves into the new movement. . . . They find themselves not in the position of bringing powerful interests round to a new way of thinking but of being met more than half way by men definitely committed to progress in all lines.[71]

Still, reformers' hopes for fulfilling this grand ambition rested uneasily in the inspiring leadership of Roosevelt. For all their fears that TR relied too heavily on large donors with ties to corporate America, and despite their worries that his persona dominated the Progressives more than was appropriate for a collective organization, those who joined the new party were deeply impressed by their leader's willingness to undertake an idealistic crusade. "I am sorry that there is so much T.R. in it," Learned Hand wrote of the nascent Progressive Party, "but that you can't help—without him, we must concede, it would cut a small figure."[72]

In the final analysis, Roosevelt's stewardship of the Progressive Party presupposed his faith in the American people's capacity to transcend traditional partisan ties. He and his supporters exalted the new party as the vehicle of a nonpartisan movement that would replace representative government with rule of the whole people. Just as Wilson attempted to join reform to the Democratic Party, so Roosevelt led the Progressive attack on those mediating institutions that came between the people and government. His future running mate, Hiram Johnson, expressed this cause soon after Wilson's nomination:

> Our platform should be radicalized, and by this I do not mean the radicalism of Debs, and his sort, but the radicalism that has obtained in such states as California. We should make clear our vision of popular rule. That we will supply to the people the weapon by which they may govern themselves; that we will give them the power to control their representatives by the initiative and referendum, even though we may think these are not national questions. When thus we have given to the people the means or weapon by which they may obtain legislation they desire, we should recognize what the past few years have rendered essential, industrial and economic reform, and that we desire to accomplish that reform.[73]

And yet, this view of the Progressive Party as the midwife of direct democracy competed with TR's position that reform leaders had the duty to transcend ordinary political interests. "There is but a limited number of my own countrymen among those of the highest education," he wrote to a friend abroad, "who understand as you do just what I am striving for. I suppose that as we grow older we naturally lose the natural feeling of young men to take an interest in politics just for the sake of strife—the same kind of interest one takes in big game hunting or football, the kind of interest quite compatible with doing excellent work but which cannot inspire the highest kind of work."[74]

Wilson claimed that democratic leaders of the new industrial age should place themselves at the service of the "man on the make." Roosevelt insisted that responsible popular leaders should call such individuals to account. "I am," he insisted,

> a practical man, and I abhor mere sentimentality; but I abhor at least as much the kind of so-called practical man who uses the word "practical" to indicate mere materialistic baseness, and who fails to see that while we of course must have a material and economic foundation for every successful civilization, yet that the fabric cannot be lasting unless a warp of lofty disinterestedness and power of community feeling is not shot through the woof of individualistic materialism.[75]

Whether this injection of idealism meant the reconstruction or denigration of American democracy remained to be seen. But as his supporters prepared to join him at the Progressive Party convention, TR's willingness to undertake a campaign that seemed to have no chance of victory provided, as Hand put it, "a kind of *vade mecum* for all true progressives."[76] Their struggle to bring forth a new political order, TR inspired reformers to believe, would determine the very fate of American civilization. "The majority of people veer one way or the other according to whether at the moment I seem to succeed or fail, and are quite incapable of believing that I am concerned with anything but my own success or failure," he wrote soon after leading his followers out of the Republican Party. "But all this is of little permanent consequence. It is a fight that must be made, and is worth making; and the event lies on the knees of the gods."[77]

The Progressive Party Convention

The tension between Roosevelt's charisma and the emergence of the new party as a collective organization that could realign political forces in the United States was palpable as the Progressives gathered at their first convention in early August. It seemed to many observers that the one controlling force was Roosevelt. His personality, rather than any one dominant issue, gave unity and coherence to the Progressive gathering. As an editorial in the *Independent* observed, "Roosevelt . . . was the only name to conjure by. He was the only aspirant for the nomination. It was his convention; it is his party."[78]

TR already had broken long-standing precedents by launching a direct primary campaign and by personally taking charge of his supporters at the Republican convention. He ignored another venerable practice of American politics by joining his running mate, California Governor Hiram Johnson, in accepting the nomination of his party before the assembled delegates of the Progressive convention. "Marking a new departure in the proceedings of national conventions," the *Chicago Daily Tribune* reported, "the two candidates immediately were informally notified of their nomination, and in the midst of deafening cheers appeared before the delegates to voice their acceptance and to pledge their best efforts in the coming campaign."[79] In the past, party nominees had stayed away from the convention to be notified officially of their nomination, a hallowed precedent to which Taft and Wilson adhered. TR's personal appearance at the convention, testifying to his dominance of the proceedings, thus gave evidence of how the Progressive Party stood for an important change in presidential campaigns, one in which candidates rather than parties would conduct and give definition to national election contests.

Indeed, Roosevelt's famous "Confession of Faith" address, delivered on the second day of the convention, offered a rousing defense of institutional changes that would make candidate-centered campaigns routine. He proposed a universal system of direct primaries that, in effect, would replace the convention as a method of nominating presidential candidates. This was the only method, he argued, to thwart the "invisible government" that silenced the voice of the people. The fraud that marked the denial of his nomination at the Republican convention, and the struggles that delayed Woodrow Wilson's nomination for forty-six ballots soon thereafter, demonstrated that the old parties had vitiated the collective power of the citizenry:

> The first essential in the Progressive programme is the right of the
> people to rule. But a few months ago our opponents were assuring us
> with insincere clamor that it was absurd to talk about desiring that
> the people should rule, because, as a matter of fact, the people actually
> do rule. Since that time the actions of the Chicago convention, and to
> only a less degree, of the Baltimore convention, have shown in striking
> fashion how little the people do rule under our present conditions. . . .
> A few years ago . . . there was very little demand in this country

for presidential primaries. There would have been no demand now if politicians had really endeavored to carry out the will of the people as regards nominations for President. But, largely under the influence of special privilege in the business world, there have arisen castes of politicians who not only do not represent the people, but who make bread and butter by thwarting the wishes of the people. . . . The power of the people must be made supreme within several party organizations.[80]

Roosevelt's dominant part in the Progressive campaign raised serious concerns about this program of pure democracy, and about how his dramatic presence at the convention subordinated the collective will of the newly formed party to his own political aggrandizement. But as the *Grand Rapids Press* insisted, in a refrain that was repeated frequently in reformist newspapers and magazines, "the Progressives turn to Roosevelt only because he is today, the chief exponent of their doctrines." Above all, TR's candidate-centered campaign summoned a collective organization committed to emancipating individual men and women from the gravitational pull of the two-party system. "It would be an absurd error to call this new party a one-man party," the *Chicago News* argued. "Equally important is the fact that it is not a one-idea party. It has its accepted leader. It stands primarily as a revolt against the fraud and bossism that marked the proceedings of the late Republican National Convention. But it is really the outgrowth of long-existing bad conditions in American party politics. Its dominant impulse is a desire to secure more power in government for the masses of the voters."[81]

Roosevelt's forceful persona and eagerness to embody the aspirations of reformers aroused a remarkable religiosity at the Progressive meeting. The appearance of TR on the platform raised this zeal to a feverish pitch, engendering a one-hour demonstration that even cynical observers described as heartfelt. As the anti-Roosevelt *New York Times* grudgingly admitted, the enthusiastic response with which the delegates greeted Colonel Roosevelt went beyond personal admiration. The delegates were "sincere enthusiasts" who were "for Roosevelt because . . . [he seemed] to embody their ideals." Roosevelt himself, the *Times* observed, appeared to be surprised by "the intense Christian feeling in the crowd all over the hall."[82] The repeated singing of hymns such as the "Battle Hymn of the Republic" and "Onward Christian Soldiers" during the three days that the convention met in Chicago revealed that virtually every delegate "unmistakably regarded himself as a soldier of the Lord."[83]

Of course, the fact that Roosevelt summoned his troops at the Chicago Auditorium with a biblical call to arms suggested that he could not have been too startled by their religiosity. As he said on that occasion,

> None of us can really prosper permanently if masses of our fellows are debased and degraded, if they are ground down and forced to live starved and sordid lives, so that their souls are crippled like their bodies and the fine edge of their every feeling blunted. We ask that those of our people to whom fate has been kind shall remember that each is his brother's keeper, and that all of us whose veins thrill with abounding vigor shall feel our obligation to the less fortunate who work wearily beside us in the strain and stress of eager modern life.[84]

In truth, Roosevelt's speeches and essays for the *Outlook,* edited by the prominent social gospeler Lyman Abbott, had conveyed to his supporters since the start of his insurgent campaign that he shared their Christian devotion.[85]

When TR concluded his "Confession of Faith" with the same line that capped his auditorium address a few months earlier, once again beckoning his troops to "stand at Armageddon" and "to battle for the Lord," his enshrinement as spiritual leader was complete. The extent to which delegates were swept off their feet by TR's inspiring presence is underscored by how the convention serenaded the nominee after his speech. In singing the chorus of a popular spiritual—"Follow, follow, We will follow Jesus; Anywhere, everywhere, We will follow on"—they remarkably substituted the name of Roosevelt for that of Jesus.[86]

The moral and religious fervor of the Progressive Party convention was its most striking characteristic. To both friends and enemies of the party this defining feature of the Chicago gathering seemed to represent the development of a new form of American democracy. As the correspondent of the *New York Sun,* a bitterly hostile paper, reported, "There was a homeliness, a heartiness, a stir in all its features which stamped the convention as one of the most remarkable gatherings of recent times. There was a seeming absence of intrigue and the chicanery of political gatherings. Some of its features resembled a tremendous religious revival."[87] This religiosity, Roosevelt's most fervent supporters insisted, distinguished the Progressive Party gathering from the more traditional party convention that nominated Wilson in Baltimore. Cast against the relatively conservative Democratic platform, the *Outlook* declared advisedly, the former professor and university president's reform candidacy was merely "academic." Comparing Wilson's Sea Girt address to TR's "Confession of Faith," the progressive journal saw a difference between a scholar's "discussion of principles" and a "reformer's [passionate] appeal to others to join him in righting the wrongs from which his fellowmen are suffering."[88]

This "revivalism" that Roosevelt's insurgency inspired sparked not admiration but concern among some observers. To the *Wall Street Journal*, Roosevelt's speech and the excitement it aroused represented a disturbing recrudescence of religious intolerance in American political life. It seemed "the most extraordinary example of successful effrontery" and appeal to the mass hysteria of "modern times." The "Confession of Faith" consisted of nothing deeper than TR's self-indulgence, it fumed, "of the forcible statement of the most obvious truisms, and vociferation of methods of remedy of the vaguest and most superficial character."[89]

But the religiosity of the Progressive Party, we have noted, went deeper than its worship of Roosevelt. The party included in its ranks many social gospelers like Lyman Abbott and Raymond Robins who saw the Progressive Party as a political expression of the movement to promote Christian social action. An official publication of the new party proclaimed it represented a "splendid idealism in the field of practical achievement," offering a "fitting medium through which the fervor, the enthusiasm, the devotion of true religion can utter itself in terms of social justice, civic righteousness, and unselfish service."[90] The practical idealism of the social gospelers was shared by academic reformers and social workers who enlisted in the new party. Few of these newcomers to party politics came to Chicago as Roosevelt worshipers or camp followers. Rather, as John Gable argues, "most had joined the new party believing that the time had come for a new strategy for reform and social change and a new day in partisan politics."[91]

The Progressive Party's embrace of the Social Gospel gave its religiosity a distinctly modern cast. Although granting that the Chicago reverential expressions "were not inaptly compared by the correspondents of conservative journals . . . to revival meetings," the *Outlook* claimed that "the religion which animates this movement is the religion of the twentieth century, not of the sixteenth or the eighteenth." In fact, conservative newspapers both respected and feared the new party precisely because they spied something new in its religiosity. The Presbyterian Reverend Dr. Mark A. Matthews told a large audience at the International Bible Conference in Winona, Illinois, that Abbott and his associate editors were a "bunch of heretics." The Social Gospel, he charged, adopted the soft denominationalism of the Unitarians, whose organizations did not deserve to be called churches. "There is no brotherhood in Jesus Christ," Matthews insisted, and "the man who would go to a Unitarian Church and unite in what they call a communion service ought to be recalled from a Protestant pulpit."[92]

Against this charge that they were apostates, TR and his supporters invoked the *civic* religion of Lincoln. Lincoln's Gettysburg Address, "the secular prayer of post–Civil War America," sanctified the Declaration of Independence as America's founding document and established its self-evident truths as the cornerstone of a new constitutional order.[93] Americans were not merely dedicated to material satisfaction, Lincoln proclaimed; they were also part of a moral community with mutual obligations. Noting the Progressives' emphasis on mass democracy rather than unalienable rights, the *New York Times* denied that the singing of the "Battle Hymn of the Republic" harked back to the political religion of the Civil War. "Hardened and experienced old political representatives looked at the shouting mob, and told each other that they were seeing something entirely new," the *Times* opined. To conservatives, the Social Gospel movement appeared to provide religious cover for a "frankly Socialistic doctrine."[94] That Roosevelt adopted the Red Banner as the Progressive Party's campaign symbol—prompting the Socialist candidate Eugene Debs to charge he had "stolen the red flag of socialism"—only reinforced conservative opinion that he preached the secular religion of "socialism and revolution."

As Debs complained, however, the Progressive Party's fight for the rule of the *whole* people deflected attention from the injustices of capitalism and the "war of the classes," which, according to socialists, were truly the cause of the people's discontent.[95] Indeed, as we shall see below, the Progressive coalition was not especially sympathetic to the concerns of African Americans, organized labor, and immigrants. The social reformers who joined the Progressive ranks were middle-class reformers whose "passionate desire" and "stern resolve to better the conditions of men and women in this present life" did not emphasize redistributing wealth or redressing injustices from which racial and ethnic minorities suffered. Their objective for the political economy was security, the protection of individual men and women from the worst abuses of industrial society.[96] More fundamentally, as their attack on traditional constitutional forms revealed, this program of social welfare rested in a commitment to supplant what the Progressive Indiana Senator Albert J. Beveridge condemned as "savage individualism" with a creed of national community. As Croly put it, those who joined the Progressive Party presumed to adopt a "New Declaration of Independence," which "affirm[ed] the American people's right to organize their political, economic, and social life in the service of a comprehensive, a lofty, and far reaching democratic purpose" (see Chapter 2).[97]

Social gospelers thus proclaimed a religious devotion that downplayed, if it did not scorn, particular theological doctrines and denominations. "I make my appeal not only to professing Christians," Roosevelt wrote in the *Outlook:*

> I make it to every man who seeks after a high and useful life, to every man who seeks the inspiration of religion or who endeavors to make his life conform to a high ethical standard; to every man who, be he Jew or Gentile, whatever his form of religious belief, whatever creed he may profess, faces life with the real desire not only to get out of it what is best, but to do his part in everything that tells for the ennobling and uplifting of humanity.[98]

Consequently, Progressive religion was broad enough to include Roman Catholics like Father J. J. Curran, champion of the Pennsylvania coal miners, and Jews like Oscar Straus, the Progressive candidate for governor in New York, who the press spied, with not a little amusement, enthusiastically joining the Progressive delegates' chorus of "Onward Christian Soldiers."[99] "We have been a wasteful nation," argued Walter Rauschenbusch in a speech praising the new party. "We have wasted our soil, our water, our forests, our childhood, our motherhood, but no waste has been so great as our waste of religious enthusiasm by denominational strife. The heed of social service is seen in the fact that as the social spirit rises the sectarian spirit declines."[100]

The social gospelers thereby invested moral fervor in Roosevelt's crusade for a new form of politics that would transform the religion of America into a national democracy. "The American nation is no longer to be instructed as to its duty by the Law and the lawyers," Croly proclaimed. "It is to receive its instruction as the result of a loyal attempt to realize in collective action and by virtue of the active exercise of popular political authority its ideal of social justice."[101]

The Progressive Party's religiosity exalted TR's attack on the bosses and conventional party politics into a moral creed. The celebration of the right of the people to rule exalted a new sense of morality that promised to replace the people's obsession with individual rights with a greater commitment to the public interest. As the Social Gospel minister James A. McDonald preached, "The new democracy is no better than the old unless there comes with it a moral dynamic. The curse of government is the inadequate morality of the people. Damn the politicians and damn as you will, back of it are the people who will have it so. . . . Love, not selfishness, is the keynote of success."[102]

No one embodied this spirit of social obligation more clearly than Jane Addams, a leading figure in the social settlement movement, which TR and his supporters praised for inspiring "many men and women . . . to give themselves to a life struggle for bettering the conditions of their fellow men and women less happily situated than themselves."[103] Addams, whose seconding nomination of TR confirmed the Progressive Party's collective identity, "was easily the most conspicuous figure present [at the Convention], save, of course one [Roosevelt]," it was reported.[104] Although Addams did not agree with TR on every issue, she saw him as indispensable to the party's reform objectives. Addams, in turn, captured the party's devotion to women's suffrage and social welfare reform.

TR's primary campaign had shown his mettle, Addams and her supporters believed. His defense of direct democracy was not a defense of public opinion per se, but an expression of faith in the people's support for social justice. He had long championed such measures as minimum wage levels, worker compensation laws, and pure food and drug policies. At the Progressive convention he went further and called for the creation of a full welfare state. Because of TR's reformist zeal, Addams noted in her nomination speech, "measures of industrial amelioration, demands for social justice, long discussed by small groups in charity conferences and economic associations . . . are at last thrust into the stern areas of political action."[105]

Addams herself was no less essential to the reform objectives of the Progressive Party. "I was delighted with your seconding nomination of Mr. Roosevelt," the progressive Republican, California Congressman William Kent, wrote to Addams soon after the Chicago convention. "I have felt that the movement was standing for much more than the disappointments or the ambitions of any one man when you felt like taking the stand that you did."[106] Addams was not only given the important task of seconding TR's nomination; the celebrated Illinois reformer was also accorded the honor of being selected as a delegate at large. In her deeds and person, she represented a group of social reformers who knew intimately the pain and complexity of social and economic problems in the United States. Having spent time laboring in the slums of Chicago, she realized that national problems were complicated, not simple. Having participated in many of the emerging civic groups that were drawn to the Progressive campaign, she recognized the painful necessity of compromise that is invariably part of building a political party. As Arthur Ruhl of *Collier's* described her at the convention, "She sat—the first citizen of Illinois—in the center of the first row, so that those looking out from the press stands over the field of men's faces, naturally saw hers first—that patient searching face, reflecting inevitably some of the endless sadness it had seen."[107]

Addams thereby added substance and depth to the party that was built around TR's dynamic presence. "There are those who think that morality does not enter into action until morality has become a problem—until, that is, the right course to pursue has become uncertain and to be sought for with painful reflection," John Dewey wrote. "There was no evidence that [TR] was ever troubled by those brooding questions, those haunting doubts, which never really leave a man like Lincoln."[108] Addams clearly was troubled by such doubts and questions. In the Progressive Party's *Bulletin* of September 1912, her picture appeared with this caption: "The burden of the sorrow of the world shows in her face as it did in the face of Abraham Lincoln."[109]

The alliance between Roosevelt and Addams would go far in determining whether the Progressive Party's marriage of direct democracy and social justice would lead to a fundamental political realignment or simply reflect a well-meaning, but unhealthy, ambition. Roosevelt himself admitted that Addams played an indispensable part in the new movement. Soon after the convention, he urged her to write a few pieces for popular magazines on "what the Progressives are striving for in the way of social justice, especially for the women and children and those men who have the hardest time in life." "I should like to have the movement, which at the moment happens to be headed by Johnson and myself, described by you," Roosevelt wrote, "because I know that no one else could describe it as well."[110]

Addams did, in fact, play a critical role during the general election. She gave numerous speeches and wrote several articles for magazines that testified to the collective mission of the Progressive Party. "A few weeks ago," Addams wrote in a piece that *American Magazine* solicited for its special election forum, "a great convention in Chicago brought together from every State in the Union men and women haunted by the same social compunctions, animated by like hopes, revealing to each other mutual sympathies and memories." Yet given the disdain reformers felt for conventional party politics and the array of viewpoints they represented, Addams conceded, their common sympathies and hopes might come to naught. From this perspective, Roosevelt's extraordinary leadership was no less necessary than it was dangerous. "Colonel Roosevelt possesses a unique power," she concluded, "to put the longing of the multitude into words that they do not forget and to banish their doubts and fears by the sheer force of his personality and the vital power of his courage." Addams was "convinced," therefore, "that no other man in America is so able to focus the scattered moral energy of our vast nation and to direct it into practical reform."[111]

The Drafting of the Progressive Platform

Then and now, those who have characterized the Progressive Party as little more than an agent for Roosevelt's ambition have devoted scant attention to the vital participation of many social reformers in the 1912 Bull Moose campaign. Indeed, few have examined the extent to which the drafting of the Progressive Party platform reflected a collective enterprise that transcended TR's coterie of followers. Moreover, few observers have taken stock of Roosevelt's own vision of collective obligation and its expression during the 1912 electoral struggle. TR and his supporters viewed the Progressive Party platform as the embodiment of their moral obligation to the American people. This, too, the *Outlook* claimed, distinguished Roosevelt and Wilson. Whereas Wilson's Sea Girt address insisted that the Democratic platform was not a program that he and his fellow partisans expected the American people to endorse, Roosevelt's "Confession of Faith" declared, "We propose to put forth a platform which shall . . . be a contract with the people; and if the people accept this contract by putting us in power, we shall hold ourselves under honorable obligation to fulfill every promise it contains as loyally as if it were actually enforceable under the penalties of law."[112]

The drafting of the Progressive platform in the summer of 1912 captures the prominence of both Roosevelt and social reformers in the life of the party. TR played a central role in mediating and shaping work on the platform, which was a ringing declaration of the principles and policies that he had espoused in his Columbus address. Indeed, to ensure that the "Contract with the People" reflected his own, controversial understanding of "pure democracy," Roosevelt struck out a plank in one of the final drafts of the platform that committed the party to a "nonpartisan judiciary." In its final form, the platform contained TR's plan to reduce the space between public opinion and court decisions. This meant direct popular control of the state courts in questions of "social welfare and public policy." The national judiciary would not be so constrained, but the platform proposed a form of constitutionalism that would be more immediately responsive to the "rule of the people." TR authored the plank entitled "Amendment of Constitution," espousing the party's belief "that a free people should have the power from time to time to amend their fundamental law so as to adapt it progressively to the changing needs of the people." How this was to be done was left open, but the party pledged "itself to provide a more easy and expeditious method of amending the federal constitution."[113]

Although Roosevelt played the lead role in drafting the platform, social reformers, who were as prominent at the Progressive Party Convention as local and state party leaders were at the Democratic and Republican gatherings, also played a critical part in formulating the "contract with the people."[114] They were especially important in developing the "Social and Industrial Justice" planks, which marked the culmination of a concerted programmatic effort begun three years earlier (see Chapter 2). As Addams declared in her speech at the Progressive Party Convention seconding the nomination of Roosevelt, her support was "stirred by the splendid platform adopted by this Convention." "A great party has pledged itself to the protection of children, to the care of the aged, to the relief of overworked girls, to the safeguarding of burdened men," she exalted. "The new party has become the American exponent of a world-wide movement towards juster social conditions, a movement which the United States, lagging behind other great nations, has been unaccountably slow to embody in political action."[115]

With the assistance of Addams, Dean Lewis of the University of Pennsylvania Law School, George Kirchway of Columbia University, Charles Merriam of the University of Chicago, and Charles McCarthy of the Wisconsin Legislative Reference Bureau, much of the Occupational Standards Committee's social justice platform became prominent planks of the Progressive Party platform. TR, who had assured social reformers of his support for their program in the aftermath of the Republican convention, now confirmed his commitment to these proposals, personally adding a critical sentence to the platform that dedicated the party to "the protection of the home life against the hazards of sickness, irregular employment and old age through a system of social insurance adopted to American use."[116] Roosevelt's embrace of social security was dramatized in his "Confession of Faith," in which he argued that "it is abnormal for any industry to throw back upon the community the human wreckage due to its wear and tear, and the hazards of sickness, accident, invalidism, involuntary unemployment, and old age should be provided through insurance." Echoing Addams's refrain that the

United States was a laggard in developing a comprehensive system of social insurance, Roosevelt added: "What Germany has done in the way of old-age pensions or insurance should be studied by us, and the system adapted to our uses, with what ever modifications are rendered necessary by our different ways of life and habits of thought."[117]

The Progressive Party's adoption of a strong social and industrial justice plank and TR's forceful defense of a comprehensive social welfare program in his "Confession of Faith" stirred reformers throughout the country. Addams had been heavily criticized for taking part in the Chicago convention, especially for championing Roosevelt's candidacy. Many social reformers doubted the sincerity of TR's commitment to a strong reform platform, a California suffragist wrote Addams. Moreover, even those who admired TR tended to hold a "non-partisan delusion" that the idealism of social movements could not be joined to a party organization. Yet the Progressive Party Convention, which summoned delegates and adopted a platform that scorned politics as usual, represented a beacon—"a great light"—that changed many minds.[118] As the prominent Chicago philanthropist Julius Rosenwald wrote Addams after the Bull Moose meeting, "May I take this opportunity to say that in choosing the political course you did, against the advice of your friends, I have no hesitancy in admitting that I now believe that you acted wisely, and that I was mistaken."[119]

To be sure, not all social reformers were converted by the dramatic events in the Coliseum. "I cannot bring myself to believe in the genuineness of Mr. Roosevelt," a leading member of the southern branch of the Consumer League wrote, or "that he will stand by the platform he has built."[120] But many others did believe that the alliance between TR and Addams meant that "social workers throughout the country [could not] well refrain from taking an active part in the campaigning in favor of the third party."[121]

Most important, the Progressive Party Convention appeared to clearly distinguish Roosevelt and Wilson in the eyes of social reformers. Lillian Wald, the founder of the well-regarded Henry Street Settlement in New York City, was heavily courted by the Wilson camp. But Wilson's Sea Girt speech, especially its deafening silence on the matter of woman's suffrage, left her with "a cold chilly feeling of disappointment." In contrast, as she wrote to Addams, TR's "Confession of Faith" "was very exciting and made us feel as if the Social Reformers' Creed was about to become the religion of the politician."[122]

Paul Kellogg, editor of the *Survey*, who drafted several paragraphs on social reform for Roosevelt's "Confession of Faith" speech, confirmed shortly after the Progressive Party Convention that social workers "had a sense of belonging there." In the Progressive Party, he noted, social workers saw "the possibility of a new alignment in American public life that may ultimately lead to a temperamental cleavage between the conservative and progressive."[123] Likewise, Raymond Robins of the Men and Religion Forward Movement believed that the Progressive Party would "make a new cleavage in American political life and . . . unite people of common purpose all over the country in behalf of a program for economic and social justice."[124] The prominence of social workers in the party was underscored by the fact that Robins was given the honor of seconding the nomination of Hiram Johnson for vice president, just as Addams had for seconding the nomination of Roosevelt for president.

In addition to reformers from social work circles and social gospelers, the new party brought together insurgent Republican politicians, conservationists, advocates of women's suffrage, various academics (most of whom were social scientists), and veterans of earlier third-party movements. To Kellogg, the "rounded social program" of the Progressive Party platform had resulted in diverse political and social insurgents joining forces in any unprecedented display of collective reform ambition.[125] Addams, as we have noted, recognized something more. What attracted disparate social reformers to the Progressive cause was not just that "we had all realized how inadequate we were in small groups," she recalled, but the "unique power" and "magnetic personality" of Roosevelt himself. The attainment of reforms so longed for by social workers, Addams thought, required the leadership of someone with Roosevelt's stature and energy. Thus Addams did not see TR as a threat to the collective responsibility of the Progressive Party and the reforms it championed: rather, as her article in *American Magazine* conceded, he was an aegis essential to social reformers' political and programmatic aspirations.

By the same token, the growing influence of social workers and other progressive reformers persuaded Roosevelt to take more advanced reform positions than he had in the past. During his 1912 campaign he enunciated a concept of reform that promised a shared vision for recasting American politics — one that was appealing to many social workers, women suffragists, social gospelers, conservationists, and other activists. They were responsive to his emphasis on the relation of social justice to not only the rights but also the *communal obligations* of citizenship. As was noted in Chapter 2, Roosevelt began his quest to return to the White House during a 1910 tour of Europe. His address at the Sorbonne in Paris on April 23, 1910, entitled

"Citizenship in a Republic," warned that "doctrines of extreme individualism" were as dangerous to a republic as those of extreme socialism.[126] He revisited the question of community and civic responsibility toward the end of the primary campaign in a Memorial Day speech on "Civic Duty and Social Justice." Calling on Americans to transcend naked self-interest, Roosevelt celebrated "the brotherhood in which all of us are joined as good citizens, each bound to think of his rights, but bound also to think of his duties toward others, and of the rights of others."[127] This appeal to duty and national community culminated in the Chicago Coliseum. Roosevelt's "Confession of Faith," which even the hostile *New York Times* granted was "the best, the ablest, the most persuasive of his public utterances,"[128] trumpeted the progressive commitment to reform as the fulfillment of the Social Gospel, as "the never-ending warfare for the good of humankind."[129]

Similarly, when TR voiced support for "equal rights as between man and woman," he advised female activists against rights-claiming that subordinated one's duties. As illustration, his February 1912 editorial in the *Outlook* pointed to the failure and terror engendered by France's first revolutionary legislature. "This body passed with wild applause resolutions declaring that the people were to have all imaginable rights," he noted, "and then voted down a resolution setting forth that the same people had grave and onerous duties." In his view, women suffragists who fought for an expansion of human rights while "assail[ing] the foundation of private and public morality" and "lower[ing] the sense of moral duty of women" were a discredit to their cause. Rejecting abstract sexual equality, TR's support for equal suffrage rested on the belief that most women would vote with a deep sense of maternal obligation. Roosevelt urged advocates of woman suffrage to remember that "the highest type of woman of the future must be essentially identical with the highest type of the woman of the present and the past—the wife and mother who performs the most important of all social duties."[130] Roosevelt's willingness to extend the ballot to women, then, was tied to what he perceived as their principally maternal role in society.

Although TR did not recognize, as he put it, "an identity of function between men and women," he did insist that there be "an equality of right" between the sexes. Just as he grew more radical in his defense of pure democracy in his quest to grasp the mantle of progressive leader, so he abandoned his circumspect support of suffrage. At the Chicago convention, he readily embraced the plank endorsed by the Resolutions Committee pronouncing that "no people can justly claim to be a true democracy which denies political rights on account of sex" and pledging the Progressive Party "to securing

CHAPTER FOUR

equal suffrage to men and women alike."[131] So as to make sure there would be no mistaking his conversion to the strongest support possible for a constitutional amendment that would secure the right of women to vote, he telegrammed Addams soon after the convention, "without qualification or equivocation . . . I am for woman suffrage. . . . The Progressive Party is for woman suffrage . . . and I believe within a half dozen years we shall have no one in the United States against it."[132]

Roosevelt's move to a more ardent support of women's suffrage strengthened his alliance with the social workers who joined the third party. He expressed deep appreciation for reformers such as Addams, Florence Kelley, and Frances Kellor, whose work took them beyond the "women's sphere" of the home and family. Most of the early concerns of the settlement-house workers fell within this sphere: the working conditions of women and children, housing, schools, and playgrounds. But settlement work offered women the opportunity to move beyond traditional domestic and maternal "duties"; moreover, the settlement workers' alliance with the Progressive Party involved them in activities that invariably posed new challenges to conventional understandings of private morality. As Roosevelt wrote Addams, in thanking her for seconding his nomination, "I prized your action not only because of what you are and stand for, but because of what it symbolized for the new movement. In this great national convention starting the new party women have . . . been shown to have their place to fill, precisely as men have, and on an absolute equality. It is idle now to argue whether women can play their part in politics, because in this convention we saw the accomplished fact."[133]

TR defended his modified understanding of equal rights soon after the Progressive convention in a campaign speech dedicated to the question of women's suffrage. Roosevelt did not disavow his belief that "the highest life, the ideal life, is the married life." But, he insisted, to deny that women such as Addams made a great contribution to "the heritage of good in this country" was not a defense of family but a slur on the "unmarried women who perform service of the utmost consequence to the whole people." Similarly, to argue that women had no proper role in politics was to ignore the importance that the rights of full citizenship could play in strengthening the family and community. That man must be "unfortunate in his list of acquaintances," TR concluded, "if he does not know women whose advice and counsel are permanently worth having in regard to matters affecting our welfare."[134] "Like Taft and Wilson," the political scientist Jo Freeman has written, "Roosevelt believed that [the] woman's place was to care for home and family. Unlike them, he did not believe that this responsibility excluded participation in public life, or that suffrage unsexed or masculinized women."[135]

As Lillian Wald's letter to Addams made clear, many women in both social work and the women's movement considered the position of Roosevelt and the Progressives on equal suffrage to be a decisive point in their favor. The National American Woman Suffrage Association had sent delegations to the Republican and Democratic conventions, only to be spurned by both parties. The Progressive Party, by contrast, not only adopted an equal suffrage plank but practiced what it called an "open door policy" toward women who wanted to participate in its organization.[136] At its national convention, an unprecedented number of women took part as delegates or watched from the gallery; keynote speaker Albert Beveridge made an impassioned case for extending new rights to women. Even a "Jane Addams' Chorus" was present to serenade the woman whose endorsement of the new party and its presidential nominee was so critical to the success of the Progressive national convention. The involvement of women in the party was not merely symbolic; they formed female state organizations and occupied key leadership positions. Kellor, for example, served as director of the National Progressive Committee's publicity and research department. To Kellor, the new party offered women a "practical opportunity" to become engaged in the day-to-day workings of a party organization. "The method of neutrality so long cherished by women has failed," she decisively announced.[137]

Roosevelt's emphasis on the maternal role of women voters posed little conflict for most of these Progressive women. In fact, they viewed the bonds of family, neighborhood, and community as the social fabric on which to base a national welfare state. When prominent women's associations supported equal suffrage, Theda Skocpol has observed, "they did so not simply for reasons of equality in the abstract, but as another tool that women might use to promote the home-protective, environmental, and child-centered reforms for which they had already been agitating for years."[138] Jane Addams suggested that it was inevitable that a party pledged to child protection, care of the aged, relief for female workers, and better protection for male laborers "should appeal to women and should seek to draw upon the great reservoir of their moral energy so long undesired and unutilized in practical politics—that one is the corollary of the other; a program of human welfare, the necessity for women's participation."[139] Indeed, she noted that it would have been in fact "unnatural" if women had been excluded from a party dedicated to social and industrial justice.[140] When a group of female party activists wrote an open letter "to the women voters of the United States from women in political bondage," they stressed the special responsibility of female voters to back a ticket that promoted "the betterment of industrial conditions and the protection of the home."[141] By emphasizing the maternal instincts of women voters, equal suffrage could be viewed as consistent with the twin pillars of the Progressive platform: direct democracy and social and industrial justice.

Many feminist scholars and participants in the women's movement would come to view the Progressive reformers' association between rights and duties as a "serious obstacle" that "undermined [women's] access to political power on the basis of equal standing with others in society." The consequence of "linking the right to vote to women's maternalist identities," Eileen McDonagh has written, "preserved women's *informal,* rather than *formal,* political status in the form of privileging women's private maternal roles as benefitting political society rather than formal political roles."[142] Yet the concept of "citizen-mothers" helped unite the Progressive Party in its advanced position on equal suffrage. As McDonagh grants, "It was precisely because women were different than men, not equal to men, that their enfranchisement seemed to many to guarantee the introduction into the voting booth of hordes of new recruits that would back legislation establishing the emerging welfare state."[143] Just as significant, the Progressive convention and campaign helped to bring to national prominence social reformers whose way of life and political activity significantly expanded women's opportunities to move beyond the traditional domain of home and family.[144]

Not surprisingly, social gospelers were especially sympathetic to Roosevelt's call for melding of civic virtue and social justice. On the front lines of settlement and social work, preeminent social gospelers like William Jewitt Tucker, Walter Rauschenbusch, and Raymond Robins offered similar messages in revival meetings, Men and Religion Forward Movement campaigns, and social work conferences throughout the early twentieth century. In 1912 the social service commission of the Men and Religious Forward Movement headed by Robins issued a report on "The Kingdom of God and the Economic Life." The report stressed the need for Americans to rediscover community and self-sacrifice, to "work out an order of industry and commerce which shall be at least an approximate expression of the fact that all men are of one great family," and which shall infuse "love and sacrifice in all the institutions of society."[145]

In turn, social gospelers were strong advocates for the conservation movement. The Conservation Congress of the Men and Religious Forward

Movement, for example, assailed the concentration of the nation's natural resources in the hands of a few financial titans. Progressive conservationists such as Gifford and Amos Pinchot also underscored the close association of economic justice and the preservation of natural resources for the general public. "The conservation movement in this country holds a position of pre-eminence in the minds of the people because it is not a political, but an economic issue, and [a] moral issue as well," Gifford Pinchot wrote during the election.[146]

What is striking about the social workers, conservationists, suffragists, and social gospelers who convened at the Progressive Party Convention in Chicago is the extent to which the membership and political agendas of these causes overlapped, as Addams, Raymond Robins, and others so vividly illustrated. From this perspective, it is easier to understand the fervent religiosity of the party and why its adherents felt justified in describing the Progressive platform as a "covenant with the people." As Robins wrote to a fellow social gospeler who doubted the viability of a party that appeared to be overshadowed by TR's "powerful and preeminent personality," the Progressive Party platform "contain[s] the three elements indispensable for constructive social progress": "a practical and effective method of popular control over machinery," "an economic and social program competent to meet the conditions of our complex modern industrial life," and "suffrage for women." Cast against the expectations of the social activists who gravitated to the Progressive Party in 1912 that their causes would be significantly advanced by such a unified national program of reform, Robins wrote, "The personality of Colonel Roosevelt . . . seems . . . unimportant in the present situation except as it helps to make the situation possible and the cleavage [between progressives and conservatives] real."[147] Having observed "the highly emotional . . . highly spectacular . . . birth of a new party," the progressive journalist William Allen White echoed Robins's point of view, insisting that the Progressive Party's strong sense of collective mission transcended TR's extraordinary charisma:

> Roosevelt, the two legged man of obvious human weakness and secondary vices, is after all only a small episode in the big event. The real significance of the event is the union of millions of American hearts in a high aspiration — partly religious in character, doubtless somewhat fanatic, but at bottom strong, clear, and as wise as the infinite impulse toward justice from which the aspiration sprang.[148]

Limits to Rule of the Whole People: Race, Commercial Power, and National Administration

"However things may turn," Paul Kellogg wrote soon after the Progressive Party Convention, "the fact remains that in the past month, we have had for the first time in American life a striking hands of political reformers, conservationists and social workers in a piece of national team play."[149] And yet the vision that inspired this team play, championed by activists who presumed to express the voice of the "whole people," paid scant attention to constituencies, such as African Americans and labor, who were not squarely in the ranks of the middle-class reformers. In part, the Progressive delegates refused to appeal openly to laborers and African Americans because they rejected the politics of rights-claiming that would become the bedrock of progressive politics—rechristened Liberalism—in the aftermath of the New Deal and Great Society. Their sense of entitlement was allied to a strong sense of duty toward one's family, neighborhood, voluntary associations, and, ultimately, the national political community.

No less important, however, many of the middle-class reformers who joined the Progressive crusade beheld an idea of national community that did not include the immigrants who made up a substantial part of the workers dwelling in major northern cities and African Americans who still awaited the freedom promised by the Fourteenth and Fifteenth Amendments to the Constitution. For many ethnic laborers and African Americans, the task was not to pronounce a new Declaration of Independence but to fulfill the promise of the old one. To be sure, reformers like Jane Addams and Frances Kellor were strong supporters of civil rights and liberal immigration policies. As we shall see below, they promoted a pro–civil rights platform plank but failed to persuade their fellow delegates to adopt it. Addams and Kellor also were influential in shaping a plank, which the delegates did approve, lamenting that "our enormous immigration population" had "become the prey of chance and cupidity" and promising to establish "industrial standards . . . to secure to the able-bodied immigrant and . . . his native fellow workers a larger share of American opportunity." At the same time, the immigration plank's promise "to encourage the distribution of immigrants away from the congested cities, to rigidly supervise all private agencies dealing with them and to promote their assimilation, education and advancement" might have struck many immigrants and the groups that championed their rights as portending dangerous paternalism. Indeed, many members of the party's high councils, including TR himself, had, at best, a mixed record on matters of race and ethnicity.[150]

More to the point, from the perspective of African Americans and immigrants, Roosevelt's New Nationalism, and its call upon Americans to abandon interest group, ethnic, and racial identities for an elusive national interest, deflected attention from America's most egregious injustices. Ostensibly, the reform coalition included too many disparate advocacy groups—several with special agendas that conflicted with the immediate programmatic ambitions of the Progressives—to harmonize under the Progressive Party banner. There was a real sense, however, in which Progressives sacrificed the rights of the dispossessed—especially of African Americans—for the false hope of forging a national interest. As Walter E. Weyl, who would become an important member of the Progressive National Committee, wrote prior to the 1912 election, "The Negro problem is the mortal spot of the new democracy." Taking note of how civil rights, especially voting rights, divided reformers, Weyl added, "Whatever the merits of this controversy as a matter of ethics or practical politics, it seems probable that the present democratic movement, uneasily recognizing the problem in its rear, will move forward, leaving the problem of Negro suffrage to one side."[151]

Lily-White Progressivism

The struggle over race pitted southern Progressives favoring a "lily-white party" against northern defenders of black rights. As president, Roosevelt had attempted to steer a middle way on the race question. He appointed a number of blacks to public office, spoke out against persecution by southern whites, and consulted Booker T. Washington at a well-publicized White House dinner. For such gestures, he drew heated criticism from southern Democratic governors and congressmen. Yet he also was assailed by many black leaders and white civil rights activists for not exercising federal government power to secure the physical safety and franchise of southern blacks.[152] In particular, advocates for black civil rights attacked Roosevelt's handling of the Brownsville Affair in 1906, in which black troops accused of firing on civilians in Brownsville, Texas, were dismissed summarily. Unlike other issues on which he abandoned previously ambivalent reform positions, such as "pure democracy" and women's suffrage, Roosevelt's stance on civil rights remained conflicted during the 1912 election. Indeed, confessing in a private letter that race represented "one of the really puzzling questions . . .

in connection with this progressive party," he attempted to obscure the civil rights issue altogether.[153]

Roosevelt's ambivalence on the race question partly reflected, no doubt, what one scholar has referred to as his "garden variety racism";[154] however, as events at the Progressive Party convention suggested, his illiberal racial views were also allied to political calculation. Throughout his career, Roosevelt had longed to shatter the Democratic stranglehold on the solid South. The sectionalism of both major parties was antithetical to his nationalistic goals, and as president he unsuccessfully attempted to make electoral inroads among southern whites. As was noted in Chapter 3, Roosevelt also failed in his effort to develop a strong Roosevelt organization below the Mason-Dixon Line during the 1912 primary contests.

After bolting the Republican Party, TR believed that southern support for the Progressive Party was critical. For his chief southern advisor he selected Colonel John Parker, a municipal reformer from New Orleans who was a contender for the vice presidential nomination. In several confidential letters, Parker warned Roosevelt that if the Progressive Party was to have any chance of finally breaking the Democratic monopoly in the South, it would have to abandon the Republican tradition of encouraging black participation in the party organizations of the southern states. "This should be a white men's party," he argued, because "the South cannot and will not tolerate the Negro."[155] In his view, a Progressive white men's party "would be a power throughout the South."[156] Yet Parker was careful to add that "a plan on these lines" should be "diplomatically arranged."[157] He recognized what Roosevelt knew all too well: that a "lily-white" party might alienate social reformers and black voters north of the Mason-Dixon Line. Jane Addams, Lillian Wald, Henry Moskowitz, Joel Spingarn, Florence Kelley, and other white social reformers with influence in the new party were among those who founded the NAACP just a year prior to the Progressive Party Convention.[158] Roosevelt and other Progressive leaders had good reason to tread delicately around the race issue, fearing that a decisive stance might sunder the party irrevocably along sectional lines.[159]

To the dismay of the Progressive strategists who hoped to make inroads on the solid South, the new party was not afforded the luxury of silently neglecting the question of black rights. In Alabama, Florida, Georgia, and Mississippi, rival white and racially integrated party conventions were held, and each sent a competing slate of delegates to the national convention. The press, especially those newspapers that saw themselves as posing principled, constitutional opposition to Roosevelt's candidacy, gave these delegate challenges expansive coverage. Getting word that Roosevelt insiders considered the contests, as James R. Garfield wrote in his diary, "very unfortunate," a potential foil to their determination to leave to the "Southern States the matter of white leadership," the *New York Times* publicized with barely disguised glee how so-called militant reformers "straddled" on such an important issue.[160] "It was learned today," the *Times* reported as the Progressive delegates began arriving in Chicago, "that a protest had already been raised by some of the negroes who sought to be delegates from Mississippi and one or two other southern states against the plan to eliminate them from the convention of the Progressives. To these protests Colonel Roosevelt and his managers have turned a deaf ear."[161] A few days later, President Taft attempted to add to TR's embarrassment by filling a minor civil service position in the Interior Department with one of the dishonorably discharged Brownsville soldiers, Sergeant Mingo Sanders.[162] Asked to comment on Sanders's appointment as he boarded the train to Chicago, Roosevelt told the press that he dismissed the soldiers on the recommendation of his secretary of war at the time, William Howard Taft.[163]

Although TR had "deflected the blow," the appointment of Sanders added to the controversy over the Progressive Party's position on the "Negro question."[164] Hounded by inquiries from the press, Roosevelt felt compelled to publicly articulate the new party's position on black rights prior to the convention. He wrote an open letter to Julian Harris, editor of *Uncle Remus Magazine,* setting forth his views on how to secure black progress. Lamenting that he had been pressured by northerners demanding black delegates from the South and by southerners seeking an exclusively white party, Roosevelt claimed that he could not abide either position. Both parties, he argued, had forsaken southern whites and blacks by sowing seeds of "race hatred." By "encouraging the hatred of the white man for the black," the Democratic Party "stirred up enmity between the white and colored men who have to live as neighbors." At the same time, the Republican Party had stoked racial conflict since the Civil War by empowering blacks who were susceptible to bribery and manipulation — "men of such character that their political activities were merely a source of harm, and of very grave harm, to their own race." The Republican Party was a "ghostly party" in the South, resting on the false belief that "the pyramid will unsupported stand permanently on its apex instead of its base."

The solution Roosevelt proposed to resolve this half-century dilemma was "to bring the best colored men [of the North] into the movement" and to entrust "the best white men in the South, the men of justice and of vision," with the fate of southern blacks. By making the "movement for social and industrial justice really nation-wide," he insisted, "we shall create a situation by which the colored men of the South will ultimately get justice."[165] Roosevelt hoped that this compromise would appeal to southern Progressive whites without sacrificing the support of northern blacks and social reformers dedicated to social justice.

In part, Roosevelt's harsh judgment of southern Republicanism expressed his view, shared by a number of Progressives, that northern blacks were more fit for political responsibility than were their southern brothers. This view, no doubt, was seared by his unhappy experience with southern delegations at the Republican convention. Black delegates from the South voted overwhelmingly for Taft. Their political lives depended on the patronage that sustained local Republican organizations, and these "spoils" were jointly controlled by the Taft administration and the party leadership in the states and localities. Tragically, however, Roosevelt's determination to keep African Americans out of southern state delegations spurned men of color who rejected patronage politics and were drawn to the Progressive Party by the allure of joining an idealistic movement.[166] One member of the contending Alabama delegation, for example, was Reverend W. H. Mixon, the very individual who had begun the stirring prayer of the Roosevelt bolters at their final meeting during the Republican convention.

Mixon and other southern black insurgents would not be silenced. Despite the best efforts of Roosevelt, Progressive National Committee chairman Joseph Dixon, and other party leaders, the race controversy could not be subdued. When the Provisional National Progressive Committee convened in Chicago a few days before the national convention, it faced the unhappy task of deciding which of the rival delegations from southern states were to be seated. Its membership, comprised of representatives of forty-eight state party organizations, did not include strong defenders of black rights such as Addams or Moskowitz. Prominent southern leaders like Colonel Parker, however, were given an important voice in committee proceedings. They had a strong ally in Chairman Dixon, who opened the committee's first meeting by explaining that South Carolina would not provide a national delegation because the "right men" had not organized a state party. Although several blacks had called for a state convention, Dixon explained that he independently disavowed the effort because it "meant suicide" for the party.[167] Before turning to the contesting delegations from the South, he also reminded members of the position expressed by Roosevelt in his letter to Harris. Having consulted with Roosevelt in a hotel room on the floor above the meeting, Dixon had orders to minimize debate and to seat the white delegates from the states in question.[168]

The Georgia delegation did die quietly, when the challengers failed to appear at the committee hearings; but rival delegations from Alabama, Florida, and Mississippi not only appeared before the committee but also made forceful arguments on their own behalf. There followed an extraordinarily candid airing of the committee members' concerns and racial views—deliberations that shed much light on the promise and limitations of the new party's reform potential. Given the Provisional Committee's composition and the tone set by Roosevelt's letter to Harris, it is not surprising that the chairmen of the white delegations were given the opportunity to speak first and at length about the allegations lodged against them. In contrast, the contending delegations, all of whom were represented at the meeting by black delegates, were subjected to icy cross-examination, sometimes from Dixon, but also from Parker, the committee member most hostile to their cause, or even from the rival white state chairmen.

The committee's inquiries discovered that lily-white delegations were arrived at differently in each of the three states. In Alabama the white state chairman, Judge Oscar Hundley, had allowed for a racially integrated state convention but made no effort to see that blacks would be considered as delegates to the national convention. Dr. Joseph A. Thomas, the spokesman for the contesting black delegation, testified that white supremacists had discouraged blacks from attending and dominated the state convention, but acknowledged that they had done their work in a "legal" manner. H. L. Anderson of Florida had done his Jim Crow work more deviously: he organized separate white and black state conventions, assuring black Progressives that both gatherings would jointly select a common slate of national delegates, only to disregard ultimately the Negro Progressive Convention altogether. Finally, the white Mississippi delegation was chosen at a convention that state chairman B. F. Fridge unabashedly explained had openly summoned only "white citizens of Mississippi."[169]

After two days of tense hearings, which were prominently covered by the press, Dixon proposed that all three white delegates be recognized as the legitimate representatives of their states. The majority of committee members, however, refused to accept such a resolution. Although most committee members were sympathetic to Roosevelt's proposal, there was sharp disagreement over whether to establish a "lily-white" party. Some northern members took exception to Parker's stark position that "we have got it understood in the south that this is a white man's party." This understanding, Parker made clear, presupposed that the exalted Progressive ideal of direct democracy applied only to white citizens. "Hereafter," he insisted, "we will have white primaries all the way through, and the white men of this country are going to rule."[170] Francis Heney, who represented California, strongly disagreed. "I know," he protested, "where we are going up against the public conscience, which Senator Dixon [and Colonel Roosevelt do not] realize the force of, and I tell you right now that we will regret it every day from now until election day if we [form a lily-white party], and I don't care whether Colonel Roosevelt himself says to do it. . . . I will say to you people that . . . we will lose ten votes in the north to every one we get in the south." Heney's protest was joined by William Flinn of Pennsylvania, one of the few machine politicians to join the third party. "Of course, I am not going to join any white man's party," he declared; "to make such rules will destroy the virility of the Roosevelt party."[171]

In truth, few committee members were bothered by the conduct of Hundley in Alabama or even the outright exclusion of blacks by Fridge in Mississippi. Indeed, many northern committee members, such as Matthew Hale of Massachusetts, the old seat of abolitionism, embraced white supremacy in the South. In a startling concession on the part of many Progressives that Reconstruction had been an abysmal failure, Hale declared that the time had come, so to speak, for the North to "surrender" to the states below the Mason-Dixon Line:

> We of the North, our fathers and grandfathers fought for the negroes, and now for the first time we are saying publicly and openly that our fathers and grandfathers were wrong and have been wrong since the Civil War. This is a mighty serious thing that we men from the north are doing. We are saying to you people from the south, "Your attitude on the negro problem is right, and ours is wrong."[172]

Although Hale was willing to concede the right of southern states to form "lily-white" delegations, he and many other northern members of the national committee did express grave reservations about the means by which racial segregation was achieved. In regard to Florida, where Anderson admitted that he had "duped" blacks, Hale maintained that the point at debate did not involve race but rather a "question of common honesty." Anderson's deception of black Progressives, in contrast to Fridge's open exclusion, represented "a plain open fraud" reminiscent of Republican steamrolling.[173]

A frustrated Dixon tried in vain to champion Anderson's cause; he argued that members were making "a mountain out of a mole hill" and reminded them that he had "submitted the case, giving all the details as to everything" to Colonel Roosevelt "upstairs in [room] 1248."[174] The chair's admonition, even though TR sanctioned it, was rejected. Although the white delegations from Alabama and Mississippi were seated, both the white and black delegations of Florida were turned away. Even this limited concession to fair play was blunted, however, by the committee's decision to leave all future disputes over the selection of delegates to the states in the hope, as Garfield's diary admits, of "avoiding contests . . . on the present Negro question."[175]

The committee's general approval of TR's southern strategy did not put an end to the Progressive Party's conflict over race. Indeed, a more heated debate arose when the "Negro question" came before the Platform Committee of the National Convention. Roosevelt's letter to Harris, and the stonewalling of the national committee, could not silence many northern blacks associated with the National Independent Political League (NIPL) and the NAACP who continued to believe that the Progressive Party should champion their civil rights.[176] W. E. B. Du Bois, the editor in chief of the NAACP's journal, the *Crisis,* composed a platform plank stating that the Progressive Party "recognizes that distinctions of race or class in political life have no place in a democracy" and that "a group of 10,000,000 people . . . deserve and must have justice, opportunity and voice in their own government." Spingarn and Alfred Hayes of Cornell Law School attempted in vain to persuade the New York delegation to endorse the plank. Nevertheless, Hugh Halbert of Minnesota, strongly supported by Jane Addams and Frances Kellor, introduced it to the platform committee. Openly challenging Roosevelt's southern strategy, Addams protested to the committee:

> Some of us are much disturbed that the Progressive party, which stands for human rights, should even appear not to stand for the rights of negroes. It seems to us to be inconsistent when on one page of our newspapers we find that this party is to stand for the working man and the working woman, and to protect the rights of the children, and to prevent usurpation of the voters' rights by special interests, and on the next we find that it denies the right of the negro to take part in the movement.[177]

Addams's plea failed to sway the convention's platform committee, which, probably with Roosevelt's approval, discarded the plank on Negro rights. In the end, even ardent defenders of civil rights, such as Addams, Kellor, Spingarn, Moskowitz, Halbert, and other white social reformers, succumbed on the race issue. Attempting to explain her forbearance several years later, Addams recalled that she and her fellow social reformers were "faced with the necessity of selecting from our many righteous principles those that might be advocated at the moment, and deciding which must still wait for a more propitious season."[178]

Few black leaders found such an argument persuasive. William Monroe Trotter, an NIPL member and editor of the *Boston Guardian* who shared Du Bois's militant commitment to the fulfillment of African American rights, wired Addams at the convention that she should refuse to second Roosevelt's nomination. "Women suffrage will be stained with Negro blood," he insisted, "unless women refuse alliance with Roosevelt."[179] Addams was deeply troubled by Trotter's indictment. She publicly agonized over whether her abolitionist father "would have remained in any political convention in which colored men had been treated slightingly." She concluded, however, that the Progressive Party offered blacks the best hope, even though its platform, like that of the Republicans and Democrats, was completely silent on the rights of African Americans. When Progressives were established on a national basis, and the solid South had been broken, Addams wrote hopefully in the *Crisis,* the new party was "bound to lift this question of the races, as other questions, out of the grip of the past and into a new era of solution."[180]

The controversy over race did not die in the platform committee. Facing considerable protest from African Americans on both sides of the Mason-Dixon Line, Roosevelt felt compelled to speak directly to the convention attendees about the controversy that grew out of his "drawing of the color line."[181] During his "Confession of Faith," TR departed from his prepared text to respond to what the press described as a "convenient query" on race shouted at him by a black delegate. Reiterating the position laid out in his letter to Julian Harris, Roosevelt assailed the Democrats for their "brutality" and the Republicans for their "hypocrisy." To offer "insincere platitudes" and meaningless southern seats to blacks, much as Republicans had for decades, "might have helped me," he conceded. However, it also "would have kept the white men of the South solidified in an angry, vindictive defensive stance against any party that did justice to the negro."[182]

The Progressive Party's commitment to racial justice was demonstrated, TR insisted, by the large number of black delegates from northern and border states. Black delegates, in fact, were elected to the convention from Rhode

Island, New Jersey, Pennsylvania, Ohio, Indiana, Illinois, Delaware, Maryland, West Virginia, and Kentucky. Progressives claimed that there were more black delegates at their convention than there had ever been in the conventions of either of the old parties. Just as important, Roosevelt told the convention, these delegates were not "forced on" the voters of their states, as was the case with Republican delegations from below the Mason-Dixon Line, but, instead, were sent with the full support of their white neighbors. Moreover, unlike the patronage hounds who represented southern states at the Republican gathering in June, the Progressive delegates from northern and border states were in "point of character, intelligence, and good citizenship" the equal of "any whites among whom they sit." These states, TR concluded optimistically, would set a standard that those south of the Potomac would attain as southern Progressives freed the old Confederacy from the thralldom of civil war issues and past party alignments.[183]

Roosevelt's response resonated with nearly all of the black delegates elected to the convention. Although a few defected, most of them stayed with the party. Indeed, at the request of concerned party strategists, they signed a statement endorsing TR's position before departing Chicago.[184] Thus, despite some heated and important battles, Roosevelt's southern strategy remained intact when the convention adjourned, owing largely to the acquiescence of Addams, Kellor, Moskowitz, Spingarn, and black delegates from the northern and border states.

Some black newspapers forgave the Progressive Party's compromise on the Negro question and indeed strongly supported Roosevelt's position on the color line. "If experience has taught us anything," an editorial in the *African-American Ledger,* located in Baltimore, Maryland, argued, "the present one party of white men, in the South, must be broken up, and a new alignment formed." Roosevelt's platform appeared to be the only practical means of achieving that goal, "an absolute necessity of the public good." Nothing else could be done "in the construction of a new party," the *Ledger* admitted, "than to make it possible for the best white men of the South, as few as they may be, to assume just such functions . . . as their character, intelligence, and general standing in the various communities would wisely suggest." In taking on the problem of Jim Crow so directly and practically, Roosevelt was "not only an independent and original thinker, but . . . also bold and courageous."[185] The editors of the *Pittsburgh Courier* agreed. Comparing Roosevelt's forthrightness to the silence of Taft and Wilson, it stated,

The only expression, we have heard, came from Theodore Roosevelt who fearlessly put himself on record at Chicago this week when he gave his views on the Negro question without dodging the issue. . . . Under the light we have to date, we must follow those who have given us the best and most safe inducement. No man has dared any of us and our cause what Mr. Roosevelt said in Chicago. He is on record, and we believe he can be depended upon to do his best to fulfill his promises and defend at all times his attitude. We have not this expression from any other party or party leaders.[186]

From the perspective of many other black newspapers, however, Roosevelt's position of civil rights was worse than the silence of Taft and Wilson. Amid the crusading atmosphere of the Progressive Party convention, it struck them as rank hypocrisy. "If there is any one group of men and women in this country suffering from oppression," editorialized the *Broad Ax,* a Chicago paper, "it is the Colored people; but the party of social justice is to think only of the wrongs done to whites!"[187] Not surprisingly, W. E. B. Du Bois echoed this sentiment on the pages of the *Crisis.* Taking note of the proposed platform plank on black rights, "written in *The Crisis* office," Du Bois fumed: "Not only was this refused, but every suggested modification, refinement and watering down was rejected, and the platform of the new Progressive party of human rights appears absolutely silent on the greatest question of human rights that ever faced America!"[188]

Du Bois's consternation, which would continue into the general election campaign, was surely understandable. Indeed, disenchantment with Roosevelt was one of the few positions that he and his principal rival for leadership in the black community, Booker T. Washington, agreed on. Washington, a gradualist who had positioned himself during the Roosevelt and Taft administrations as the chief dispenser of federal patronage for African Americans in the South, had struggled since February to resist the defection of black Republicans to the new party. "I cannot refrain from a little 'I told you so' in connection with Roosevelt's kicking the Southern negro delegates out of the Progressive Party," he wrote to the social activist Oswald Garrison Villard in early August. "I do hope now that the bulk of the colored people who have still clung to this man will realize the falsity of his nature, and will no longer follow his leadership."[189]

Nonetheless, many African Americans remained deeply interested in if not fully supportive of the Progressive Party. Like many white voters, they saw Roosevelt as the embodiment of new political era, a national democracy that beheld a more promising future than did the business as usual that the Democrats and Republicans practiced. To be sure, the Progressive Party Convention had demonstrated clearly enough that racial prejudice still held considerable sway over Roosevelt and many Progressive reformers. The failure of Reconstruction only served to justify their belief that most non-whites, especially southern blacks, were inferior to whites. The program of the Progressive Party Convention shows that the delegates were treated not only to choruses of the "Battle Hymn of the Republic" but also of "Dixie," thus demonstrating that even the most advanced reformers in the country were willing to sacrifice the rights of blacks for the false alluring promise of reuniting white America.[190] Moreover, as the striking parallels between the delegate selection battles of 1912 and those over the challenge of the Mississippi Freedom Party at the 1964 Democratic Convention suggest, the trauma of reconciling African American rights and civic nationalism would endure. As the historian Gary Gerstle has written, "It is not too much to say that the refusal to seat black delegates set a precedent that would haunt liberal politics for much of the rest of the twentieth century."[191]

In fact, the Progressive Party's celebration of "the right of the people to rule" marked the emergence of a leader and a movement that rejected the "liberal tradition," which cast aspersions on rights-based politics. To be sure, Addams and other social reformers embraced a more capacious civic nationalism that disavowed distinctions based on race. Nonetheless, the Progressives' disdain for traditional rights-based politics and the way the judiciary buttressed them tended toward a celebration of mass democracy that was all too willing to disregard the fundamental liberties of minorities. As the *Philadelphia Bulletin* astutely observed, in a passage invoked approvingly by the *African-American Ledger*:

> The Progressive policy on the Negro question as declared from
> Oyster Bay is of a kind. To be sure, the Fourteenth Amendment to
> the Constitution was intended to give equal political rights to men
> regardless of the color of their skin and the courts have interpreted
> the language literally; but . . . one of the cardinal principles of the
> Progressive party . . . is . . . that the people shall rule, even in the
> interpretation of the Constitution. The colored brother must accept the
> measure of his Constitutional rights by the sentiment of the community
> in which he lives.[192]

Given their celebration of the modern state as the embodiment of popular will, the struggle among reformers at the Progressive Party Convention over how to approach the regulation of big business was perhaps even more profoundly divisive than was the race question. The fight over monopoly, in fact, produced a cleavage that cut into the very core of its leadership. Although this struggle was for the most part *sub rosa,* it exposed a debilitating split in the reformers' ranks that Wilson and the Democrats would exploit in the general election, especially in making their effective overtures to labor.

The conflict over monopoly first arose in a platform battle regarding the composition of the party's business plank. A number of luminaries—including scholars George Kirchway, William Draper Lewis, and Charles McCarthy, as well as William Allen White, Chester Rowell, and Amos and Gifford Pinchot—were invited to prepare preliminary drafts of the platform. Several conferences of social workers and academics were held in July to help in the formulation of the drafts, and Learned Hand, George Rublee, and Herbert Croly provided revised drafts. Just prior to the Chicago convention in early August, a resolution committee of Lewis, White, Dixon, Rowell, Kirchway, and Merriam was organized to hammer out a final version of the Progressive platform. Senator Beveridge, the Pinchots, McCarthy, and George Perkins, a former associate of J. P. Morgan and generous contributor to the party who had run the party's business affairs since June, were given access to committee deliberations, and Roosevelt remained close at hand to resolve disagreements as they emerged.

Conflicting drafts of a plank concerning trusts betrayed an important ideological schism within the party councils. The Pinchot brothers and McCarthy, who responded very favorably to Wilson's antimonopoly position, advocated "strengthening the Sherman Law" and listed an array of "unfair trade practices" that the party would seek to legally bar. All three, especially McCarthy of Wisconsin's Legislative Reference Bureau, were once close supporters of La Follette and strident proponents of trust busting. Amos Pinchot passionately endorsed the Sherman Act and strong antitrust policies because he believed that large corporate units had imposed a "high cost of living" on most Americans by undermining competition in the marketplace. Economic competition could and should be restored, he argued, with a full-scale assault on trusts. As Pinchot wrote TR,

We are today solemnly pledged to carry on an active campaign against the system of exploitation which the trusts have fastened upon the American people. It is the same old struggle for economic justice which has gone on from the beginning of time, — the few who are strong and rich organized against the many who are poor, weak and unorganized. In the old days it was the Crown . . . against the people. Today it is the industrial oligarchy, the trusts, against the people.[193]

To his brother Gifford, antitrust policy represented "the eternal question of the people's bread."[194]

Scorning this assault on big business, Beveridge, Perkins, publisher Frank Munsey, and others supported a plank that characterized "the concentration of modern business" as "both inevitable and necessary for national and international efficiency." In their view, the Sherman Act and antitrust suits were counterproductive: large corporations were here to stay and could be regulated in a manner that was economically beneficial to the country. "Nothing of importance is gained by breaking up a huge inter-state and international organization *which has not offended otherwise than by its size*," Perkins noted in 1911.[195] Their plank on interstate corporations made no mention of the Sherman Act, instead emphasizing TR's proposal for a federal trade commission that would distinguish between economic combinations that behaved responsibly and those that did not.

Amos Pinchot and the other antitrust Progressives were skeptical of the regulatory commission plan. They endorsed the Populist position of Bryan and La Follette that centralized administrative power was hostile to self-rule. "The people will not for a moment stand for a commission, even of arch-angels, with power to fix prices of necessaries of life and say which are good trusts and which are bad trusts," Pinchot wrote.[196] Roosevelt, however, believed that centralized administration, established within the executive branch, could be allied to the national democracy that Progressives championed. "The only effective way in which to regulate the trusts," he said in his "Confession of Faith," "is through the exercise of the collective power of our people as a whole through the governmental agencies established by the Constitution for this very purpose."[197] He was thus aligned more closely to the Perkins-Beveridge camp regarding business regulation. TR favored a federal trade commission over antitrust legislation and court suits; moreover, he doubted the claim of the Pinchots that large corporations had caused inflation and high prices. "I disagree with you absolutely when you say that the trust question means the cost of living question, the bread question," Roosevelt wrote Amos Pinchot.[198] Similarly, Roosevelt scrawled the words "utter folly" next to the paragraph on "high cost of living" prepared by Pinchot as a platform plank.[199] Like Perkins and Beveridge, TR opposed "making mere size of and by itself criminal" and preferred "a policy of just and efficient control" over "strangulation" of business.[200]

Although Roosevelt did not believe that a vigorous antitrust campaign to recover economic competition could be a substitute for democratic administration, he recognized that public opinion, supportive of trust busting and renewed competition, required him to back government action against systematic exploitation by irresponsible trusts.[201] Since the Democratic convention, William Jennings Bryan had been attacking Roosevelt's support for an interstate trade commission. In words strikingly similar to those of Amos Pinchot, he insisted that such an administrative tribunal would place more power in the hands of a few individuals than a representative democracy could tolerate.[202] Bryan's assault on the Progressives' commitment to expanding national administrative power echoed Woodrow Wilson's militant antimonopoly position and anticipated the Democratic candidate's pronouncement of a rival political philosophy, which, in contrast to TR's New Nationalism, he dubbed the New Freedom. Even the self-styled conservative Taft joined the antimonopoly chorus, pointing to his administration's record of many antitrust suits.

The conflict over the business plank became a *cause célèbre* among party leaders when the rival factions each became convinced that their position had won out in the platform battle. On the night before the nomination, Roosevelt sought a compromise between the Perkins and Pinchot camps on the business plank. Although there is confusion as to the actual events, the platform committee appears to have passed a plank that contained both a long statement on interstate corporate regulation advocated by Perkins and Beveridge *and* the Pinchot-McCarthy endorsement of the Sherman Act and list of illegal practices. During these prolonged negotiations, it seems Perkins was misinformed as to the final version approved by the resolutions committee. When the platform was read to convention delegates the next day, a stunned Perkins met with Dixon, Beveridge, Lewis, and Roosevelt to point out that a grievous error had occurred. "That [the Sherman Act statement] doesn't belong in the platform," Perkins insisted. "We cut it out last night."[203] The hastily assembled group determined quickly that the Pinchot-McCarthy language would be removed from all printed versions of the platform.

Amos Pinchot and McCarthy later protested that their proposals had been "stolen" by Perkins.[204] For antitrust Progressives, the incident exemplified the danger of having a "trust magnate" like Perkins in a position of power in the party. His leadership role was unseemly, they charged, because he was intimately connected to some of the nation's most prominent corporate trusts—trusts that lay at the heart of America's suffering. "His name will bring to mind . . . the New York Life Insurance Company, J. P. Morgan and Company, the United States Steel Corporation, and the International Harvester Company," warned Pinchot.[205] At the first meeting of the New York delegation at the Chicago convention, Pinchot unsuccessfully opposed the nomination of Perkins to the Progressive National Committee. Shortly after the convention adjourned, Harold Ickes and William Allen White tried to no avail to derail Perkins's selection as chairman of the Progressive Executive Committee.[206] Perkins was buoyed by the unflinching support of Roosevelt, who had enormous respect for his organizing skills (not to mention his wallet).

In the end, the antitrust plank controversy brought to the surface fundamental differences concerning business regulation and the leadership role of Perkins. These issues would cause considerable damage to Roosevelt's general election campaign; indeed, the fight over the antitrust plank cut to the very core of the modern state that, ostensibly, the programmatic initiatives touted by Progressives anticipated. As Croly acknowledged, the Progressive program presupposed national standards and regulatory powers that "foreshadowed administrative aggrandizement."[207] And yet, some Progressives, mindful of—indeed, sympathetic to—Americans' traditional hostility toward centralized administration, were diffident in their defense of state-building. Unlike those who would embrace Wilson's New Freedom, McCarthy insisted there could be no restoration of equality of opportunity under modern conditions without a strong "state"—comprised of national commissions—that could underpin it.[208] Nonetheless, he insisted, shorn of the antitrust plan or any legal standards to guide national administration, the idea for an interstate trade commission "was too great a power to give any commission" and "gave the opponents of the Progressive party an opportunity to excite suspicion against it."[209] In particular, like Amos Pinchot, McCarthy fretted that the prominent position of Perkins in the third-party movement would arouse fear that the Progressives favored an alliance of federal administration and corporate power.[210] This concern would prove prescient, especially with respect to the Progressive Party's failure to forge strong ties with labor.

There were additional sources of conflict within the Progressive ranks with respect to how administrative power should be used. Progressives aligned with the Prohibition movement pressured the platform committee to accept a temperance plank. When the committee turned a deaf ear to their demands, only TR's personal appeal persuaded prohibitionists not to launch an embarrassing fight on the convention floor. The fact that foreign affairs did not figure prominently in the election averted splits that would emerge after 1915 between Roosevelt and peace activists. Addams and other Progressives associated with the peace movement had difficulty stomaching Roosevelt's proposals for the annual construction of two battleships and the fortification of the Panama Canal.[211] Ultimately, many social reformers like Addams, the Pinchot brothers, and McCarthy acquiesced to unpalatable positions of the new party on race, business regulation, and foreign affairs because they had faith that goals such as racial justice, business competition, and international peace could be achieved at a more hospitable moment—after the preeminent agenda of social and industrial justice was realized. However, the critics outside the Progressive Party would be less forgiving on the questions of race and antimonopolism. During the general election they would expose the serious disagreements that divided reformers who presumed to represent the vanguard of a new political era.

Conclusion: The Candidates and the Parties

Soon after the Progressive National Convention adjourned, Roosevelt's friend and critic Learned Hand sent him a letter that was unusual in its unequivocal praise. "It is the most inspiring time in my own political experience, and has the largest premise for good," he wrote. "You have succeeded in switching the radical movement from the mere distribution of political power to the actual issues for which political power exists at all. . . . You will immensely raise the tone of American politics for a generation."[212] Even Taft admitted that the convention had "in a certain sense been a success," that it had been more than a rump movement in protest against the Republican Party's defiance of Roosevelt's personal aspirations. At the same time, Taft took some consolation from the profound challenge Roosevelt faced in bringing together the disparate strands of social reform that gathered in Chicago. As he wrote in a letter to his secretary Charles Hilles, "It has been a conglomeration of elements, as varied, as impossible of mixture and as impossible of accomplishment as the platform which [Roosevelt] enunciates in his 'Confession of Faith.'"[213] For all their differences, however, the reformers who backed Roosevelt shared a commitment to overcome the limits of the decentralized republic, the constitutional order shaped by party organizations and legal doctrines that formed a wall of separation between the federal government and society. Progressives of all stripes, even those like the Pinchots and McCarthy, who hoped to find nonbureaucratic and noncentralized ways to expand the responsibilities of the national government, were committed to breaching that wall.

Given the traditional American hostility to centralized administration, Progressives' hope of building a modern state depended ultimately on somehow transforming the decentralized republic into direct rule of the people. At the time, and ever since, skeptics have puzzled over the apparent contradiction between Progressives' celebration of direct democracy and their hope to achieve more disinterested government, which seemed to demand a powerful and expert national bureaucracy. In spite of this apparent contradiction in Progressive doctrine, TR's charismatic leadership and his exalted defense of direct democracy gave New Nationalists hope that administration could be reconciled with and even strengthen self-rule in the United States. The diverse array of reformers who allied with Roosevelt agreed that the government, and the constitutional forms that shaped it, "should be subject to and not above the final control of the people as a whole."[214] That sentiment captured the moral high ground of the campaign. Indeed, as the dramatic events in Baltimore suggested, the Democrats felt they had little choice but to come to terms with the tenets of progressive democracy.

There is a real sense in which the emphasis on forging a direct link between the president and public opinion—recasting the executive as "the steward of the public welfare"—obviated fundamental questions about what the modern state should do. Both Wilsonians and New Nationalists, in fact, downplayed the importance of their respective party platforms, stressing instead the need to establish a vital connection to popular will. As Charles McCarthy wrote Roosevelt soon after the Progressive Party's national convention, "The people are jealous of losing control of the situation. They have had four years of Mr. Taft, have seen him constantly thwart their will, and they wish to have greater control over the presidency."[215] TR's candidate-centered campaign exalted this wish into a creed. Believing that "pure democracy" was the glue that held together the movement Roosevelt sought to lead, McCarthy urged him to go further than the platform and support a popular recall of the president. "In the platform you have called for the recall principle," McCarthy wrote. "I do not see why, then, it is not consistent for you to follow it out in your own case, especially as this is not a platform but a covenant with the people. What is a covenant with the people? To my mind it is a far more solemn thing than a platform." A statement by Roosevelt, McCarthy concluded, that he would subject himself to a recall of the American electorate if he did not live up to that covenant was "consistent [with Progressive principles] and at the same time extraordinarily good policy."[216]

TR was not ready to support such a radical measure this early in the campaign, but his cousin and close advisor, George Emlen Roosevelt, assured McCarthy that the colonel believed in "the principles of the Recall of the President" and would "bring it forward if he thinks it necessary."[217] In truth, the dramatic peroration of TR's "Confession of Faith" more than hinted at his belief that the people had a right to recall the president. "I hold that a man cannot serve the people well unless he serves his conscience," he declared, "but I also hold that where his conscience bids him refuse to do what the people desire, he should not try to continue in office against their will."[218] This right demanded more than writing into law measures such as the direct primary, recall, and referendum. It also required, as McCarthy put it, "inaugurating a custom that [would] become firmly rooted in unwritten law", that presidents derived their authority "directly" from the people.[219]

The Progressive Party's program thus tended to subordinate collective partisan responsibility and party platforms to a candidate-centered campaign that worshipped at the court of public opinion. The excitement this program aroused, moreover, signaled an important transformation of American politics—a shift from a decentralized republic to mass democracy—that none of the contenders for the presidency in 1912 could afford to ignore. To many observers, "the memorable and colorful conclave at Chicago had given the country the promise of a realignment and restructuring of the party system."[220] To others, however, especially many foreign correspondents covering the exciting American presidential election, such a contest looked less like a realignment of parties than it did a triumph of a cult of personality that gave the illusion of democratic accountability. Lampooning the emergent candidate-centered campaign in the United States, a cartoon in the German newspaper *Lustige Blaetter* depicted the three major contenders—Taft, Roosevelt, and Wilson—as three large birds carrying flypaper. "There are now in North America three flycatchers abroad," read the caption. "In one way or another the people will get caught!"[221]

Nonetheless, Taft, Roosevelt, and Wilson proved to be impressive candidates. Along with Eugene Debs, the most effective socialist candidate in the nation's history, they conducted a campaign, as a distinguished historian of the period has noted, of "serious ideas and elevated discourse."[222] Prodded by TR and the Progressive Party, which proposed to harness representatives, including members of the judiciary, more tightly to mass public opinion, they debated the most fundamental questions about the future of constitutional government in the United States. That this debate became inextricably entwined with a contest of character and personality only confirmed that the transformation of democracy that the leading reformers of the day championed beheld both great promise and dangerous possibilities.

꙳

FIVE

"The Constitution Is a Living Thing": The Progressive Party and the Great Campaign of 1912

The general election of 1912 recalled other great presidential contests in American history, most notably the elections of 1800, 1832, and 1860, that challenged voters to think seriously about the meaning of their rights and the Constitution that promised to fulfill them.[1] Some of the most important changes foretold by this campaign would not take place until the arrival of the New Deal political order in the 1930s. But the contest among Taft, Roosevelt, Wilson, and Debs was a critical prelude to the political realignment of the 1930s, setting in motion developments that have been important ever since. TR and the Progressive Party played the most important part in stirring these developments. Beholding a program that would "purify" democracy and strengthen national administrative power, the Bull Moose campaign signaled major changes in the relationship between representatives and the public.

President Taft was the strongest opponent of these changes. He stood like Horatio at the Bridge in opposing the Progressive Party program, insisting, as he had throughout the primary contests, that it betrayed "an entire willingness to destroy every limitation of constitutional representative government."[2] Against this charge, Progressives retaliated that their reform proposals would not radically change but, rather, "harmonize with the intent and scope of the Constitution," with the "stated object" pronounced in the Preamble.[3] As Albert Beveridge put the issue in his keynote address at the Progressive National Convention in Chicago,

> The Progressive party believes that the constitution is a living thing, growing with the people's growth, strengthening with the people's strength, aiding the people in their struggle for life, liberty and the pursuit of happiness, permitting the people to meet all their needs as conditions change. The opposition believes that the constitution is a dead form, holding back the people's growth, shackling the people's strength, but giving a free hand to malign powers that prey upon the people. The first words of the constitution are these: "We the people," and they declare that the constitutional purpose is "to form a more perfect union and to promote the general welfare." To do just that is the very heart of the Progressive cause.[4]

In proposing to make the election a mass constitutional convention, Roosevelt and his followers drew inspiration from the parallels they perceived between the first national campaign of the Republican Party and their own. "As the Progressive party sprang into existence in 1912 to meet the demand of the people for a 'new party' standing cleanly and aggressively on the supreme issue of the day," proclaimed the program of the Progressive convention, "exactly so sprang up the Republican party in the year 1856."[5] In truth, as was noted in Chapter 3, there was a real sense in which the Progressive delegates, in subordinating natural rights philosophy to "pure democracy," stood for more fundamental change than their Republican forbears. The Republican Party was conceived to change the Constitution so that it would be more consistent with the unalienable rights of the Declaration of Independence; the Progressive Party pledged, as Roosevelt stated in his "Confession of Faith," to make "the people themselves . . . the ultimate makers of their own constitution," the "equivalent," as Herbert Croly, acknowledged, of a "new Declaration of Independence" (see Chapter 3).[6]

Moreover, despite the Progressives' insistent comparison of their campaign with the origins of Lincoln's Republican Party, the fate of the nation did not hang on the outcome of the 1912 election as it did on the results of the 1860 campaign. Nonetheless, the 1912 campaign "crackled with excitement."[7] All of the candidates, even Taft, who championed constitutional sobriety, agreed that momentous changes were occurring in American politics and that they had an obligation to provide leadership that would meet the profound challenges raised by the new industrial order. Roosevelt would command the agenda of the general election by standing most resolutely for a new political era, by calling on the American people to look beyond interest and class toward, as Croly put it, "a comprehensive, a lofty, and far reaching democratic purpose."[8] Indeed, TR considered Progressives more fortunate than the Republicans who followed Lincoln, for their movement had the opportunity to transcend the traditional schisms of American electoral politics. The task of the new party, he told those who joined his bolt from the Republican convention, was to appeal "to all honest citizens, East and West, North and South," and "all right thinking men, whether Republicans or Democrats, with regard to their previous affiliation."[9]

The intense conflicts at the Progressive Party Convention had revealed all too clearly, however, that schisms among progressive-minded reformers were no less formidable than the traditional ones. Indeed, the conflict over race had caught Roosevelt in a rank compromise with states' rights and Jim Crow. And yet in the face of these challenges, he placed greater emphasis on the Progressive Party's most radical and unifying theme, direct plebiscitary democracy. That Wilson's formidable candidacy, which offered a more moderate version of reform, probably doomed the new party to electoral defeat did not deter Roosevelt's assault on existing constitutional forms. Instead, the likelihood of short-term defeat only appeared to further encourage Roosevelt and militant Progressives to embrace radical reform. As Charles McCarthy, one of the most ardent defenders of "pure democracy," wrote to a friend of Robert La Follette at the start of the general election, the attacks of the Wisconsin senator and Wilson on TR were "a constant spur to him." Comparing Roosevelt's position to that of a war-like South African tribe, McCarthy predicted an aggressive campaign: "The Matabeles get killed when they go home after a defeat, and they have a saying: 'We go forward and die, we go backward and die, we might as well go forward and die.' Mr. Roosevelt is in that position."[10]

Rule of "the Whole People" and the Rights of the Dispossessed

Roosevelt opened his campaign on August 16 in Providence, Rhode Island. Determined to show himself as the prophet of a national democracy, the Progressive candidate first took his message to New England, which was considered a Taft stronghold: "I was told only six months ago that there was not a Progressive in Rhode Island," Roosevelt told a large enthusiastic audience. "I think the statement was erroneous."[11] New England, he continued, had taken the lead in the great contests of the nation's founding and the Civil War, and the American people had "a right to look to New England to stand at the forefront and not merely follow along in this third great movement to make and keep this a government of the people themselves, to be used in getting justice for the people themselves." Only boss rule stood in the way of New England playing a vital part in the Progressive movement. Roosevelt regretted, he told his audience, that the Republican machine had rejected the adoption of the direct primary in Rhode Island, which made a visit to the state "a waste of time" prior to the national convention. But the birth of a new party gave him the vehicle to "get at the people," and the Progressives championed a program that would, if enacted, establish an enduring, vital connection between representatives and public opinion.[12]

Indeed, repeating his promise to Charles McCarthy that he would defend a more unvarnished form of majority rule during the general election, Roosevelt confessed that as the Progressive movement developed, "instead of growing less radical, I have grown more radical. I would be content to go further than our platform in some directions, because I know from my own experience in the Presidency all I was able to accomplish was accomplished by getting at the people and getting them back of me." McCarthy had urged TR soon after the Progressive Party Convention to defend the recall of all representatives, including the president, and the colonel strongly implied that he supported such an idea. With his Providence speech, he began to make his own, less compromising support for direct democracy known to the public. Just as he had learned that the president's usefulness was conditioned on his having public opinion on his side, so Roosevelt "felt this was true of every public servant."

Even as his commitment to "pure democracy" grew more enthusiastic, Roosevelt continued the tortured effort he had made during the primary contests to balance statesmanship—republican responsibility—and plebiscitary governance: "The public servant cannot be a good public servant unless he serves his conscience first, yet this usefulness as public servant ceases as soon as he ceases to represent the deliberate and conscientious judgment of the people." Roosevelt would "develop that thought," he promised his audience, just as he had assured McCarthy that he would amplify his defense of the recall. "At present," however, he chose not to go "any further than the platform."[13]

Instead, Roosevelt chose to elaborate on the principles that informed his understanding of progressive democracy. In the rest of the Providence address he rejoined the debate with Taft over the future of constitutional government: Roosevelt denied Taft's charge that he was a demagogue; like Lincoln's calling, he insisted, his task was to appeal to the "better angels" of the American citizen. "We hold that no man can be permanently benefited unless we make it easier for him to get for himself and his wife and his children what is necessary for their bodies," Roosevelt acknowledged. But the Progressive program of economic and social justice, although of paramount importance, was not enough. "We insist no less upon each man taking thought for his soul as well as for his body."[14] Invoking the philosopher Grotius (heavy stuff for a campaign address!), he argued that the Progressive idea of justice rested in a "social impulse," "the source of . . . natural law—the basis of property and contract." Grotius stressed the importance of "sociability" in addressing international relations; Roosevelt suggested that Progressives hoped to extend the morality displayed by the soldier in defending his country to domestic affairs, especially in moderating the Gilded Age's obsession with property rights:

> We are opposed to the sordid views of those who base morality and therefore law only on fear and on greed and who have twisted a just regard for property rights into the erection of noxious fetichism [sic] which would make of privilege masquerading as property an ideal before which the rights of men, women and children are to be sacrificed without remorse. We stand for popular government, for the overthrow of the crooked boss and the crooked financier. We stand against the dictation which has corrupted the political management and the economic policy of this republic and which treats with sneering derision every attempt to replace our government on a basis of human equity.[15]

As the British press recognized, there were important similarities between Roosevelt's New Nationalism and Lloyd George's Liberal Party program.[16] This approach did not emphasize natural rights, as Lincoln did, or "economic rights," as New Deal Liberalism would in the aftermath of the Great Depression. Rather, the Progressive Party's program, as least as Roosevelt and Croly interpreted it, sought national administration "not so much out of compassion for or identification with the individuals affected, as in the interest of social harmony and national strength."[17] There were also some similarities between the Progressives' and British Liberals' pursuit of major "constitutional" reforms—for example, the Liberals curbed the power of the House of Lords whereas the Progressives prescribed direct election of senators. Nonetheless, neither "radical" liberalism in Great Britain nor social democracy in Europe attacked party politics in the service of direct democracy. Roosevelt's great challenge—and what gave Progressive reform a sui generis American caste—was to meld centralized administration and mass democracy. As Croly described this seemingly "absurd and contradictory" task, "If the two party system is breaking down as an agency of democratic government, the remedy is not to democratize the party which was organized to democratize the government, but to democratize the government itself. Just in proportion as the official political organization becomes genuinely democratic, it can dispense with the services of the national party."[18]

Although cynics like H. L. Mencken and even sympathetic allies like Learned Hand scoffed at such a formula for reform, it stirred a great deal of excitement among the American people. The enthusiastic response that Roosevelt received in Providence threw "the scare into the camp of the Taft leaders," the *New York Times* reported. In fact, Roosevelt's appeal seemed to transcend class or other traditional political identities, and it appeared to be drawing out "men from all ranks of life who never before took much interest in politics"—"many from the textile mills, many from the shops, lawyers, and business men." To be sure, most of the 1,800 men and women who heard Roosevelt's Providence address probably did not understand the references to Grotius; however, the crowd responded warmly to his description of the new movement and cheered most loudly "when he slashed out at the 'rule of the bosses' and appealed for aid in bringing about the rule of the people."[19]

In the face of such a powerful celebration of a new political order, the ancien régime seemed to be in full-scale retreat. Vice President James S. Sherman could not campaign due to a severe illness that took his life before election day, and Taft, although in good health, appeared to have expired politically. When asked early in the campaign about the incumbent president, Roosevelt responded cheekily, "I never discuss dead issues."[20] In truth, Taft chose to stand—or hide—behind the Republican Party. Having been badly rebuked in his effort to match Roosevelt's direct appeal to voters during the primary contests, Taft decided to withdraw to the customary presidential practice of leaving the general election to the party organization. "I am not going to make any speeches in this campaign," he wrote a friend soon after the Republican convention. After his speech of acceptance in early August, Taft hoped to "be done, so far as speaking activity in the canvass is concerned."[21]

The president did make one exception. He briefly emerged from the splendid seclusion of routine executive duties to deliver a conservative salvo in late September in Beverly, Massachusetts. Repeating the theme of his acceptance address, Taft stated what he took to be the campaign issue that was of the most "fundamental and permanent importance to the Government and the people": "the preservation of the institutions of civil liberty as they were handed down by our forefathers in the constitution of the United States and the state constitutions which are modeled after it." Although his acceptance speech had excoriated both Roosevelt and Wilson as dangerous radicals, he devoted special attention in his one general election address to the "third party" (Taft refused to dignify TR's party as a "progressive" organization). Dismissing the insurgent campaign as the embodiment of Roosevelt's demagogy, built "merely to gratify personal ambition and vengeance," he added,

> In the gratification of that personal ambition and vengeance, every new fad and theory, some of them good, some of them utterly preposterous and impractical, some of them as socialistic as anything that has been proposed in the countries of Europe, many having no relation to national jurisdiction of policy, have been crowded into a platform in order to tempt the votes of the enthusiastic supporters of each of these proposed reforms.

In the end, Taft predicted, in spite of the "acclaim" and "hero worshipping" that boosted Roosevelt's candidacy, the "movement would not succeed." For "the great bulk of the people are not emotional, undiscriminating, superficially-minded, non-thinking or hero-worshipping." The American people, with the Declaration and the Constitution as their guide, had "the virtue of the second sober thought. They [had] the underlying common sense that after full disclosure enables the scales to fall from their eyes, and to see the danger of a movement that must depend for its success on holding forth impossible promises of a millennium to be effected through legislation only and by no change in human nature, or the character of the individual member of society."[22]

After this brief interlude, Taft was content to remain on the sidelines during the dramatic campaign of 1912, attending to presidential responsibilities in a "business as usual" fashion.[23] His forbearance did not follow merely from his distaste and lack of talent for "modern" campaigning, however. The president's refusal to become actively involved in the general election—his decision to suspend participation in the candidate-centered contest—was part and parcel of his belief in the party system and his view that it had become a keystone of constitutional democracy. "I would like to be elected, but that wish is secondary to the main purpose which I have already alluded to," he wrote in a letter that sought to explain his campaign objectives. Having thwarted Roosevelt's effort to capture the Republican Party—"nothing [that had] occurred in his life had given [him] more gratification"—Taft felt that the most important task remaining was to uphold the two-party system. "If we are to be defeated by the Democrats," which the president admitted was the likely outcome, "we can still retain the Republican Party, and it may not suffer from defeat." Defeat was likely to increase the GOP's "discipline." More to the point, Taft added, the election and its aftermath were likely to impart an important lesson on the value of political parties.

> There are a good many people who ought to learn what they are not now likely to learn, that we must have parties in the country if we are going to accomplish anything through popular government. The people must subordinate their views on the less important subjects, in order that the main purpose of government may be subserved by the adoption of measures of reform and progress and normal development; but as long as we are going to have merely groups and not pass the measures that ought to be passed, we will have mere compromises, not framed by any logical principle, and accomplishing little.[24]

In demurring so, of course, Taft risked subordinating any effective defense of limited constitutional government and the party system to a contest for the soul of the Progressive movement. This was Wilson's view of the campaign. "The contest is between [Roosevelt] and me, not between Taft and me," he confided to a friend. He was not certain, however, that this contest would involve a test of whether the voters preferred his tempered version of progressivism or Roosevelt's more emphatic defense of social justice and direct democracy. Wilson worried that the emergence of a new form of politics would deflect attention from the contest of ideas to one of dueling personalities, a fight he feared that he could not win. Persuaded of the need to appeal directly to public opinion, Wilson was less confident than was Taft that the people could resist Roosevelt's charisma. TR captured the imagination of the American people, Wilson admitted; "I do not. He is a real, vivid person, whom they have seen and shouted themselves hoarse over and voted for, millions strong; I am a vague, conjectural personality, more made up of opinions and academic prepossessions than of human traits and red corpuscles. We shall see what will happen!"[25]

In the end, Wilson would be helped in this battle for the mantle of reform leader by two unlikely allies: civil rights activists and labor unions. Roosevelt declared at the Progressive Party National Convention that the plight of black Americans could be alleviated only if a strong, nationalistic party displaced the tenacious sectional politics that served as the bulwark of racial hatred and Jim Crowism. But the vitality of such a party, he insisted, required "white leadership" in the South. From the moment this race policy was articulated in August until election day, it drew intense criticism from the press, civil rights leaders, and segregationists in the South. The *Atlanta Journal* printed a blistering editorial against Roosevelt's southern strategy shortly after the Julian Harris letter was made public. "If you fancy that the pharisaic pose you have recently assumed on the Negro question will win you this section's support, you are pitiably deceived. You have straddled the issue in both the North and the South, fraternizing with the Negro there and execrating him here," the editors charged. "Do you think that we are so stupid as not to see through this two-faced and impudent game? . . . Go home, Colonel, go home and apologize as best you can to the colored brethren, whom you consider your 'equals' in the North; but as for the South, what you have done speaks so loudly that we cannot hear what you say."[26]

As early as June 1912, TR knew that Booker T. Washington—"the arbiter of Federal appointments for Negroes under Roosevelt and Taft"—had pledged support to President Taft and the Republican Party.[27] A number of African American leaders, however, disenchanted with Taft's disinterest in enforcing the Fourteenth and Fifteenth Amendments, the decline of black patronage on his watch, and the president's frank declaration that he would not appoint blacks to office in the South where local whites objected, rejected Washington's counsel to stick with the GOP. Indeed, a number of younger black leaders of the National Independent Political League and the NAACP scorned Washington's "policy of gradualism, his acceptance of segregation, and his soft-pedaling of the franchise and higher education."[28] Those more "radical" black leaders like William Monroe Trotter, editor of the *Boston Guardian* and a prominent figure in the National Independent Political League; W. E. B. Du Bois, the noted editor of the NAACP's *Crisis;* and even those at the forefront of Washington's own National Negro Business League were hopeful that the new party would advance black civil rights. In the wake of the black delegates and civil rights plank battles at the Progressive convention, however, Du Bois, Trotter, and J. Milton Waldron, also a representative of the National Independent Political League, expressed a sense of betrayal (see Chapter 4). Scandalized by the deafening silence of the Progressive Party platform on civil rights, Du Bois scoffed in the *Crisis,*

> Lest there should be any misinterpretation of this silence, the party proceeded to bar practically every representative of 8,000,000 Southern Negroes and to recognize delegates chosen by Southern conventions open "to white people only." To seal this compact these Hosts of Armageddon stood and sang: "Mine eyes have seen the glory of the coming of the Lord!" Selah! Now, Mr. Black Voter—you with 600,000 ballots in your hand, you with the electoral vote of Illinois, Indiana, Ohio and New York in your pocket—WHAT ARE YOU GOING TO DO ABOUT IT?[29]

Du Bois's disenchantment with the Progressive Party was in all likelihood aggravated by his suspicion that white suffragists, especially those associated with the National American Woman Suffrage Association (NAWSA), had forsaken the rights of black men and women. In August 1911, he charged, NAWSA had refused to allow the introduction of a resolution at its Louisville convention stating that "women who are trying to lift themselves out of the class of the disenfranchised, the class of the insane and criminal, express their sympathy with the black men and women who are fighting the same battle and recognize that it is unjust and as undemocratic to disenfranchise human beings on the ground of color as on the ground of sex."[30]

The Progressive Party tried to counter the charge of hypocrisy that civil rights leaders lodged against it by launching an ambitious publicity campaign and by creating new bureaus to reach out to black voters. Roosevelt wrote an essay in the *Outlook* entitled the "Progressives and the Colored Man," which repeated his defense of the color line the third party drew at his behest between the northern and southern delegations. Referring to his letter to Julian Harris that set the tone for the Progressives' deliberation on black rights, Roosevelt once again defended his party's third way. "Unlike the Democratic party, the Progressive party stands for justice and fair dealing toward the colored man," he wrote,

> and unlike the Republican party, it proposes to secure him justice and fair dealing in the only practical way, by encouraging in every part of

the country good feeling between the white men and the colored men who are neighbors, and by appealing in every part of the country to the white men who are the colored man's neighbors, and who alone can help him, to give him such help, not because they are forced by outsiders to do so, but as an honorable obligation freely recognized on their own part.[31]

This rendition of compromise with Jim Crow, however, prepared for the general election campaign, was hitched to a strong stand on civil rights. Departing from his customary emphasis on the duties of the "whole people," Roosevelt committed the Progressive Party to the natural rights of black Americans. "We feel with all our hearts that in a democracy like ours, and above all, in such a genuinely democratic movement as ours, we cannot permanently succeed except on the basis of treating each man on his worth as a man," Roosevelt argued. "The humblest among us, no matter what his creed, his birthplace, or the color of his skin, so long as he behaves in straight and decent fashion, must have guaranteed to him under the law his right to life and liberty, to protection from injustice, to the enjoyment of the fruits of his own labor, and to do his share in the work of self-government on the same terms with others of like fitness." Roosevelt also strayed from the position on the "Negro question" that he took at the Progressive Party convention by implicating the North, as well as the South, in the unjust treatment of African Americans. "There have been plenty of lynchings and race-riots in the North," he admitted, "and we intend to make a serious and conscientious effort to do away with the conditions which have brought about these race-riots and lynchings."[32]

Roosevelt's explanation for the Progressive color line was endorsed by *Outlook* editors. As they argued in championing TR's position on civil rights,

He has, in fact, taken the ground of reason and justice—the ground that in a representative government no man is to be accepted as a representative unless he does in fact represent the community from which he comes; and no representative is to be rejected if he does in fact represent such a community. It is perfectly notorious that the Negro delegates who have claimed to represent the extreme South in Republican conventions have not truly represented the community; in the Progressive convention every Negro delegate accepted did represent the community and came with the good will of his white neighbors.[33]

Du Bois responded disdainfully to Roosevelt's essay and the *Outlook*'s endorsement of it. "If anyone will substitute in the [editorial statement] 'white community' for 'community,'" he scoffed, "the meaning of the editors will be clear."[34] Nor was he impressed with the importunities of James Hayes of the Negro Suffrage League, who was named director of the Progressive Party's "Colored Bureau." Du Bois and his allies in the National Independent Political League disagreed with Hayes's contention that the black voter had "everything" to gain and "nothing" to lose "by casting his lot with the new party."[35] Since 1908, in fact, they had been tempted to throw their support to the Democratic Party. Du Bois urged blacks to vote for Bryan in that election, not on the basis of purely racial considerations but because "the Democratic party today stands for the strict regulation of corporate wealth, for the freedom and independence of brown and black men in the West Indies and the Philippines, for the right of labor to strive for higher wages and better working conditions, for a low tariff, and for the abolition of all special privileges." By abandoning the reactionary Republican Party, Du Bois acknowledged, some blacks might lose patronage positions, but that was a small matter when cast against the chance to transform the party system. Should they join the Democrats, black voters could tilt the party's center of gravity toward its northern wing, which treated Negroes "better" than did northern Republicans. "The Negro voter, today, therefore has in his hand the tremendous power of emancipating the Democratic Party from its enslavement to the South."[36]

Du Bois thus anticipated the New Deal realignment, which saw Franklin D. Roosevelt and northern Democrats, aided by the desperate conditions of the Great Depression, persuade many African Americans to switch party allegiance by appealing to them along economic and class lines. No change of this magnitude took place during the Progressive era, when economic circumstances were far less dire, but due to the efforts of the NAACP and the National Independent Political League, the Democratic Party began to court black voters. This was especially so in 1912, when the Progressive Party shook the foundations of the party system, challenging traditional loyalties in a way that had not been the case since the end of Reconstruction. Bishop Alexander Walters, of the AME Zion Church, organized the National Colored Democratic League to rally black support for Wilson. Urging African Americans to "Make Friends of Thine Enemies," Walters warned his colored brethren not to join the new party. Their rights as a minority, already greatly weakened, would become even more so, should the Progressives become a dominant political force. "If Mr. Roosevelt's policies triumph," he wrote in an advertisement placed in the *Crisis,* "the Constitution of the United States will be subject to amendment and repeal by any temporary majority of the people enjoying the right to cast a ballot. The ballot then is the bulwark of our property, our liberties, and our lives." Nor did it make sense to stick with the Republicans. "For forty-years the Negro had supported the Republican party in the hope that the party which stood sponsor for his freedom would stand as the guardian of his constitutional rights," Walters wrote. Yet the GOP had proven itself "confessedly unable to secure for the black man the enforcement of the laws, which the founders made nearly a half century ago."

Understandably, Walters observed, Negroes feared "that should the Democrats come into power some greater misfortune would befall them." The decisive argument against that fear was the record of the Democrats in Congress from 1910 to 1912, when they controlled the House and, with the support of Republican progressives, had a working majority in the Senate. This Congress passed "the greatest of all pension bills, which included among its beneficiaries, thousands of old negro soldiers." More important, the Democratic Party created the National Colored Democratic League, "the first bona fide national political organization of colored men ever formed" in the country. The Democratic Party had thus demonstrated that it wanted to include blacks in its ranks, Walters assured his readers: "it has met us half way." With the invitation offered, "reason and intelligence command us to lay aside our prejudice and fears and reach out for the friendship and support of the people who are today oppressing us because of our political hostility toward them."[37]

Du Bois was more measured in his support of the Democrats. He openly admitted that the Democratic candidate, born in Virginia, shared the antiblack sentiments of many of his contemporaries. Not once in Wilson's entire career before 1912 had he expressed any interest in the rights of black Americans; indeed, as president of Princeton University he had refused to challenge—in truth, evaded—its failure to admit African Americans. "On the whole," Du Bois understated, "we do not believe that Woodrow Wilson admires Negroes." Nonetheless, Du Bois, a distinguished sociologist, expressed faith that the New Jersey governor's academic credentials would temper him. Wilson's scholarly demeanor, Du Bois insisted, at least made him a better candidate than the unreliable populist Roosevelt:

Woodrow Wilson is a cultivated scholar and he has brains. . . . We have, therefore, a conviction that Mr. Wilson will treat black men and see their interests with farsighted fairness. He will not be our friend, but he will not belong to the gang of [Southern racist Democrats of] which Tillman, Vardaman, Hoke Smith, and Blease are the brilliant expositors. He will not advance the cause of oligarchy in the South, he will not seek further means of "Jim Crow" insult, he will not dismiss black men wholesale from office, and he will remember that the Negro in the United States has a right to be heard and considered; and if he becomes President by the grace of the black man's vote, his Democratic successors may be more willing to pay the black man's price of decent travel, free labor, votes, and education.

Of the four candidates, Du Bois believed that the socialist Eugene Debs was the ideal candidate—"he alone, by word and deed, stands squarely on a platform of human rights regardless of race or class"—but Wilson was the only realistic choice. [38]

Du Bois's support for Wilson expressed his faith that the Democratic candidate, and not Roosevelt, was the more reliable progressive. Indeed, as Wilson Carey McWilliams has written, the shame of Jim Crow veils "how thoroughly Du Bois fits the Progressive paradigm—raised in Protestant New England culture, educated at Fisk [in ethics and philosophy], and trained at Harvard and Berlin in the most advanced social science." [39] While a student at Harvard, Du Bois later wrote, he was "a devoted follower of William James at the time he was developing his pragmatic philosophy," and he credited James with converting him from "the sterilities of scholastic philosophy to realist pragmatism." Once Roosevelt and the Progressives so violated his hopes for the new party, Du Bois probably was drawn to Wilson for the same reasons that attracted James's personal friend Louis Brandeis to the Democratic candidate: "his rigorous mind, his uneasiness with the shibboleths of backward-looking agrarians within the Democratic Party, and his passion for exposing the excessive power of big business." [40]

Since the Democratic convention, in fact, Wilson had been meeting with and seeking to reassure civil rights leaders on the race question. The Democratic nominee was on fairly close terms with Oswald Garrison Villard, grandson of William Lloyd Garrison, crusading editor of the *New York Evening Post* and one of the founders of the NAACP, who "was in 1912 unquestionably the leading white champion of Negro rights in the United States." [41] Villard had supported Wilson's gubernatorial campaign in 1910 and appreciated the New Jersey governor's reform program. He hoped the commitment to economic and political reform that Wilson had demonstrated as governor could be extended to the Negro question. This hope was encouraged in a meeting between Villard and Wilson about a month after the Baltimore convention. Although he had doubts about Wilson's attitude on matters pertaining to international relations and women's suffrage, the civil rights activist was "delighted" with the Democratic nominee's attitude on racial politics. As Villard wrote in his diary of the meeting, "He said that, of course, he should be President of all the people, that he would appoint no man to office because he was colored, any more than he would appoint one because he was a Jew or a Catholic, but that he would appoint them on the merits." Wilson acknowledged to Villard that he and the crusading reformer would "differ . . . as to where the entering wedge [on race relations] should be driven." But the governor promised fair dealing for black Americans, albeit in vague terms. "He said of course he would speak out against lynching," Villard reported, admitting that "every honest man must do so." At the same time, Wilson "did not wish the colored people to get the impression that he could help them in that matter as President, as the President had no power." Finally, the Democratic candidate promised Villard a statement for the *Crisis* or *Evening Post,* "or if not, one to . . . help me in writing a letter to the negro newspapers and otherwise helping his candidacy."[42]

Meanwhile, Wilson met with the Reverend J. Milton Waldron and William Monroe Trotter of the National Independent Political League. Anxious to consummate an alliance with the Democratic Party, Waldron stated what he took to be Wilson's attitude on race in an unauthorized statement that was printed in the September issue of the *Crisis.* Wilson's position, as Waldron interpreted it, went further than the understanding that he had conveyed to Villard. The governor was quoted as stating that he needed and would seek the support of black voters and would pledge himself to fair dealing with black Americans in executing the laws and making appointments. Moreover, and more surprising given Wilson's cautious commitment to Villard, he allegedly "assured Waldron and Trotter that Negroes had nothing to fear from a Democratic congress and that if, by some accident, congress should enact legislation inimical to the Negro's interest, he would veto such laws."[43]

The publication of the Waldron statement caught Wilson completely off guard. "In haste," the governor wrote Villard that he "read with amazement Dr. Waldron's version of the conversation." He did assure his visitors, Wilson acknowledged, that if elected he would be president of the "whole Nation and would know no differences of race or creed or section, but to act in good conscience and in a Christian spirit through it all." Wilson also admitted to assuring that they had nothing to fear "in the way of inimical legislation" should a Democratic president and Congress be elected. But he insisted that he did not promise Waldron and Trotter "that if by accident such legislation should be passed," he would veto it. Neither did he "give them any assurance about patronage, except that they need not fear discrimination." Wilson confessed that he was greatly "distressed" by Waldron's account of their conversation, because he had not discussed the matter with party leaders; moreover, he "would, of course, make no such general promise to anybody" about his executive action. "If you can advise me as to any way in which I could put out a general statement along the line I have just written," Wilson concluded, "I would be very glad to act upon your advice, for I want these people to be reassured."[44]

A few days later, Villard responded to Wilson's request for a general statement with one that Du Bois drafted. Obviously agitated by Wilson's disavowal of Waldron's statement, he urged the governor to embrace Du Bois's memorandum in the most "frank" terms:

I feel strongly that nothing important can be accomplished among the colored people until we have an utterance from you which we can quote. They not unnaturally mistrust you because they have been told that Princeton University closed its doors to the colored man (and was about the only Northern Institution to do so) during your presidency. They know that besides yourself both of [your close campaign advisors] Mr. [James] McAdoo and Mr. [William] McCombs are of Southern birth, and they fear that the policy of injustice and disenfranchisement which prevails not only in the Southern States, but in many of the Northern as well, will receive a great impetus by your presence in the White House.

As Villard had previously explained to Wilson, and as Du Bois's draft statement confirmed, African Americans wanted "some assurance that they will not wholly be excluded from office, office meaning so much to them because the bulk of their race are absolutely deprived of any self-government, even in the smallest matters such as schools and the making of the town ordinances in which they live."[45]

Wilson did not respond to Villard's importunity. He refused to endorse Du Bois's suggestion that the Democratic Party was "not in favor of unfair discriminating laws against any class or race" and that "the qualifications for voting should be the same for all men." Nonetheless, so distraught were

Du Bois, Waldron, and Trotter at what they understood to be the rank hypocrisy of Taft and Roosevelt that they "swallowed" Wilson on the basis of his claim to be a "Christian gentleman" and the vague promise that he would be a president of the "Whole Nation" who would deal fairly with black citizens.[46]

Many African Americans refused to follow their lead, however. Just as black opinion was badly divided about Roosevelt's color line at the time it was drawn, so it was on whom to support in the general election. Several black newspapers urged African Americans to stick with the Republican Party, for Taft was the only major candidate who stood for individual rights, although, admittedly, he expressed far more commitment to property rights than to the rights of black citizens. The *Cleveland Gazette,* for example, although it was a "'radical' anti-Bookerite organ," felt that Taft was the least of the three evils that had a chance to win the election.[47] But the *African-American Ledger,* located in Baltimore, Maryland, joined many black newspapers in strongly endorsing Roosevelt. "You have not been ashamed in all these years to call yourselves Republicans," it editorialized. "Now show your colors and let the folks know you are Progressives. The very name sounds good. It has a ring about it that makes one feel that he is a part of the community in which he lives, and that he is up to the times. Progress is the watch word."[48] Characterizing Roosevelt's essay in the *Outlook,* "The Progressives and the Colored Man," as the "2nd Emancipation Proclamation," the *Ledger* claimed that the "new emancipation includes a severance of business and political manipulation, the bringing about of better conditions for the great average of men, women, and children, be they black or white." It was a good sign, the editorial added, that "enlisted in this battle with Col. Roosevelt are many of the best known exponents of social justice in the country." And yet, the *Ledger* admitted, "the colored voters have not all heeded this argument, and the present campaign has resulted in the greatest division of the Negro vote during the forty odd years that the race has had the right to vote."[49]

The fracturing of the black community in the 1912 election gauged the limits of the Progressive Party's reform potential. As noted in Chapter 4, these limitations followed from a tortured combination of narrow strategic concerns and exalted principle. Roosevelt and his Progressive allies had "pledged themselves to a quest for a nationalist America liberated from the forms, prejudices, and slogans of the old order." Yet the stubborn persistence of racial prejudice that afflicted not just the South but all regions of the country revealed the profound difficulty of achieving such an enlightened form of liberation. More fundamentally, the conflict over the "Negro question" in 1912 exposed a dark side of progressive democracy. As Taft struggled to show, the national democracy Roosevelt championed, grounded so much on majoritarian principles, risked denigrating the core principles of political life in the United States, the unalienable rights that Lincoln characterized as the "jewel of liberty." For all the compromises and strange bedfellows that resulted from the "Negro question," therefore, the battle over race relations further defined the 1912 campaign as a serious contest over the meaning of rights and community in the United States.

New Freedom versus New Nationalism

Rights talk that savaged the trusts and championed the labor movement also damaged Roosevelt and the Progressive Party. Roosevelt and the reformers who joined him at Armageddon were confident that their social and industrial justice program would prove irresistible to working-class voters. At the start of the campaign, Roosevelt wrote an interested observer abroad, "Wilson . . . is a strong candidate. I shall not draw any of the silk stockings away from him, but I shall draw many of the workingmen and the like away, because these think, quite rightly, that he does not understand them."[50] Yet, as David Thelen wrote in his study of the Wisconsin legislature, "the 'typical' progressive and conservative came from the same social background."[51] Indeed, the social reformers who figured significantly in the formulation of the Progressive platform were for the most part educated, professional, and well-off. By the same token, representatives of organized labor generally were not important participants in platform deliberations, the national convention, or even state organizations. The Progressive Party's most notable exponent from organized labor was Timothy Healy, president of the International Brotherhood of Stationary Firemen. Little wonder that Roosevelt elicited almost no endorsement from labor unions.

Samuel Gompers, president of the American Federation of Labor (AFL), chose to endorse Woodrow Wilson in 1912, even though he agreed with Roosevelt that "[the Democratic candidate's] earlier academic writings indicated that he did not understand labor problems."[52] As president of Princeton, Wilson delivered a baccalaureate address in 1909 criticizing organized labor for inducing overly burdensome business regulation of hours and wages. "Our economic supremacy may be lost because the country becomes more and more full of unprofitable servants," he fretted at the time.[53] Wilson also was quoted in a March 1907 address as saying, "We speak too exclusively of the capitalistic class. There is another as formidable an enemy to equality and freedom of opportunity as it is, and that is the class formed by the labor organizations and leaders of the country, the class representing only a small minority of the laboring men of the country, quite as monopolistic in spirit as the capitalist, and quite as apt to corrupt and ruin our industries by their monopoly."[54]

Despite Wilson's past diatribes against organized labor, several factors conspired to steer Gompers and labor to the Wilson camp. Many urban union members had well-established relationships with Democratic machines. Moreover, with William Jennings Bryan as its candidate, the national Democratic Party committed itself to a pro-labor program in 1908, including a plank in the platform stating, "The expansion of industry makes it essential that there should be no abridgement of the right of wage-earners and producers to organize for the protection of wages and the improvement of labor conditions, to the end that such labor organizations and their members, should not be regarded as illegal combinations in the restraint of trade." This commitment to the right of labor to bargain collectively and other pro-labor planks were reaffirmed in the 1912 platform; moreover, the House passed a number of labor-friendly bills after the Democrats secured a majority in the 1910 congressional elections.[55] Perhaps most important, organized labor was suspicious of Roosevelt. Gompers and other labor leaders believed that he had not done enough during his presidency to protect workers and attack trusts. Their concerns about TR were confirmed when he sent an address he planned to deliver on Labor Day to Gompers for his review and suggestions. Gompers recalls that he found the speech "not only defective in many respects but manifesting a tendency to pursue a mistaken course, and I wrote him to that effect, pointing out what I believed should be corrected."[56] It was the final exchange between the two men on labor issues during the election.

The strained relations between Gompers and Roosevelt frustrated the Progressive Party's efforts to win labor's endorsement. "The planks contained in the Progressive platform are what labor unions have been contending for for more than thirty years," Healy wrote during the election. He noted as evidence the Progressive Party's commitment to the initiative, referendum, and recall, which labor had been championing since the end of the nineteenth century, as well as to "the procurement of laws . . . for the prevention of suffering from industrial accidents, occupational diseases, overwork, involuntary employment, and other injurious effects incident to modern industry." Given these pro-labor proposals, Healy concluded,

"What could ring more true to the hearts of the American working man, either among skilled or unskilled labor, men or women, organized or unorganized, employed in the factory, mine or mill, or in the great agricultural pursuits or among those engaged in the avenues of distribution or in fact to every person who works for a living, by either hand or brain, than the declaration of the Progressive party for Social and Industrial Justice."[57]

Gompers admitted, albeit rather grudgingly, that the Progressive Party had incorporated many of labor's demands.[58] Nonetheless, in a report on "Labor's 1912 Political Program" published in September, the Executive Council of the AFL concluded that though the Progressive platform was "outspoken and favorable," Roosevelt "failed during his administration to secure any remedial legislation in the interest of labor."[59]

Although the Executive Council's report helped the Democratic cause, it did not mention Wilson, nor did it mark a bright line between the Democratic and Progressive parties' industrial programs. Given the candidate-centered nature of the campaign, it was necessary for Wilson to counteract the image formed by his past anti-labor statements, which the Progressive Party was highlighting in its appeal to workers.

The transformation of Wilson's image was greatly facilitated by Louis Brandeis, "the People's Lawyer," a valued ally of Gompers, who often solicited his advice on the AFL's legislative program.[60] Brandeis and Wilson met for the first time on August 28 at the Democratic candidate's summer residence in Sea Girt, New Jersey. After a three-hour meeting, the crusading lawyer announced his support for Wilson and indicated that he was likely to make a number of speeches on Wilson's behalf, with particular attention to the trusts and the tariff. Brandeis had supported La Follette during the primary contests, during which he attacked Roosevelt for being insufficiently attentive to the dangers of monopoly and too optimistic about the ability of the national government to regulate big business in the public interest. That same concern, he announced in Sea Girt, explained why he supported Wilson instead of "the new party" (like Taft, Brandeis and Wilson refused to accept Roosevelt's insurgent campaign as "Progressive"). "The new party," Brandeis told the press, "must fail in all the important things which it seeks to accomplish, because it rests on a fundamental basis of regulated monopoly." He continued, "Our whole people have revolted at the idea of monopoly, yet the third party comes along and proposes to make legal what is illegal. Let us undertake to regulate competition, instead of monopoly, for our industrial freedom and our civic freedom go hand in hand, and there is no such thing as civic freedom in a state of industrial absolutism."[61]

CHAPTER FIVE

Those arguments, which Amos Pinchot and Charles McCarthy had hurled at Roosevelt and George Perkins during the Progressive Party's convention, would now form the cutting edge of Wilson's New Freedom. Indeed, Brandeis was more opposed to the New Nationalism's emphasis on expanding regulatory power than were TR's recalcitrant Progressive allies. The core principles that would comprise Wilson's doctrine were laid down in a lengthy memorandum Brandeis sent the Democratic candidate in late September. Stating how he understood the essential differences between the Democratic Party's solution to the trust problem and that of the Progressive Party, Brandeis wrote:

> The two parties differ fundamentally regarding the economic policy which the country should pursue. The Democratic Party insists that competition can be and should be maintained in every branch of private industry; that competition can be and should be restored in those branches of industry in which it has been suppressed by the trusts; and that, if at any future time monopoly should appear to be desirable in any branch of industry, the monopoly should be a public one—a monopoly owned by the people and not by the capitalists. The New Party, on the other hand, insists that private monopoly may be desirable in some branches of industry, or at all events, inevitable; and that existing trusts should not be dismembered or forcibly dislodged from those branches of industry in which they have already acquired a monopoly, but should be made "good" by regulation. In other words, the New Party declares that private monopoly in industry is not necessarily evil, but may do evil; and that legislation should be limited to such as should attempt merely to prevent the doing of evil. The New Party does not fear commercial power, however great, if only methods for regulation are provided. We believe that no methods of regulation ever have been or can be devised to remove the menace inherent in private monopoly and overweening commercial power.[62]

A few days later, Wilson gave a speech in Indianapolis that exalted the principles of regulated competition into a Democratic creed. He excoriated Taft and Roosevelt for tolerating "excessive tariffs" and "almost universal monopoly." With respect to the business regulation, Wilson argued, the Republicans and Progressives offered a choice between "Tweedledum and Tweedledee": "They do not so much as propose to lay the knife at any one of the roots of the difficulties under which we now labor. On the contrary, they intend to accept these evils and stagger along under the burden of excessive tariffs and intolerable monopolies as best they can through administrative commissions." "Therefore," Wilson proclaimed, "it is inconceivable that the people of the United States, whose instinct is against special privilege and whose deepest convictions are against monopoly, should turn to either of these parties for relief when these parties do not so much as pretend to offer them relief." It would fall to the Democrats, he concluded, and especially the Democratically elected president, to carry out the fundamental tasks that challenged industrialized America: "And there will be no greater burden in our generation than to organize the forces of liberty in our time in order to make conquest of a new freedom for America."[63]

As John Milton Cooper rightfully cautions, scholars should not exaggerate Brandeis's contribution to the New Freedom. After all, Wilson had been seeking to rally supporters to enlist in a campaign against monopoly since he was anointed in Baltimore. Just as Croly helped Roosevelt refine thoughts he already had expressed, so Brandeis helped Wilson clarify a direction in which he was already moving.[64] Brandeis most clearly influenced Wilson's thinking about how New Freedom principles could appeal to labor. Following his meeting with Brandeis, Wilson began to emphasize two points that reflected the influence of the People's Lawyer: the threat that big business posed to the worker's independence, and the need to protect the right of labor to organize.[65] In a Labor Day address delivered to the United Trades and Labor Council in Buffalo, New York, the Democratic candidate warned workers that the welfare measures promised by the Progressive Party would be worthless, indeed, would destroy the laborer's dignity, if Roosevelt's regulatory program was enacted. "These monopolists that the government, it is proposed, should adopt are the men who have made your independent action most difficult," he observed. "They have made it most difficult that you should take care of yourselves, and let me tell that the old adage that God takes care of those who take care of themselves is not gone out of date." Wilson went on to argue that no federal legislation could tame ruthless corporations. Instead, the attempt to regulate these "cars of Juggernaut" was likely to empower them: "The minute you are taken care of by the government, you are wards, not independent men. And the minute [monopolists] are legalized by the government, they are protégés and not monopolists. They are the guardians and you are the wards."[66]

Wilson made a direct connection between the New Freedom and workers' rights in his September 26 address, "To Working Men," in Fall River, Massachusetts. Many workers in the textile factories of Massachusetts were attracted to the Progressive Party's social and industrial justice planks, celebrated with much fanfare during Roosevelt's tour of New England at the outset of the general election. Wilson chose the Fall River speech to make the right of workers to organize a principal feature of the New Freedom and to make clear the failure of Roosevelt and the "third term party," with their stress on duties and obligations, to attend adequately to labor's collective interest. Suggesting, without directly admitting, that he had changed his mind about unions, Wilson stated:

> Organized labor has been unwise in some things, but the point is this, that the right of organization on the part of labor is not recognized even by the laws of the United States. And nowhere in the third term platform is it promised that right will be granted. There is a plank in which it is said, "We are in favor of the organization of labor"—I have forgotten the exact words, but that is what it means— "We are in favor of the organization of labor," that is to say, "We approve of the practice." But it doesn't anywhere promise to buttress that practice with the structured steel of law. . . . And I believe that we ought to hold a brief for the right, the legal right, to organize.[67]

Wilson's speech in New England echoed many features of an address that Brandeis gave the week before in Fitchburg, Massachusetts. Speaking before the Massachusetts AFL convention, Brandeis offered a detailed critique of the Progressive Party platform. Although he praised the "social and industrial justice" planks of the new party, Brandeis noted pointedly that its "solemn covenants" did not include the right of labor to organize:

> Nowhere in that long and comprehensive platform, neither in its nobly phrased statement of principles, nor in its general recommendations, nor in its enumeration of specific measures, can there be one word approving the fundamental right of labor to organize, or even recognizing this right, without which, all other grants and concessions for improvement of the conditions of the workingman are futile. The platform promises social and industrial justice, but it does not promise industrial democracy.[68]

When challenged to explain how he could claim the Progressive Party denied labor rights in light of its platform favoring "the organization of workers" and pledging "to establish a Department of Labor," Brandeis modified his statement, so that it acknowledged this "friendly approval of the practice" of collective bargaining. Nonetheless, much as Wilson would do a week later, he insisted that a definitive statement of the "right" of labor to organize, through legislation or a constitutional amendment, was necessary, "in view of the Court's [hostile] decisions."[69] For the new party to support the "practice" of organization without explicitly sanctioning the "right" of labor to organize was tantamount to saying, "I am in favor of the law, but against its enforcement."[70]

Like Wilson, too, Brandeis argued that this was an especially egregious omission, given that the "trust policy of the New Party [proposed giving] capital [an] immense advantage over labor." Amplifying his comments to the press at Sea Girt and anticipating the key points of his memo to Wilson a few weeks later, Brandeis charged that the new party's proclamation that it "did not fear commercial power" would encourage "the development of new capitalistic combinations, fundamentally hostile to organized labor and determined by the huge powers of combined resources to exterminate unionism from the industries they would control."[71] As he told the Fitchburg audience, the Progressive platform advocated "a policy of legalizing private monopoly and regulating it: or, in other words, domesticating industrial monsters and taming them." Allowing for "the perpetuation and extension of private monopoly in industry," Brandeis argued, would lead to a "dethronement of the people" by the "benevolent despotism" of corporate trusts—an economic concentration from which "the few have ever profited at the expense of the many."[72]

Personalizing his assault more than Wilson was willing to do, Brandeis underscored his attack on the Progressive regulatory program by devoting eleven of the fourteen pages of his speech to discussion of the business activities of George Perkins, chair of the executive committee of the Progressive Party, whom he dubbed the "Father of Trusts." The Progressive stance on corporate trusts, combined with the prominent role played by Perkins in the new party, was sufficient evidence that Roosevelt and the Progressives favored private monopoly over economic competition.[73]

Brandeis's assault on the Progressive platform burnished Wilson's reform credentials. The views of the celebrated reformer found an immediate platform in the Democratic campaign. His speech to the Massachusetts AFL was made available to Democratic strategists, who published thousands of copies as pamphlets.[74] Throughout the general election campaign, Brandeis submitted articles to newspapers and journals across the country stressing similar themes. In many, he defied Roosevelt's contention that regulating large economic units with an interstate commission would nurture industrial democracy. Confirming the anxiety of Charles McCarthy and Amos Pinchot that cutting the antitrust plank from the final version of the Progressive Party platform would come back to haunt the Roosevelt campaign, Brandeis insisted that "the cost of living" could not be reduced by merely controlling trusts: it would require a restoration of economic decentralization and competition. "If the government is powerful enough to control monster monopolies," he asked, "why is it not powerful enough to prevent them? That the Sherman law has failed to suppress monopolies is no answer, for there has been no serious attempt to enforce the law and no thought of making it effective by adding essential legal and administrative machinery."[75]

Brandeis found an especially important platform for his views and the New Freedom in the pages of the progressive journal *Collier's*. Prior to the publication of Brandeis's missives, *Collier's* had supported Roosevelt, reflecting the position of the magazine's publisher, Robert J. Collier, and its associate editor, Mark Sullivan. But Norman Hapgood, editor of *Collier's* and an enthusiastic supporter of Wilson, enlisted Brandeis to write two articles on the trust questions, which, echoing the arguments of his Fitchburg address, condemned Roosevelt for proposing to legalize monopoly. Brandeis also wrote five editorials attacking the Progressive Party, which appeared anonymously on Hapgood's editorial pages during September and October.[76]

The Brandeis-Hapgood alliance did great damage to Roosevelt's campaign. Not only did the articles and editorials amplify the New Freedom indictment of the Progressive Party's economic program, but they also seemed to show that one of the country's most important reform magazines had renounced its former view that Roosevelt was the heroic leader of the Progressive movement. "It seems to me there is decidedly something wrong with a lot of men who ought naturally to be with us heart and soul, like Norman Hapgood," Gifford Pinchot lamented. "So far as I can find out, it is a willingness to let essentials be crowded out by non-essentials."[77]

And yet, as the bitter fight over the business plank of the Progressive Party showed, the split between New Nationalism and New Freedom cut to the core of the modern state that, ostensibly, the programmatic initiatives touted by reformers appeared to anticipate. Wilson and Brandeis argued that Americans must maintain their hostility to centralized administration, no matter how complex the social and economic problems had become in the United States. Roosevelt's followers, even those who were keener on antimonopolistic practices than he, insisted that the concentration of private economic power required the creation of "administrative machinery" to uphold economic justice. "We have all read with great interest your article[s] in *Collier's*," Amos Pinchot wrote to Brandeis in early October. "I sincerely approve of your plan of trust regulation," he acknowledged, "only why not add to it the industrial commission, so as to get results while the process of restoring competition is going on. It seems to me that it would take quite a while, if only your plan is put in force, to break down the power that big business has to fix prices and wages."[78]

Underlying this disagreement about national administrative power was a philosophical dispute between Roosevelt and Wilson on the social contract—on the appropriate balance between rights and duties in American political life. Noting that the New Freedom's rights-based approach left the courts as the ultimate arbiters of business practices, Charles McCarthy complained to Hapgood that Brandeis's distinction between "regulated monopoly and regulated competition" missed the point. "*The state must provide . . . equality of opportunity*," he wrote:

> It can do so no other way except by a commission. . . . In the hundred and one changing conditions of our modern life, this commission must make its rulings on the actual facts as they are found and they change from day to day. If a man complains that he is not given a fair chance to compete all he has to do is to apply to this commission, who will at once take his case up and give him that chance if his case is a good one.

Roosevelt's economic program, McCarthy added, did not reject antitrust laws, such as the Sherman Act, but rather was dedicated to enforcing them more vigorously than the judiciary had, or possibly could. The idea behind New Nationalism "simply means that when a particular case arises the case can be dealt with vigorously, *not by the courts, but by this economic commission*."[79]

Just as Wilson and Brandeis did not face up to the aggrandizement of administration that would follow from progressive principles, so the New Nationalists could be charged with underestimating the difficulties entailed in holding administrative tribunals accountable. In taking this issue up with Hapgood, McCarthy proposed making commissioners "subject to recall by Congress," as was the case in English parliamentary government. McCarthy and Roosevelt also put a lot of stock in linking the reconstituted modern executive, of which such commissions would be a part, to mass public opinion.

But these provisions were not in the Progressive platform. Moreover, Wilson and Brandeis argued effectively that the New Freedom would restore, rather than depart from, self-government as traditionally understood in American political life. Wilson's most devastating indictment of Roosevelt was that his emphasis on duties and administration was essentially paternalistic.[80] The third-party platform, Wilson argued in his Labor Day address, presumed to"[act] as a Providence for you . . . but I want to say frankly to you that I am not big enough to play Providence, and my objection to the [New Nationalism] is that I don't believe there is any other man that is big enough to play Providence." Repeating the position he took during the contest for the Democratic nomination, Wilson pledged to rest reform in the constructive use of—rather than the denigration of—interests. "What I fear," he declared, is a government of experts. "God forbid that in a democratic country we should resign the task and give the government over to experts. . . . Because if we don't understand the job, then we are not a free people. We ought to resign our free institutions and go to school . . . to find out what it is we are about."[81]

In attempting to counter the devastating assaults of Wilson and Brandeis, the Progressive Party was not above appealing to interests. Timothy Healy attempted to win labor votes by writing an essay in the *Progressive Bulletin* and distributing upbeat campaign literature on Roosevelt's "Square Deal for Labor" and the anti-labor statements of Wilson. This appeal praised Roosevelt's courage in intervening in a 1902 coal strike, in which TR became the first president to recognize the rights of labor in an industrial dispute.[82] Particularistic appeals also were extended to the conservation and women's movements.[83] TR and the Progressive Party began their campaign with a unified national reform program that emphasized the responsibilities of citizens to the national community. In the heat of the election, however, TR and party strategists felt compelled to compromise this "covenant" in favor of special appeals to elusive social movements and interest groups.

This compromise rested in something more fundamental than campaign strategy. Like the battle over the "Negro question," the fight over the rights of labor exposed the tension between progressive democracy and the natural rights tradition—between the hope to build a national community and the exigency of recognizing particular interests and movements. As the Brandeis assault showed, the Progressive Party's claim that New Nationalism stood for principles that transcended private interests was undermined especially by its dependence on George Perkins. Perkins's critical role in financing the

Progressive Party and Roosevelt's solicitude for his opinions, most notably in the dispute over the trust plank at the convention, abetted Brandeis's charge that the new party was beholden to corporate interests.

Perkins's relationship to the Progressive Party in particular, and question of campaign contributions generally, came into sharp focus in late August. *Hearst's Magazine* published letters showing that Senator Boies Penrose, the potentate of the Pennsylvania Republican Party, had received a $25,000 contribution for the 1904 election from Standard Oil. Penrose, who had become the Senate Republican leader in 1904, insisted that the money did not benefit him but, rather, Roosevelt's 1904 election campaign. Understandably, Penrose was as eager to tarnish Roosevelt as he was to divert attention from his own role in negotiating an alliance between the oil trust and the Republican Party. TR's insurgent campaign had formed a partnership with Penrose's principal Pennsylvania rival, William Flinn, whose organization contributed significantly to Roosevelt's important primary victory in the Keystone State during the previous April (see Chapter 3). Flinn, moreover, was one of the few practical politicians to join TR's bolt from the Republican Party. With the support of Flinn's strong organization, Penrose feared, Roosevelt's third-party movement could very well win Pennsylvania and further weaken the senator's grip on that important Republican state.

Hoping to kill two birds with one stone—to fend off Roosevelt's powerful insurgency and to deflect *Hearst's Magazine*'s charges of corruption—Penrose self-righteously claimed on the floor of the Senate that the money was part of funds contributed by Standard Oil to the GOP in 1904 and that, in effect, he had merely been acting on behalf of Roosevelt and the national committee. In 1904, contributions from corporations were not illegal, as they were in 1912 due to the passage of the Tillman Act in 1907. But the real purpose of the Senate investigation was to discredit the leaders of the Progressive Party.[84] Indeed, Penrose's Senate speech also charged that Perkins had "underwritten for $3,000,000 the attempt to procure the nomination of the Colonel at the [1912] Republican convention." Given his well-deserved reputation for graft, Penrose's testimony alone probably would not have amounted to much. But he formed an unlikely modus operandi with Senator La Follette, characterized by the press as "the strangest alliance in the history of modern politics." Joined by their common hatred of Theodore Roosevelt, "the most violent reactionary in the Senate and its most pronounced progressive" cosponsored a resolution during the waning days of the congressional session that called for a probe of campaign spending in 1904, 1908, and 1912. The charge of the investigation was to examine "all correspondence and financial transactions between John D. Archibald [of Standard Oil], George W. Perkins, Theodore Roosevelt, and members of the Senate from 1900 to the time of the investigation."[85]

Senator Moses E. Clapp of Minnesota, a Progressive, was named chairman of the special Senate investigating committee, but the other members were enemies of Roosevelt and the new party. The press speculated, in fact, that the earnestness with which the Senate carried out this probe "made plain . . . that the Democrats and Taft contingent [were] in mortal dread of Roosevelt as a political factor."[86] The principal focus of the Clapp investigation was the indictment of both Penrose and Archibald that TR knew of the contribution; in fact, that he demanded a larger sum in exchange for the promise not to bring antitrust action against Standard Oil. That the Roosevelt administration did prosecute the company after his election was retribution for its failure to pour more money into TR's campaign coffers. The more immediate task, however, at least for most members of the committee and Senate, was to substantiate the charge of Wilson and Brandeis that the Progressive Party was the captive of Wall Street. To be sure, major corporate and finance figures, such as International Harvester's Cyrus H. McCormick and Wall Street's Bernard Baruch, also supported Wilson and the Democratic Party. Nonetheless, neither McCormick nor Baruch was a leading figure in the Democratic campaign, whereas Perkins was the executive secretary of the Progressive Party.

Although the Clapp committee found time to question Penrose and Archibald before its members left Washington, TR, when he expressed a desire to testify before the panel, was told that he would have to wait until Congress was back in session. Roosevelt feared, quite reasonably, that delaying his day in court until early October would allow the Senate investigation, which was given saturated coverage by the press, to undermine the Progressives' objective of challenging the major parties on fundamental questions about the relationship between the Constitution and American democracy. Unable to have his day in court, Roosevelt turned with characteristic alacrity to the stump and newspapers. Determined to reaffirm his party's dedication to duty and responsibility, the Progressive standard-bearer, to the consternation of many supporters—including his vice presidential candidate, Hiram Johnson—decided to meet head on the indictment of his campaign finance practices and Perkins's role in the Progressive Party.

Taking advantage of a campaign stop in Wilkes-Barre, Pennsylvania, Roosevelt noted that Penrose's charges were based "on hearsay"—no checks or receipts were produced—and were belied by the fact that most big business executives and the newspapers over which they had influence opposed his Progressive Party campaign. Furthermore, Roosevelt referred to letters made public the previous day, which he had sent to George B. Cortelyou, chairman of the Republican National Committee in 1904, "directing that no campaign contribution be received from Standard Oil Company." More broadly, Roosevelt tied his defense against charges of corruption to a symbolic display of his support, not for the rich but the downtrodden. The very purpose of his trip to Wilkes-Barre was to participate in the golden jubilee of Father J. J. Curran, the noted Social Gospel reformer who had long championed the cause of coal miners. Roosevelt had joined forces with Curran in 1902 when he arbitrated the bitter coal miners' strike of that year. In renewing that political friendship, he meant to show the Progressive Party's dedication to economic justice and to principles that celebrated a new idea of national democracy that transcended narrow interest-group politics.[87]

Similarly, Roosevelt defended his relationship with Perkins in terms that highlighted the new party's dedication to public service. He should not have to apologize for having Perkins with him, he argued when confronted with the issue during an address in Boston. "On the contrary, he should be proud of having started a progressive movement that can attract successful men, and not merely hacks and the failures of other political parties." Roosevelt's remarks, which were celebrated in the first issue of the *Progressive Bulletin,* portrayed Perkins's financial and administrative support of the third party as a generous act of citizenship. As the *Bulletin* reported, Roosevelt said that Perkins, although a rich man, "had joined the Progressive party and interested himself in politics BECAUSE HE HAS CHILDREN AND FELT IT WAS HIS DUTY TO DO WHAT HE COULD TO MAKE CONDITIONS BETTER IN THE COUNTRY IN WHICH THE CHILDREN WOULD LIVE AFTER THEIR FATHER'S DEPARTURE." Unlike the financial titan J. P. Morgan, who was only interested in making money, Roosevelt argued, Perkins was "giving to the business of the people." That Perkins was now devoting the energy and talent that he had once given to private business undertakings to the public interest was "a good, new thing in politics." Such an individual, TR concluded, would also "be a useful man in government." The people were bound, therefore, "until they [had] proof to the contrary," to assume that Perkins [was] sincere in his advocacy of the new party—which [had] antagonized and [was] denounced by most of the men [who were as] rich and influential as [was] Perkins."[88]

Nor did Roosevelt shirk from his position that national administration could serve the people. Even more than the tortured appeals for the African

American vote, the conflict between New Nationalism and New Freedom revealed that reformers were sharply divided over the virtues of big government—whether the principles and practices of local self-government could be sustained in the gale storm of the industrial revolution. Roosevelt brought this important issue to the fore in defending the Progressive Party's position on the trust against the hammer blows of Wilson and Brandeis. Noting the Democratic candidate's recent conversion to progressivism, Roosevelt and his political allies had sought to portray Wilson as a sham reformer. In early September, Wilson's extemporaneous remark during the course of an address to the New York Press Club seemed to confirm that he was a wolf in sheep's clothing, an insincere reformer whose progressive utterances hid a conventional allegiance to states' rights and private property. Seeking to elaborate his critique of Roosevelt's ambition to establish a "Providence over the people," Wilson stated, "the history of liberty is a history of the limitation of government power, not the increase of it."[89]

With the help of the press, Roosevelt pounced on this statement. Before a large, boisterous crowd in San Francisco, where the atmosphere resembled the religious fervor of the Bull Moose convention, he ridiculed Wilson's "platonic devotion to the principles of the Progressive party."[90] "It was idle," he insisted, to profess devotion to these principles and "at the same time to antagonize the only methods by which they can be realized in actual fact." Wilson's New Freedom left the federal government impotent in the face of the social and economic injustices that plagued the country. As TR put it, the New Freedom was "a bit of outworn academic doctrine which was kept in the schoolroom and the professorial study for a generation after it had been abandoned by all who had experience in actual life."[91] Although the Democratic candidate pretended to be a reformer, Roosevelt argued, no less than Taft, he was an advocate for "the *laissez-faire* doctrine," which "English political economists [had championed] three-quarters of a century ago." This nostrum made sense so long as the people were enslaved by a monarchy. But the rule of "We the People" changed the equation dramatically: "now the governmental power rests with the people, and the kings who enjoy privilege are the kings of the financial and industrial world; and what they clamor for is the limitation of government power, and what the people sorely need is the extension of governmental power."[92]

Seeking to extend the constitutional debate he waged with Taft to his battle with the purveyors of a "new" freedom, Roosevelt attacked Wilson's attachment to natural rights as shopworn. "He is not thinking of modern American history or of present day American needs," TR said of the

Democratic candidate. "He is thinking of *Magna Carta,* which limited the power of the English king, because his power over the people had before been absolute. He is thinking of the Bill of Rights, which limited the power of the governing class in the interest of the people, who could not control the governing class."[93] Just as Wilson had sought to pair TR with Taft and distinguish himself as the only progressive in the race, so Roosevelt now sought to tar the Democratic candidate as conservative. Wilson, Roosevelt concluded, proposed to "throw away" the "one great weapon" of the people; he was "against using the power of the government to help people to whom the government belongs." Taking "flat issue" with Wilson's understanding of liberty, Roosevelt returned to the core theme of his campaign—the essential connection between mass democracy and a new, more meaningful understanding of freedom:

> We propose to use the government as the most efficient instrument for the uplift of our people as a whole; we propose to give a fair chance to the workers and strengthen their rights. We propose to use the whole power of the government to protect all those who, under Mr. Wilson's *laissez faire* system, are trodden down in the ferocious, scrambling rush of an unregulated and purely individualistic industrialism.[94]

Roosevelt had adeptly drawn the philosophical differences between the New Nationalism and New Freedom, but he had not adequately answered the concerns of many reformers that big business might capture a federal trade commission. Roosevelt denied that he would destroy free enterprise or legalize monopoly. He, too, favored strengthening the Sherman Act but thought that harnessing private power, whether in the form of antitrust measures or proscribing abusive business practices, required the creation of administrative tribunals. It was folly to believe that effective control of big business could be achieved through lawsuits arbitrated by the courts. Roosevelt might have better withstood the assault of Brandeis and Wilson, however, had the Progressive platform specifically endorsed strengthening the Sherman Act. The omission of an antitrust plank, especially given the charge that Perkins had excised one from the final version of the platform, McCarthy lamented, allowed Roosevelt's rivals to claim that "it would be an easy thing to have the commission appointed by the president under corporation influences and then have this commission, without any responsibility to Congress or to the people, make what rulings it would see fit." The way the Progressive platform and, for most of the campaign, Roosevelt championed a national commission cut against the grain of American core values that shunned centralized power, McCarthy knew. "It was too great a power to give to any commission and it gave the opponents of the Progressive Party an opportunity to excite suspicion against it."[95]

"The People Themselves Must Be the Ultimate Makers of Their Constitution": The Progressive Faith in Public Opinion

Although there were many questions on which reformers were deeply divided, there was one party doctrine that unified the disparate strands of progressivism: faith in public opinion and direct democracy reform. As Roosevelt said in his "Confession of Faith," "the first essential of the Progressive programme is the right of the people to rule." This meant, Roosevelt made clear, strengthening the ties between constitutional forms and public opinion. "The people themselves must be the ultimate makers of their own constitution," he proclaimed, "and where their agents differ in the interpretation of the constitution, the people themselves should be given the chance, after full and deliberate judgment, authoritatively to settle what interpretation it is that their representatives shall thereafter adapt as binding."[96]

Just as surely as the Progressive Party's program to reform the political economy betrayed fundamental disagreements in its ranks, so this program of direct government, advocating the universal use of the direct primary; the direct election of senators; the initiative, referendum, and recall; and a more expeditious mechanism to amend the Constitution, elicited a shared sense of endeavor. During the general election, therefore, Roosevelt made the recall of judicial decisions, the most controversial plank of the Progressives' direct government program, a central part of his 1912 campaign. Indeed, Roosevelt announced toward the end of September, in a speech in Denver, Colorado, that he "should be glad to have the recall for the president." "It is not in the Progressive platform, and this is merely the expression of my opinion," Roosevelt admitted. But his own experience

> was that I could do nothing as President except when the people were heartedly with me. The minute I ceased to have them with me, whether it was my fault or theirs, I ceased to have power. Under such conditions I would prefer to leave the Presidency, unless in fair open fighting on the stump I could bring the people around to my way of thinking. Such a course, I think, would be to my advantage and theirs.

"Roosevelt tonight exceeded the speed limit in radicalism," a startled *New York Times* correspondent reported. "He went further in his speech at the Denver Auditorium than he has ever gone before, by declaring his willingness to have the recall extended to the Presidency."[97]

In fact, Roosevelt's support for the recall of the president was not made without considerable forethought. As noted in Chapter 4, it had been discussed at the time the Progressive Party platform was being prepared, and the Wisconsin reformer, Charles McCarthy, concerned that the people would fear the administrative aggrandizement prescribed by the new party, urged TR to make it part of his convention speech. Such a proposal, McCarthy argued, was consistent with the Progressive program, which was "not a platform but a covenant with the people." TR decided not to make his support for the recall of the president explicit in his "Confession of Faith," but his admonition that leaders should "not try to continue in office against the will . . . of the people" more than hinted at his agreement with McCarthy. As TR's cousin and personal aide, George Emlen Roosevelt, responded to the Wisconsin reformer, "You know perfectly well that [TR] believes in the principles of the Recall of the President." The "great question," he added, was when TR should announce his support for such a proposal. "I know that this subject is prominently in the Colonel's mind, as I talk with him about it frequently, and you may be sure that he will bring it forward if he thinks it necessary." At McCarthy's urging, Gifford Pinchot also agreed "to take that matter of Presidential recall up with the Colonel the first time I see him, and shall try to see him very soon. It seems to me it ought to be very fully considered just at this time."[98]

Roosevelt came close to publicly proclaiming his support for recall of the president during his kickoff address in Providence, Rhode Island, yet stopped short of explicitly stepping beyond the commitments of the Progressive Party's platform. But the constant attack of Wilson and Brandeis on his plan to expand the responsibilities of the executive prompted Roosevelt to elaborate on his strongly held view that the solution of America's ills was not to restrain presidential power, which the Democratic platform explicitly prescribed, but, rather, to democratize it. TR's choice of Denver to amplify the idea of "pure democracy" was provoked by William Jennings Bryan, who toured Colorado just before Roosevelt's swing through the state. During a stop in Pueblo, Bryan challenged TR to answer a question that had haunted the colonel since he threw his "hat in the ring": "How many terms may a President serve?" Roosevelt's answer to the Great Commoner was to let the people decide. After announcing his support for presidential recall,

TR added, "Mr. Bryan professes to believe in the people. It was to the people that I made my appeal, and in the primaries by votes varying from two to one to fifteen to one the people decided that the talk of a third term in this case was the veriest bugaboo ever held up to frighten political children." To another query from Bryan, suggesting that such plebiscitary measures as the referendum and recall should be confined to the states, Roosevelt observed, in what the press described as a "note of finality," "They are national and State issues both. The Democratic Party has dodged them, but the Progressives are not afraid of them."[99]

Roosevelt repeated, indeed further expanded, his unflinching support for direct government a few days later. In a speech in Phoenix, Arizona, he pledged, "I would go even further than the Progressive Platform. I should like to have the recall applied to *everybody,* including the President." TR "stands upon the bald doctrine of unrestricted majority rule," the *Nation* responded. "But it is just against the dangers threatened, by such majority rule, in those crises that try the temper of nations, that the safeguard of constitutional government as the outgrowth of ages of experience has been erected."[100] The *New York Times,* the most fervent journalistic guardian of constitutional sobriety, was, if possible, even more scandalized than the *Nation* editors. Comparing Roosevelt to radicals in France, its editors scorned militant Progressives who were "eager to remove all constitutional limitations in the way of enacting social justice." Given Roosevelt's stated desire to go beyond the Progressive platform, the *Times* warned, his election would mean that "the proposals of the Progressive platform are likely to be a starting point instead of a goal, and whoever limits himself to the platform will be in danger of arguments such as are unfamiliar to the participants in parlor debates on Socialism as a route to social justice." In excoriating Roosevelt, the editorial did not deny the need for reform. Alluding to Wilson's New Freedom, which proposed to combine progressive economic policies and constitutional conservatism, the *Times* urged reformers to exercise restraint: "If the Progressive crusaders would distinguish between opposition to their aspirations and their methods, perhaps they would find that many who are unable to approve their methods would support a more reasonable programme toward the same end."[101] Still, Roosevelt would never have the opportunity to remake America, the conservative newspaper predicted: "He was a lawless President for seven years. The country had enough of him in his two terms."[102]

Roosevelt would not be elected, of course. But the third party's pledge to forge a national democracy and Roosevelt's expressed willingness to go even further than the Progressive platform in empowering the court of public opinion stirred considerable enthusiasm in the country. Although the Progressives' faith in unmediated, national mass public opinion appeared to threaten valued traditions in the United States, such as federalism and the separation of powers, their celebration of the rights of the people resonated with the public at a time when industrial capitalism and urbanization threatened the integrity of local and state governments. The Progressive defense of direct rule of the people, in fact, capitalized on the commitment to popular sovereignty in the tradition of local self-government, embodied in such institutions as New England town meetings, which coexisted uneasily with strong local and state party organizations. Indeed, one early progressive tract that defended direct government made this connection between the nineteenth-century concept of self-government and the progressive idea of democracy explicit:

> Direct legislation is law-enacting by the electors themselves as distinguished from law-enacting by representatives or by some aristocratic body, or by a single ruler, such as the king, emperor, or czar. In small communities this is accomplished by electors meeting together voting on every law or ordinance by which they are to be governed. This is done in New England town meetings. . . . In communities too widespread or too numerous for the voters to meet together and decide on the laws by which they are to be governed, Direct Legislation is accomplished by the use of imperative petitions, through what is known as the Initiative and Referendum.[103]

Interestingly, conservatives abroad saw the appeal of direct democracy more clearly than their American brethren. Roosevelt was not a radical, the conservative *Le Figaro* insisted. "M. Roosevelt's role in American politics in the last seven or eight years, his position seemingly so strange in the current struggle, are the result of the current situation caused by [the Progressive] movement," the French newspaper's American correspondent wrote. "M. Roosevelt has understood that this middle-class movement, although complicated because gathering different interests and passions, is tied in one point to the simple but strong and healthy idealism that characterized the Union at its beginnings. And he has also understood that this movement was in part the reaction of puritan and democratic tradition against the excesses and disorder of a civilization which is very powerful and brilliant but also full of vices and impure desires." Roosevelt's strategy to mobilize middle-class support to undertake reforms necessary to meet important economic and social changes was not unlike those "adopted by all conservative parties when they felt threatened by the growing discontent of working classes. And this can explain the anger, mistrust, [and] enthusiasm that M. Roosevelt fans in the Union; the blame for demagoguery put on him by many of his old friends; but also the surprises that came in this struggle and those that will come." Like those who scorned his attempt to return to past political mastery in the United States, many French statesmen and intellectuals "saw Roosevelt as a sort of future dictator" before his visit to the Sorbonne during the 1910 European tour. But most of these skeptics "were disappointed when they could watch him closely in Europe. He was very simple and naïve, this so-called despot! But it is precisely this simplicity of ideas, with a determined and self-confident will, which has generated his immense popularity."[104]

Roosevelt was neither simple nor naïve. He knew that in America conservatism was defined, as James Madison anticipated, by the sort of "veneration" for the Constitution without which "the wisest and freest governments would not possess the requisite stability."[105] And yet, American social and economic conditions, remade by the industrial revolution, provided an opening for doctrinal and institutional change that Roosevelt brilliantly exploited. Highlighting what it termed the "new tendencies of the old spirit," the conservative London *Times* observed that the Progressive Party's political program helped explain the wide appeal of Roosevelt's reformist politics in the midst of relatively prosperous conditions in the United States. "Just as in England it is probably the case that many who call themselves Conservatives have found themselves in unexpected sympathy with the principles of parliamentary reform," the *Times* correspondent wrote, alluding to the Liberal Party's reform of the House of Lords, "so in America the most salient result of that 'national stocktaking' which Mr. Roosevelt has done so much to bring about has been the sudden distrust of the infallibility of American institutions." This national debate, fueled by TR's popular insurgency, roiled venerable ideas and political practices—subjecting them to doubt and experimentation that were fundamentally transforming America:

> It is no longer taken for granted that American institutions are "the best in the world." . . . The Constitution is no longer universally sacrosanct: the drawbacks of a somewhat atrophied system of representative government are no longer accepted simply because the "Fathers of

the Country" decreed such government; the limitations of federal power are criticized; and there are doubts as to whether the legislative authority of the Courts is, after all, the main bulwark of American liberty. Can a system of government conceived when industries were local, when steam and electricity were unknown, still be all sufficient when single enterprises bestride the continent, and when colonization is beginning to roll back from the Pacific into the congested areas of 20th century industrial cities? Such is the main question propounded by Mr. Roosevelt's New Nationalism and the unequivocal affirmative of leaders of conservative thought fails to hide Mr. Roosevelt's uncanny grasp of the essentials of a problem that is vexing many minds.

Roosevelt's insurgency, the *Times* boldly declared, had intensified unrest that "utterly destroyed the old time complacent conservatism of the Republicans."[106]

We should be reluctant to dismiss these observations as the whimsy of international journalists. Observing Roosevelt's tour on the ground, the prominent Progressive Benjamin Lindsey, admittedly not an unbiased source, expressed surprised delight at how enthusiastically crowds responded to TR's Denver speech. Whereas Bryan had drawn barely five thousand people to an auditorium in the western city, Roosevelt enticed a throng of fifteen thousand to the same venue, and "just about as many more" were turned away. Whereas Colorado tradition dictated that people did not turn out for political events during bad weather, Lindsey enthused that the gathering that transpired despite poor weather conditions "made the enormous out-pouring all the more significant." More to the point, he reported, "Our people were delighted with all that the Colonel had to say. I haven't heard a single criticism."[107]

Of course, there were serious criticisms of Roosevelt's "drastic departure," as the *San Francisco Examiner* put it.[108] Moreover, for all the enthusiasm Roosevelt generated in the state, Colorado Progressives conceded that he could do no more in all likelihood than split the Republican ranks and ensure a Democratic victory. Nonetheless, Roosevelt's effective campaign for direct government set the tone of the election. It not only relegated Taft's unstinting campaign for constitutional sobriety to virtual irrelevance but also forced Wilson and his political allies to come to terms with the Progressive Party's political program. Amid the celebration of pure democracy, Samuel Gompers pointed out with pride "that the American Federation of Labor was the first organized body of men in the United States officially to endorse direct legislation and to demand that the Initiative, Referendum, and Recall be added to the political tool chest of the people." Without directly crediting Roosevelt or the Progressive Party, the *American Federationist* noted the dramatic change in popular support for direct government in 1912. "In 1892 Labor could not get the old party politicians within a mile of a pledge to support Direct Legislation, save in rare instances," Judson King, field secretary of the National Referendum League, wrote in an essay that appeared in the October 1912 edition of the AFL's magazine. "In 1912 thousands of old party and new party politicians are imploring voters to elect them to State Legislatures, or make them governors, presidents, or what not, because they are in favor of the Initiative and Referendum. . . . The stone which politicians once rejected has become the threshold of entrance to the political temple."[109]

Nor was the matter of direct government simply a local and state matter, as Bryan had claimed in shadowing Roosevelt during the general election campaign. As a matter of informal practice, progressive principles had transformed the executive. Whether or not the measures he advocated were enacted, Roosevelt's candidacy signaled a critical change in American constitutional government. As Gompers wrote toward the end of the campaign, "In discussing problems of American legislation for great reforms, it must be borne in mind that one of the most significant developments in the unwritten constitution of the United States, is the increasing prestige and authority attached to the office of the President." Even as it rejected Roosevelt's insurgent candidacy, therefore, the AFL embraced the premise of his campaign: "As a result of popular distrust of Federal legislative bodies and of the fact that of Congress only the House of Representatives is directly responsible to the people, the people have come to look upon the President as their representative and defender against what is often a gigantic merger of political 'holdings' and financial 'holdings,'" Gompers observed. "Thus backed by the sanction of public opinion, the President has had more power to shape the course of legislation and to stamp policies with his own convictions and personality." More than ever before, Gompers concluded, "choosing the man who is to wield this tremendous power for four years, is a matter of grave importance and consequence."[110]

In the wake of the excitement stirred by Roosevelt's western tour, Wilson and his political allies recognized that the Democratic candidate would have to stake out his own strong position on political reform. Encouraged by Brandeis, the New Jersey governor had emphasized a militant antitrust program as the proper avenue to restore self-government in the United States.

But during his tour of New England in late September, Wilson began to identify himself more clearly as a champion of the whole people. With his "Speech on New Issues," delivered in Hartford, Connecticut, on September 25, the press reported, Wilson "went further . . . toward defining his ideas toward progressive principles than he has since he became the Democratic nominee." This address, which "was received with enthusiasm," saw Wilson strongly defend the direct election of senators; popular primaries; and the "extreme doctrines of the initiative, the referendum, and the recall."[111] Wilson pointedly stopped short of embracing Roosevelt's proposal to give voters the right to recall judicial decisions, even as he accepted the Progressives' indictment of courts restricting the authority of the federal government and states to curb the abuses of big business. The judiciary, Wilson said to loud applause, "is the last and ultimate safeguard of the things that we want to hold stable in this country." "If I did not believe that to be a progressive was to preserve the essence of our institutions, I for one could not be progressive," he insisted.[112]

And yet Wilson did not emphasize the Constitution in his defense of "ancient rootages," as Taft did. Instead, he celebrated the Declaration of Independence, which he claimed as the "foundation" of his progressive principles. He argued that the direct primary, which most self-styled conservatives skewered as an attack on representative government, followed logically from the creed Americans celebrated on Independence Day:

> What do you talk about on the Fourth of July — if you are talking in public? You talk about the Declaration of Independence . . . and there we read this uncompromising sentence, that when at any time the people of a commonwealth find that their governments are not suitable to the circumstances of their lives or the promotion of their liberty, then they are privileged to alter them at their pleasure. That is the foundation, that is the central doctrine, that is the ancient vision of America with regard to affairs, and this arrangement of the direct primary simply squares with that. If they cannot find men whom they can trust to select their tickets, they will select them for themselves.[113]

Wilson extended his defense of a progressive measure that would change an unwritten rule of the American Constitution, attenuating the buffer that party organizations established between mass opinion and candidate selection, to the written Constitution. Invoking Walter Bagehot's refrain that the

U.S. Constitution worked so well "not because it was an excellent constitution" but because the "Americans could run any constitution," Wilson strongly advocated the direct election of senators. This was a "compliment, which lay like sweet unction to our souls," the Democratic candidate told his audience; nonetheless, it was also "a criticism which ought to set us thinking." As they had done throughout their history, he instructed, the American people ought to think constitutionally, to deliberate on how to improve on the formal law given changing political and economic circumstances. Alluding to the role he alleged "bosses" played as a conduit between state legislatures and big business, Wilson granted that "when American forces are awake they can conduct American affairs without serious departure from the ideals of the Constitution." Nonetheless, he added, it was impossible to deny that "we have many shameful instances of practices which we can absolutely remove by the direct election of senators." No one who knew history, the former professor stated, could say "that I am acting inconsistently with either the spirit or the form of the American government in advocating the direct election of senators."[114]

Similarly, although measures of direct legislation—the initiative, the referendum, and the recall—made "most men shrink," Wilson insisted that these reforms had been adopted in various states to strengthen, rather than weaken, representative government: "The most eager advocates of these reforms have always said that they were intended to recover representative government, that they had no place where those who were elected to legislative chambers were really representative of the communities which they professed to serve." Wilson more than hinted, however, that these measures would establish a direct link between representatives and public opinion. Like the militant advocates of pure democracy in the third party, he argued that the initiative, referendum, and recall were an extension of institutions like the New England town meeting, applying the virtues of local self-government to mass democracy:

> Nobody in New England ought to find any very grave objections to the recall of administrative officers, because in most parts of New England the ordinary administrative term is a single twelvemonth. You haven't been willing in New England to trust any man out of your sight more than twelve months, so that your elections are a sort of continuous performance based on the very fundamental idea that we are discussing—that we will not take your own hands off your own

affairs. That is the principle of the recall. I don't see how any man who is grounded in the traditions of American affairs, particularly as they derive their origins from New England, can find any valid objection to the recall of administrative offices.[115]

In defending measures of direct legislation, Wilson surpassed the Democratic platform in championing popular government. Indeed, he came close to Roosevelt in defending a constitutional position that would greatly reduce the space between representatives and public opinion by rooting in legislation and custom the principle that public officials derived their authority directly from the people. William Randolph Hearst, whose newspapers had strongly supported Champ Clark during the Democratic primaries, had been reluctant to endorse Wilson. Although the Hearst papers had been very critical of Roosevelt's ostensible support of big business, their editorial pages had consistently defended his program of pure democracy. It is probably no coincidence, then, that Wilson's tour of New England coincided with the news that Hearst was throwing his support to the Democratic candidate.[116] Applauding Wilson's stepped-up attack on the "bosses," a Hearst editorial stated, "Progressives of all parties—Democratic, Independent and Republican—note with eminent satisfaction that Governor Wilson in his recent speeches is swinging into the aggressive campaign which deserves and will win success."[117]

To be sure, Wilson's defense of natural rights and the courts circumscribed his defense of direct government. Not only did he stop short of calling for popular referenda on court decisions, he also said nothing about the need to modify the amendment process so as to expedite constitutional change. Still, his defense of individual rights and limited government wavered somewhat during the New England tour. Clarifying his position on restricting the powers of the national government, which Roosevelt had attacked with such alacrity, Wilson stated in New Haven, where he kicked off the Connecticut campaign, that Jeffersonian principles and the Democratic Party had to change in order to address the problems of the twentieth century: "I feel confident that if Jefferson had lived in our day, he would see what we see—that the individual is caught in a great confused nexus of all sorts of complicated circumstances, and that to let him alone is to leave him helpless as against the obstacles with which he has to contend, that, therefore, law in our day must come to the assistance of the individual." Nonetheless, Wilson insisted, the expansion of government in the states and at the national level should empower, not denigrate the dignity of, the democratic individual. It followed, therefore, that the expansion of the national government had to be governed by laws, not administrative fiat. "We [the Democratic Party] want to see the law administered; we are not afraid of commissions. . . . But I am absolutely opposed to leaving it to the choice of those tribunals what the process of law shall be and the means of remedy."[118]

In the view of Roosevelt and Croly, of course, Wilson's position was a fairy tale—it ignored the necessity of administrative aggrandizement, which could only be ameliorated by reconstituting the executive so that it would be immediately accountable to public opinion. But Wilson wanted to reform and not diminish the law. As he had acknowledged in the Hartford address, Wilson joined his Progressive opponents in believing that the courts—the "safeguard" of American liberty—had been "corrupted," so much so that judges tended to guard "merely the interests of a very small group of individuals." But the waywardness of judges was "the symptom instead of the disease." Not surprisingly, Wilson attributed the disease to an unsavory partnership between business and government. Disentangling this alliance, and removing big business from the "seat of privilege" it enjoyed in the councils of government, was the exalted yet practical mission for an expanded federal government. Tariff reform, Wilson proposed, would mark the first battle in this campaign to restore individual opportunity and economic competition. "The Democrats . . . propose to unearth those special privileges and to cut them out of the tariff. They propose not to leave a single concealed private advantage in the statutes concerning duties that can possibly be eradicated without affecting the part of the business that is sound and legitimate and which we all wish to see promoted."[119]

During his New England tour, then, Wilson clarified his differences with Roosevelt and stated emphatically that he proposed an alternative program of reform. As he concluded his Hartford address, "You have your complete series, therefore, of suspicions about nominations for office, about the election of United States senators, about the rejection of laws traced down to the taproot—this great colossal system of special privilege, on account of which men feel obliged to keep their hands upon the sources of power."[120] Nonetheless, in going so far to embrace progressive democracy, in stepping up his critique of existing constitutional forms in the name of the people, Wilson joined Roosevelt in worshiping at the court of public opinion. For all the differences between the Progressive and Democratic candidates, it was now clear that both championed the expansion of national adminis-trative power, and both insisted that national representatives must use this power in the name of the whole people.

Progressivism at the High Tide of Socialism

Since the start of his long campaign, Roosevelt had argued that unless his call to make political parties and constitutional arrangements more responsive to public opinion was heeded, the American citizenry might look favorably on a more radical alternative. This view was supported by the distinguished Harvard government professor Albert Bushnell Hart during the general election campaign. Noting the growing strength of the Socialist Party in California, he wrote,

> Unless [the] movement is checked, within sixteen years, there will be a Socialist president in the United States. . . . There is only one way to head off that danger, and that is the formation of a party which will take over the reasonable part of the Socialist programme. Neither the Republican nor Democratic party shows any disposition to protect the Nation from this serious danger, and the Progressive party must therefore become the bulwark of the Nation by satisfying the just demands of the people before they go over to Socialism as the only remedy that they see.[121]

Wilson and, even more vehemently, Taft rejected this foreboding and insisted that the vast majority of people in the United States rejected class consciousness and honored a creed that privileged property and individualism. Conservative observers abroad were less sure. As the London *Times* warned, general conditions of prosperity in the country had not stalled increasing unrest among American workers: "Socialism is growing, syndicalism has broken out, violence in industrial disputes is all too common."[122]

The rise of socialism in 1912 was abetted considerably by a January strike of textile workers, many of them immigrants, in Lawrence, Massachusetts. Sparked by a group of Polish female laborers who abandoned their looms rather than accept a wage cut, more than ten thousand textile laborers, organized by the radical Industrial Workers of the World (IWW) and representing "both sexes of all ages, and numerous nationalities," quit work. Despite their ethnic differences, the ominous presence of state militia, and a brutal police attack on striking families, the workers remained united and stayed the course for eight weeks. IWW head William "Big Bill" Haywood, an advocate of syndicalism, nonetheless counseled against violence and urged workers to seek satisfaction of specific demands through negotiation with the mill owners. By mid-March, the workers won all of their key demands in a labor victory hailed throughout the country.

This triumph had a "stunning effect" on the Socialist movement. Hitherto, the Socialist Party in America had been bitterly divided between two major factions. One was led by Haywood, who rejected Gompers's emphasis on organizing craft (skilled) workers and working with mainstream business and political leaders. Haywood and the IWW celebrated "direct action," which urged industrial workers to ignore politics and to challenge their employers militantly, using violence if necessary. The other was led by Victor Berger, elected to Congress in 1910, who was a strong critic of direct action and an enthusiastic proponent of party-building. These two factions, despite their sharp differences, appeared to come together in the Lawrence strike. Haywood counseled peaceful negotiation while Berger cooperated in the Socialist Party's support of the textile workers, even demanding and obtaining a congressional investigation of the strike that shed unfavorable light on the labor practices of the mill owners. Lawrence Socialists were active in the strike, and the national party gave over $18,000 to the strike fund. The coming together of the two enemy factions and the effective role the Socialist Party played in the Lawrence strike prompted the *International Socialist Review* to exult that the Massachusetts battle "is only the beginning. Its importance lies in the fact that winning tactics have been discovered and have already received the virtual endorsement of the Socialist party of America. Industrial Unionism is no longer an untried theory. Henceforth progress will be swift and sure."[123]

Eugene Debs, the Socialist candidate for president in 1912, also made an important contribution to the growing popularity of the party. Born to immigrant parents in Terre Haute, Indiana, Debs's radicalism was expressed in terms that revealed his Midwestern small-town origins. In fact, the most distinctive feature of Debs's socialism was its sui generis American form. Debs styled himself as the champion of the working class but urged middle-class Americans to join the Socialist crusade, which he portrayed as the fulfillment of the Declaration of Independence. Whereas Wilson invoked the Declaration to inspire moderate reform, Debs celebrated its revolutionary potential. "I like the Fourth of July," Debs said. "It breathes the spirit of revolution. On this day we affirm the ultimate triumph of Socialism."[124] As Debs described this revolutionary sentiment in a rousing address, published in the socialist newspaper the *New York Call,* "The Socialist party exists . . . to . . . place the worker in full command of his natural powers and faculties, so that he may exercise his God-given right as a human being to utilize the resources of his nature, art and invention for the benefit of himself and those dependent upon him."[125]

In celebrating the "unalienable rights" of the Declaration, Debs styled himself as a modern-day Lincoln who rose from humble beginnings to become a great champion of an American cause that appealed to universal principles. "All the world knows Lincoln's [Gettysburg address]," he told the *Brooklyn Daily Eagle,* "because it was made to all the world. And yet Lincoln came from the depths. From the depths Lincoln rose—from poverty and misery, and by the greatness of his heart and soul he raised all mankind with him."[126] Just as the Progressives took heart from the realignment of the 1850s, which witnessed the triumph of a new party, so Debs viewed the abolition of slavery as inspiration for the fulfillment of America's toiling masses:

> That a realignment of political forces in this country is inevitable must be apparent to even the most superficial observer. The situation is similar to the one which existed previous to the Civil War. The issue then was chattel slavery; it is now wage slavery. The basis of the conflict then was the right of the black man to own himself and to control his own destiny: to be regarded as something higher than a brute, and to enter upon the struggle for existence upon moral terms with his white brother. . . . The issue of chattel slavery, which was . . . settled at such an enormous cost of human life pales into insignificance besides the question of wage slavery which confronts the nation today. The question of chattel slavery involved merely the limited and qualified liberty of three million wealth producers of the black race. The question of wage slavery involves the complete liberty of every producer of wealth without reference to race or color. Whether this vastly greater question of wage slavery shall be settled without another terrible physical conflict will depend largely upon the action of the workers in the present campaign.[127]

Under Debs's leadership, the Socialist Party reached its peak of national popularity, so much so that by 1912 a growing number of reformers had come to view it as a reasonable alternative to the two major parties. Debs was a stirring orator who drew large crowds to his campaign events, even though the Socialist Party, unlike the other contenders in 1912, charged admission to hear their presidential candidate speak. In Philadelphia, eighteen thousand people crammed into Convention Hall, where Debs praised the modern relevance of the Declaration; at Madison Square Garden in New York, people paid from twenty-five cents to a dollar to hear Debs, thus contributing an estimated $10,000 to the campaign.[128]

Although the 1912 presidential campaign was the fourth time that Debs had run for president—he also was the Socialist standard-bearer in 1900, 1904, and 1908—this was the first in which his oratorical gifts and popularity were matched with a strong organization. Between 1910 and 1912, Ira Kipnis has written, "the Socialist party reached the zenith of its power, prestige, and influence. . . . In dues paying membership, in national and local union influence, in votes polled, and in members elected and appointed to political office the party attained new and sudden stature."[129] In 1910 Victor Berger became the first Socialist elected to Congress; the 1911 elections saw Americans elect some 450 Socialist officials, including 56 mayors and 305 aldermen and city councilmen. Part and parcel of this electoral success was the development of a strong Socialist press: the party had 5 English-language dailies and 262 English-language weeklies as well as many foreign-language newspapers. The most popular Socialist paper, *Appeal to Reason,* included Debs as a contributing editor: soon after Debs joined the *Appeal* in 1907, its circulation rose from 250,000 to half a million; by 1912 its circulation reached 761,747.[130]

Most important, the Socialist Party seemed poised in 1912 to flower into an American social democratic organization, to play the same sort of role in remaking politics in the United States that social democrats were undertaking in Germany and Great Britain. For the first time, the Socialists would have full party slates in every state. No less critical, for the first time the Socialist platform pronounced against "violence as a weapon of the working classes," signifying that the moderate wing of the party, committed to political rather than "direct" action, had secured control of the campaign.[131] The adoption of this plank at the Socialist convention in May built on the momentum of the successful settlement of the Lawrence strike through peaceful negotiation. Nevertheless, the rejection of direct action and the embrace of electoral politics did not take place without a heated debate, which ended with the expulsion of the party's most radical elements. Although Haywood sanctioned moderation in the Lawrence strike, he refused to give general approval of peaceful tactics. Indeed, in the middle of the Lawrence episode, the IWW leader gave a speech at the Cooper Union in New York City, published by *International Socialist Review,* that took a swipe at Berger and denigrated party-building efforts by stating that he would rather workers could elect a factory superintendent than a congressman. Haywood then told the Cooper Union audience that his formative organizing efforts in the western mines had taught him to scorn peaceful negotiation. "No Socialist can be a law abiding citizen," Haywood insisted. "When we come together . . . to overthrow the capitalist system, we become conspirators then against the United States government." "Coercion," he concluded, was the best way to achieve industrial democracy.[132]

Debs, who usually stayed out of factional battles, took on Haywood and his radical IWW allies directly. In the same issue of the *Review* that carried Haywood's speech, Debs insisted that the Socialist Party must employ tactics "adapted to the American people and to American conditions." He understood the contempt that some of his labor brethren had for laws, such as the tariff, that protected capitalism, but he would not "make an individual lawbreaker" of himself. Moreover, Debs insisted that American workers were "law-abiding" and would never support a party that prescribed direct action. Measures of coercion were "reactionary, not revolutionary," he argued. Such tactics played directly "into the hands of the enemy": secrecy and stealth would expose industrial unions to anarchists, fracture the movement, and leave those remaining loyalists "responsible for the deed of every spy or madman."[133]

Debs did not attend the Socialist convention, held in Indianapolis—a testament to his determination to stay out of factional party struggles—but his strong opposition to Haywood bestowed on moderates like Berger and Morris Hillquit, a New York City labor lawyer, the moral authority they needed to pass the motion that rejected direct action. Moreover, Emil Seidel, a political ally of Berger who had recently been mayor of Milwaukee, was chosen as Debs's running mate. Another moderate, J. Mahlon Barnes, was named campaign manager. Following the convention, the New York State Socialist Party sponsored a national referendum to punish Haywood for his Cooper Union address by expelling him from the National Executive Committee: the referendum passed easily, with Haywood receiving less than one-third of the votes cast and carrying only ten state organizations, all but Tennessee and West Virginia in the far West or Southwest.[134]

Consequently, for the first time since its founding at the turn of the century, the Socialist Party and its popular standard-bearer ran a campaign dedicated to peaceful negotiation and participation in the electoral process. This change was duly noted in the mainstream press. "Debs is not a revolutionist in the sense of social warfare," the *Brooklyn Daily Eagle* trumpeted. "He believes in a social revolution through the gospel of politics."[135] A lengthy favorable profile of Debs in the conservative *New York Sun* also expressed approval of the Socialist Party's evolution. Those advocating "methods of violence as a weapon of the working class, to aid in its emancipation, shall be expelled from membership in the party," the *Sun* reported. "Political action shall be construed to mean participation in elections for public office and practical legislative and administrative work along the lines of the Socialist platform."[136]

Given the growing strength of the Socialist Party, it is not surprising that Roosevelt and the Progressive Party deliberately sought to steal its thunder. Invoking the red flag of socialism, Roosevelt chose the crimson bandana handkerchief as the symbol of his campaign, thus hoping to signal to potential Debs supporters that the Progressives represented an alternative form of radicalism, one more likely to take root in America. Adopted as the "Roosevelt battle flag" soon after TR and his followers bolted from the Republican Party, the bandana, insurgents told the press, "stands for the plain people who ordinarily use them."[137] Symbolism was joined to programmatic ambition. The Progressive Party platform, especially the plank on "Social and Industrial Justice," endorsed many of the objectives championed by the Socialist Party: the regulation of hours and wages; the prohibition of child labor; support for a graduated income tax; the adoption of a system of social insurance that would protect against the hazards of old age, sickness, and unemployment; and equal suffrage for men and women. As Fred Warren, the managing editor of *Appeal to Reason,* wrote Debs after the Progressive Party convention, "My prediction that Roosevelt would steal our platform bodily has been fulfilled. I am also firmly convinced that he is to be the central figure around which the campaign will be waged this year."[138]

Warren and Debs could not have been comforted by a report in the *New York Times* that Robert W. Bruere, a prominent New York Socialist, participated in the development of the Progressive Party's platform and Roosevelt's "Confession of Faith" address. Bruere and TR gently refuted this story: Bruere would only admit that he "heard Mr. Roosevelt read a section of [his convention] speech one afternoon in July at Oyster Bay"; Roosevelt would only acknowledge that he hoped to make his campaign acceptable to "the social workers in the big cities" and thus invited a number of reformers, including Bruere, to review the Progressive platform and to hear his "Confession of Faith." But these mild rejoinders did not impress most members of the New York County Executive Committee of the Socialist Party, who, the *Times* reported, were "highly incensed" to learn of Bruere's complicit behavior.[139]

Fearful that the Progressives would short-circuit the Socialist movement just as it had begun to emerge as an important rival to the Democrats and Republicans, Debs spent a good part of the general election campaign attempting to refute Roosevelt's reform credentials. Debs's fixation was no doubt intensified by "inquiries pouring into Terre Haute" asking the Socialist leader "to express his opinion of the Progressive party platform."[140] "The really progressive planks in the Progressive platform were taken from the Socialist platform," he responded to such an inquiry from the *New York Times*, "and even the Red flag of Socialism was appropriated, or at least imitated by the red bandana of the Roosevelt followers." Like Robert La Follette, whom Roosevelt outflanked as a reform leader during the Republican primary contests, Debs warned "the many honest and progressive spirited people" who were attracted to his rival that the new party could not last. The Progressive Party was "built largely upon the personality of one man and no great party has ever been reared upon that kind of a foundation," he insisted.[141] Like La Follette, too, Debs scorned Roosevelt for being a late convert to progressive democracy and for embracing planks in the new party's platform "which he denounced as treason and anarchy when he was President." But the Socialist candidate insisted that progressive democracy itself was fool's gold. "Mr. Roosevelt has shrewdly seized upon the prevailing popular unrest and has baited his platform like a trap to catch the votes of the discontented people," he stated. In fact, Debs argued, the Progressive Party was "reactionary." "In the aggregate it is a middle class protest against trust domination," he insisted.[142]

From Debs's perspective, the fact that Roosevelt made "pure democracy" the centerpiece of his crusade confirmed the Progressive Party campaign as retrograde. To be sure, Debs and the Socialists strongly advocated political reform. The Socialist platform called for the "adoption of the initiative, referendum and recall and of proportional representation nationally as well as locally"; the "abolition of the Senate"; and the "election of the President and Vice President by direct vote of the people." These planks showed that, unlike the radical wing of his party, which he helped to purge from the Socialist councils, Debs privileged persuasion over coercion. Nonetheless, Debs feared that exalting direct democracy as the centerpiece of reform risked obscuring the injustices of capitalism that were at the root of the people's discontent. Whereas Gompers celebrated the AFL's enduring commitment to direct legislation, Debs had long cast skepticism on investing too much faith in public opinion. "You will never be able, in my opinion, to organize any formidable movement upon [the referendum] or any other single issue," he wrote in 1898. "The battle is narrowing down to capitalism and socialism, and there can be no compromise or half-way ground. In the present state of ignorance of the masses the referendum would probably be a suicidal weapon in their hands. Not until the workingman comprehends the trend of . . . economic development and is conscious of his class interests will he be fit to properly use the referendum, and when he has reached that point he will be a Socialist."[143]

The excitement stirred by Roosevelt's "covenant" with the people during the 1912 election could only have heightened the urgency that Debs and his comrades felt to highlight the choice between capitalism and socialism. Just as the Progressive platform began with a paean to popular rule, so the Socialist platform started with a denunciation of capitalism. "The capitalist system has outgrown its historical function," the platform read, "and has become utterly incapable of meeting the problems now confronting society. We denounce this outgrown system as incompetent and corrupt and the source of unspeakable misery and suffering to the whole working class." The repudiation of capitalism was also the theme of Debs's passionate essay "Why You Should Vote for Socialism," which the *Appeal to Reason* published in late August. "You must either vote for or against your own material interests as a wealth producer," he began; "there is no political purgatory in this nation of ours despite the desperate efforts of so-called progressive capitalist politicians to establish one. Socialism alone represents the material heaven of plenty for those who toil and the Socialist party alone offers the political means for attaining the heaven of economic plenty which the toil of the workers of the world provides in unceasing and measureless flow."

That only the Socialist Party stood for the collective ownership of production, Debs stated, distinguished his campaign as the distinctively meaningful voice of progress in the election. "Beside the terrible facts of capitalism, how puerile, how utterly imbecile is the chatter [of the Republicans, Democrats, and Progressives] about the 'tariff,' the 'control of the corporation,' the 'dignity of the courts,' 'the theft of delegates to national conventions of capitalist parties' and a hundred other so-called 'issues' with which capitalism seeks to cozen the worker out of his vote." A vote for Socialism, Debs added, would truly fulfill the country's democratic potential. "Can you, my fellow workers, justify a vote of confidence in capitalism in the face of this terrible indictment?" he asked. "Surely the daily experience of your own life and the experience of those who are dear to you is a more terrific indictment of capitalism than mortal man can pen."[144]

And yet, the American people were interested in these "puerile issues." Indeed, next to New Nationalism and New Freedom, Socialist doctrine, even when conveyed in Debs's "Americanized" version, seemed elusive. In the struggle for the mantle of reform leader, Debs was simply outflanked by Roosevelt and Wilson. In the final analysis, their faith in public opinion and their willingness to come to terms with the puerilities of American democracy represented a necessary compromise with the widespread fear of a centralized state in the United States. Debs, too, understood this fear, and he sought to address it by denouncing the executive aggrandizement that Roosevelt's program appeared to portend. For example, the Socialist platform, proscribing the veto, sought to restrain presidential power. Nonetheless, the Socialists' insistence on "collective ownership" threatened a radical assault on deeply ingrained American values such as individualism, private property, and local self-government.

The Progressive celebration of public opinion thus short-circuited the development of a social democratic party in America. As Herbert Croly explained in *Progressive Democracy*, many well-meaning social democrats in England or France, as well as the United States, favored the formation of a national programmatic party as a vanguard of social and economic reform. Such devotees of a permanent social democratic party disdained direct popular government, Croly pointed out, because they expected that, at least in the near future, direct popular government, dependent on the vagaries of public opinion, would increase the difficulty of securing the adoption of many items in a desirable social program. Herein they were right, Croly acknowledged. But reformers of this sort attached too much importance to the accomplishment and maintenance of specific results and not enough to the permanent social welfare of democracy: "An authoritative representative government, particularly one which is associated with inherited leadership and a strong party system, carries with it enormous prestige. It is frequently in a position either to ignore, to circumvent or to wear down popular opposition. But a social program purchased at such a price is not worth what it costs."[145]

Debs received more than 900,000 votes in 1912, around 6 percent of the total, which was more than double the support he had garnered four years earlier (see Chapter 6 for a detailed analysis of the voting results). This was the best showing of a socialist party in a presidential election in American history. By most accounts, however, the Socialists' vote would have been greater still in 1912 had the Progressive Party not stolen its thunder. Roosevelt's intervention seemed to be especially effective in gaining the support of moderate social democrats, like Learned Hand, toward whom the Socialist Party made a deliberate appeal during the 1912 campaign. Those addressing the timeless question of why no socialism exists in America would thus be well served to consider Roosevelt's appeal to middle-class reformers. The Progressive Party campaign of 1912 suggests that America's liberal tradition and constitutional heritage only partially inoculated the country against social democracy.[146] Roosevelt's millennial appeal to the people gave important political effect to these cultural and institutional dimensions of American politics.

Conclusion: The Triumph of the "Modern" Campaign

The Progressive Party's celebration of direct rule of the people was not reactionary, as Debs charged. Roosevelt's insurgent campaign united disaffected Republicans, muckraking journalists, Social Gospel evangelists, progressive academics, and social workers behind a program of middle-class radicalism that posed fundamental challenges to social contract theory and constitutional forms. Of course, as Roosevelt's mating dance with moderate socialists suggests, the middle-class character of the Bull Moose campaign circumscribed the extent of its assault on the old order. Indeed, the Progressive Party's rejection of natural rights, in the name of a national democracy, contributed to its compromises with Jim Crow and big business, thus giving it the appearance of a "hybrid aggregation," as Debs put it, composed of reformist and reactionary elements.[147] Moreover, Taft's virtual abdication during the general election reduced the contest to a choice between New Nationalism and New Freedom, which some reformers dismissed as insignificant. These two reform programs, the Progressive journalist William Allen White claimed many years later, were separated by "that fantastic imaginary gulf that always has existed between tweedle-dum and tweedle-dee."[148]

Nonetheless, the contrast between the constitutional sobriety of both the Taft and Wilson campaigns, on the one hand, and the Roosevelt campaign, on the other, points to the great significance of the 1912 election. As one of Wilson's important academic champions, Charles W. Eliot, emeritus president of Harvard University, wrote in a letter to the *New York Times*,

> The Democratic Party and the Progressive Party both advocate serious changes in the political usages of the people, [but] the Progressive party's proposals [are] more numerous and more serious than those of

the Democratic party. Some of these changes are expected to extend the direct control of the people over legislation, over the election of representatives in legislative assemblies, and over executive officers during the terms for which they were elected; while others are intended to diminish the power of the courts both absolutely and relatively to that of other Governmental Departments. These are grave matters for they touch subjects which were critical at the time of the adoption of the existing Constitutions, and have been critical at several later epochs. They also touch the question of how far the centralization of power in the national executive may go. On these questions the Democratic party and its candidates seem unquestionably more trustworthy than the Progressive party and its candidates, so far as one can judge from their public declarations and the personal history of the candidates themselves.[149]

In response to the charge that they represented a reckless and mongrel radicalism, Progressives insisted, with considerable effect, that the political reforms they championed were not a radical rejection of the American constitutional tradition but an effort to strengthen it in the face of the hard challenges thrown up by the new industrial order. The obstacle to progressive democracy, they insisted, was not the Constitution; rather it was the extra-constitutional party system, which perverted constitutionalism and individualism, properly understood. Respectfully, but forcefully, taking issue with the former president of his university, Professor Hart insisted that Roosevelt and his followers did not express "an impulsive desire for popular government." Rather, their protest was "simply a determination to secure the birthright of which [the American people] had been deprived." For the past three decades, this protest had been spreading from city to city and state to state, demanding reforms such as the secret ballot, direct election of senators, women's suffrage, and the popular primary, as well as measures of direct legislation such as the initiative, referendum, and recall. "Not a single one [of] these great reforms," Hart noted, "had been the work of either of the two National parties"; in fact, he continued, "the forces in control of these parties have, with all their might and to the last ditch, resisted those reforms, each in their own state." Hart acknowledged that individual Democrats and individual Republicans had pursued reform at the local and state levels; however, he concluded, "the Progressive Party is the first great National organization in our history to commit itself and all its voters to a programme of general reform."[150]

Put simply, the Progressive campaign of 1912 was an attack on the whole concept of political parties. Roosevelt's unabashed promotion of dramatic electoral and constitutional reform reflected an unwavering devotion to direct democracy. Furthermore, the direct democracy reforms he championed, most of which were endorsed by the Progressive platform, became the central issue of his campaign. In its celebration of devices such as the direct primary, initiative, recall, and referenda (even on court rulings), the Progressive Party was a party to end party politics. This was not an attack on the Constitution, Progressives insisted, but a rejection of the way Jeffersonians and Jacksonians interpreted it. Theirs was a "neo-Hamiltonian" interpretation of the Constitution, as Hand had put it to Roosevelt. Claiming to celebrate the national democracy called for by the Preamble of the Constitution, Progressives presumed to make practical the elusive but powerful idea of "We the People."

The Progressive Party received welcome acknowledgment of its support for American democracy with the well-publicized endorsement of its cause by Thomas Edison. Edison's allegiance was announced with great fanfare by the *New York Times* in an article with the appropriate headline, "Edison Discovers He's a Bull Mooser."[151] Although constitutional conservatives feared progressive democracy's faith in public opinion, Edison saw it as a virtue, especially as it would free the country to experiment politically. His experiments led to electric bulbs replacing gaslights; by the same token, the Progressive Party heralded the displacement of party politics by democratic innovations such as the referendum and recall. Such political experimentation, Edison insisted, celebrated rather than diminished American individualism.[152] Edison's testimony was echoed by other celebrities who were enlisted in the Progressive crusade: William Gillette, the dashing "Sherlock Holmes" of the stage, went on speaking tours for the new party, and Lillian Russell, wife of the Pennsylvania Progressive Alexander P. Moore, appeared in a publicity photograph purchasing Bull Moose buttons at the party's New York headquarters.[153]

That Thomas Edison and other celebrity endorsements became an important feature of Roosevelt's crusade sheds light on how the Progressive Party marked a critical transformation of American politics. With its emphasis on candidates rather than parties, direct appeal to voters through new methods of publicity, and reliance on civic groups and celebrity endorsements, the Bull Moose campaign embodied a shift in American politics from localized party politics to mass democracy. Of course, Roosevelt was an extraordinary celebrity in his own right. As president, he pioneered major innovations in publicity techniques that began to forge strong ties between the White House and public opinion. His Progressive Party campaign brought to fruition and bestowed legitimacy on campaign practices and institutional changes that privileged a direct relationship between presidential candidates and voters.

As Chapter 3 shows, the primary contest between Roosevelt and Taft had demonstrated the perils as well as the virtues of "pure democracy." So the general election campaign, which was dominated by Roosevelt and Wilson, aroused serious concerns about the consequences of candidate-centered campaigns for American democracy. A central theme of the story of the Progressive Party campaign of 1912 — and, more broadly, the wayward legacy of progressive democracy — is that reformers' doctrinal faith in a more plebiscitary form of democracy constantly threatened to rob the insurgent movement of the organization necessary for surviving in the absence of its larger-than-life leader. Moreover, Roosevelt and the Progressive Party set the tone of the 1912 campaign, so much so that the important doctrinal differences represented by this extraordinary four-cornered contest were at times reduced to a personality contest, which obscured these distinctions.

Foreign observers, especially, recognized and were amused by this feature of the election. "What has inspired enthusiasm on the one side and vehement opposition on the other is not so much . . . the program of the Progressive Party," the *Manchester Guardian* reported toward the end of the campaign, "as the personality of its leader. To his supporters, Mr. Roosevelt is St. George fighting the dragon. To his opponents he is the most dangerous man that has ever appeared in American politics. He is acclaimed as the chivalrous leader of a new crusade against the entrenched forces of greed and wrong-doing. He is denounced as a reckless adventurer who is ready to sacrifice friends to his own inordinate ambition." By the side of such a charismatic figure, the *Guardian* observed, President Taft appeared "commonplace." The mention of the forlorn incumbent's name incited "no fanaticism, either for or against." But Wilson, although hardly as "vivid a character" as Roosevelt, possessed the sort of qualities that made for statesmanship: "Mr. Wilson has been a much shorter time in the public eye than either of his rivals, but he has already given proof of both brilliance and stability. He has a far better grasp of political questions than either of the other two, and excels them also in exposition and debate. He approaches much more nearly than Mr. Roosevelt or Mr. Taft to the British type of statesman."[154]

Wilson, in fact, had long demonstrated a keen interest in British party government and reforms that would make American politics resemble it. In his final address of the general election, a speech at Madison Square Garden, he urged his supporters not just to support him but to "vote the Democratic ticket." Only a "unified government" could reform America, the governor insisted, which consisted of "a House of Representatives, of a President, and of something that in my time the people have not yet captured—a Senate." Moreover, Wilson continued, it was important for the Democratic Party to capture control of state governments. "If you have a Democratic government at Washington and don't have a Democratic government in New York," he said, "you haven't got any conducting medium by which to signal to Washington." In contrast to Roosevelt's excoriation of parties, Wilson thus presented himself as a party leader. "You have got to have a vital organization of purpose, spreading throughout the United States," he concluded, "in order that great bodies of men may be united together for the great project of emancipation."[155]

Nonetheless, since his nomination, Wilson had made clear that he hoped to place his own stamp on the Democratic Party. No less than Roosevelt, he attacked the party "bosses" and promised to govern with the authority bestowed on him by a popular mandate. As the *Nation* pointed out with appreciation, Wilson had captured the Democratic nomination with the support of a personal organization formed to his own image and programmatic concerns (see Chapter 4). Even more notable, however, was the manner in which this organization continued its effective campaigning into the general election. Relying heavily on the support of Princeton alumni, William McCombs constructed an elaborate network of Wilson supporters that represented a major innovation in president politics. The Wilson machine was significant, the *Nation* observed, not only because the candidate could "depend upon it for political work"; its real contribution was that he could rely on it "almost exclusively." The Woodrow Wilson College Men's League, as it was called, "which, both financially and otherwise stood on its own feet from the start," marked the "triumph of the amateur," a good thing in the eyes of the independent magazine's editors: "Despite its name, it looks upon itself as nonpartisan, and aims to be a permanent factor in national political campaigns, since it proposes to throw its influence on the side of the most worthy, regardless of his party badge. It has already enrolled thousands of men who had never belonged to a political organization and by so doing has rendered a valuable service, not only to its candidate and his party, but to the whole country."[156]

By the end of the general election campaign, Wilson had come to portray himself not as a more moderate reformer than TR but, rather, as a more reliable progressive. In part, this reliability rested in Wilson's artful balance of insurgent and accommodating positions toward the party system and the Constitution. Wilson styled himself not merely a party leader, the *New York World* editorialized, but "a leader of all the people regardless of party"; he would be a "president who is against arbitrary personal government, but who knows how to make constitutional government an instrument of progress, not of reaction."[157] And yet, the *San Francisco Examiner,* a Hearst paper that supported the Democratic Party but embraced the Progressive creed of "pure democracy," argued that Wilson had beaten Roosevelt at his own game. "It has passed into a commonplace, agreed upon by all companies, by friends and enemies alike, that Mr. Roosevelt was the foremost man of his generation in the arts of practical politics," the editorial acknowledged. Nonetheless, it continued, "nothing in current events and common conversation is more noteworthy than the lapse of legend. Mr. Roosevelt has been outclassed." Hearst had warmed slowly to Wilson, doubting his bona fides as a popular leader. By the final month of the campaign, however, he celebrated the former professor and university president as a "Leader Who Knows the People":

> Who can doubt that the judgment of history will find in Mr. Roosevelt
> something eccentric and anomalous—an aberration from the straight
> line of common feeling and national development? Who can doubt,
> on the other hand, that history will recognize in Mr. Wilson a man of
> exceptional normality—one of those rare characters who represent
> an age or a country just because there is nothing peculiar about them,
> except the immense range of their mental correspondence with other
> men. . . . Wilson knows the United States. He interprets the country
> correctly, because in his mental habit he identifies himself with it. Thus
> he sees the nation from inside the nation's mind. Roosevelt would be a
> kind of super-age. He stands aloof and apart—watching the nation's
> mental processes with a lynx eye, but never really understanding
> them.[158]

As if on cue, a few days later Wilson returned to an important theme of his primary campaign that squared with this idea of a leader who embraced "normality." Once again contrasting himself with Roosevelt's self-styled heroic leadership, Wilson presented himself as the champion of ordinary interests. "What this country needs above all else is a body of laws which will look after the men who are on the make rather than the men who are already made," he declared. Only from them, the people with "the average enterprise, the average initiative," could the nation gain renewal and strength.[159]

Thus an election that asked American voters to make principled and programmatic choices of far-reaching consequences, a great contest that would determine the fate of constitutional government, was sometimes reduced to dueling styles of popular leadership. Americans, it seemed, were asked not to invest their faith in New Nationalism or New Freedom but, rather, to select the individual candidate who best embodied the ambitions of the "whole people."

The candidate-centered nature of the campaign was accentuated by the use of movies in the 1912 election. Both the Roosevelt and Wilson campaigns contracted with companies to produce films that would be shown in theaters around the country. Both campaigns hoped to take advantage of the new popular medium of motion pictures to communicate directly with voters. Even the party of conservatism and solemn William Taft spent some of its very limited funds on motion pictures.[160] Although Taft refused to stump during the general election, Charles D. Hilles, head of the Republican National Committee, ran ads in 1,200 movie theaters that defended the GOP's protectionist policies by offering a pictorial comparison between the conditions of labor abroad and in the United States. Hilles appreciated the political possibilities of film at least as much as his rival campaign managers.[161] But the hopelessness of Taft's campaign and the reluctance of the incumbent president to engage in a contest of personalities diminished the importance of the Republican cinematic appeals.

Besides, these films, which marked the first extensive use of movies as political advertisements in presidential elections, proved most effective in supplementing the whirlwind tours the candidates and their surrogates made throughout the general election campaign. Roosevelt hired the General Film Publicity and Sales Company to help publicize his important western tour, during which his enthusiasm for direct government reached the peak of enthusiasm. Although Roosevelt had been shown on film frequently before the Bull Moose campaign, the movies made by General Film Publicity and Sales were specially crafted as political messages, with the speeches flashed on the screen in tandem with pictures of his delivering them. "This was the first time that anything of this kind has been attempted," the trade magazine the *Moving Picture News* enthused, "and only goes to demonstrate the unparalleled usefulness of the motion picture film."[162] One of the more popular Progressive campaign films, *Theodore Roosevelt: Fighter for Social*

Justice, showed the colonel giving speeches in North Dakota and Colorado, with excerpts from these addresses that highlighted the Progressive themes of direct democracy and economic justice. Roosevelt's vigorous appearance on the stump, punctuated by the symbol of a flaming sword, conveyed the urgency of his campaign.[163] Although these campaign movies were shot during the silent film era, voters could hear Roosevelt's voice by listening to four sound recordings made by the Edison Company, a contribution in kind from the celebrated inventor. Among these recordings was Roosevelt's lively rendition of the dramatic peroration of his "Confession of Faith."[164]

Wilson's campaign countered by enlisting the services of Universal Studios to make a political satire, *The Old Way and the New,* which depicted Roosevelt and Taft as the handmaidens of big business. Significantly, Universal had taken the lead in opposing the existing film trust, the Motion Pictures Patents Company, which had been created by several leading moving companies, including the Edison Company, to monopolize the burgeoning film industry.[165] Charles R. McCauley, the lead cartoonist for the *New York World*—a strong supporter of Wilson—wrote the script for the eight-minute movie. Most of the film depicts the "old way," showing the nefarious activities in the plush offices of a corpulent manufacturer, who is labeled, on his shirtfront, as "The Trust." He rejects a request for a donation to a hospital that treats men injured in his own factories; dismisses with disdain the timid request of two workers for a raise—"you ought to be glad you're living," he snorts; and happily greets a villainous character, labeled the "High Tariff Boss," whose request for "a million dollars to swing 100,000 votes" is eagerly granted. All of these activities are overseen by large portraits of Taft and Roosevelt. Tellingly, Roosevelt's picture remains in view for the entire scene while Taft's portrait is only visible to the audience during the opening sequence. It is Roosevelt and the new party, the film suggests, not the moribund Taft, that are most likely to perpetuate, indeed enhance, the power of trusts.[166]

The Wilson film ends with a dramatic portrayal of "the new way." One of the laborers who asked The Trust for a raise is shown on his way home from work. He first passes a large poster on a wall that features another obese figure, this one labeled "protected interests," who has his arms around the shoulders of the smiling figures of Taft and Roosevelt. Rejecting these three figures with a dismissive wave, the worker comes to a campaign poster for Wilson and Marshall: he enthusiastically gestures toward the Democratic ticket and responds immediately to the masthead's appeal for "100,000 earnest citizens to contribute each one honest dollar" to elect a president "for and of the people." Befitting the purpose of the film, the Wilson and Marshall poster makes no reference to the Democratic Party. The political advertisement is intended to be a direct appeal to public opinion that poses a choice among three candidates: Taft and Roosevelt, who serve the trusts, and Wilson, who is prepared to fight them. "We stand for pictures and not politics," the *Universal Weekly* assured its readers in a "nonpartisan" promotion of the campaign film, "and in standing for pictures we would like to go on record as saying that Governor Wilson's advisors have, we think, shown a great wisdom in taking advantage of the motion picture for campaign purposes. . . . We are glad to have enlisted the approbation of the enlightened Democratic candidate for the Presidency."[167]

Similarly, the General Film Publicity and Sales Company focused its campaign movies on Roosevelt himself: "Roosevelt, the Great Regenerator," an advertisement targeting theater owners trumpeted. "YOU owe the people of your district the right to see the great American statesman at close range, regardless of *your* political creed. Thousands and thousands of people of your territory love Roosevelt. REALIZE THAT THEY WILL PAY TO SEE HIM!"[168]

Because the distribution data for these campaign films have been lost, there is no way to accurately determine the size of the audience that viewed them or what effect they had on the campaign. But the use of commercial political films remained a staple of elections until they were replaced by television commercials in the 1950s.[169] They thus provide another measure of the important change in American politics signaled by the 1912 election—a contest in which issues and candidates elevated mass public opinion as the master of presidential politics.

Although Wilson would win the election, Roosevelt would become the apostle of progressive democracy. Ironically, on the very day the *San Francisco Examiner* editorialized about his "lapsed legend," Roosevelt gave a performance that would immortalize the Progressive Party campaign. Having campaigned in thirty-two states and every section of the country, delivering over 150 speeches, Roosevelt arrived in Milwaukee on October 14, his voice hoarse and his strength depleted. He had cancelled speeches the day before in Illinois, Indiana, and Wisconsin, but he insisted on keeping the speech scheduled for Milwaukee, a stronghold of socialism and, therefore, a critical battleground in his plan to steal Deb's thunder.

Shortly before eight in the evening, Roosevelt's party left their hotel and went to an open-topped automobile that would take them to the site of the Milwaukee Auditorium. While the Roosevelt group settled into the car, a crowd that had assembled to greet him cheered, and the Progressive standard-bearer rose to acknowledge his admirers. Suddenly one of the on-lookers raised a gun and fired, at a distance of about seven feet, hitting TR in the chest. Roosevelt's secretary, Elbert Martin, dove over the side of the car and tackled the would-be assassin, John Schrenk, a New York saloon keeper. The deranged Schrenk would tell police that he wanted to kill Roosevelt "because he did not believe any President ought to have more than two terms." In his pocket, police found a letter addressed "To the People" that told of a dream in which President McKinley accused Roosevelt of his murder.[170]

Philip Roosevelt, who was near the car when the pistol fired, reported that his cousin "had dropped at the force of the shot without sound," and he feared that TR "would never get up again." But Colonel Roosevelt "got up again in a second" and insisted on keeping his date with the audience waiting at the Auditorium. Roosevelt had put his fingers to his lips, saw that he was not bleeding from the mouth, and concluded that the wound had not perforated his lung. Moreover, as Philip described his cousin's stubborn refusal to go to a hospital, Roosevelt's determination to make the speech was based "on the theory that 'once in a while you can finish in style.' The chances against his being mortally hurt, he thought, were about twenty to one, and if he was mortally hurt then he wanted to take advantage of that opportunity to say things that he could not otherwise have said without having his sincerity questioned."[171] Having been accused throughout his idealistic campaign of being a hypocrite, Roosevelt now spied an extraordinary opportunity to confess his faith in a form that could not be questioned. "I would not speak to you insincerely within five minutes of being shot," he told his startled listeners.[172]

Roosevelt abandoned his prepared remarks, typed out on a fifty-page manuscript and folded in his coat pocket, which, by deflecting the flight of the bullet as it struck him, might have saved his life. The colonel occasionally rambled during his ninety-minute impromptu performance, and he frequently interrupted his oration with allusions to the shooting, even unbuttoning his coat and vest to show those who were in attendance that his white shirt was badly stained with blood. Nonetheless, the speech was a forceful presentation of his belief that he and the Progressive Party represented the country's best hope against a radical assault on the ramparts of the American way of life. "To hear him speak," a correspondent for the *San Francisco Examiner* wrote admiringly, "with all the vigor he displayed in his whole campaign, no one would have imagined, had he not known it, that the plucky candidate carried a freshly fired bullet."[173] Roosevelt's performance, Patricia O'Toole writes, was "an astonishing effort to capitalize on the moment."[174]

Roosevelt denied, as he would repeatedly afterward, that the attempt on his life was the random act of a madman. "I wish to say seriously to the speakers and newspapers representing the Republican and Democratic and Socialist parties, that they cannot, month in and month out, year in and year out, make the kind of slanderous, bitter, and malevolent assaults that they have made and expect that brutal and violent characters—especially when the brutality be accompanied by a not too strong mind, will remain unaffected by it," he stated. More to the point, Roosevelt added, "this effort to assassinate me emphasizes to a peculiar degree the need of this Progressive movement." The movement he led was "endeavoring to forestall [an] evil" development, the advent of raw and disruptive class conflict: "Every good citizen ought to do everything in his or her power to prevent the coming of the day when we shall see in this country two organized greeds fighting one another; when we shall see the greed of the 'have-nots' arrayed against the greed of the 'haves.' If ever that day comes such incidents as this tonight will be commonplace in our history."

The Progressive movement, Roosevelt argued, would prevent the polarization of rich and poor by appealing to the whole people, by forming "a movement for justice now, a movement in which we ask all just men of generous hearts to join—all men who feel in their souls that lifting upwards which bids them refuse to be satisfied themselves while their fellow countrymen and countrywomen suffer from avoidable injustice and misery." Having invoked the Social Gospel that had infused his campaign, TR spoke of the new party's effort "to rally decent men, rich or poor, whatever their social or industrial position, to stand together for these elementary rights of good citizenship, and for those elementary duties which must underlie good citizenship in this great republic of ours." Responding to his audience's obvious anguish over his wound, Roosevelt insisted that this was a cause worth suffering, even dying for: "Never in my life was I in any movement in which I was able to serve with such wholehearted devotion as in this—in which I was able to feel as I do in this that, come weal, come woe, we have fought for the good of our common country."[175]

At the start of the general election campaign, Roosevelt spoke in Rhode Island of extending the patriotism one finds in war among soldiers to domestic affairs. Leavening the country's rights consciousness with a stronger sense of duty, he reaffirmed during the course of his Milwaukee remarks, would underscore the essence of the American nation. "We do not regard

Americanism as a matter of the way in which a man worships his God, or as being affected by where he was born," he said of the Progressive Party. "We regard it as a matter of spirit and purpose."[176] Roosevelt's performance with a bullet in his chest gave dramatic testimony to his message that class and ethnic differences (he did not mention the peculiar American problem of race) should be transcended by an appeal to a warlike spirit of sacrifice and common purpose.[177] Joining a cult of personality to the collective identity of the movement he led, TR wired his supporters from his hospital bed two days later, "Tell the people not to worry about me, for if I go down another will take my place. For always, the army is true."[178]

The press's saturated coverage of Roosevelt's recovery from his chest wound dominated the rest of the campaign. Indeed, Roosevelt's principal rival, Wilson, immediately announced, over the objections of his campaign managers, that he would halt speaking until the Progressive candidate recovered.[179] "The country has been profoundly stirred," the London *Times* reported. "Press of all shades of politics is unanimous in its horror at the crime and relief that the results are no worse. . . . Small as the consolation must be to Mr. Roosevelt's friends and admirers, probably the incident, if all goes well, will benefit politically. Once more Mr. Roosevelt has given signal evidence of that pluck, physical endurance and disregard for his personal well being which have done so much to endear him to people."[180]

TR's recovery did seem to go well, and by October 30 he was strong enough to address a boisterous rally in New York City's Madison Square Garden, the final important speech of his campaign. At the first sight of Roosevelt, the sixteen thousand men and women in attendance broke into shouting and song that lasted forty-five minutes: the celebration would have lasted longer—sixty or seventy minutes—the press reported, save for TR's "perfectly obvious" signal that he was anxious to begin this important address.

Although somewhat stiff and unable to raise his right arm, Roosevelt looked remarkably fit and, refusing the chair one of his aides offered, smiled at "such a tossing sea of red bandannas as might have made Debs jealous," said the *New York Evening Post*.[181] "It cannot be denied," the unfriendly *New York Times* acknowledged, "that nobody else ever got such a wonderful reception in the Garden. How much of it was due to the sympathy which most people instinctively feel for a brave man who has shown his courage, and how much of it was due to his principles cannot be told. It is nevertheless astounding that 16,000 persons should go absolutely crazy for forty five minutes as these men and women in the Garden did." The Roosevelt they heard was more grave than usual, the *Times* correspondent noticed—determined to take advantage of the afterglow of the Milwaukee episode to give a serious statement of the collective mission of this campaign. "Colonel Roosevelt wanted to make it plain in his last important speech during this campaign that he was going to take just so many steps towards radicalism as could be safely taken, and that he meant to devote the rest of his life to that, but that he did not intend to take one single step prematurely." The surprising solemnity of Roosevelt's tone was underscored "by one striking fact borne home on many of his listeners": TR's "failure to use the first personal pronoun singular which he has made so famous, substituting for it almost invariably the words 'we Progressives' or the plain and apparently not editorial 'we.'"[182]

Returning to many of the themes of which he spoke seven months before in Carnegie Hall, Roosevelt gave a concise defense of the Progressive platform, both defending and joining its commitments to social and industrial justice and pure democracy. Although they challenged the prevailing understanding of the Declaration and Constitution, these causes, he insisted, were not new: "They reach back to the Golden Rule and the Sermon on the Mount. They reach back to the commandments delivered at Sinai." All the Progressives were doing, Roosevelt insisted, was "to apply these doctrines in the shape necessary to make them available for meeting the living issues of our own day."[183] The economic and social reforms they defended would not create a paternalist government that would sap the spirit of individual responsibility. Such a view grossly underestimated the character of the American people. Rather, these measures would nurture a shared sense of endeavor that would foster, for the first time, a national community in the United States:

Our people must work hard and faithfully. They do not wish to shirk their work. They must feel pride in the work for the work's sake. But there must be bread for the work. There must be a time for play when the men and women are young. When they grow old there must be the certainty of rest under conditions free from the haunting terror of utter poverty. . . . We must shape conditions so that no one can own the spirit of a man who loves his task and gives the best there is in him to that task, and it matters not whether man reaps and wrests his livelihood from the reluctance of the soil or whether with the hand or brain he plays his part in the tremendous industrial activities of our great cities. We are striving to meet the needs of these men, and to meet them in such a fashion that all alike shall feel bound together in a bond of a common brotherhood, where each yet feels that he must also think of his brother's rights because he is in very truth that brother's keeper.[184]

The "bond of common brotherhood," which the Progressives made clear must include men and women, presupposed a new understanding of the Declaration and the Constitution. This meant emphasizing the nationalizing features of these documents, so that reasonable welfare measures would not be obstructed by "a fetich" [sic] for the protection of property and state rights. Most important, Roosevelt insisted, enunciating the political reform that he had made the centerpiece of his campaign, law and custom must be reinterpreted so that the people themselves became the masters of the Constitution. "We forbid any man, no matter what their official position may be, to usurp the right which is ours, the right which is the people's," he stated. "We recognize in neither court nor Congress nor President, any divine right to override the will of the people expressed with due deliberation in orderly fashion and through the forms of law." This meant, TR made clear, Croly's proposition that Progressives believed in, so to speak, a new Declaration of Independence. "In very truth," he said solemnly to his now hushed audience, "this is a government by the people themselves, that the Constitution is theirs, that the Courts are theirs, that all the government agents and agencies are theirs." Then, once more seeking to strike the difficult balance between leadership that led and yet remained beholden to public opinion, Roosevelt claimed, "We believe that all true leaders of the people must fearlessly stand for righteousness and honesty, must fearlessly tell the people what justice and honor demand. But we no less strongly insist that it is for the people themselves finally to decide all questions of public policy and to have their decision made effective."[185]

With this last sermon, Roosevelt cut through the obsession of the press and public with the personalities of the campaign. He made clear how much was at stake in the great contest of 1912; he enunciated principles that effectively framed the election as a popular constitutional convention. In portraying his own constitutional vision, heralding a new sense of national community, Roosevelt insisted—as he had throughout the long campaign—that the high ideals he saw in the American people required "visionary" leadership. Repeating the dramatic words he had uttered in Carnegie Hall the previous March, TR pledged to sacrifice himself—to enlist as a "soldier"—in the cause of righteousness. But Roosevelt's admonition that the "watchword" in the long fight for justice was "spend and be spent" took on new meaning in the aftermath of his near martyrdom. The phrase came from Paul's second letter to the Corinthians. Condemning their hedonism, Paul wrote, "And I will very gladly spend and be spent for you, even though the more abundantly I love you, the less I be loved." Roosevelt's persuasive claim that he was "ready to spend and be spent . . . for the welfare of mankind" helps to explain the remarkable influence he had on the election of 1912 and the enduring legacy of the Progressive Party campaign. "Roosevelt in the year of the Bull Moose," O'Toole writes, "was as zealous as Paul and as convinced of his selflessness."[186] Playing this role with panache, he enshrined the Progressive program of political and social reform as an enduring feature of American political discourse and electoral struggle.

SIX

⮽

Back to the Future: The
Progressive Party's Legacy for
American Politics

Roosevelt's friend and critic Learned Hand had been very supportive of the New Nationalism program. At the same time, the distinguished jurist's enthusiasm for TR's candidacy had been somewhat diminished by his scorn for the Progressives' infatuation with direct government, especially the platform's support for recalling judicial decisions. But after attending Roosevelt's performance at Madison Square Garden, Hand was deeply inspired. So effective was Roosevelt's defense of the two major planks of the Progressive platform—social and industrial justice and pure democracy—that even the colonel's steadfast support for popular referenda on the constitutional judgments of the state courts did not restrain Hand's enthusiasm. Two days later, he wrote an emotional note to Corinne Roosevelt Robinson, TR's sister, expressing how much "he was moved" by the Madison Square Garden meeting. "Your brother certainly never appeared more gallant," Judge Hand wrote. "The occasion absolutely suited his genius, and he showed himself most truly a great leader of men." Confirming reports in the press that Roosevelt's display of urgency, which, following in the wake of defying a would-be assassin's bullet, transcended the cult of personality and firmly tied his candidacy to a shared sense of endeavor, Hand added, "I shall never forget the lofty and inspiring phrases in which he put our aims, nor his solemn fervor as he assured us now with the added emphasis on the last two weeks of his consecration to a great cause." Sensing the likelihood of Roosevelt's impending defeat, Hand closed the letter with a virtual post-mortem. "I hope, and I believe, that when history comes to be written, the greatest service he would have done his country—and even his worst enemy admits there are many—will be said to be when he became the inspiration and the leader, as he had been the real creator, of the Progressive Party."[1]

Roosevelt did, indeed, lose the election; however, the results partly vindicated Hand's high esteem for his candidacy. Wilson easily defeated a fractured Republican party, capturing forty states and 435 electoral votes. Nonetheless, although Wilson's victory was an electoral college landslide, his 6,301,254 popular votes were only about 42 percent of the total. In winning over 27 percent of the popular vote and running a strong second, Roosevelt did remarkably well, especially when considering that he was the candidate for a party that had only been in existence for three months. Not since the emergence of the Republican Party in the 1850s had a third party been so successful; now that party's future seemed in jeopardy. Taft came in third in the popular vote (with fewer than 3.5 million votes to Roosevelt's 4-million-plus) and only managed to capture two states, Utah and Vermont. Never before or since 1912 has a Republican presidential candidate been so widely defeated or run third in popular and electoral votes. In historical perspective, then, Roosevelt's showing was extraordinary. In coming in second, he not only carried five states—Michigan, Minnesota, Pennsylvania, South Dakota, and Washington—and won eleven of California's thirteen electoral votes but also came close to victory in nine additional states and was second in twenty-three states.

Significantly, Roosevelt did especially well in urban and industrial counties with the highest rates of population growth. As such, his support appeared to reveal how the Progressive commitments to political and social reform appealed to those voters who best represented the future of the country, just as Wilson and, even more so, Taft tended to celebrate the virtues of the decentralized republic of the past.[2] The national rate of population growth in the first decade of the twentieth century, as determined by the 1910 census, was 21 percent. Fourteen cities in the North and West (excluding Oklahoma and Idaho) with a population of or exceeding 25,000 had grown at a rate of more than 100 percent in the years 1900–1910. Taft did not carry any of the counties in which these cities were located, Wilson won four, and Roosevelt captured eight. Except for Schenectady, New York, Huntington, West Virginia, and Flint, Michigan, all of the fastest-growing cities were west of the Mississippi. These years had witnessed a boom in western urban growth, thus increasing the political importance of this section of the country.[3]

Arguably, California, which experienced roughly a 60 percent increase in population during the first decade of the century, was the most important site of this western boom. Roosevelt's success there had much to do with the effective Progressive Party organization in the state that TR's running mate, Hiram Johnson, played the principal part in forming. Because Taft was not on the ballot in California, the results in the state provide an interesting gauge of the distinctive appeals of Roosevelt's New Nationalism and Wilson's New Freedom. Of the eight California cities with populations larger than 25,000, Roosevelt captured the counties in which five of the eight were located, including the two cities with the highest rate of growth: Pasadena, 232 percent, and Los Angeles, 221 percent. Of the three major cities, he lost only one, San Diego, which had a growth rate of over 100 percent. By contrast, Wilson captured San Francisco, then the largest city in California, which had the lowest growth rate among the state's major cities (21.6 percent). Repeating the trend set by Hiram Johnson's gubernatorial contest in 1910, Roosevelt drew his greatest support in southern California, which had experienced the fastest growth in the state.[4]

Because of Roosevelt's strong second-place showing, and the success he achieved in the rising urban and industrial areas of the country, most Progressives shared Learned Hand's view that the 1912 election was only the beginning of the New Nationalist crusade. "As a result of the elections yesterday," Progressive Party chairman Joseph Dixon announced in the *Progressive Bulletin* of November 11, "the Progressive party is now the dominant party in opposition to the Democratic party." On account of the "tremendous responsibility thus devolving upon us," Dixon continued, the national committee planned to meet in Chicago on December 10 to discuss the future of the party.[5] At this meeting, TR managed to head off an effort by the more militant reform leaders to remove the financier George Perkins—one of the party's most important financial angels—as the head of the executive committee.[6] The party reformers were assuaged by the creation of a Progressive National Service, chaired by the prominent New York social worker Frances Kellor. The service was dedicated to establishing the Progressive Party as the first truly nationalized and programmatic party in the United States. Its work would be done by four bureaus: Jane Addams became the director of the Bureau of Social and Industrial Justice; Gifford Pinchot, the champion of enlightened management of natural resources, headed the Conservation

Division; George Record, the militant New Jersey reformer, assumed command of the Department of Popular Government; and Charles J. Bird, a Massachusetts industrialist, led the Bureau of the Cost of Living and Corporation Control. The "First Quarterly Report of the Progressive National Service," issued in March 1913, stated its high purpose:

> It is political organization in the highest sense of the term. It is unbound by statutory forms and legal technicalities which combine men into mere political machines. It is unhampered by election law discrimination which makes it difficult and well nigh impossible for the independent voter to express his will. It places the burden not upon voting on election day but upon civic responsibility and duty year round, locally and nationally. Voting then becomes one expression of patriotism rather than the sum total of civic expressions.[7]

Many Progressive leaders viewed the 1912 election and the creation of the Progressive National Service as the signal for a major realignment of the American political system. Prior to the election, Herbert Knox Smith, who helped organize the Progressive forces in Connecticut, wrote an article in the *Yale Review* that cast the current party battles against the history of major political developments in the United States. The Progressive Party, Knox argued, was "a protest against the entire American political alignment, and for the forcing of a new and better one." Within eight years, he predicted, the Progressives would be in power, with the Democrats as the party of opposition. The new alignment, signaling a major transformation of political life in the United States, was foreordained and defined clearly in the Progressive Party's platform: "It raises specifically great vital modern issues that will themselves divide our people into Progressives and Conservatives."[8] The election results confirmed Knox's prediction for most Progressive leaders, and the organizational efforts that followed further encouraged bold predictions of realignment. As William Hinebaugh, who was elected to the House in 1912 and served as the chairman of the Progressive Congressional Committee, wrote to a local party leader in New York City, "The election results of 1912 gave the death-blow to the Republican party, just as the election of 1856 gave the death blow to the Whig party. The Whig party died the servant and tool of the aristocracy of slavery, and the Republican party died the servant and the tool of the aristocracy of wealth. It entered upon its last administration March 14, 1909, and is now facing final dissolution."[9]

Two years later, the Progressives, not the Republicans, faced their final dissolution. In truth, Roosevelt's strong showing obscured the weaknesses of the Progressives in the states and localities. The Progressives did run strongly in some states. The new party won a gubernatorial election in Wisconsin, where Francis McGovern, Roosevelt's ally at the Republican convention, was reelected. Moreover, gubernatorial candidates Albert Beveridge in Indiana and Oscar Straus in New York won more votes than TR received in their states. The Progressives' determination to field a full slate of candidates also proved to be important, as those who contested for the House and Senate won enough votes to guarantee that the Democrats would enjoy huge majorities in both congressional chambers in 1913–1914, thus setting the stage for the enactment of the reform program that the Wilson administration would pursue during its first term. In general, however, the third party carried far fewer votes in gubernatorial, congressional, and state legislative races than did the national ticket. Although badly beaten in the presidential race, the Republicans still controlled fifteen governorships and the mayoralties of twenty of the fifty-five largest cities in the nation. In the historical situation that the Progressives hoped to emulate—namely the Whig-Republican split of 1856—the Whigs had no such solid base of political strength in the states and the localities. As a result, the Whig state party organizations had a strong incentive to march into the new Republican Party. In 1913, the situation was reversed.[10]

The relative weakness of Progressive insurgency below the presidential level allowed Taft to hope that Wilson's victory might simply represent "the normal political change from one party to another." As the incumbent president had insisted throughout the campaign, he believed that electoral competition between two great parties was "the sheet anchor of popular government"—fortification against petty and virulent interest-group politics. Indeed, he admitted that the Democrats' immense victory might be good for the country, especially after the Republican Party had been in power so long that "jealousies and faction in it [had] destroyed the discipline and the loyalty of its members and [had] injured its political prestige." Still, Taft admitted, "he was surprised at . . . Roosevelt's strength, as compared with the regular Republican ticket." TR's strong showing, he feared, might portend more dramatic change. "When a party like the Bull Moose party comes forward and proposes to utterly tear down all the checks and balances of a well-adjusted, democratic, constitutional, representative government, to destroy the limitations on the executive and legislative power as between the majority and minority, as between the majority and the individual, then the issue becomes a capital one, and it affects the permanence and continuance of our government."[11]

Roosevelt, too, was uncertain of the Progressive Party's future. "No one can tell the future of the Progressive Party, as a party," he wrote the philanthropist Alexander Smith Cochran after the election. "I hope, and I am inclined to believe, that it will even as a *party* play a very important part in our social and industrial development."[12] Roosevelt's ego was such, however, that he had no trouble believing the interpretation that the 1912 election was a testament to the remarkable spell his personality and reputation cast on the electorate. "There was no human being who could have saved the whole movement from collapse if I had not been willing to step in and take a hammering," he wrote his British friend Arthur Hamilton Lee.[13] This feeling of being indispensable made TR uncertain about the future of the Progressive Party. Nonetheless, Roosevelt insisted, the principles he and the party championed would not die. "I do not merely hope, I know," Roosevelt opined in the letter to Cochran, "that the *principles* for which we stand will and must receive an extraordinary development and application within the next few years."[14]

And yet the fragile base of the Progressive Party reflected more than Roosevelt's indispensability. The inverted pyramid of Progressive support also can be attributed to the doctrinal schism that afflicted the Progressive movement—the fundamental differences on matters of race and trusts that attenuated the party's unity. The tortured compromise that Roosevelt struck at the Progressive Party convention on the "Negro question" did not hurt his candidacy as much as the press or black activists predicted it would; nevertheless, the lily-white policy on southern delegates and the Progressive platform's deafening silence on the rights of African Americans hobbled the party's efforts to establish substantial ties with black voters in the North. In spite of the importunities of civil rights leaders like W. E. B. Du Bois and William Monroe Trotter that blacks vote for Wilson, Roosevelt appeared to have won most of their support. Writing in May 1913, for example, Kelly Miller estimated that possibly 60 percent of the African American vote went to Roosevelt, with the rest divided roughly equally between Wilson and Taft.[15] Although such estimates are not particularly reliable, some of the results of the Chicago vote suggest that Miller might not have been far off. In the two precincts with substantial black populations (Wards 2 and 3), Roosevelt won nearly 57 percent of the vote, to Taft's 33 percent and Wilson's 9 percent. Roosevelt won Chicago, but only with 39 percent of the vote, to Wilson's 31 percent and Taft's 18 percent. The results of the 1914 Senate race, however, in which the social gospeler Raymond Robins ran on the Progressive ticket, showed that the third party failed to lure African Americans away from the Republican Party. Robins only managed to gain 9 percent of the vote in these two precincts as compared to 78 percent for the Republican candidate and 9 percent for the Democrat.[16]

For all its risks, Roosevelt's emphasis on allying national administration and mass opinion might have been more attractive to many African American voters than the hollow promises of Taft and Wilson to respect minority rights. But the split between New Nationalism and New Freedom proved more debilitating to Roosevelt and the Progressive Party than did the conflict over race, betraying fundamental differences over the relationship between the individual and the state. In part, the Progressive schism over how to regulate the trusts touched on whether to grant workers the *right* of collective bargaining. Although TR and his allies advocated an expansive program of industrial reform, including support for the "organization of workers," they were reluctant to make the sort of particularistic appeals to laborers or ethnic groups that marked the Democratic campaign. Moreover, the religiosity of the Progressive Party left many labor leaders and immigrants cold. Although Social Gospel leaders such as Walter Rauschenbusch insisted their movement was nonsectarian, the national community they celebrated struck many non-Protestants as inhospitable to their way of life.

Roosevelt thus polled badly in those five eastern and New England states—Connecticut, Massachusetts, New Jersey, New York, and Rhode Island—with the highest percentage of foreign-born voters. The largest immigrant groups in these states were Irish, Italians, Eastern Europeans, and French Canadians, those populations most likely to view the Progressives' call for a New Nationalism as a threat to their ethnic identity. These groups found it easier to follow the familiar party leaders in their neighborhoods than the elusive siren call of the new party. Roosevelt came in third in four of these five states; only in New Jersey, which had a strong state Progressive organization, did he manage to beat out Taft for second place. Roosevelt polled reasonably well in those states with large Northern European populations, such as Minnesota, one of the five states he captured. But aside from Germans and Scandinavians, who tended to assimilate more easily into the American nation, the Progressive appeal to immigrant and ethnic groups was severely restricted, especially so in the East.[17]

The limited appeal of the Progressive Party was not exclusively due to the threat its aspiration for a new sense of nationhood posed to minority groups in the United States. Reformers themselves were deeply divided on how what John Dewey called the "Great Community" should be constructed. The great cause of progressivism, as Judge Ben Lindsey of Colorado proclaimed at the Progressive convention, was that "property rights shall not be exalted over human rights."[18] Yet Wilson's victory, as well as the visceral fight over antitrust policy within the Progressive Party, seemed to indicate that Progressives remained diffident in the face of collective government power. The underlying issue in the battle over regulating big business was not really a matter of New Nationalism succumbing to special interests, as Wilson and Brandeis charged. Instead, it was agitated by conflict over how much the United States could tolerate centralized administration without destroying the American people's love of property and their celebration of the independence of the democratic individual. Jane Addams spoke to Progressives' ambivalence about national administrative power in a speech delivered at the Second Annual Lincoln Day dinner of the Progressive Party, held in 1914:

> We are trying to bring about in America something in the way of much needed control of large industrial undertakings. We are trying to repair some of the inevitable disasters . . . of modern industry as have been done in older countries . . . with centralized government. We could easily cite the attempt to take care of the unemployed in Belgium, the whole series of social insurance for all old age and sickness in Germany, or a dozen other things which appeal to us all. But, we have the difficulty of doing that in America, in such ways, that the institutions of self government shall not be impaired.[19]

Addams's uneasiness about constructing a modern American state exposes the central Progressive dilemma and helps to explain why the Progressive Party failed to achieve the same unity in the face of the trust that the Republicans were able to achieve against slavocracy. "The great danger for us," TR wrote to Gifford Pinchot a week after the election, "is that with no clear purpose and no adequate organization our party may make so poor a showing in the local and state Congressional elections during the next three years as to be put out of the ring."[20]

Indeed, for all the excitement engendered by the Progressive Party campaign, it had failed to mobilize a large turnout of voters. The number of voters participating had grown slightly since 1908—from 14,889,239 to 15,048,834—but the percentage of the voting-age population that turned out declined from 65.4 percent to 58.8 percent. Voting had generally been declining since the 1896 election, although there was a very slight increase between 1904 and 1908. But the 1912 campaign, dominated by the Progressives' celebration of direct democracy, failed to reverse—indeed, appeared to accelerate—this trend. In part, the decline in turnout might have reflected the near certainty that Wilson would win the election. The hopelessness of Taft's campaign, not to mention the incumbent president's virtual absence during the general election, might have discouraged some voters, especially loyal Republican partisans, from participating. As was noted in Chapter 3, there is a sense in which the primary contest among La Follette, Taft, and Roosevelt was the most decisive part of the campaign, and once that unprecedented, dramatic struggle was resolved by the GOP's steamroller tactics, some of the excitement aroused by the election might have dissipated. More fundamentally, Roosevelt's crusade championed a direct relationship between candidates and voters—candidate-centered campaigns—that made for good theater but might have undercut the ability of parties to act as agents of mass mobilization.[21] Many reform leaders recognized the risks that progressive politics posed to mass voter participation, but Roosevelt's concerns about the future of the third party expressed the dilemma reformers faced in reconciling charismatic leadership and an enduring collective organization.

The Demise of the Progressive Party

The 1914 election confirmed TR's worst fears. Weak party organization at the state and local levels left Progressives with incomplete slates in many districts, and most of those who did run fared poorly. In every state but California, where Hiram Johnson was reelected governor, the Progressives had been badly defeated, and in most states they had come in a distant third. The disastrous results of the midterm election focused the Progressives' attention on the 1916 presidential campaign, when they hoped Roosevelt could rejuvenate the party. But with the outbreak of war in Europe, TR's attention turned from domestic reform to military preparedness. As war approached, the issue of America's place in the world, which was hardly mentioned in the 1912 campaign, further aggravated the disagreement among Progressive leaders over the appropriate role of the national state. Whereas Addams and her fellow social reformers were willing to swallow the two battleships a year to which TR committed the party in 1912, they could not abide his militaristic stance toward the European theater. Many Progressive stalwarts, including Addams, Amos Pinchot, Lillian Wald, and Paul Kellogg, joined the American Union Against Militarism, which lobbied Wilson and Congress against expanded funding for war preparation and legislation that authorized the president to conscript in time of war.[22] Wilson showed more sympathy for these antimilitaristic concerns than TR, who deeply resented the "pacifists"; they would make it impossible for Progressives to do their "duty in . . . a crisis," he fumed. Roosevelt wrote to Raymond Robins in June 1915, soon after the sinking of the *Lusitania*:

> During the last five years the professional pacifists have wrought greater mischief to the American character than either the corrupt politicians or the crooked business men. Their stand tells for unrighteousness. It tells for hideous wrongdoing at the expense of the helpless and innocent. Our position should be the position of the just man armed, the man who scorns to wrong others and is fearless in the face of the wrongdoer.[23]

Addams left the party once the national outrage over the *Lusitania* made war preparations the central issue within the Progressive councils. But the majority of party leaders stayed with TR, many of them embracing his view that progressivism involved the righteous use of superior force not only in domestic affairs but in the international arena as well. In urging Roosevelt to run again in 1916, Robins assured the colonel that he shared his view of America's duty to world affairs.

> The events of the last months and those of the next months will make American foreign policy of more moment both at home and abroad for the higher interests of domestic and world civilization than at any previous time in our history. . . . In this supreme hour, our national leadership is in danger of betrayal between the kindly but ignorant and feeble Democracy on the one hand and the selfish and wholly materialistic dollar diplomacy of the Standpatters on the other. From neither can the nobler genius of our people expect such service and vindication. Through neither can the true genius of our people find expression in this most vital period in the history of the western world.[24]

In spite of the support of Robins and other Progressive leaders for military preparedness, the party was a shell of itself, more than ever dependent on the whims of its heroic standard-bearer. When TR refused the Progressive nomination in 1916, returning to the Republican fold, the party dissolved, albeit not without considerable bitterness. As William Allen White described the convention delegates' reaction to Roosevelt's public letter of refusal,

> The last words, "But your candidate I cannot be," fell upon them like a curse. For a moment there was silence. Then there was a roar of rage. It was a cry of a broken heart such as no convention ever had uttered in this land before. . . . I saw hundreds of men tear the Roosevelt picture or the Roosevelt badge from their coats and throw it on the floor. They stalked out buzzing like angry bees.[25]

The unhealthy reliance of the Progressive Party on TR appeared to confirm the warnings of his critics that he had merely used it as a tool to further his own ambition. The fragility of the Bull Moose organization went deeper than Roosevelt's ample ambition, however. It is naïve to deny Roosevelt had great ambition for power; by the same token, it is simplistic to reduce the party's travails to a political maneuver. In part, the demise of the Progressive Party is attributable to its failure to find an issue that could overcome its fractious tendencies; at the same time, finding a unifying issue was made more difficult by its unstinting dedication to direct government. Indeed, there is a real sense in which the demise of the Progressive Party followed naturally from its doctrine, its celebration of "pure democracy," which was not congenial to party politics. Measures such as the direct primary subordinated parties as collective organizations with a past and a future to the ambitions of candidates and the issues of the moment. Moreover, measures of direct government, such as the initiative, recall, and referendum, presupposed an ongoing dialogue between representatives and their constituents about issues that denied parties their traditional responsibility of securing harmony in the ranks of its supporters. "If the parties are . . . to continue to do as they have done for the last fifty years, make the issues, then the Progressive party would probably little show," Progressive congressman Victor Murdock of Kansas wrote George Perkins in March 1914. "But the nature of the times and the pressing new problems are such that the issues are going to make the parties."[26]

Given the Bull Moose party's celebration of pure democracy, it is not surprising that the Progressive National Service never fulfilled the high ideals that informed its creation. By the end of 1913, the party's national committee cut back on the service's funding so as to devote more resources to the local and state elections that would occur in the following year. More problematic, the social workers and academics connected with the service shunned the more practical tasks involved in organizing election campaigns. They dedicated themselves to the long-term objective of public education—to the cultivation of a "progressive conscience." But the more practical organizers of the Progressive Party, such as Roosevelt, Albert Beveridge, and George Perkins, doubted that the new party could survive long enough to wait for social and political views to change. Either it would prove itself as a party in the near future by winning more offices, or it would cease to be a party.[27] Roosevelt and his more practically inclined allies agreed that the service played a valuable part in developing and publicizing progressive programs, but they believed that it did little to further the party's urgent need for grassroots organization and that those who ran it little understood the necessities involved in building and maintaining a party.

Still, the Progressive National Service, embodying the high ideals that Roosevelt himself so effectively championed during the 1912 campaign, offers important clues as to why certain features of progressive politics would endure even as the party faded away. Alice Carpenter, a member of the Progressive National Service's Department of Popular Government and the architect of the Working Man's Progressive Party League, dedicated to enlisting the support of labor in the cause, pointedly reminded Perkins of the principles that led militant reformers to join Roosevelt's crusade. Carpenter objected to Perkins's efforts to control her organization, in large part because she felt his direction, often impugned as the handmaiden of big business, would weaken the league's objective of strengthening the Progressives' ties with the labor movement.[28] Her protests against his interference, however, emphasized the Progressives' celebration of public opinion. "The principle upon which I have organized my League is the principle inherent in the direct primary, and is the principle above all others upon which the progressive movement is based; namely, that the people themselves should have the power to name their own candidates, and the PEOPLE not the political organizations should rule."[29]

The Progressive Party dedicated itself to the welfare state; at the same time, it stood for the proposition that any program of social control, social insurance, and standardization of industry could not be adopted until it was well digested by public opinion. There was no prospect in the United States—where centralized administration was a cardinal vice—that the people would grant legitimacy to a welfare state that was not attuned to the preferences, even biases, of public opinion. It was on these grounds that

Croly rejected the possibility of a social democratic party playing the same role in the United States that it was beginning to play in Western Europe and Great Britain (see Chapter 5). The popularity of the direct primary in the United States, Croly noted, revealed how centralized and disciplined parties went against the looser genius of American politics. To the extent that government became committed to a democratic program that was essentially social in character, the American people would find intolerable a two-party system that stood between popular will and government machinery. As Jane Addams noted in her Lincoln Day address, a fundamental principle of the Progressive Party was that a welfare state could not be created in the United States "unless the power of direct legislation is placed in the hands of the people, in order that these changes may come not as the centralized government [has] given them, from above down, but may come from the people up; that the people should be the directing and controlling force of legislation."[30]

So dedicated, the Progressive Party was a party to transcend party politics. Its death was not attributable simply to the caprices of TR or to the checkbook of George Perkins, or even to the fundamental disagreements over race, trusts, and foreign policy that divided its leaders. In large measure, it followed from the almost hopeless task of reconciling loyalty to the progressive ideal with loyalty to a particular organization. As Croly wrote in an editorial for the *New Republic*, a magazine founded in 1914 with the purpose of keeping Progressive principles alive,

> In our opinion progressivism is having and will continue to have a tendency to undermine the traditional two party system. That system was created to meet the needs of a democracy whose conditions and ideals differed radically from the conditions and ideals of modern democracy, and which had no social aspirations that were not sufficiently expressed in an individualistic bill of rights. It wanted to be protected against the government rather than to use the government as an instrument for the attainment of positive public ends. . . . The American democracy will not continue to need the two-party system to intermediate between the popular will and the government machinery. By means of executive leadership, expert administration, independence and direct legislation, it will gradually create a new governmental machinery which will be born with the impulse to destroy the two party system, and will itself be thoroughly and flexibly representative of the underlying purposes and needs of a more social democracy.[31]

Viewed in this way, as has been noted throughout this book, the Progressive idea of democracy was not a radical rejection of the American tradition. Rather, it marked an important effort to reconcile the country's celebration of individualism and reformers' recognition of the need to strengthen the national government. Building on, or more accurately, attempting to restore, the traditional disdain for parties in the United States, the Progressives presumed to provide individual men and women with the opportunity to vote patriotically, to free them from traditional partisan ties formed on local attachments, and to inoculate them from national attachments cultivated by class or racial conflicts. As Croly wrote in an essay prepared for a forum, which the *American Magazine* published in late October, on the critical nature of the 1912 election,

> The formation of the new national Progressive party has emancipated the progressive voter from . . . difficult and discouraging alternatives. The sincere and ardent reformer has finally been given a chance to exercise a decisive and momentous choice. The new party, devoted exclusively to his own cause of progressive democracy, has not merely freed him from meaningless and embarrassing partisan ties, but it has given life and power to the exercise of his will as an elector. He need no longer vote with a discretion that kills enthusiasm. His vote becomes an affirmation of faith—a dedication to personal service.[32]

This "dedication to personal service" distinguished the Progressive Party from the fledgling Socialist Party in 1912. Chapter 5 discussed how a growing number of reformers and voters were coming to see the Socialists as a viable reform alternative to the Democratic and Republican parties. Eugene Debs was an enormously appealing candidate who passionately articulated a vision of social democracy in traditional American terms. Invoking Lincoln, he depicted the industrial worker as the victim of an economic system that denigrated natural rights—the right of property—properly understood. As Victor Berger, the first Socialist elected to Congress, bluntly put it in his contribution to the *American Magazine* forum, "Political liberty and economic despotism are incompatible." Yet Berger, who played a critical part in strengthening the Socialists' national organization, which fielded a full slate of candidates and proscribed syndicalism, rejected the candidate-centered campaign that Roosevelt and Wilson identified as a critical ingredient of progressive reform. "As good a man as Eugene V. Debs is I am not going to vote for him in the sense one is voting for Wilson, Taft or Roosevelt," he wrote. "I simply vote the ticket of the Socialist party. I have no hope that the Socialist party will elect its candidate for president in this election. With us the Socialist movement and its principles are paramount—not the candidate." More fundamentally, the Socialists, as Debs himself had long argued, scorned the Progressives' faith in mass democracy:

> Why should we wait with our work until the majority of votes is with us? The majority is always indolent and often ignorant. We cannot expect them to be anything else with their present social surroundings. . . . The majority have never brought about consciously and deliberately any great social change. They have always permitted an energetic minority to prepare the way. But the majority was always there when the fact itself was to be accomplished.[33]

Roosevelt and the Progressives' willingness to invest in mass democracy gave them an advantage over their Socialist rivals. As John Dewey understood, Roosevelt's enormous popularity followed from his ability to embody the country's ambition during the first two decades of the twentieth century to undertake public action "on a large scale." "The ordinary politician," Dewey observed, "is fortunate when by dint of keeping his ear to the ground he can catch and reflect in articulate speech the half formed sentences of the people." "Roosevelt did not have to resort to this undignified posture"; he emerged as leader of the Progressive movement because "he was the phonograph in whose emphatic utterances the people recognized and greeted the collective composition of their individual voices."[34] In urging reformers to stand with him at Armageddon—to battle for the Lord—Roosevelt gave political effect to the alluring idea of "We the People." He posed hard challenges to the grand limited politics that Lincoln sanctified as an extension of the Declaration's "unalienable rights." Under his auspices, the Progressive Party invented a novel reform tradition that dramatically changed the way Americans thought about the Constitution and that paved the way for the creation of a national democracy buttressed by a modern executive that Roosevelt memorably ordained as the "steward of the public welfare." Such leadership did not bring voters to the polls in great numbers; nonetheless, reforms such as the direct primary, initiative, referendum, and recall were generally popular among the electorate. More important, the Progressive Party's idea of democracy, no matter how flawed, bestowed legitimacy on the unwritten law that the representatives derived their authority "directly" from the people, that American democracy would reach its fulfillment in an alliance between public opinion and the autonomous political executive, now freed from the constraints of traditional party organizations and practices.

As was noted in Chapter 5, the Progressive idea of a reconstituted executive joined directly to public opinion stole the thunder of the Socialist Party just as it was evolving as a force to reckon with in American politics. What Debs and Berger failed to understand in dubbing the Progressives "a reactionary protest of the middle classes, built largely upon the personality of one man," was that the middle classes would enlist in radical reform if the threat to their interests and values became severe enough. The fascist movements that emerged in Europe after 1918 would demonstrate just how radical and virulent middle-class political movements could become. No such pathological strain would arise in the United States of 1912, where generally prosperous conditions and resilient institutions prevailed. Nonetheless, the Progressive Party was anything but reactionary. Debs and his Socialist allies simply lacked the vocabulary and insight to formulate a clear view of the 1912 Progressives, for they really did represent something brand new in American politics.[35]

Indeed, many conservatives viewed Roosevelt and the Progressive Party as more radical and dangerous than the Socialists. Debs, at least, honored the natural rights tradition and recognized the critical importance of party organization. In contrast, Roosevelt, as Croly insisted, stood for a new declaration, which celebrated mass democracy and encouraged a fixation on leaders that threatened to sweep mediating institutions like interest groups and parties off the stage. As the GOP loyalist from Pennsylvania, Samuel Harden Church, argued in a letter to the *New York Times,* the claim of Roosevelt's supporters that the Progressive Party would staunch the country's growing support for socialism should not comfort conservatives. "If that is the choice, better far to have Debs in the White House," Church claimed, "yielding grudgingly to the control of immovable safeguards than to elect this insatiable adventurer, whose passion stays neither for the law nor precedent nor the binding honor of his own sacred promise."[36]

As Taft's poor showing revealed, however, there was not much sympathy in the country for such constitutional sobriety. Roosevelt's challenge to existing constitutional forms appeared to many people a message that would strengthen, rather than destroy, the dignity of the democratic individual. Moreover, Debs's rendition of natural rights, although powerful, was overshadowed by the Progressives' invocation of the whole people. Although Debs more than doubled the popular support he received in 1908, attaining over 900,000 votes, George Harvey, the editor of *Harper's Weekly*, estimated that if Roosevelt had not run, Debs would have had 500,000 more votes than he obtained.[37] It is not possible to determine precisely how many votes Roosevelt received that otherwise would have gone to Debs. In fact, Roosevelt and Debs shared relatively strong support in states such as California: Roosevelt won the state with nearly 42 percent of the vote, and Debs received nearly 12 percent of the vote, well above the 6 percent he received nationally. Nonetheless, Roosevelt appears to have won the support of many middle-class reform-oriented voters who otherwise would have been attracted to the moderate social democracy for which Berger, who lost his congressional seat in 1912, stood. For example, Roosevelt won Pennsylvania, doing especially well in those counties that tended to be urban, prosperous, and growing in population. In contrast, Debs's support (he won nearly 7 percent of the vote) tended to be concentrated in heavily industrialized areas, such as Allegheny County, where his vote increased over 300 percent from his 1908 total. As the *International Socialist Review* explained, the Socialist Party had been very active in Allegheny, "fighting side by side with other workingmen, pointing out new methods of Class warfare in every strike and lending a hand in very struggle." Not only did the *Review*, which had a close relationship to Debs, acknowledge that Roosevelt had taken votes from the Socialists, its editors celebrated this loss as a purifying experience. "Fortunately for us," they wrote, "the Progressive party is here to stay. It will steadily drain off muddle-headed members of the dying middle class advocates of government ownership, leaving only a band of class conscious Socialists who can be depended upon."[38]

So obsessed with the Progressive Party, Debs and the Socialist Party became a marginal force in American politics: the 6 percent of the vote Debs received in 1912 proved to be the Socialists' high-water mark in the United States. In contrast, although the Progressive Party collapsed, progressive democracy lived on and became the foundation of America's twentieth-century reform tradition. At the end of the day, the Progressives outflanked American Socialists not only because they offered more moderate measures that would ameliorate working conditions. Many Progressives' ideas also prevailed due to their less equivocal celebration of political reforms that most Americans accepted as necessary to restore public accountability to government.

The Enduring Importance of Progressive Democracy

The Progressive Party's "compromise" with public opinion in the United States points to its legacy for American politics and government. For nearly four decades, the scholarly effort to define progressivism or identify the principles and organizational forms of the Progressive movement has been under full-scale attack. Peter Filene has argued that the Progressive movement is an intellectual construct, a mere semantic device that never existed as a historical reality.[39] Although unwilling to go this far, Daniel Rodgers acknowledges that "the trouble with comprehending 'progressivism' as a list of beliefs" is that "progressives did not share a progressive creed or a string of common values." This era, he suggests, exemplified a new fragmented and issue-oriented politics in which often-contradictory reform movements sought to capitalize on the declining influence of traditional party control on politics and government. After all, as Daniel Rodgers notes, "those whom historians have labeled progressives shared no common party or organization."[40]

Still, there was a Progressive Party, and its brief existence involved an impressive effort, "an experiment," TR called it, to articulate a coherent progressive philosophy and comprehensive progressive program. Arguably, the failure of the 1912 experiment and the party's subsequent decline underscore the incoherence of the Progressive movement. Nevertheless, the Progressive Party can be viewed as an effort to define progressivism, temporarily housing a movement of public opinion rather than party, affecting the prestige and fortunes of all political leaders. It was neither the Democrats, the Republicans, nor the Socialists who set the tone of the 1912 campaign. It was the Progressives. "Roosevelt's platform," Arthur Link and Richard McCormick have written, "constituted a remarkable compendium of almost every social and economic reform then talked about in the United States—all bound together by one of the boldest visions in the history of mainstream American politics."[41] Beyond the 1912 election, the third party's program of political and social reform, including most of the Progressive era's reform agenda, has been an enduring feature of American political discourse and electoral struggle. The Progressive Party forged a path of reform that left both social democracy and conservatism—the constitutional sobriety of Taft—behind. Similarly, TR's celebrity, and the popularity of the Progressive doctrine of the people's right to rule, tended to subordinate the more populist prescriptions for "grassroots" democracy to the plebiscitary schemes in the platform—such as the initiative, the referendum, and the direct primary—that exalted mass opinion.

Of course, Wilson won the election, championing a New Freedom that was far more sympathetic to the decentralized state of courts and parties than was New Nationalism. Wilson warned that big government would not be accountable to public opinion, as Roosevelt promised. Instead, it would establish a ruling class that inevitably would be beholden to powerful interests. By lending assistance to the New Nationalist program, Wilson told an audience in Kansas, the reformer "is playing false to the very battle in which he has enlisted, for that battle is a battle against monopoly, against control, against the concentration of power in our economic development, against all those things that interfere with absolutely free enterprise." Urging progressives not to trust the "label" of the new party, Wilson, invoking Kansas's pivotal role in resisting the expansion of slavery, proclaimed that "monopoly shall never rear its head in this soil fertilized by the blood of martyrs in the cause of liberty!"[42] He insisted that his campaign, not Roosevelt's, was truly progressive, because it would bring needed change through such measures as tariff reform and antitrust policy, without sacrificing self-rule, which was sustained by America's foundational belief in local self-government and decentralized administration. He concluded that progressivism, properly understood, required an artful melding of received wisdom and innovative policy:

I believe for one that you cannot tear up ancient rootages and safely plant the tree of liberty in soil which is not native to it. I believe that the ancient traditions of a people are its ballast, that you cannot take a *tabula rasa* upon which to write and determine what your life shall be tomorrow. You must knit the new into the old. And you cannot put new patches on ancient garments without destroying, or endangering the destruction of, the ancient garment. It must be something woven into the fiber, of practically the same pattern, of the same texture and intention.[43]

The contrasting appeals of Roosevelt and Wilson gave the nation, Link and McCormick suggest, "its fullest opportunity to decide what progressivism meant."[44] At the same time, these divergent views appeared to defy the existence of a coherent progressive movement, especially as, in the aftermath of this contest for the mantle of reform leader, progressivism resided primarily in the much more pluralistic Democratic Party. Wilson's victory, Alonzo

Hamby has observed, ratified a compromise between progressivism and the self-interested nature of traditional American politics that "transmuted . . . the drive to restore the ideal of democratic citizenship working for the common interest . . . into the most fully elaborated system of pluralist coalition politics in American history."[45]

And yet, as Chapter 5 shows, Wilson's reform message had moved very far in Roosevelt's direction by the end of the campaign. Seeking to establish his own credentials as servant of the people, Wilson championed mass opinion almost as fervently as did Roosevelt, although the Democratic candidate stopped short of calling for referenda on court decisions and the recall of all public officials. "I would rather be the voice of a nation than the voice of a class," he announced in one of his final campaign speeches. "I would rather interpret the common feeling; I would rather know the common impulse of America than to originate. I would rather be the spokesman of the men who have confidence in me in any crisis, and who I know will stand behind me in any crisis, than to pride myself in the belief that I alone could devise a plan to redeem and restore the strength of the human race." Like Roosevelt, Wilson styled himself as an interpreter of public opinion who could transcend particular interests and parties. "America was coming out of the leading strings of parties and was beginning to transact the great business of humanity. Men and measures are the only things worthy of the thought of a great people who are not going to school to politicians, but going to school to their own consciences, following their own visions, realizing their own dreams of what American manhood means and must achieve."[46]

Wilson's New Freedom campaign was thus gradually eclipsed by Roosevelt's bolder defense of the "whole people." Indeed, in the wake of the excitement the Progressive Party aroused, Wilson felt compelled, or saw the opportunity, to govern more as a New Nationalist than a New Freedom progressive. As was observed in Chapter 4, this was not a radical shift in Wilson's politics. His attachment to conservative British thinker Edmund Burke did not lead to a firm embrace of traditional American values and institutions. It issued, instead, in an organic theory of political development that implied both a "disposition to preserve" and a "willingness to adjust."[47] The first sign of Wilson's flexibility came with his disregard for the plank of the Democratic Party that called for a constitutional amendment to limit the president to one term. This proposal reflected the fears of William Jennings Bryan and his Populist supporters of executive power. Wilson said nothing about the term limits provision prior to election day, but he now argued, much as Roosevelt had throughout his insurgency campaign, that it would betray the critical need for a strong executive in a nation transformed by the industrial revolution. The proper task, he insisted, was to reconstitute the executive as the embodiment of popular will. As he wrote to his attorney general, Alexander Mitchell Palmer, in February 1913, progressives "are seeking in every way to extend the power of the people, but in the matter of the Presidency we fear and distrust the people and seek to bind them hand and foot by rigid constitutional provision." Hoping to deflate support for a single term, Wilson proposed a national primary that would make more democratic, rather than diminish, the exercise of executive power.[48]

Wilson also took steps to enhance the power of public opinion over the councils of government.[49] Most notably, he revived the practice, abandoned by Thomas Jefferson, who believed it resembled too closely the British monarch's annual speech from the throne, of appearing before Congress to deliver important messages, including the State of the Union Address. With the rise of the mass media, Wilson believed, such occasions would help concentrate public attention on the actions of the president and Congress.[50] Overcoming the resistance of Democrats who still revered Jefferson as the patron saint of their party, Wilson addressed Congress frequently, beginning with an important address on tariff reform, a central issue of his presidential campaign. Well received by most members of Congress and the press, the president's precedent-shattering speech, delivered on April 8, 1913, launched the first successful campaign for serious tariff reform since before the Civil War.

Having embraced Roosevelt's concept of the executive as the steward of the people, Wilson also supported the idea of a regulatory commission with broad responsibilities for overseeing business practices, resulting in the creation in 1915 of the Federal Trade Commission. In addition, Wilson and the Democratic Congress enacted in 1913 the Federal Reserve Act, which established a board to oversee the national banking and currency system. Under the editorial leadership of Croly, the New Republic celebrated rather than scorned the inconsistency of Wilson and the Democrats: "The whole record ignores and defies the Jeffersonian tradition. Its tendency is to use Hamiltonian nationalism in the interest of a democratic social policy which is, of course, precisely what the Progressives proposed to do four years ago. The Progressive party is dead, but its principles are more alive than ever, because they are to a greater extent embodied in the official organization of the nation."[51] With the exception of the Underwood Tariff Reform Act, which became law in October 1913, Croly happily reported, "the New Freedom had been discarded." He thus joined many other erstwhile Progressive leaders in supporting Wilson's reelection. As he wrote in an editorial for the *New Republic* toward the end of the 1916 campaign, Wilson's "program no longer seeks the restoration of a regime of incoherent, indiscriminate, competitive, localistic individualism." "It foreshadows rather," Croly added, "a continuing process of purposive national reorganization determined in method by the realities of the task but dedicated to the ultimate enhancement of individual and associated life within and without the American commonwealth."[52]

To Amos Pinchot, who organized a group during the 1916 election, dubbed the Wilson Volunteers, to convert Roosevelt Progressives into Wilson supporters, the incumbent's victory over the Republican candidate, Charles Evans Hughes, marked a critical triumph for reform politics. Roosevelt had urged Progressives to support Hughes, but Pinchot, echoing Croly, insisted that Wilson "had embraced and put into execution progressive principles just as fast as, or a little faster than, Roosevelt had dropped them." Indeed, TR's return to the Republican fold signaled his embrace of imperialism, which many of his former allies could not abide. "The saber rattling conception of national honor that Mr. Roosevelt advances," Pinchot wrote, in a statement released for publication by the Democratic National Committee during the campaign, "to wit, that it is credible to seize the first opportunity to physically injure anyone who has in the slightest degree injured you, has no larger following among intelligent, patriotic foreigners than it has among intelligent patriotic Americans. It is the dying idea of trial by violence."[53] Taking pleasure in the critical part that erstwhile Bull Moosers played in Wilson's close but decisive victory, Pinchot wrote a congratulatory note to the reelected president: "It is hard for me to get used to the idea of your victory and Mr. Hughes' defeat, for I have hardly ever been on the winning side. Representing as he does the forces, which one might sum up as the Mammon of righteousness, Mr. Hughes certainly should have won, according to the precedent of practical politics. It is a beautiful thing to see the country heaving overboard past precedents and finding out that practical politics are no longer practical."[54]

Not all reformers agreed that Wilson's embrace of New Nationalist principles marked the triumph of progressive democracy. Most disappointed were civil rights activists, like W. E. B. Du Bois and William Monroe Trotter, who had thrown caution to the wind and supported Wilson in 1912. They had gambled that the election of an "enlightened Democrat" promised fairer treatment of blacks than the choice of Taft, who represented the broken promises of the Republican Party, or Roosevelt, who, in their view, had struck a shameful compromise with Jim Crow at the Progressive Party's convention. To be sure, as has been noted, most African Americans ignored their advice and voted for Roosevelt. Nonetheless, the support of civil rights activists, by most accounts, helped Wilson attain about 20 percent of the black vote, more than any Democratic candidate had received since the Civil War. Moreover, their attacks on Roosevelt—the charge that he was a rank hypocrite—badly tarnished the luster of the Progressive Party campaign.

After the inauguration, civil rights leaders quickly became disillusioned with the new president. Roosevelt accepted "Lily White" Progressive state delegations and the third party's deafening silence on the "Negro question" in its platform because he acknowledged the popularity of Jim Crow in the South. Wilson, a native of Virginia elected to the White House in large part because of white southern support, allowed his administration to actively promote racial segregation in the national government's departments and agencies. Some segregation had been introduced in the Roosevelt and Taft administrations, but these discriminatory practices were limited and took place without the direct support of these Republican presidents. Yet Wilson, who had promised black Americans "absolute fair dealing" during the election, knew and approved of the extension of segregation to several government departments, most notably in the Treasury and the Post Office. Moreover, Wilson bowed to pressure from southern Democrats in his patronage appointments: he appointed only two blacks during his first term while he dismissed many incumbents and put pressure on several others to resign.[55]

Civil rights leaders who wagered on Wilson rising above his southern roots and party expressed a strong sense of betrayal. Oswald Garrison Villard, who had played the principal part in wooing black support for the Democratic candidate, wrote a strong letter of protest in July 1913. The president replied summarily that segregation was not a movement against black Americans but, rather, something that served their best interests. Even Roosevelt, who certainly could be accused of pandering to racial prejudice, never defended segregation as a positive good. It was a necessary evil, he insisted, which must be confined to the South and gradually rolled back as racial attitudes allowed.

Things came to a head when a delegation, led by Trotter, obtained an audience with the president on November 12, 1914. In a confrontation that made the front page of the *New York Times*, Wilson once again argued "that the policy of segregation had been enforced for the comfort and best interests of both races in order to overcome friction." The president also told his visitors that the practice would continue, assuring them that segregation would nurture "the independent development . . . of the negro race." When Trotter protested vehemently, Wilson expressed his willingness to investigate individual cases of discrimination; however, the president stuck adamantly to his belief that separate but equal was good for the races; indeed, he insisted that segregation of blacks and whites, although enforced by the government, "had no place in politics." Angry at Trotter's persistent criticism of this attitude, Wilson interrupted the civil rights leader, who had praised the Democratic candidate as the "second Abraham Lincoln" during the 1912 campaign, and asked him to leave the White House. "What the President told us was entirely disappointing," Trotter told the press as he left. "His statement that segregation was intended to prevent racial friction is not supported by facts. For fifty years negro and white employees have worked together in the government departments in Washington. It was not until the present Administration came in that segregation was drastically introduced, only because of the racial prejudices of [Assistant Secretary of the Treasury] John Skelton Williams, Secretary [of the Treasury] William McAdoo, and Postmaster General [Joseph] Burleson."[56]

So the strange alliance between "radical" black leaders and the Democratic Party came to an end. Du Bois and Trotter found themselves in the political wilderness as the 1916 election approached. At first, Du Bois supported Hughes, albeit with little enthusiasm. "Under ordinary circumstances," he wrote in the *Crisis,* "the Negro must expect from him, as chief executive, the neglect, indifference and misunderstanding that he has had from recent Republican presidents. Nevertheless, he is practically the only candidate for whom we can vote." Near the end of the campaign, however, miffed at Hughes's deafening silence on the issues of lynching, disenfranchisement, and segregation, Du Bois "called a plague" on both major presidential candidates: he suggested that blacks should either lodge a protest vote for the Socialist Allen I. Benson or stay home on election day. But most African Americans joined Roosevelt in returning to the Republican Party, even though the GOP was hardly less anxious to cater to southern whites than was the Democratic Party.[57]

Although their support for Wilson was bitterly disappointed, it is difficult to argue that African American leaders missed the boat in failing to support the Progressive Party. To a point, Wilson's support for Jim Crow followed from the Democratic Party's perverse view of individual rights; in their reading of the Declaration, "unalienable rights" applied only to whites. But the Progressive Party, and Wilson's embrace of progressive principles, threatened to add a more assertive justification for ignoring the claims of those who were not part of the American community. Those who championed progressive democracy held that public opinion, not nature, supplied the standard of rights. Although Roosevelt and his followers heralded their intention to call Americans to a more noble calling, the principles and institutional reforms they advocated came to betray in many instances the biases and prejudices of public opinion.

Progressive Democracy Goes to War

The intertwining of moral purpose and repression were revealed dramatically during World War I. Wilson's position of neutrality had endured for two years after the sinking of the *Lusitania* and became the core theme of his reelection campaign: "He kept us out of war." But Germany's declaration of unlimited submarine warfare in February 1917, a practice it had been willing to renounce in the immediate aftermath of the *Lusitania* crisis, pushed Wilson to lead the United States into war. Just as the politics of military preparedness had divided Progressives, so the declaration of war deepened the schism over America's role in the world. For Addams and many of her social worker colleagues, who believed that the United States could use its "vast neutral power to extend democracy throughout the world," Wilson's decision was a terrible tragedy.[58] For Roosevelt and social gospelers like Lyman Abbott and Raymond Robins, the war would not only place the United States on the side of democracy against autocracy abroad but also weaken the forces of reaction at home. The hope that the Great War would promote a sense of public responsibility at home was not limited to the Social Gospel movement. John Dewey spoke for many progressive intellectuals in anticipating that the coming battle was "full of social possibilities." It would, he predicted, constrain "the individualistic tradition" that dominated America's past and teach its people "the supremacy of public need over private possessions."[59] Even Du Bois renewed for a time his faith in Wilson's progressivism and embraced the social promise of total war. As his July 1918 *Crisis* editorial "Close Ranks" read, "Let us, while this war lasts, forget our special grievances and close our ranks shoulder to shoulder with our white fellow citizens and the allied nations that are fighting for democracy. We make no ordinary sacrifice, but we make it gladly and willingly with our eyes lifted to the hills."[60]

Wilson's war message to Congress on April 2, 1917, clearly linked the country's entry into the European fray as the fulfillment of progressive democracy. "The world must be made safe for democracy," the president stated in a famous phrase. Only total war would advance the cause of self-government and "achieve the ultimate peace for the world and for the liberation of its peoples, including the German peoples," who were suffering under the Prussian autocracy. Thus, Wilson, who once professed a modest reformism dedicated, as the press put it, to American "normality," now infused American foreign policy with the same idealistic zeal that Roosevelt expressed in summoning his Progressive troops for a battle against domestic autocrats. "We have no selfish ends to serve," he insisted. "We desire no conquest, no dominion. We seek no indemnities for ourselves, no material compensation for the sacrifices we shall freely make. We are but one of the champions of the rights of mankind. We shall be satisfied when those rights have been made as secure as the faith and the freedom of nations can make them."[61]

As the *New Republic,* a strong defender of what Croly characterized as the "righteous use of superior force," predicted, the Great War proved "a pretext to foist innovations upon the country." Under the pressure of total war, the executive was transformed for a time into the steward that Progressives prescribed. Wilson instituted a draft that provided the bulk of the 4.8 million men who served in the military during the war. This was an important victory over the "easy going American individualism," the *New York Tribune* enthused—the mischievous "idea that one may serve the State or not, as he pleases."[62] But the president's duties went well beyond his responsibilities as commander in chief. Wilson also became responsible for organizing and controlling the industrial economy and for coordinating the transportation and communication industries so they could meet the requirements of military commitment. The exigencies of economic and social mobilization appeared to establish the very form of expert administration that Wilson had scorned in attacking Roosevelt's New Nationalist ambitions during the 1912 campaign. Extraordinary powers were invested in wartime administrators such as Bernard Baruch, who chaired the powerful War Industries Board; Herbert Hoover, who served as food administrator; and Secretary of the Treasury McAdoo, who managed the railroads. Nonetheless, as the historian Michael McGerr has written, "even though the Wilson administration greatly expanded and employed the coercive power of the federal government, the war managers, in typical progressive fashion, preferred to manipulate or cajole, rather than strong arm the American people."[63]

Whenever push came to shove with respect to gaining the cooperation of big business in the war effort or confronting dissent among the citizenry, the Wilson administration was determined to bring the recalcitrant to the attention of public opinion, and bring the moral authority of the "whole people" to bear against recusant individuals, groups, and businesses. In order to arouse the patriotism of Americans, Wilson formed the Committee on Public Information (CPI). Led by the passionate muckraker George Creel, the CPI enlisted seventy-five thousand speakers to persuade the public that war was a crusade for freedom and democracy against the Germans, a people corrupted by a barbaric government bent on world domination. Most Americans supported the war. But a significant minority opposed it, including not only progressive pacifists such as Addams but also many German and Irish Americans, whose ethnic ties disposed them to doubt the cause of the Allied powers. The CPI and several self-styled patriotic groups sought to discourage and sometimes repress dissent. Creel established a Division of Work with the Foreign-Born, which produced pamphlets and also monitored foreign-language newspapers and magazines for disloyalty. People who refused to buy war bonds were often ridiculed; some were even assaulted. Those with German names, scorned as "hyphenate Americans," were prosecuted indiscriminately. Some school boards outlawed the teaching of the German language.

Wilson's progressive principles did not deter this wave of oppression. Indeed, his view that war was a moral crusade for democracy actually inspired intolerance toward those who disagreed. The president signed the Espionage Act of 1917, which imposed fines of up to $10,000 and jail sentences as long as twenty years for persons convicted of aiding the enemy or obstructing the recruitment of soldiers. Wilson also authorized the postmaster general to ban from the mails material that seemed treasonous or seditious. In May 1918, at Wilson's urging, Congress passed the Sedition Act, an amendment to the Espionage Act, which made "saying anything" to discourage the purchase of war bonds a crime. The act also made it illegal to "utter, print, write, or publish any disloyal, profane, scurrilous, or abusive language" about the government, the Constitution, or the uniforms worn by soldiers and sailors. Not surprisingly, this assault on dissent was leveled most aggressively on Socialists. The Progressive Party campaign of 1912 isolated the Socialist Party; the progressive crusade during the First World War persecuted its leaders. A federal court sentenced Eugene Debs to ten years in jail for making an antiwar speech. Thus, a Socialist, dedicated to nationalizing the means of production, became the champion of natural rights. In his statement to the court Debs scorned a law that he charged was in "flagrant conflict with democratic principles and the spirit of free institutions."[64] Meanwhile, Wilson, a progressive champion of the American way of life, seemed indifferent to civil liberties.

The atmosphere of intolerance aroused by the war eventually spread to industrial relations. The critical support that the leader of the American Federation of Labor, Samuel Gompers, gave Wilson and the Democratic Party during the 1912 campaign resulted initially in important gains for labor: "collective bargaining rights began to be guaranteed, trade union membership soared, and an increasing number of large corporations agreed to establish consultative committees with their workers."[65] Once the United States entered the European theater, Gompers negotiated a voluntary no-strike deal in exchange for the Wilson administration's promise of greater union recognition. This deal collapsed, however, as wartime economic hardships, subjecting workers to rampant inflation and stagnant wages, led to an unprecedented outbreak of industrial conflict. In response, the Wilson administration abandoned its support of collective bargaining rights and turned instead to industrial repression. It clamped down especially hard on the Industrial Workers of the World, sentencing its leader, "Big Bill" Haywood, who had refused to join Debs in rejecting syndicalism (see Chapter 5), to twenty years in prison. Haywood escaped this fate only by fleeing to the Soviet Union.[66]

The fate of Jane Addams during the war most dramatically illustrated the reactionary potential of progressive democracy. The alliance formed between Roosevelt and Addams at the Progressive Party convention appeared to mark a political merger of charisma and communal virtues that would ensure the triumph of progressive democracy. By 1919, Roosevelt was dead, his reform legacy tarnished by a militarism that showed no more tolerance for dissent than did Wilson and his war managers. Addams, celebrated as the ideal democratic citizen during the Progressive Party campaign, was not prosecuted for her opposition to the Great War, but she suffered terribly from the intolerance of public opinion, which she had so fervently championed. Maude Royden, a British pacifist, described the radical changes in attitude toward Addams during the war:

In America in 1912 I learned that it was unsafe to mention Jane Addams's name in public speech unless you were prepared for an interruption, because the mere reference to her provoked such a storm of applause. They told me Jane Addams's mere promise of support to Mr. Theodore Roosevelt was worth a million votes to him. . . . And I was in America again after the war, and I realized with a shock how complete was the eclipse of her fame. . . . Her popularity had swiftly and completely vanished. . . . How well I remember, when I spoke in America in 1922 and 1923, the silence that greeted the name of Jane Addams.[67]

Many of Addams's Progressive colleagues and friends joined that silence. The "red scare" that followed the triumph of Bolsheviks in Russia intensified the assault on dissenters in the United States, affecting not only Socialists like Debs but also mainstream reformers like Addams who had been active in progressive organizations that opposed the war. "Many of us," wrote a regretful Donald Richberg, a Chicago lawyer and an active participant in the Bull Moose campaign, "now can look back upon the heroic efforts [of pacifists] like Jane Addams, and feel a little small and ashamed that, even if we did not join with those who scowled and spat upon them . . . yet we watched them through troubled, puzzled eyes." That silence, Richberg admitted, sucked the vitality out of Progressive reform. "Thus we prepared for the final dissolution of the progressive movement," he wrote. "To doubt, to question the wisdom of the powers that be, to advance new and disturbing ideas, had ceased to be an act of virtue, the proof of an aspiring spirit. Such attitudes were 'radical' and 'destructive.'" With the red scare, things only got worse. "Progressivism," Richberg concluded sadly, had "lost its supreme asset—respectability."[68]

Conclusion: Return to Normalcy and the Resurrection of Progressive Democracy

The 1920 election appeared to confirm the death of progressivism. It occurred in the aftermath of Wilson's abortive campaign for the League of Nations, which offered dramatic evidence that the "modern" executive—enthroned as the "steward of the public welfare"—had limited sway over the American people. Given the enactment of the Nineteenth Amendment just prior to the election, the presidential campaign might have been a Progressive triumph—the first national contest under women's suffrage. Instead, the election of Republican Warren G. Harding, the conservative anti-League Republican senator from Ohio, appeared to be a major setback for progressivism and its commitment to popular presidential leadership. Ostensibly, the landslide election, in which Harding won 60 percent of the national popular vote, was fought on the League of Nations. But in rejecting the League, so closely identified with Wilson and his aspirations for national and international reform, voters were expressing their desire for quieter times after two decades of far-reaching and unsettling political change. Harding, not Wilson, who inspired the press to use the term during the 1912 election, would forever be identified with a yearning for "normalcy."[69] In May 1920, the Republican candidate told the Home Market Club in Boston, "America's present need is not heroics, but healing; not nostrums but normalcy; not revolution but restoration . . . not surgery but serenity." The word *normalcy,* in particular, attracted immediate and lasting attention, and "a return to normalcy" became the theme of the 1920 presidential campaign.

Having won a great landslide on no small part due to their candidate's identification with the nation's longing for a moratorium on change, the Republicans resumed power in March 1921, militant in their determination to rehabilitate constitutional sobriety, rugged individualism, and party organization to their former stature. And yet, the critical election of 1912, and its aftermath, had irrevocably changed American politics. It is interesting to note in this regard that President Harding commuted Debs's sentence in December 1921, not on grounds of civil liberties or law but, rather, as a result of the perception, supported by "an overwhelming mass of letters, petitions, and resolutions," that public opinion had come to view his imprisonment as unjust.[70]

Without question, Wilson's failures and the wayward path of progressivism during the First World War testified to the limits of New Nationalism. Nonetheless, the changes wrought by the Progressive Party campaign ensured that localized parties were no longer the principal agents of democracy and that the alliance between decentralization and democracy was gradually weakened in favor of a relationship between the individual and the "state." The advance of the ideas and institutions of progressive democracy invariably followed. Robert La Follette's insurgent campaign of 1924, which captured 16 percent of the popular vote, reveals that progressivism did not go into hibernation during the 1920s. Indeed, La Follette's independent campaign, lacking any semblance of a party organization, advanced further the Progressive concept of direct democracy. That La Follette received such an impressive vote despite a booming economy and the popularity of incumbent president Calvin Coolidge testified to the growing fragility of the two-party system.[71] With the celebration of public opinion spawned by the Progressive Party campaign of 1912, even conservatives like Coolidge were forced to go directly to the public to ensure support for themselves and their policies. Coolidge, in fact, was the first president to make use of a new medium, the radio, which he used effectively to enhance his image and to enlist support for his tax reform plan. The decentralized party system would endure as an important institution until the 1970s, yet it would never again be a bulwark of a decentralized republic—a "wall of separation" between the national community and the many communities at the state and local level.[72]

Emancipated from the "wheelwork" of the two-party system, the surges of progressivism endured throughout the 1920s. As became clear during World War I, these episodes were as likely to bring policies that appeared to be reactionary as reformist.[73] Thus women's suffrage triumphed, but so did immigration restriction and Prohibition, which many, if not a majority of, progressives supported. Some New Nationalists, especially more provincial social gospelers such as Raymond Robins, tended to equate the improvement of American democracy with the triumph of the Protestant faith. In urging Roosevelt to run in 1916, he wrote, "there are two issues upon which the utmost care should be exercised. The one is Romanism and the other Prohibition. Both are powerful, treacherous, hidden currents in the stream of national life." Referring to some of the colonel's recent utterances that proscribed anti-Catholicism and temperance, Robins urged TR to avoid writing articles or giving speeches that championed religious toleration or cast doubt on the wisdom of prohibiting the consumption of alcohol. "No man can be nominated in a Republican national primary who is a pro-Romanist," Robins insisted. "No man can be elected President in 1916 who is believed to be against the vigorous control and ultimate suppression of the open saloon for private profit."[74]

Roosevelt's reply suggested that he feared public opinion on these issues, especially on the Catholic question. TR revealed, in fact, that the religious intolerance he sensed, along with the public's resistance to military preparedness, was an important reason for his refusing to run again in 1916. Roosevelt acknowledged that he was not strongly opposed to Prohibition, although he argued, presciently, that the plan to enact national restrictions through a constitutional amendment "was in advance of the people," without whose support such a measure would backfire. But Roosevelt took strong exception to Robins's criticism of his "Romanism." His attack on anti-Catholicism, he wrote, was part of a general belief in maintaining some separation between the state and religious practice. Just as Roosevelt refused to countenance religious intolerance, so he stood "openly and aggressively for non-sectarian Public Schools and against any diversion of the public money to sectarian schools." His opposition to mixing church and state, Roosevelt added, included an open "stand against reading the Bible in Public Schools when Catholics and Jews might object to its being read." Thus Roosevelt concluded:

> I do not care whether the discrimination is for or against a man because of his creed; it is equally un-American in either case. . . . This is not an issue upon which I can compromise; it is not an issue on which I would feel it was right to compromise. . . . But with the anti-Catholic public feeling as you describe it, and as I have no doubt it actually is, I think this is another reason why it would be hopeless and mischievous even to consider putting me forward for the Presidency at this time.[75]

Roosevelt's response to Robins suggests that had he not been so distracted by the foreign situation, the Progressive standard-bearer might have rethought substantially his support of pure democracy, to acknowledge that in their rejection of traditional constitutional remedies and their indifference to political associations, reformers risked the manipulation of progressive means for ends that badly fractured the Progressive movement—ends that some reformers abhorred. The mere fact that immigration restriction and Prohibition "were potentially or actively regressive does not mean that they were not progressive," Arthur Link insisted. "On the contrary," he continued, "they superbly illustrated the repressive tendencies that inhered in progressivism precisely because it was grounded so much upon majoritarian principles."[76]

Many Progressives, in fact, began to rethink their celebration of New Nationalism during the Great War.[77] Notably, one of these revisionists was Herbert Croly, the prophet of progressive democracy. Toward the end of 1917, his essays in the *New Republic* began to warn that the war accentuated a tendency in all modern nations to attribute "moral sovereignty to physically powerful states without sufficient assurance of the use of the power for genuinely social purposes." America was not immune from this trend; indeed, the emphasis on individualism in the United States "savagely prevented the growth of corporate bodies," such as labor unions and other types of interest groups, that would stand between citizens and the central government. As a result, the emergence of a modern American state was leading to a "contradictory combination of individualism and indivisibility." Unless this trend was ameliorated, Croly feared, America's "liberal democracy" risked becoming a "Jacobin democracy." Just a few years before,

Croly had urged the creation of a national commonwealth that would join mass democracy and social purpose. But the sobering lessons of the war made him challenge "the assumption that existing states, merely because they claim to embody the common concerns of the whole community, can be trusted as consummate servants of the moral progress of humanity." The "experimental and chiefly educative character" that constituted the "peculiar merit" of a national commonwealth would be lost, Croly insisted, unless it "invited the competition which is necessary for its own moral vitality." If the choice were one between an "indivisible state and a dismembered society," he would choose the former, Croly conceded. But American democracy was not confined to such a choice. The moral vitality of the modern state, he concluded, could be strengthened with the toleration—indeed, fostering—of "competition" from intermediary organizations:

> [The country's] leaders have failed to understand to what extent a strong and coherent national organization must be the reflection not only of independence of character on that part of individual citizens, but of equally genuine independence on the part of those associations which represent its fundamental industrial and social activities. The legal recognition of such associations constitutes the best possible guarantee against the arrogance of abuse either of state power or of power of any particular professional or trade association.[78]

Croly's concern about progressive democracy degenerating into plebiscitary politics was given a more complete elaboration in John Dewey's struggles during the 1920s to reconcile individualism with progressive ideals. Like Croly, Dewey was sobered by the oppressive impulses that progressivism displayed during the First World War. Like Croly, too, he feared that centralized administration threatened to destroy, rather than strengthen, the dignity of the democratic individual. As Dewey conceded in 1927,

> The same forces which have brought about the forms of democratic government, general welfare, executive and legislatures chosen by majority vote, have also brought about conditions which halt the social and human ideals that demand the utilization of government as the genuine instrumentality of an inclusive and fraternally associated people. "The new age of human relationships" has no political agencies worthy of it. The democratic public is still largely inchoate and unorganized.[79]

CHAPTER SIX

Reflecting on the abusive power of "the American democracy" during the Great War, Croly looked to industrial and social organizations to connect vitally national administration and individuals; in the midst of the fractiousness of the 1920s, Dewey spied a crisis of community that could only be remedied by revitalizing and reconstituting locality. The attachment of democratic individuals, Dewey held, had to shift from the emotive grounds of local ties to "the cumulative and transmitted intellectual wealth of community." As Dewey put it optimistically, "the Great Community, in the sense of free and full intercommunication," would do "its final work in ordering the relations and enriching the experience of local associations."[80] Yet this faint optimism left unanswered the question of how such a cosmopolitan idea of localism could be made effective. Just as Croly's concept of a corporate state threatened to reduce progressivism to an interest-group society, so Dewey's vision of a Great Community appeared to subsume local self-government into vague declarations of the public interest.

The historian Robert Wiebe has observed that during the 1920s, "Dewey became just another voice in the chorus declaring a crisis in democracy."[81] By the eve of the Great Depression, however, his search for a synthesis between traditional American virtues and national reform settled on the more confident prescription that progressivism could re-create itself as a "new individualism."[82] For Dewey, progressivism could have an enduring and salubrious effect on the American polity only insofar as it could be transformed into a new liberal tradition. New Liberalism did not embrace "rugged individualism," celebrated by Herbert Hoover as the foundation of America's "unparalleled greatness," which abhorred state interference with private property, but instead viewed the state as the guarantor of social and democratic welfare.[83] In his influential *Liberalism and Social Action,* a book he dedicated to the memory of Jane Addams, Dewey wrote, "These new liberals fostered the idea that the state has the responsibility for creating institutions under which individuals can effectively realize the potentialities that are theirs." It had the duty to advance social welfare policy and foster community participation in the "cause of the liberty of the human spirit."[84]

At the peak of New Nationalist enthusiasm, Croly had anticipated that a purposive national democracy would supplant rights consciousness in the United States and mark the adoption of a veritable "new declaration of independence." From the ashes of the crisis of democracy that progressivism wrought, Dewey discovered a more traditional rendering. "The great tradition of America is liberal," the philosopher H. M. Kallen wrote in his review of *Liberalism and Social Action*, which Dewey "restates in language under the conditions of his time what Jefferson's Declaration of Independence affirmed in the language and under the conditions of his."[85]

Although the hope of many social reformers that the Progressive Party would serve as an instrument for unifying disparate groups and causes came unraveled, Dewey's celebration of a new conception of liberalism underscores the important ties between the Progressive Party of 1912 and the New Deal's programmatic and institutional aspirations. Indeed, the New Deal realignment marks the consolidation of many significant changes begun by the Progressive Party campaign of 1912. The so-called purge campaign and other partisan practices during the New Deal period suggest a political program to create a national programmatic two-party system. The system of party responsibility, Franklin Roosevelt argued, "required that one of its parties be the liberal party and the other be the conservative party."[86] Ultimately, however, FDR and his New Deal allies, many of whom were former Bull Moosers, took action and pursued procedural reforms that would establish candidate-centered elections and executive-centered party organizations. Like the Progressive Party, the New Deal Democratic Party was formed to advance the personal and nonpartisan responsibility of the executive at the expense of collective and partisan responsibility. The New Deal—like its successor in the 1960s, the Great Society, which extended new liberalism to the cause of civil rights—was less a partisan program than an exercise in extending the president's responsibility to fulfill popular aspirations for social and economic welfare.[87]

This is not to deny that there are very significant differences between New Nationalist progressivism and New Deal liberalism. In calling themselves liberals, rather than progressives, New Dealers borrowed from Dewey, but FDR's version was more in keeping with the American constitutional tradition. Most important, it asserted more directly the connection between a strong national government and rights. Beginning with his 1932 campaign speech at the Commonwealth Club and at each key rhetorical juncture thereafter, FDR stated that the purpose of modern government was "to assist in the development of an economic declaration of rights, an economic constitutional order."[88] Just as the Progressive Party platform of 1912 proclaimed an inextricable connection between an expansive welfare state with direct democracy—a "covenant with the people"—so the 1936 Democratic platform was written as a pastiche of the Declaration of Independence and emphasized the need for a more capacious understanding of natural rights. If the national government was truly to protect liberty, the natural rights

CHAPTER SIX

tradition had to be enlarged to include programmatic rights. With respect to the 1935 Social Security legislation, the platform claimed:

> We hold this truth to be self-evident—that the test of representative government is its ability to promote the safety and happiness of the people. . . . We have built the foundations for the security of those who are faced with the hazards of unemployment and old age, for the orphaned, the crippled, and the blind. On the foundations of the Social Security Act we are determined to erect a structure of economic security for all of our people, making sure that this benefit shall keep step with the ever-increasing capacity of America to provide a high standard of living for all its people.[89]

The New Deal task of pronouncing a progressive understanding of rights culminated during the Second World War. As FDR stated in his 1944 State of the Union Address, constructing a foundation for economic security meant that the inalienable rights protected by the Constitution—speech, press, worship, due process—had to be *supplemented* by a new bill of rights "under which a new basis of security and property can be established for all—regardless of station, race, or creed." Included in the second bill of rights were the right to a useful and remunerative job; the right to own enough to provide adequate food, clothing, and recreation; the right to adequate medical care; the right to a decent home; the right to adequate protection from the economic fears of old age, sickness, accident, and un-employment; and the right to a good education.[90]

The defense of progressive reforms in terms of extending the rights of the Constitution marked an important development in the advent of the pro-gressive understanding of government responsibility. FDR bestowed greater legitimacy on progressive principles than did his cousin by his willingness to embed them in the language of constitutionalism and interpreting them as an expansion rather than rejection of the natural rights tradition. Practi-cally speaking, New Deal liberalism represented a more secular and less idealistic program of reform, albeit one that had more appeal to African Americans, Catholics, and blue-collar workers than did New Nationalism. When FDR signed the Beer-Wine Revenue Act in March of 1933, he sig-naled his support for reversing the temperance policy, which had been sup-ported by many Progressives and which had alienated many ethnic groups in the country. The ratification of the Twenty-first Amendment in December of that year represented a setback for the intolerant Protestantism that had a powerful influence on progressivism during the 1920s. Moreover, it anticipated the New Dealers' success in winning the support of ethnic groups in the Midwest and Northeast who could not abide the 1912 third-party movement. Similarly, FDR's interpretation of New Deal programs as programmatic rights led eventually to the recognition of collective bargaining rights that helped nurture a strong union movement, which became a principal constituency of the liberal coalition.

By 1936, it was clear, the New Deal economic constitutional order appealed to African Americans as well. At first, as W. E. B. Du Bois prescribed in supporting Wilson in 1912, African Americans were drawn to the New Deal for economic reasons—because it promised more relief from the harsh conditions under which they labored than Hoover's idea of "rugged individualism." Like his progressive forbears—TR and Wilson—FDR hoped the South could be enlisted in progressive reform. Consequently, in its early days, New Dealers, true to the Progressive tradition, did not show much concern for the rights of African Americans. For example, the 1938 Federal Housing Administration Act required that government-insured home mortgages have racially restrictive covenants.[91] Only two years later, however, the Roosevelt administration, pressured by a growing civil rights movement, established the Fair Employment Practices Committee (FEPC), which was charged with eliminating discrimination in the employment of workers in the defense industry or in the government because of race, color, creed, or national origin. As the wartime internment of Japanese Americans and the continued racial segregation of the armed forces showed, this action did not mark a sea change in civil rights policy. Nor was the FEPC an adequate response to racial discrimination. Nevertheless, it was the first federal government effort since Reconstruction that was specifically aimed at alleviating racial discrimination.

Befitting New Deal liberalism's support for rights talk, these administrative efforts were joined to judicial politics. As the court-packing plan and Roosevelt's subsequent judicial politics revealed, the problem of conservative jurisprudence was treated not through a program to weaken the courts' institutional power but with a direct assault on extant legal doctrine. This strategy was extended to civil rights in 1939, when the attorney general Frank Murphy, at FDR's behest, set up the Civil Liberties Section of the Justice Department. Later called the Civil Rights Section, this office played a critical part in beginning and successfully adjudicating Supreme Court cases that challenged white supremacy in the South. The most important case, *Smith v. Allwright*, decided in 1944, declared the white primary, a critical foundation of Jim Crow electoral practices and a perverse application of progressive reform, unconstitutional.[92] FDR's successor, Harry S Truman, built on the New Deal's cautious early efforts to extend the idea of programmatic rights to African Americans, most notably with his 1948 executive order demanding that "there shall be equality of treatment and opportunity in the Armed Services without regard to race, color, or national origin." From this perspective, as the historian Morton Keller has observed, the Great Society civil rights legislation of the 1960s was "the fulfillment of much that was implicit in the New Deal."[93]

New Deal liberalism, then, aimed not at forging a direct tie between public officials and popular opinion but, rather, at "redefining the social contract," as FDR put it, thus preserving many features of American constitutional tradition—especially a commitment to individual rights and a strong, independent judiciary—that TR and his moralistic followers scorned. Nevertheless, the new rights that FDR and his New Deal political allies championed were never formally ratified as part of the Constitution. Nor did most militant New Dealers want them to be. To transform the "second bill of rights" into a constitutional program would deny New Deal liberals the discretion to administer programs prudently and would bind the New Deal constitutional order in a legal straightjacket. The Constitution, FDR insisted in his address celebrating its sesquicentennial, "was not a lawyer's contract."[94]

No less than New Nationalist progressives, therefore, New Deal liberals embraced a pragmatic understanding of governance that rejected traditional constitutional and legal forms. As the astute New Dealer Chester Bowles observed in urging Roosevelt to pronounce a new understanding of rights during the Second World War, the most important objective was to articulate "a program which everyone can understand, and will bring to all men in our Armed Forces and the millions of men, women and children here at home, new hope for the future that lies ahead."[95] As Bowles hoped, although the New Deal idea of rights was not adopted into the Constitution, it resonated with the American people. Significantly, Roosevelt not only made effective use of the radio in taking the people to school on the new idea of rights, he also was the first president to make extensive use of surveys and pollsters. This gave the president a direct source of information about what the people were thinking and how they were responding to his program. With the help of the respected pollster Hadley Cantril, the Roosevelt administration learned that the American people viewed the idea of a "second bill of rights" favorably.[96] These polls no doubt encouraged FDR to make the economic bill of rights the centerpiece of his 1944 State of the Union Address, and he returned to the new idea of rights during the presidential election campaign, making it the principal theme of his most important campaign address. Beyond the 1944 election, the new bill of rights became the foundation of political dialogue, redefining the role of the national government.

New Deal liberalism thus became the surrogate for the second Declaration that Croly had prescribed. It redefined in important respects the social contract, so that rights became associated with collective endeavors such as social security, consumer and environmental protection, civil rights, and education. Moreover, just as Progressives championed internationalism that would make the world safe for democracy, so New Deal rhetoric stressed collective international rights. As FDR put it in his famous 1941 Four Freedoms speech, the traditional liberal freedoms of speech and religion were to be supplemented by two new freedoms. "Freedom from Want" was a commitment to "economic understandings which [would] secure to every nation a healthy peace time life for its inhabitants." "Freedom from Fear" was dedicated to "a world-wide reduction of armaments to such a point and such a fashion that no nation will be in a position to commit an act of physical aggression against any neighbor."[97] Like the Progressive understanding of national community, these domestic and international collective rights presupposed an expansion of national administrative power and an inclusive popular nationalism.

Understood within the context of the Progressive tradition, the New Deal is appropriately viewed as the completion of a realignment that would make future partisan realignments unnecessary. Far more than was the case with Wilson, under the leadership of FDR the Democratic Party became an instrument of greater national purpose. Ultimately, however, this purpose was dedicated to the creation of a progressive national state that would displace partisan politics with "enlightened administration." Like the Progressive Party, the New Deal Democratic Party was forged as an organization to transcend rather than reform the American party system. Having witnessed the rapid demise of the Progressive Party, FDR and many of his top advisors understood that a major partisan effort was necessary to generate popular support for the economic constitutional order. To a point, this made partisanship an integral part of New Deal politics, for it was necessary to remake the Democratic Party as an instrument to free the councils of government, particularly the president and bureaucracy, from the restraints of traditional party politics and constitutional understandings. But the Democratic Party was to be but a way station on the road to progressive democracy, where, to quote the important Brownlow Committee report, "Our national will must be expressed not merely in a brief exultant moment of electoral decision, but in persistent, determined, competent day-by-day administration of what the nation has decided to do."[98]

Nonetheless, the ambition reformers invested in progressive democracy, the hope of creating self-government on a grand scale, was ultimately disappointed. The expansion of national administrative power that followed the New Deal realignment did not result, after all, in the form of national state progressive reformers had championed—one enshrining regulation and social welfare policy as expressions of national unity and popular commitment. Progressive and New Deal reformers sought to circumvent the American antipathy to the expansion of national administrative power by rooting the idea of a national state in constitutional language: "We the People," in the case of Progressives, and "Economic Bill of Rights," the exalted purpose of New Deal liberalism. For all the success progressive reformers had in formulating an indigenous reform tradition, however, they left their programs exposed to the vagaries of public opinion and to the capture of interest groups. The New Deal commitment to new freedoms, in particular, left liberal initiatives vulnerable not only to the interference of Congress and the courts but also to the "public" interest groups that formed to protect these programs. Consequently, particular programs, such as Social Security and Medicare, have achieved popular support, but New Deal liberalism was never defined and defended in such a form that could withstand the rights-based claims of favored constituencies.

At the end of the day, a study of the Progressive Party sheds light on the love-hate relationship Americans forged with the state in the twentieth century, a profound ambivalence that seeks refuge in forms of participation, such as the direct primary, referendum, and initiative, that expose national and state governments to the uncertain fortunes of mass public opinion. The direct form of popular rule championed by the Progressive Party of 1912 became newly relevant with the emergence of the Great Society in the 1960s and 1970s, as reformers attempted to revive the Progressive aspiration for national administrative power to serve as an agent of democracy. For all the failures these reformers experienced, their call for "participatory democracy" would have an enduring influence on politics and government in the United States.[99] By the early 1970s, direct primaries and caucuses would replace the national party conventions as the principal means of nominating presidential candidates. During the past four decades, moreover, the initiative process has become a routine way of making critical government decisions in the twenty-four states that provide voters the opportunity to participate in these exercises of direct democracy. Furthermore, the belief in direct democracy has affected the rest of the nation as well as the work of the federal government, by advancing the notion that representatives should be beholden to public opinion.[100]

Conservatives, no less than liberals, now choose to draw on progressive solutions. The strand of conservatism that arose in opposition to the Progressive movement, represented by Taft's support for constitutional forms like separation of powers and federalism, embraced a settled standing body of law, upheld the right of property, and resisted popular and populist solutions to political and social discontents. This Whiggish defense of traditional institutions and values has largely been eclipsed by a modern form of conservatism that prescribes a less defensive strategy in the war against the progressive state. Indeed, ballot initiatives became a favorite tactic of conservative activists in California to challenge its progressive establishment. Beginning with Proposition 13, an anti–property tax measure passed in 1978, conservative activists enacted a number of initiatives constraining government revenues, reducing welfare benefits for illegal aliens, and prohibiting public universities and state agencies from using affirmative action programs in admissions and hiring practices. The popular enthusiasm generated by these measures soon spread beyond California, helping to propel Ronald Reagan to the White House in 1980 and to push taxes to the forefront of the national political agenda. Reagan was the first president in nearly fifty years who appealed to natural rights and limited government. And yet, his assault of the liberal state deployed the rhetorical and administrative powers of the modern executive in a way that reinforced rather than challenged the progressive idea that the president, rather than Congress or political parties, was the steward of popular rule in the United States. In his hands, the Republican Party was not reborn as the guardian of limited government. Rather, as one commentator astutely observed toward the end of his presidency, Reagan "did not reinvent the Republican party so much as transcend it. His primary political instrument was the conservative movement, which inhabited the party out of convenience."[101] Without question, Reagan and the conservative groups that supported him strengthened the Republican Party; indeed, the Reagan administration's assault on liberal programs and organizations contributed to the revitalization of party politics in the United States. Nevertheless, his administration's view that the entrenchment of the liberal state required a strong countermobilization to dislodge it led it to rely on presidential politics and unilateral action in ways that ultimately compromised the president's party leadership as well as his support for limited constitutional government.[102]

Modern conservatives' embrace of Progressive politics is not merely instrumental. Many applaud TR's call for greatness and his vigorous use of executive power, especially in foreign affairs. Moreover, a large number of contemporary conservatives have concluded that the government—even the federal government—has the responsibility to shape proper habits and behavior. Such a view permeates proposals to restrict abortion, require work for welfare, and impose performance standards on secondary and elementary schools.[103] Most notably, conservatives have embraced progressive aspirations in foreign affairs with far more alacrity than their liberal counterparts. The Iran-Contra scandal, for example, was not merely a matter of President Reagan being asleep on his watch. Rather, it revealed the Reagan administration's determination to assume a more forceful anti-Communist posture in Central America in the face of a recalcitrant Congress and bureaucracy.

The War on Terror, which the administration of George W. Bush extended with such controversy to Iraq, illustrates especially well conservatives' embrace of certain features of progressivism. It was defended in the service of promoting democracy in the world. Wilson led the United States into World War I to "make the world safe for democracy." The Bush administration exalted the War on Terror into a crusade that would empower people in the Middle East and throughout the world to form democratic nations. "It is the policy of the United States to seek and support the growth of democratic movements and institutions in every nation and culture," President Bush pronounced in his second inaugural address, "with the ultimate goal of ending tyranny in our world."[104]

Contemporary conservatism owes much, therefore, to the Progressive Party. The faith that Taft expressed in limited constitutional government has given way to support for ambitious programmatic initiatives that are pursued through political methods that corrode political and governmental institutions. Some conservatives, to be sure, scorn Progressive-style conservatism as apostasy, as confirmation of progressivism's triumph at the hands of the very prophets who presume to call it to account.[105] But these voices of restraint have been all but drowned out amid the populist uprising against the progressive state, abetted as it has been by activists who rest their hopes for change in the possibility that progressive institutions and politics can be reinvented as agents of conservatism. Many, if not most, contemporary conservatives express little faith in a program to restore constitutional space between government and the people.[106] For example, one leading conservative intellectual, frustrated by the courts' failure to roll back liberal constitutional doctrines, proposes "to implement term limits for federal judges."[107]

The very pervasiveness of the Progressive tradition calls for a reconsideration of its moral foundation. Because of its dedication to direct democracy and the way it cast discredit on the two-party system, the Progressive movement never clearly existed as a recognizable organization with common goals. Rather, it is better understood as a movement of public opinion that has been aroused episodically to our own time by powerful issues, domestic and international crises, and dynamic leaders. Progressivism advanced a new concept and practice of democracy in which candidates and public officials would form more direct ties with the public. At the same time, progressive democracy weakened constitutional constraints and political associations that nurtured a sense of collective responsibility among individual men and women. It was precisely on these grounds that the 1912 Progressive campaign elicited such an extraordinary debate about the country's future. It forced the nation to confront for the first time the question of whether constitutional forms and mass democracy could be reconciled, to consider whether the executive could be reconstituted as a "steward of the public welfare" that promoted popular leadership. Roosevelt's critics warned that presidential democracy was a chimera, a mischievous formula that would prosecute a cult of personality. Those who joined TR's Bull Moose campaign were not unmindful of the possibility that mass democracy would confound statesmanship and charisma. They knew that loosening constitutional constraints and partisan ties risked breeding an apathetic public that was susceptible to plebiscitary appeals; it was in this very respect that TR's dominant presence posed the greatest challenge to Progressive ideals. Nonetheless, Progressives believed that this risk had to be taken, lest government remain impotent in the face of major changes taking place in the economy and society. The democratic principle, the Progressive Miles Poindexter wrote during the 1912 campaign,

has been kept warm and vigorous in the hearts of the people, but in both the Democratic and Republican organizations it has become so encumbered by machinery and loaded with the ball and chain of obsolete governmental dogmas that it has ceased to find expression in the Government through either of these organizations. . . . Both parties are verbose in declaring for a government of the people, but the power of the people is so diluted through an indirect choice of officials, a division of powers of government under the Constitution, and an irresponsible party government wholly outside the Constitution that it largely disappears before it is applied to the actual making and administration of the laws.[108]

The wayward path of progressive democracy invites us to consider a dilemma as old as the republic: How can a state that is strong enough to protect our rights allow for an active and competent citizenry? From the start, the original Constitution placed public officials at such a distance from popular influence that it risked a dominant and dominating executive that would not simply "refine and enlarge the public views," as the Federalists hoped, but rather render them moot, as the Anti-Federalists feared. In the nineteenth century, Americans sought answers to this dilemma in a natural rights version of liberalism that celebrated localism. Traditional party organizations and newspapers rectified the Constitution's insufficient attention to civic matters and moderated presidential ambition. But there was no "golden age" of parties. Progressive and New Deal reformers had good reasons to view localized parties and the provincial liberties they upheld as an obstacle to economic, racial, and political justice. By the same token, the modern presidency—born of progressive reformers' inspired, awkward effort to wed national administration and popular rule—has weakened political parties and fostered a more active, better equipped national state: one that can tackle problems such as forced segregation at home and communism, or terrorism, abroad, but one without adequate means of common deliberation and public judgment, the pillars of a vital civic culture. Can the presidency in a vast modern nation-state be a truly democratic institution? Can it represent the values or interests of a political party, let alone a large and diverse nation? Can a distant president, no matter how eloquent or popular, forge meaningful links with the public?

These are the profound and unsettling questions that troubled the critics of Theodore Roosevelt's crusade. Nearly a century after the election of 1912, a new dynamic leader has inspired a large following with his charisma. Calling on the people to trust in the "audacity of hope," Senator Barack Obama of Illinois mounted an idealistic quest for the Democratic nomination and White House in 2008, and did so in a political atmosphere that was strikingly similar to the one that Roosevelt called to account in his Bull Moose campaign. Many of those features of contemporary politics that often are deemed so new—the distrust of politicians, aspirations for direct democracy, self-styled public-interest groups, "culture wars," investigative reporting, scorn for the "malefactors of great wealth," and a messianic view of America's role in the world—had their critical start during the Progressive era. The political and economic conditions that raised the stakes of the 2008 presidential contest—a global war on terror, prosecuted with such controversy in Iraq, and a worldwide financial crisis that rivaled in its severity the Great Depression—encouraged especially intense scrutiny of the state of American democracy, remade by the progressive idea of popular rule.

So far had this idea advanced by the dawn of the twenty-first century that there was no longer much debate about the authority of mass opinion. Both Democrats and Republicans have embraced national administrative power and claimed that this power must be used in the name of the whole people. Both parties have accepted the verdict of popular primaries in selecting their presidential candidates. Indeed, the candidate who triumphed in the Republican contest for the nomination in 2008, Senator John McCain of Arizona, often expressed his admiration for Theodore Roosevelt and sought the nomination of his party and election to the presidency by winning the support of moderate partisans and independents who scorn the partisan maneuvers, corrupted by selfish interests, that appeared to ensnare national politics.[109]

Senator Obama, however, sounded the loudest trumpet for progressive democracy. "In the face of despair, you believe there can be hope," he told the large, enthusiastic audience that gathered in Springfield, Illinois, in February 2007 to hear him announce his candidacy for the presidency. "In the face of politics that's shut you out, that's told you to settle, that's divided us for too long, you believe we can be one people, reaching for what's possible, building that more perfect union."

Although he chose Springfield to throw his hat in the ring and drew on Lincoln's hope for "a new birth of freedom" to sanctify his message, Senator Obama did not mention the Declaration of Independence or unalienable rights in launching his presidential campaign. Instead he voiced the strains of the "second Declaration," calling on the power of the whole people. The child of a white mother from Kansas and a black father from Kenya, a man of color raised in Hawaii and Indonesia, and a reformer schooled in Chicago politics as a member of the post–civil rights generation, the Illinois senator seemed perfectly poised to embody the aspirations of the whole people—to rise above, as Roosevelt never could, racial, ethnic, religious, and economic differences. To be sure, Obama aroused considerable opposition among conservatives, who dismissed him as a wolf in sheep's clothing, a doctrinaire liberal posing as a statesman who could rise above and lift the nation out of the muck of partisan rancor. His candidacy was also heavily criticized by his chief rival for the Democratic nomination, Senator Hillary Clinton of New York, the former first lady, who as the first strong woman candidate for president also had a legitimate claim to inherit the Progressive mantle. To a remarkable degree, however, Obama inspired the admiration of the country: he was cast perfectly as the leader of "inspired idealism" that Roosevelt exalted and sought to embody at the birth of progressive democracy. Warming to this role, Obama closed his remarks in Springfield with a challenge to his supporters to believe not just in *his* ability to remake American politics, but also in *their* ability to empower him to do so:

> That is why this campaign can't only be about me. It must be about us—it must be about what we can do together. This campaign must be the occasion, the vehicle, of your hopes, and your dreams. It will take your time, your energy, and your advice—to push us forward when we're doing right, and to let us know when we're not. This campaign has to be about reclaiming the meaning of citizenship, restoring our sense of common purpose, and realizing that few obstacles can withstand the power of millions of voices calling for change.[110]

With his quest for the presidency, which ended in a decisive victory for himself and the Democratic Party, Barack Obama's campaign vividly reminds us that the progressive democracy championed by TR in 1912 has become a powerful, enduring part of our political life. In this sense, the Progressive Party campaign provides important insights into the impressive and troubling influence of the Obama phenomenon. Such leadership, scholar of religion and politics Alan Wolfe argues, is an essential part of satisfying a yearning in contemporary American democracy. "Politics is about policy," he acknowledges, "but it is also about giving people some kind of sense of participating in a common venture with their fellow citizens." Just as Roosevelt spoke the language of the Social Gospel, which presumed to defy denominational differences, so Obama articulates "a soft civil religion . . . that our country desperately needs at a time of deep partisanship." To other students of American democracy, however, Obama threatens to bring to a culmination a "cult of personality" that denigrates self-government. "What is troubling about the campaign," the historian Sean Wilentz claims, "is that it's gone beyond hope and change to redemption. [Obama] is posing as a figure who is the one person who will redeem our politics. And what I fear is, that ends up promising more from politics than politics can deliver."[111]

More broadly, these views of a campaign that appeared to mark the apotheosis of progressive democracy highlight how the attempt to make practical the elusive ideal of "We the People" has rendered more intractable the dilemma inherent in the American experiment to create self-government on a grand scale. Even in their most noble aspirations, Progressives tended to discount the value of family, place, and partisanship. They failed to appreciate, Wilson Carey McWilliams wrote, that "we all begin in a world of particulars, from which the human spirit ascends, on any account, only slowly and with difficulty." Still, he concludes, "while the Progressives may have overestimated the reach of the spirit, unlike so many of our contemporaries, they never forgot that its yearning perennially strains against the possibilities."[112] Thus, the Progressive Party campaign of 1912 provides important insights into contemporary and future developments in American politics. For only by revisiting the origins of progressive democracy and tracing its unsteady path through the twentieth and twenty-first centuries can its fundamental challenge to deep-rooted American values be fully understood — and its compelling unsettling demand that Americans transcend themselves be properly appreciated.

CHAPTER SIX

$\backsim$

Notes

Preface

1. Arthur S. Link and Richard L. McCormick, *Progressivism* (Wheeling, IL: Harlan Davidson, 1983), 41.

2. Sidney M. Milkis and Daniel J. Tichenor, "'Direct Democracy' and Social Justice: The Progressive Party Campaign of 1912," *Studies in American Political Development* 8, 2 (Fall 1994): 282–340.

3. "Roosevelt Favors the Recall of the President," *New York Times,* September 20, 1912, 1.

Chapter One. The Critical Year of 1912

1. "Gilded Age" was coined by Mark Twain and Charles Dudley Warner in their book *The Gilded Age: A Tale of Today,* which was published in 1873. The term originates in William Shakespeare's *King John:* "To gild refined gold, to paint the lily . . . is wasteful and ridiculous excess."

2. John Milton Cooper Jr., *The Warrior and the Priest: Woodrow Wilson and Theodore Roosevelt* (Cambridge, MA: Harvard University Press, 1983), 141.

3. Francis L. Broderick, *Progressivism at Risk: Electing a President in 1912* (Westport, CT: Greenwood Press, 1989), 4–5.

4. The only book-length treatment of the Progressive Party is John Gable's *The Bull Moose Years: Theodore Roosevelt and the Progressive Party* (Port Washington, NY: Kennikat Press, 1978). Gable offers a carefully researched blow-by-blow account of the history of the Progressive Party but does not provide any detailed evaluation of the constitutional debates it engendered or the legacy of these debates for politics and government in the United States.

5. Significantly, the Progressives mounted the last third-party campaign in American history. No third party since 1912 has fielded a full slate of candidates. Insurgent candidates have challenged the two-party system frequently since the Progressive Party campaign, but their followers have not made any serious effort to form an enduring collective organization.

6. In coming to this conclusion, I am picking up on an important but undeveloped observation that Arthur Link and Richard McCormick made in 1983: "The use of the direct primaries, the challenge to traditional party loyalties, the candidates' issue orientation, and the prevalence of interest-group political activities all make the election of 1912 look more like 1980 than that of 1896." Arthur S. Link and Richard L. McCormick, *Progressivism* (Wheeling, IL: Harland Davidson, 1983), 43–44.

7. In accepting the Progressive Party's nomination in person, Roosevelt followed the example of previous third-party candidates who scorned the two-party system. Soon after being nominated by the Populist Party in 1892, James B. Weaver was summoned to address the convention. Weaver did not formally accept the nomination until a month later, however. Fred Emory Haynes, *James Baird Weaver* (Iowa City: State Historical Society of Iowa, 1919), 310–343. Eugene Debs went a step further. He attended the Socialist Party convention in 1904, where he proclaimed his acceptance before the delegates. Bernard J. Brommel, *Eugene V. Debs: Spokesman for Labor and Socialism* (Chicago: Charles H. Kerr Publishing, 1978), 79–80; and H. Wayne Morgan, *Eugene V. Debs: Socialist for President* (Syracuse, NY: Syracuse University Press, 1962), 67–68. Roosevelt's stature made his appearance at the Progressive Party convention all the more dramatic; TR's popularity and the significant support of his newly formed party highlighted his acceptance of the nomination at the Progressive Party convention as a pathbreaking event. "Marking a new departure in the proceedings of national conventions," reported the *San Francisco Examiner* (August 8, 1912, p. 1), "the two candidates were notified of their nominations, and in the midst of deafening cheers they appeared before the delegates to voice their acceptance and to pledge their best efforts in the coming campaign." See also Gable, *The Bull Moose Years*, 108.

8. On the antipartisan character of the Progressive Party, see Sidney M. Milkis and Daniel J. Tichenor, "'Direct Democracy' and Social Justice: The Progressive Party Campaign of 1912," *Studies in American Political Development* 8 (Fall 1994): 282–340; and Eldon Eisenach, *The Lost Promise of Progressivism* (Lawrence: University Press of Kansas, 1994), 241.

9. Proceedings of the First National Convention of the Progressive Party, August 5, 6, and 7, 1912, Progressive Party Archives, Theodore Roosevelt Collection, Houghton Library, Harvard University. Roosevelt's "Confession of Faith," delivered on the second day of the convention, was actually the keynote address of the Progressive convention. His remarks on accepting the nomination were far shorter and less formal. The party nominee's acceptance address, which has now become the climax of national conventions, began with Franklin Roosevelt's appearance at the 1932 Democratic convention. See Sidney M. Milkis, *The President and the Parties: The Transformation of the American Party System since the New Deal* (New York: Oxford University Press, 1993), 53–54.

10. James Montague, "Roosevelt and Johnson Nominated: Moose Lift Voices in Hymn Singing," *San Francisco Examiner*, August 8, 1912. The delegates' religiosity

owed much to the many social gospelers who joined the campaign, to individuals such as Raymond Robins of the Men and Religious Forward Movement and the *Outlook* editor Lyman Abbott, who saw the Progressive Party as a political expression of their commitment to promote Christian social action. But this practical idealism was not unique to social gospelers; it was shared by the academic reformers and social workers who enlisted in the new party. For an illuminating interpretation of the Social Gospel movement's centrality to American political development, see James A. Morone, *Hellfire Nation* (New Haven, CT: Yale University Press, 2004).

11. Elmer E. Cornwell Jr., *Presidential Leadership of Public Opinion* (Bloomington: Indiana University Press, 1965), 10 (emphasis in original).

12. Sidney M. Milkis and Michael Nelson, *The American Presidency: Origins and Development, 1776–2007*, 5th ed. (Washington, DC: CQ Press, 2007), 208–226; and Gerald Gamm and Renée M. Smith, "Presidents, Parties, and the Public: Evolving Patterns of Interaction," in Richard J. Ellis, ed., *Speaking to the People: The Rhetorical Presidency in Historical Perspective* (Amherst: University of Massachusetts Press, 1998).

13. Editorial, "What Roosevelt Believes in 1912," *San Francisco Examiner*, August 8, 1912.

14. Eisenach, *The Lost Promise of Progressivism*, 239.

15. On the importance of this strategy for the modern presidents, see Samuel Kernell, *New Strategies of Presidential Leadership*, 4th ed. (Washington, DC: CQ Press, 2006).

16. Milkis, *The President and the Parties*, chapters 3–6.

17. In addition to the foothold it established for merit hiring and the bar it erected against on-the-job solicitations of campaign funds from federal employees, the Pendleton Act established a bipartisan three-member Civil Service Commission, to be appointed by the president and confirmed by the Senate.

18. For example, see John F. Reynolds, *The Demise of the American Convention System* (New York: Cambridge University Press, 2006).

19. Michael McGerr, *The Decline of Popular Politics: The American North, 1865–1928* (New York: Oxford University Press, 1986), 70. McGerr traces the start of the candidate-centered campaign to the election of 1876. The contest between Democrat Samuel Tilden and Republican Rutherford B. Hayes marked the emergence of a new, more issue-based appeal to independent voters through pamphlets as well as the independent press. Reynolds argues, with considerable evidence, that party leaders' acceptance of reforms was not just a matter of campaign strategy. By the 1890s they feared losing control of the convention system and hoped to restore order and gain "semiofficial status" by embracing the regulation of their organizations. Primary laws, for example, converted nomination contests into official elections, which transformed the Democrats and Republicans from private associations into semipublic agencies. See Reynolds, *The Demise of the American Convention System*, 3. As the "progressive movement's prophet," Herbert Croly recognized, however, such semi-official status came at a steep price: "By regulating it and by forcing it to select its leaders in a certain way, the state is sacrificing the valuable substance of party loyalty and party allegiance to the mere mechanism of party association. Direct primaries will necessarily undermine partisan discipline and loyalty." Croly, *Progressive Democracy* (New York: Macmillan, 1914), 343.

20. Gamm and Smith, "Presidents, Parties, and the Public."

21. Gil Troy, *See How They Ran: The Changing Role of the Presidential Candidate*, rev. and expanded ed. (Cambridge, MA: Harvard University Press, 1996), 104.

22. Matthew Crenson and Benjamin Ginsberg, *Presidential Power: Unchecked and Unbalanced* (New York: Norton, 2007), 114–120.

23. Troy, *See How They Ran*, 106. on the role that McKinley and Mark Hanna played in establishing the president as a party leader—in particular, in enhancing the ability of the president to shape the content of national electoral campaigns—see Daniel Klinghard, "Grover Cleveland, William McKinley, and Emergence of the President as Party Leader," *Presidential Studies Quarterly* 35, 4 (December 2005): 736–760.

24. The decentralized polity might better be described as a state of parties and courts, for party politicians, empowered by a "highly mobilized, highly competitive, and locally oriented democracy," had the commanding voice in late-nineteenth-century American politics and government. The federal judiciary molded the political character of the nineteenth-century state into a formal legal tradition. See Stephen Skowronek, *Building a New American State: The Expansion of National Administrative Capacities, 1877–1920* (New York: Cambridge University Press, 1982), 41. See also Morton Keller, *America's Three Regimes: A New Political History* (New York: Oxford University Press, 2007), chapter 8.

25. Troy, *See How They Ran*, 112–125. Roosevelt did jump into the fray in 1900, when McKinley refused to redo the front-porch campaign. Matching Bryan's campaign activity, the vice presidential candidate appeared to bestow bipartisan legitimacy on the rear-platform campaign. Apparently, however, Roosevelt felt the taboo against incumbent presidents actively campaigning was too great to ignore. By the 1908 campaign, which did not include an incumbent, the taboo against presidential candidates stumping had all but disappeared, but the emphasis on candidates, although now a standard party strategy, had not yet evolved into a full-throated assault on the party system itself. That the Progressive Party campaign represented such a challenge demarcates the 1912 election as a milestone in undermining the constitutional and political foundation of the traditional two-party system.

26. Louis Hartz, *The Liberal Tradition in America* (New York: Harcourt, Brace & World, 1955). On the constitutional changes brought by the rise of the two-party system, see Sidney M. Milkis, *Political Parties and Constitutional Government: Remaking American Democracy* (Baltimore: Johns Hopkins University Press, 1999), especially chapter 2. For a concise and persuasive account of Lincoln's reinterpretation of the Constitution, see James M. McPherson, *Abraham Lincoln and the American Revolution* (New York: Oxford University Press, 1992).

27. *The Works of Theodore Roosevelt*, national ed. (New York: Scribner's, 1926), vol. 17, 19.

28. For example, see George Mowry, *Theodore Roosevelt and the Progressive Movement* (Madison: University of Wisconsin Press, 1946), 220–255; Samuel P. Hayes, *The Response to Industrialism, 1885–1914* (Chicago: University of Chicago Press, 1957), 92–93; Peter Rechner, "Theodore Roosevelt and Progressive Personality Politics," *Melbourne Historical Journal* 8 (1969): 43–58; and James Chace, *1912: Wilson, Roosevelt, Taft, and Debs—The Election That Changed the Country* (New York: Simon & Schuster, 2004).

29. The most recent study of the 1912 election, Lewis S. Gould, *Four Hats in the*

Ring: The 1912 Election and the Birth of Modern American Politics (Lawrence: University Press of Kansas, 2008), grants that Roosevelt's insurgency gave this election its importance, just as it sees political practices such as the primary, candidate-centered campaigns, and the emergence of a mass media as signaling the arrival of modern politics. But Gould devotes little attention to development of Roosevelt's ideas as he raced to get at the head of a burgeoning Progressive movement, nor does he recognize that the Progressive Party not only practiced but also *championed* a new form of politics, which sparked a debate, engaging all four candidates, that truly demarcates the 1912 election as a critical contest. Indeed, Gould argues that Roosevelt's "impulse"—in challenging Taft and becoming the standard-bearer of the Progressive Party—was personal, not ideological (75). At the same time, he observes, without much explanation or evidence, that "the Progressives and Roosevelt had put at the center of the public agenda a group of ideas that would concern American politics throughout the rest of the twentieth century" (146). This leaves open the question of how the Progressive Party—seemingly consumed by the personal ambition of its celebrated candidate—achieved a collective identity, dominated the 1912 election, and had an enduring legacy for American politics and government.

30. Paul Allen Beck, "The Electoral Cycle and Patterns of American Politics," *British Journal of Political Science* 9 (1979): 138. Beck's excellent work on electoral developments, like most of the historical labors on the American party system, has emphasized the importance of so-called critical partisan realignments. The study of realignments has made an unquestionable contribution to our understanding of the rhythms of political history in the United States; at the same time, it has deflected attention from long-term secular changes that have weakened the influence of parties in the electorate and rendered the concept of *partisan* realignment far less relevant to contemporary political developments. The two seminal presentations of critical realignment theory are V. O. Key Jr., "A Theory of Critical Elections," *Journal of Politics* 17 (February 1955): 3–18; and Walter Dean Burnham, *Critical Elections and the Mainsprings of American Politics* (New York: W. W. Norton, 1970). Historians and political scientists have recently become more critical of the realignment approach to the study of the historical development of parties. Some argue that the emphasis on critical elections and realigning eras has ceased to offer much explanatory power in an era when the electorate appears to be weakly associated with political parties. Others argue that the concept of realignment skews the study of the past as well, that it has led scholars to group earlier developments that are really quite distinctive. See, for example, Byron Shafer, ed., *The End of Realignment? Interpreting American Electoral Eras* (Madison: University of Wisconsin, 1991). For the most comprehensive critique of realignment theory to date, see David Mayhew, *Electoral Realignments: A Critique of an American Genre* (New Haven, CT: Yale University Press, 2002).

31. Burnham, *Critical Elections and the Mainsprings of American Politics*, 27–28. Burnham does not mention the election of 1912 in this passage, but he has conveyed to the author in private correspondence his view that the Progressive Party campaign represents an extraordinary event, but one that did not fundamentally disrupt the Republican majority born of the 1896 realignment.

32. In one sense the 1912 election shows, as Mayhew emphasizes, that important developments of the party system have occurred independently of "realigning elections."

Mayhew, *Critical Realignments*, 39–40. More broadly, developments during the Progressive era around 1912 cry out for an alternative "periodization" of party and electoral history, one that focuses less on cyclical patterns and more on what Stephen Skowronek calls "secular time"; Skowronek, *The Politics Presidents Make: Leadership from John Adams to Bill Clinton* (Cambridge, MA: Harvard University Press, 1997), 30. As Skowronek and Karen Orren note, in calling for "periodization schemes that are more variable and multiform and less well aligned with one another," recent research "has shown that changes in the ideologies of America's two parties do not move in tandem with changes in their coalitional alignment with one another but seem to follow a different logic with consequences of its own." Karen Orren and Stephen Skowronek, *The Search for American Political Development* (New York: Cambridge University Press, 2004), 15–16. For a sweeping treatment of parties that employs a period scheme that does not conform to the realignment approach, see John Gerring, *Party Ideologies in America: 1828–1996* (New York: Cambridge University Press, 1998).

33. De Witt, *The Progressive Movement*, 4.

34. For the classical statement of this position, see Peter Filene, "An Obituary for the Progressive Movement," *American Quarterly* 22 (Spring 1970): 20–34.

35. Alonzo L. Hamby, "Progressivism: A Century of Change and Rebirth," in Milkis and Mileur, *Progressivism and the New Democracy*, 43.

36. Ibid.

37. Jane Addams, *Twenty Years at Hull House* (New York: Macmillan, 1910), 288.

38. On the reformist zeal of progressive reformers, see Eisenach, *The Lost Promise of Progressivism*; and Michael McGerr, *A Fierce Discontent: The Rise and Fall of the Progressive Movement in America, 1870–1920* (New York: Free Press, 2003).

39. Theodore Roosevelt, introduction to S. J. Duncan-Clark, *The Progressive Movement: Its Principles and Its Programme* (Boston: Small, Maynard, 1913), xiii.

40. Croly, *Progressive Democracy*, 12.

41. Jeffrey Tulis describes TR's leadership of national public opinion as the beginnings of the "rhetorical presidency." See his *The Rhetorical Presidency* (Princeton, NJ: Princeton University Press, 1987). But this celebration of popular leadership was connected to a program to reform the political economy. As such, it was not merely popular leadership progressives wanted, but national leadership freed from the provincial, special, and corrupting influence of political parties.

42. John Dewey, "Theodore Roosevelt," in Jo Ann Boydston, ed., *John Dewey: The Middle Works, 1899–1924* (Carbondale: Southern Illinois University Press, 1982), vol. 2, 146.

43. Hiram Johnson to TR, October 20, 1911, Theodore Roosevelt Papers, Manuscript Division, Library of Congress, Washington, DC.

44. White cited in Rechner, "Theodore Roosevelt and Progressive Personality Politics," 54.

45. Jane Addams, Speech Seconding the Nomination of Theodore Roosevelt, Proceedings of the First National Progressive Party, 1912, pp. 194–195.

46. Johnson to TR, October 20, 1911.

47. "I have still the feeling," Johnson wrote, "that you are sort of political father-confessor to whom many of us turn in times of grave doubt and difficulty." Ibid.

48. Night Press Message to Fred W. McKenzie, c/o *La Follette's Magazine*, no date (July 1912), Robert M. La Follette Sr. Papers, La Follette Family Collection, Manuscript Division, Library of Congress, Washington, D.C.

49. Erving Winslow to Jane Addams, August 7, 1912, Jane Addams Papers, Swarthmore College Peace Collection, series 1, Swarthmore, Pennsylvania. Until the summer of 1912, TR's support for woman's suffrage was lukewarm at best. Instead of a constitutional amendment that would give women the right to vote, Roosevelt called for a series of state referenda in which women themselves would decide the issue. See Roosevelt, "Women's Rights; and the Duties of Both Men and Women," *Outlook*, February 3, 1912, 262–266.

50. Jane Addams to Lillian D. Wald, August 15, 1912, and Addams to Anna Howard Shaw, August 20, 1912, Jane Addams Papers, series 1.

51. William Allen White, "The Party Bigger Than the Man," from a personal letter to the editor, *American Magazine*, November 1912.

52. Samuel P. Hays, *Conservation and the Gospel of Efficiency*, new ed. (Pittsburgh, PA: University of Pittsburgh Press, 1999).

53. Croly, *Progressive Democracy*, 347.

54. For example, see Filene, "An Obituary for the Progressive Movement"; and Daniel T. Rogers, "In Search of Progressivism," *Reviews of American History* (December 1982): 114–123.

55. H. L. Mencken, "Roosevelt: An Autopsy," in James T. Farrell, ed., *Prejudices: A Selection* (New York: Vintage Books, 1958), 61.

56. On the limits of progressive democracy, see Robert H. Wiebe, *Self-Rule: A Cultural History of American Democracy* (Chicago: University of Chicago Press, 1995), chapter 7.

57. On the connection between popular leadership and national administration, see Sidney M. Milkis, "The Rhetorical and Administrative Presidencies," *Critical Review* 19, 2–3 (2007): 379–401.

58. Robert Wiebe is surely correct that a strain of progressivism involved a "search for order." See *The Search for Order: 1877–1920* (New York: Hill & Wang, 1967). Nevertheless, to claim that "the heart of progressivism was the ambition of the new middle class to fulfill its destiny through bureaucratic means" misses the sincere, if chimerical, commitment of Progressives to ally national administration with public opinion, as well as the harsh criticism that reformers such as Woodrow Wilson and Louis Brandeis leveled at the new party's dedication to administrative aggrandizement. See Link and McCormick, *Progressivism*, 3–10.

59. Woodrow Wilson, "Constitutional Government in the United States," in Arthur S. Link, ed., *The Papers of Woodrow Wilson* (Princeton, NJ: Princeton University Press, 1974), 197–198.

60. George E. Mowry, *The Era of Theodore Roosevelt and the Birth of Modern America, 1900–1912* (New York: Harper & Row, 1958); and Richard Hofstadter, *The Age of Reform: From Bryan to FDR* (New York: Knopf, 1955).

61. George M. Forbes, "Buttressing the Foundations of Democracy," *Survey*, November 18, 1911, 1231–1235. On the Social Centers movement, see Kevin Mattson, *Creating a Democratic Public: The Struggle for Urban Participatory Democracy during the Progressive Era* (University Park: Pennsylvania State Press, 1998).

62. Alexis de Tocqueville, *Democracy in America*, ed. J. P. Mayer (Garden City, NY: Doubleday, 1969), 68, 82, 95.

63. Mary Parker Follett, *The New State: Group Organization of Popular Government* (New York: Longmans, Green, 1918; reprint Gloucester, MA: Peter Smith Publishers, 1965).

64. Forbes, "Buttressing the Foundations of Democracy," 1232.

65. Croly, *Progressive Democracy*, 264.

66. William Helmstreet, "Theory and Practice of the New Primary Law," *Arena* 28, 6 (December 1902): 592 (emphasis in original).

67. Duncan-Clark, *The Progressive Movement*, 26, 28.

68. Editorial, "The Political Use of School Buildings," *Outlook*, September 14, 1912.

69. Woodrow Wilson, "Constitutional Government in the United States," 213–214.

70. Keller, *America's Three Regimes*, 174.

71. Charles Merz, "Progressivism: Old and New," *Atlantic Monthly* 132 (July 1923): 106 (emphasis in original).

72. De Witt, *The Progressive Movement*, 215.

73. Croly, *Progressive Democracy*, 27.

74. Wilson Carey McWilliams, "Standing at Armageddon: Morality and Religion in Progressive Thought," in Milkis and Mileur, *Progressivism and the New Democracy*, 104.

75. George Mowry, "The Election of 1912," in Arthur Schlesinger Jr. and Fred I. Israel, eds., *History of American Presidential Elections* (New York: Chelsea, 1971), 2160.

76. Barry Karl, *The Uneasy State: The United States from 1915 to 1945* (Chicago: University of Chicago Press, 1983), 234–235.

77. Mowry, *Theodore Roosevelt and the Progressive Movement*, 217. See also Gould, *Four Hats in the Ring*, 58–59.

78. Address of William Howard Taft, April 25, 1912, Senate Document 615 (62-2, vol. 38, 2), 3–4.

79. Taft, address at the banquet of the Republican Club, February 12, 1912.

80. Theodore Gilman, "The Progressive Party Comes Not to Destroy, but to Fulfill, the Constitution," address delivered at a public rally in Yonkers, New York, September 27, 1912, Progressive Party Publications, 1912–1916, Theodore Roosevelt Collection, Harvard University, Cambridge, Massachusetts.

81. Croly, *Progressive Democracy*, 54–55.

82. Gilman, "The Progressive Party Comes Not to Destroy, but to Fulfill, the Constitution," 5–6.

83. Debs cited in "The New Party Gets Itself Born," *Current Literature*, September 1912, 256.

84. Eugene V. Debs, "The Greatest Political Campaign in American History," St. Louis Campaign Opening Speech, July 6, 1912, Eugene V. Debs Papers, Indiana State University, Terre Haute, Indiana.

85. Croly, *Progressive Democracy*, 281–282.

86. James T. Kloppenberg, *The Virtues of Liberalism* (New York: Oxford University Press, 1998), 119.

87. James T. Kloppenberg, "James's Pragmatism and American Culture, 1907–2007," unpublished manuscript. On the development of pragmatic thought during the late nineteenth and twentieth centuries, see Louis Menand, *The Metaphysical Club: A Story of Ideas in America* (New York: Farrar, Straus & Giroux, 2001).

88. Herbert Croly, *The Promise of American Life* (New York: Macmillan, 1909; reprint, New York: Dutton, 1963), 278.

89. On the American struggle to reconcile individual autonomy and national administration, see Barry Karl, *The Uneasy State*.

90. "Letters of Cato," in Herbert J. Storing, ed., *The Complete Anti-Federalist*, 7 vols. (Chicago: Chicago University Press, 1981), vol. 2, 112.

91. Croly, *The Promise of American Life*, 338.

Chapter Two. Roosevelt, Progressive Democracy, and the Progressive Movement

1. Theodore Roosevelt, *The Works of Theodore Roosevelt*, 26 vols. (New York: Charles Scribner's, 1926), vol. 20, 378.

2. Theodore Roosevelt to George Trevelyan, June 19, 1908, Theodore Roosevelt Papers, Manuscript Division, Library of Congress, Washington, D.C. (hereafter, Roosevelt Papers).

3. Gifford Pinchot to TR, December 31, 1909, Gifford Pinchot Papers, Manuscript Division, Library of Congress, Washington, D.C. (hereafter, Pinchot Papers).

4. John A. Gable, *The Bull Moose Years: Theodore Roosevelt and the Progressive Party* (Port Washington, NY: Kennikat Press, 1978), 8.

5. The press gave front-page coverage to TR's address; for example, see "Acclaim Roosevelt at Paris Lecture," *New York Times*, April 24, 1910, 1.

6. Theodore Roosevelt, "Duties of the Citizen," printed in *Theodore Roosevelt's Speeches in Europe* (New York: C. S. Hammond, 1910), 2.

7. Ibid., 4–11.

8. Ibid., 6.

9. "Acclaim Roosevelt at Paris Lecture," 2.

10. *Le Temps* quoted in "Mr. Roosevelt in Christiana: Ceremony at the University," *Times* (London), May 7, 1910.

11. *Liberté* cited in "Mr. Roosevelt in Paris: Reception at the Hotel De Ville," *Times* (London), April 26, 1910.

12. Roosevelt cited in Mark Hulliung, *Citizens and Citoyens: Republicans and Liberals in America and France* (Cambridge, MA: Harvard University Press, 2002), 74.

13. Henry Cabot Lodge to Theodore Roosevelt, September 3, 1910, Roosevelt Papers.

14. "The World's Development," in *Theodore Roosevelt's Speeches in Europe*, 83.

15. Ibid., 120–125.

16. Ibid., 123.

17. Cited in Joseph L. Gardner, *Departing Glory: Theodore Roosevelt as ex-President* (New York: Charles Scribner's, 1973), 167.

18. Theodore Roosevelt, *The Works of Theodore Roosevelt*, vol. 8, 79.

19. Hulliung, *Citizens and Citoyens,* 172.

20. "The World's Development," 87, 124, 126.

21. "Some Reflections of the Tour," *Times* (London), May 16, 1910.

22. "Mr. Roosevelt's Visit to Oxford," *Manchester Guardian,* June 8, 1910.

23. "Mr. Roosevelt's Home-coming," *Manchester Guardian,* June 20, 1910.

24. Theodore Roosevelt, "The Uplift of Nations," in *Theodore Roosevelt's Speeches in Europe,* 69.

25. "A Journey of Education: Correspondent Thinks Much Good Will Result from Mr. Roosevelt's Tour," *New York Times,* May 17, 1910.

26. Eldon J. Eisenach, ed., *The Social and Political Thought of American Progressivism* (Indianapolis: Hackett, 2006), XVI.

27. For example, see Jane Addams, "The Thirst for Righteousness," in Jean Bethke Elshtain, ed., *The Jane Addams Reader* (New York: Basic Books, 2002). Speaking of "those youths who so bitterly arraign . . . the present industrial order," she wrote: "It would be an interesting attempt to turn that youthful enthusiasm to the aid of one the most conservative of the present social efforts, the world wide movement to secure protective legislation for women and children in industry, in which America is so behind other nations . . . In one year in the German Empire one hundred thousand children were cared for through money paid from the State Insurance fund to their widowed mothers or to their invalid fathers. And yet in the American states it seems impossible to pass a most rudimentary employers' liability act, which would be but the first step towards that code of beneficent legislations which protects 'the widow and fatherless' in Germany and England" (140–141).

28. "The Uplift of Nations," 67–68.

29. Philip James Roosevelt, "Politics of the Year 1912: An Intimate Progressive View," unpublished manuscript, Theodore Roosevelt Collection, Houghton Library, Harvard University, Cambridge, Massachusetts (hereafter, Roosevelt Collection).

30. Learned Hand to Theodore Roosevelt, April 8, 1910, Learned Hand Papers, Harvard University Law School, Cambridge, Massachusetts (hereafter, Hand Papers).

31. Herbert Croly, *The Promise of American Life* (New York: Macmillan, 1909; reprint, New York: Dutton, 1963), 170, 172–173.

32. Hand to Roosevelt, April 8, 1910.

33. Theodore Roosevelt to Frederick Scott Oliver, August 9, 1906, in Elting E. Morison, ed., *The Letters of Theodore Roosevelt* (New York: Charles Scribner's, 1926), vol. 5, 351.

34. Roosevelt, *Works,* vol. 20, 414.

35. Croly, *The Promise of American Life,* 169.

36. Martha Derthick, "Federalism," in Peter H. Schuck and James Q. Wilson, eds., *Understanding America: The Anatomy of an Exceptional Nation* (New York: Public Affairs, 2008), 123–127.

37. Croly, *The Promise of an American Life,* 168.

38. "The New Nationalism," in Roosevelt, *Works,* vol. 17, 19–20.

39. Ibid., 8–9.

40. Ibid., 10–19.

41. David Green, *The Language of Politics in America: Shaping Political Consciousness from McKinley to Reagan* (Ithaca, NY: Cornell University Press, 1987), 59.

42. Roosevelt, *Works,* vol. 17, 12.

43. Robert M. La Follette, "The Beginning of a Great Movement, Address Before the Wisconsin Legislature, Announcing the Formation of the National Progressive Republican League," *La Follette's,* February 4, 1911.

44. Theodore Roosevelt, "Wisconsin: An Object Lesson for the Rest of the Union," *La Follette's,* February 4, 1911.

45. Learned Hand to Herbert Croly, February 6, 1911, cited in Gerald Gunther, *Learned Hand: The Man and the Judge* (New York: Alfred A. Knopf, 1994), 205.

46. Roosevelt, *Works,* vol. 17, 20.

47. Ibid., 22.

48. Henry Cabot Lodge to Theodore Roosevelt, September 3, 1910, Roosevelt Papers.

49. Editorial, "At Osawatomie," *New York Times,* September 1, 1901.

50. Roosevelt quoted in Gardner, *Departing Glory,* 200.

51. Roosevelt to La Follette, September 29, 1911, Roosevelt Papers.

52. Hulliung, *Citizens and Citoyens,* 170.

53. Alexis de Tocqueville, *Democracy in America,* edited by J. P. Mayer (Garden City, NY: Doubleday, 1968), 258–259.

54. "Letters of Theodore Roosevelt and Charles Dwight Willard," February to April 1911, *American Scholar* (Autumn 1934): 465–481 (emphasis in original).

55. Ibid. (emphasis in original).

56. Ibid.

57. Roosevelt, *Works,* vol. 20, 342.

58. For a discussion of Roosevelt's campaign on behalf of the Hepburn Act, and its constitutional consequences, see Jeffrey Tulis, *The Rhetorical Presidency* (Princeton, NJ: Princeton University Press, 1987), 97–116. Of Roosevelt's presidential leadership of public opinion, Tulis writes, "Roosevelt abandoned nineteenth century practice, to be sure, but he did so in a way that retained nineteenth century objectives and accommodated the 'nineteenth' century institution, the Senate" (106–107).

59. "Progressives from Thirty States Get Together," *La Follette's,* October 28, 1911.

60. Ibid.

61. James Garfield to Theodore Roosevelt, October 17, 1911, Roosevelt Papers.

62. James Garfield to Robert La Follette, October 18, 1911, Roosevelt Papers.

63. Roosevelt to Lodge, December 13, 1911, Roosevelt Papers.

64. Ibid.

65. "Roosevelt Won't Reassure Taft," *New York Times,* January 2, 1912.

66. "La Follette Fails with Progressives," *New York Times,* January 2, 1912.

67. James Garfield to Theodore Roosevelt, January 2, 1912, Roosevelt Papers.

68. Robert La Follette to Sol H. Clark, January 15, 1912, the La Follette Family Collection (Robert M. La Follette Sr. Papers), Manuscript Division, Library of Congress, Washington, D.C. (hereafter, La Follette Papers).

69. Robert La Follette to Sol H. Clark, January 27, 1912, La Follette Papers.

70. Robert La Follette to Gilbert Roe, February 6, 1912, La Follette Papers.

71. "La Follette Jars Publishers' Feast by 2½ Hour Talk," *Philadelphia Evening Bulletin,* February 3, 1912.

72. E. P. Powell to Phillips, September 23, 1911, La Follette Papers.

73. "La Follette Jars Publishers' Feast."

74. Ibid.

75. Gardner, *Departing Glory,* 214.

76. "Roosevelt Jumps into Arena," *San Francisco Chronicle,* February 26, 1912.

77. "Roosevelt Gives out Platform in Ohio Address," *San Francisco Chronicle,* February 22, 1912.

78. "The Week," *Nation,* March 22, 1912, 173.

79. "A Charter for Democracy," address before the Ohio Constitutional Convention at Columbus, Ohio, February 21, 1912, Roosevelt Collection.

80. Diaries, Papers of James Garfield, February 21, 1912, Manuscript Division, Library of Congress, Washington, D.C.

81. John C. O'Laughlin to Roosevelt, March 28, 1912, Roosevelt Papers.

82. Mowry, *Theodore Roosevelt and the Progressive Movement,* 217.

83. Lodge to Roosevelt, February 28, 1912, from *The Correspondence of Roosevelt and Lodge, 1884–1914* (New York: Charles Scribner's, 1925), 423–424.

84. Gunther, *Learned Hand,* 210; Learned Hand to Mr. Whitridge, February 21, 1912, Hand Papers.

85. Roosevelt, *Works,* vol. 16, 206.

86. Hand to Roosevelt, November 20, 1911, Hand Papers.

87. 201 N.Y. 271; 94 N.E. 431 (1911).

88. Hand to Roosevelt, November 20, 1911, Hand Papers.

89. Roosevelt to Hand, November 22, 1991, Roosevelt Papers.

90. Roosevelt to Stimson, February 5, 1912, in Elting E. Morison, ed., *The Letters of Theodore Roosevelt* (Cambridge, MA: Harvard University Press, 1952), vol. 7, 494.

91. Hand to Roosevelt, March 15, 1912, Hand Papers; and Roosevelt, *Works,* vol. 17, 157–158.

92. William Howard Taft, Address to the General Court of the Legislature of Massachusetts, Boston, Massachusetts, March 18, 1912, William Howard Taft Papers, Manuscript Division, Library of Congress, Washington, D.C. (hereafter, Taft Papers).

93. Address of President Taft at the Bequest of the Republican Club of the City of New York, February 12, 1912,Taft Papers.

94. Roosevelt, *Works,* vol. 17, 155.

95. Ibid., 156, 157–164.

96. Roosevelt to Hand, November 28, 1911, Hand Papers.

97. Roosevelt, *Works,* vol. 17, 166.

98. Ibid., 152, 170.

99. Mowry, *Theodore Roosevelt and the Progressive Movement,* 213.

100. "Taft Will Answer Roosevelt Speech," *New York Times,* February 23, 1912.

101. Roosevelt to Pinchot, February 15, 1912, in Morison, *The Letters of Theodore Roosevelt,* vol. 7, 515.

102. Charles G. Washburn, *Roosevelt and the 1912 Campaign,* Proceedings of the Massachusetts Historical Society, Boston, Massachusetts, May 1926, 8 (emphasis in original).

103. Lodge cited in ibid. (emphasis in original).

104. John Dewey, "Theodore Roosevelt," in Jo Ann Boydston, ed., *John Dewey: The*

Middle Works, 1899–1924 (Carbondale: Southern Illinois University Press, 1982), vol. 2, 146.

105. Hiram Johnson to Theodore Roosevelt, October 20, 1911, Roosevelt Papers.

106. Gifford Pinchot to Hiram Johnson, March 29, 1912, Pinchot Papers.

107. "Which? Taft, Roosevelt, La Follette—Judged by Their Records," address delivered at San Diego, California, March 24, 1912, La Follette Papers.

108. Louis Brandeis, "Are Trusts Efficient," *La Follette's*, February 3, 1912.

109. Smythe, "Which? Taft, Roosevelt, La Follette."

110. Jane Addams, *The Second Twenty Years at Hull House: September 1909 to September 1929* (New York: Macmillan, 1930), 12–27; "The Christ Answer to the Cry of the City," *Survey*, May 4, 1912, 184–187; Paul Kellogg, "The Industrial Platform of the New Party," *Survey*, August 24, 1912, 668–670; and Allen Davis, "Social Workers and the Progressive Party, 1912–1916," *American Historical Review* (April 1964): 672.

111. As recalled by Julian Mack in his 1912 President's Address, "Social Progress," in Alexander Johnson, ed., *Proceedings of the National Conference of Charities and Correction: 1912* (Fort Wayne, IN: Fort Wayne Printing, 1912), 1.

112. "Jane Addams Relates the Steps by Which She Became a Progressive," *Progressive Bulletin*, December 28, 1912, 2.

113. In fact, many social reformers believed that there was a "need for action on an international basis"; see Addams, *The Second Twenty Years at Hull House*, 20.

114. Ibid.

115. Ibid., 23–24.

116. Paul Kellogg, "Report of the Committee," *Proceedings of the National Conference of Charities and Correction, 1910* (Fort Wayne, IN: Fort Wayne Publishing, 1910), 391.

117. "A Case for the Recall," *Survey*, March 30, 1912, 1989.

118. Owen Lovejoy, "Standards of Living and Labor: Report of the Committee," *Proceedings of the National Conference of Charities and Correction: 1912*, 376, 379–394.

119. Julian Mack, "Social Progress," 1, 6.

120. Kellogg, "The Industrial Platform of the New Party," 688.

121. Gifford Pinchot to Robert La Follette, February 17, 1912, Pinchot Papers.

122. "Mr. Taft and Mr. Roosevelt," *Manchester Guardian*, May 16, 1912; "After the Conventions: Mr. Roosevelt and the Old Parties," *Times* (London), July 4, 1912; "The Struggle for the Presidency," *Times* (London), November 4, 1912; and "The Progressives in the United States," *Times* (London), November 22, 1912.

123. Edward J. Ward, *The Social Center* (New York: Allenton, 1913), 87.

124. Roosevelt, *Works*, vol. 17, 105.

125. Mack, "Social Progress," 11.

126. Eldon Eisenach, *The Lost Promise of Progressivism* (Lawrence: University Press of Kansas, 1994), 62.

127. James Morone, *The Democratic Wish: Popular Participation and the Limits of Government*, rev. ed. (New Haven, CT: Yale University Press, 1998).

128. Alexis de Tocqueville, *Democracy in America*, ed. J. P. Mayer (Garden City, NY: Doubleday, 1969), 68, 82, 95.

129. Abbott cited in Eisenach, *The Lost Promise of Progressivism*, 62, n25.

130. Croly, *Progressive Democracy,* 167–169.

131. Robert Wiebe, *Self-Rule: A Cultural History of American Democracy* (Chicago: University of Chicago Press, 1995), 264.

132. Learned Hand to Felix Frankfurter, April 4, 1912, Hand Papers.

133. Alexander Hamilton, James Madison, and John Jay, *The Federalist Papers,* edited by Clinton Rossiter (New York: New American Library, 1960), 432.

Chapter Three. The First Primary Campaign: Candidate-Centered Politics and the Battle for the Republican Presidential Nomination

1. Gifford Pinchot to Robert La Follette, April 13, 1912, Box 472, Folder: 1912, Robert M. La Follette Papers, Manuscript Division, Library of Congress, Washington, D.C. (hereafter, La Follette Papers).

2. "The Right of the People to Rule," address at Carnegie Hall, New York City, March 20, 1912, from Roosevelt, *Works,* vol. 17, 151.

3. On the development of the direct primary at the local and state levels, see Alan Ware, *The American Direct Primary: Party, Institutionalization, and Transformation in the North* (Cambridge, UK: Cambridge University Press, 2002); and John F. Reynolds, *The Demise of the American Convention System* (New York: Cambridge University Press, 2006).

4. McKinley and Campbell cited in Roosevelt to Senator Joseph Dixon, March 8, 1912, in Elting E. Morison, ed., *The Letters of Theodore Roosevelt* (Cambridge, MA: Harvard University Press, 1952), vol. 7, 521–524.

5. Andrew Jackson to James Gwin, February 23, 1835, *Niles' Registrar,* April 4, 1835, 80.

6. Roosevelt to Dixon, March 8, 1912.

7. George Mowry, *Theodore Roosevelt and the Progressive Movement* (Madison: University of Wisconsin Press, 1946), 228.

8. Editorial, "The First Fruits," *New York Times,* April 28, 1912, part III, 16.

9. La Follette to Fred McKenzie, Editorial for *La Follette's,* no date, Box 107, Folder: June 1912, La Follette Papers.

10. The *New York World* estimated that more than $1 million had been spent by the Roosevelt campaign on the nomination contest by the middle of May, and that expenditures were increasing as the time for the Republican National Convention was approaching (May 19, 1912).

11. Editorial, "Taft and Roosevelt," *Evening Star* (Washington), April 8, 1912.

12. La Follette to Fred McKenzie, editorial for *La Follette's;* for a detailed description of the Roosevelt organization, which would eventually provide much support for the Progressive Party, see Morison, *The Letters of Theodore Roosevelt,* vol. 7, 502.

13. George Kibbe Turner, "Manufacturing Public Opinion: The New Art of Making President by Press Bureau," *McClure's Magazine,* July 1912.

14. Editorial, "Dr. Bryan's Opinion," *New York Times,* February 14, 1912,

15. "Taft Has Reward in People's Rebuke," *San Francisco Chronicle,* May 28, 1912, 22; and "Let the Popular Will Prevail," *San Francisco Chronicle,* May 31, 1912, 24.

16. "Tomorrow's Presidential Election," *Manchester Guardian,* November 4, 1912.

17. Walter Weyl, *The New Democracy* (New York: Macmillan, 1912), 5.

18. Roosevelt's first national exposure to national politics was the Republican National Convention of 1884, when, as a delegate at large from New York, he joined a

small number of reformers in backing Senator George Edmunds from Vermont for the nomination. When the convention nominated James Blaine of Maine—a captivating man of great ability but also of questionable integrity—a sizable minority of Republicans defected to the Democratic candidate, Grover Cleveland. These "mugwumps" (so called because their mugs were on one side of the fence and their wumps on the other) included many people Roosevelt had collaborated with in supporting Edmunds. But Roosevelt refused to join the bolters, claiming that his effectiveness as an independent Republican depended on his reputation for being a solid party man. Without denying that he supported Edmunds and opposed Blaine, Roosevelt acknowledged that he had been beaten in a fair fight and reaffirmed his attachment to party: "I am by inheritance and by education a Republican; whatever good I have been able to accomplish in public life has been accomplished through the Republican party; I have acted with it in the past, and wish to act with it in the future." Roosevelt quoted in H. W. Brands, *TR: The Last Romantic* (New York: Basic Books, 1997), 177. On the 1884 campaign, see 167–179.

19. "Roosevelt Says He's No Bolter; 'Best Man Wins,'" *San Francisco Chronicle*, February 27, 1912.

20. George E. Mowry, *Theodore Roosevelt and the Progressive Movement* (New York: Hill & Wang, 1946), 226.

21. Ibid., 232.

22. *Times* (London), May 23, 1912.

23. *New York World*, March 27, 1912; and *New York Times*, March 28, 1912.

24. Gilbert Roe, "The Meaning of the North Dakota Primary," *La Follette's*, March 30, 1912.

25. Robert La Follette, letter to supporters in Wisconsin who were going to North Dakota to campaign on his behalf, no date, Robert M. La Follette Sr. Papers, Folder: March 1912.

26. Bonaparte cited in Mowry, *Theodore Roosevelt and the Progressive Movement*, 232.

27. "The Illinois 'Primaries,'" *Times* (London), April 11, 1912; and "Taft, Defeated in Illinois, to Be Ditched," *San Francisco Examiner*, April 11, 1912.

28. "Illinois Swept by Roosevelt and Champ Clark," *San Francisco Examiner*, April 10, 1912.

29. *Times* (London), April 15, 1912.

30. Editorial, "To Mr. Taft's Managers," *New York Times*, April 15, 1912.

31. Editorial, *Nation*, April 18, 1912.

32. Editorial, "Up to the National Convention," *Boston Herald*, May 1, 1912.

33. *Boston Evening Transcript*, May 1, 1912.

34. *San Francisco Examiner*, May 24, 1912.

35. Editorial, "Taft's Duty," *New York World*, April 23, 1912.

36. Address of President Taft, April 25, 1912, Boston, Massachusetts, William Howard Taft Papers, Manuscript Division, Library of Congress, Washington, D.C. (hereafter, Taft Papers).

37. William Howard Taft to L. O'Brien, January 21, 1911, Taft Papers.

38. Ibid.; Taft to Frank P. Flint, February 15, 1911, Taft Papers.

39. William Howard Taft, "The Sign of the Times," address given before the Electrical Manufacturers Club, Hot Springs, Virginia, November 6, 1913, Taft Papers.

40. William Howard Taft, address at Boston, Massachusetts, April 25, 1912, Taft Papers.

41. In appealing to African American voters during the Ohio primary contest, Taft did warn "his colored friends" that TR's call for popular referenda on court decisions would amount "to writing your constitutional restrictions in water." But this claim was not likely to mean much to his audience, who were more than likely aware of the judiciary's complicity in the country's failure to fulfill the promises of the Fourteen and Fifteenth Amendments. "Campaign Crisis Seen in Ohio Fight," *New York Times*, May 9, 1912.

42. William Howard Taft, address at the banquet of the Republican Club, New York, February 12, 1912, Taft Papers.

43. Taft, "The Sign of the Times."

44. Address of William Howard Taft, April 25, 1912, Senate Document 615 (62-2, vol. 38, 2), 3–4.

45. Taft, address at the banquet of the Republican Club, New York, February 12, 1912.

46. Taft, address of April 25, 1912.

47. Theodore Roosevelt Address, Omaha, Nebraska, April 17, 1912, Theodore Roosevelt Collection, Houghton Library, Harvard University, Cambridge, Massachusetts.

48. The Recall of Judicial Decisions, address at Philadelphia, PA, April 10, 1912, in Roosevelt, *Works*, vol. 17, 191.

49. Address at Omaha, Nebraska, April 17, 1912.

50. Ibid.

51. Roosevelt to Sydney Brooks, June 4, 1912, Morison, *The Letters of Theodore Roosevelt*, vol. 7, 552–553 (my emphasis).

52. Taft address, February 12, 1912.

53. Abraham Lincoln, "The Perpetuation of Our Free Institutions," address before Springfield's Young Men's Lyceum, January 27, 1838, in Richard N. Current, ed., *The Political Thought of Abraham Lincoln* (Indianapolis, IN: Bobbs-Merrill, 1967), 11–21.

54. Lincoln, First Inaugural Address, in Current, *The Political Thought of Abraham Lincoln*, 175–176.

55. Taft address, February 12, 1912.

56. Roosevelt address, April 17, 1912.

57. Abraham Lincoln to Henry L. Pierce and others, April 6, 1859, *Abraham Lincoln On-Line*, http://showcase.netins.net/web/creative/lincoln/speeches/speeches.htm (emphasis in original).

58. Roosevelt address, April 17, 1912.

59. Daniel Walker Howe, *The Political Culture of the American Whigs* (Chicago: University of Chicago Press, 1979), 291.

60. Abraham Lincoln, address to a Special Session of Congress, July 4, 1861, in Current, *The Political Thought of Abraham Lincoln*, 187–188.

61. "Roosevelt Assailed by Robert Lincoln," *New York Times*, April 29, 1912.

62. Herbert Croly, *The Promise of American Life* (New York: Macmillan, 1909; reprint, New York: Dutton, 1963), 278–279.

63. Charles E. Merriam, *A History of American Political Theories* (New York: Macmillan, 1903), 305–333.

64. Theodore Roosevelt, *Citizenship in a Republic*, address delivered at the Sorbonne, Paris, April 23, 1910 (New York: Review of Books, 1910), 2204.

65. Taft cited in Kathleen Dalton, *Theodore Roosevelt: A Strenuous Life* (New York: Vintage Books, 2002), 386.

66. "Colonel's Victory Matter of Majority," *San Francisco Chronicle*, May 15, 1912.

67. "Mr. Taft and Mr. Roosevelt," *Manchester Guardian*, May 16, 1912.

68. Turner, "Manufacturing Public Opinion."

69. Ibid.

70. "Mr. Taft and Mr. Roosevelt."

71. "Victory Surely His, Roosevelt Boasts," *New York Times*, May 16, 1912; and Joseph L. Gardner, *Departing Glory: Theodore Roosevelt as Ex-President* (New York: Charles Scribner's, 1973), 234.

72. "Roosevelt Read Out, with His Followers," *New York Times*, May 17, 1912.

73. "Principles and Personalities," *Outlook*, May 25, 1912.

74. "Roosevelt Unsafe, Taft Tells Ohioans," *New York Times*, May 14, 1912.

75. Roosevelt to Chase Salmon Osborne, April 16, 1912, in Morison, *The Letters of Theodore Roosevelt*, vol. 7, 534.

76. "Strain Tells on Taft," *New York Times*, May 21, 1912.

77. "Taft Names Bosses Who Aid Roosevelt," *New York Times*, May 7, 1912.

78. "Colonel Has Throat Treated," *New York Times*, May 18, 1912.

79. William Howard Taft, *Popular Government* (New Haven, CT: Yale University Press, 1913), 117–121.

80. "Presidential Primaries," *Outlook*, May 11, 1912.

81. "Crowds Watch the Bulletins," *New York Times*, May 22, 1912.

82. Editorial, "Ohio," *New York Times*, May 22, 1912.

83. James R. Garfield, diary entry, May 22, 1912, Diaries, Papers of James R. Garfield, Box 9, 1912, Manuscript Division, Library of Congress, Washington, D.C.

84. Roosevelt to Joseph Moore Dixon, May 23, 1912, in Morison, *The Letters of Theodore Roosevelt*, vol. 7, 546.

85. Delos F. Cox, "The New Irrepressible Conflict," *Independent*, June 13, 1912.

86. Editorial, "The Compromise Delusion," *New York Times*, May 23, 1912.

87. "The Campaign as a School of the People," *Outlook*, June 8, 1912.

88. Learned Hand to Felix Frankfurter, April 4, 1912, Learned Hand Papers, Harvard University Law School, Cambridge, Massachusetts.

89. Turner, "Manufacturing Public Opinion."

90. Editorial, "The Menace in the Presidential Primary," *McClure's Magazine*, July 1912.

91. Wilcox, "The Irrepressible Conflict."

92. Editorial, "The Presidential Issue," *Outlook*, April 27, 1912.

93. Wilcox, "The New Irrepressible Conflict."

94. Taft quoted in Gable, *The Bull Moose Years*, 16.

95. Theodore Roosevelt, editorial, "A Naked Issue of Right and Wrong," *Outlook*, June 14, 1912.

96. "Steam Roller Crushes T. R. but He Bobs Up Fighting," *San Francisco Chronicle*, June 7, 1912.

97. Governor Hiram Johnson, on behalf of the California delegation, to the Delegates of the Republican National Committee, June 17, 1912, James A. Stone Manuscripts, Wisconsin Historical Society, Madison, Wisconsin (emphasis in original). The author is grateful to Professor Lewis Gould, Department of History, Texas University, for sending him this memo.

98. Philip James Roosevelt, "Politics of the Year 1912: An Intimate Progressive View," unpublished manuscript, Theodore Roosevelt Collection, 13–17.

99. Taft received 31 delegates and Roosevelt 9 from the national committee. According to Lewis Gould's detailed analysis, Taft deserved 19 and Roosevelt 21. See Gould, "Theodore Roosevelt, William Howard Taft, and the Disputed Delegates in 1912," *Southwestern Historical Quarterly* 80 (July 1976): 33–56.

100. "Help TR's Men Cry; and He's Coming," *San Francisco Examiner,* June 8, 1912.

101. Roosevelt, "A Naked Issue of Right and Wrong."

102. *Chicago Daily Tribune,* June 18, 1912.

103. Editorial, "The Spectacle at Chicago," *New York Times,* June 17, 1912.

104. "Mr. Roosevelt's Strength," *Times* (London), June 17, 1912.

105. Quoted in Gardner, *Departing Glory,* 240.

106. Ibid.

107. Patricia O'Toole, *When Trumpets Call: Theodore Roosevelt after the White House* (New York: Simon & Schuster, 2005), 177.

108. Ibid., 176.

109. All quotes come from "The Case against the Reactionaries," speech at the Auditorium, Orchestra Hall, Chicago, Illinois, June 17, 1912, typed manuscript, Theodore Roosevelt Collection.

110. Walter Rauschenbusch, *Christianizing the Social Order* (New York: Macmillan, 1912), 282.

111. Norman Wilensky, *Conservatives in the Progressive Era,* University of Florida Monographs (Gainesville: University of Florida Press, 1965), 65.

112. Roosevelt cited in O'Toole, *When Trumpets Call,* 178.

113. Philip C. Jessup, *Elihu Root* (New York: Dodd, Mead, 1938), 188.

114. Harry Wilbur, Executive Clerk to McGovern, to A. Gulickson, July 9, 1912, Box 7, Folder: June 25–30, 1912, Francis McGovern Papers, Wisconsin State Historical Society Collections, Madison, Wisconsin (hereafter, McGovern Papers).

115. "La Follette's Lost Chance," *New York Times,* June 25, 1912.

116. McGovern to M. W. Zeidler, July 6, 1912, Box 8, Folder: July 1–July 12, 1912, McGovern Papers.

117. Robert La Follette to Charles R. Crane, August 21, 1912, La Follette Papers.

118. Root quoted in William A. Schambra, "Elihu Root, the Constitution, and the Election of 1912," Ph.D. dissertation, Northern Illinois University, DeKalb, 1983, 248.

119. Ibid., 252.

120. Root quoted in Jessup, *Elihu Root,* 182–183.

121. Ibid., 182.

122. Ibid., 186.

123. Ibid., 197.

124. Address of the Temporary Chairman, Official Report of the Proceedings,

Fifteenth Republican National Convention, Chicago, Illinois, June 18–21, 1912, 89, Research Library, Republican National Committee, New York City.

125. Ibid., 94; see also Schambra, "Elihu Root and the Constitution," 296–298.

126. Address of the Temporary Chairman, 97, 98.

127. Ibid., 99.

128. Ibid., 99–100.

129. Ibid.

130. Jessup, *Elihu Root*, 197.

131. Ibid., 199–200.

132. As the GOP loyalist Camillus G. Kidder wrote his disgruntled friend Charles Bonaparte, a strong Roosevelt supporter, after the Republican National Convention: "You see, in the action of the steamroller, a deliberate cheating of your candidate to deprive him of the nomination; but is it not conceivable that the 'Old Guard' believed that the majority of the party had not yet spoken and that [TR's] success, upon the platform stated, would be bad for the country and might be fatal for the party and that, therefore, it was right to use all technical points to defeat him." Kidder to Bonaparte, Charles J. Bonaparte Papers, Manuscript Division, Library of Congress, Washington, D.C. I thank Lewis Gould for bringing this letter to my attention.

133. Ibid., 197.

134. White cited in Schambra, "Elihu Root and the Constitution," 299.

135. Jessup, *Elihu Root*, 197–198.

136. "Taft Rejoices That the Party Is Saved," *New York Times*, June 23, 1912.

137. Amos R. E. Pinchot, *History of the Progressive Party, 1912–1916*, edited by Helene Maxwell Hooker (New York: New York University Press, 1958), 165.

138. Speech at Orchestra Hall, Chicago, Illinois, June 22, 1912, typed manuscript, Theodore Roosevelt Collection.

139. "Mr. Roosevelt's Strength."

140. Root speech, as printed in *New York Times*, August 2, 1912; see also Schambra, "Elihu Root, the Constitution, and the Election of 1912," 301.

141. Taft's speech, as printed in *New York Times*, August 2, 1912.

142. Croly, *Progressive Democracy*, 14.

143. "The World We Live In."

144. "The Progressive Party," *Literary Digest*, August 17, 1912, 244.

Chapter Four. *"Enthroned on the Seat of Righteousness":*
The Formation of the National Progressive Party of 1912

1. Nicholas Roosevelt, "Account of the Republican Convention, 1912," no date, Theodore Roosevelt Collection, Houghton Library, Harvard University, Cambridge, Massachusetts, 53 (hereafter, Roosevelt Collection).

2. Ibid.; and John Pratt, "Third Party Dons Fighting Togs for Battle to Finish," *San Francisco Examiner*, June 24, 1912.

3. Ibid.

4. Philip J. Roosevelt, "Politics of the Year 1912: An Intimate Progressive View," Roosevelt Collection, 21.

5. Ibid.

6. "Flinn Lays Plans for State Battle," August 8, 1912, *Philadelphia Evening*

Bulletin, August 8, 1912; and Editorial, "An Impossible Coalition," *Philadelphia Evening Bulletin,* August 9, 1912.

7. "Mr. Roosevelt and the Old Parties," *Times* (London), July 4, 1912.

8. John Allen Gable, *The Bull Moose Years: Theodore Roosevelt and the Progressive Party* (Port Washington, NY: Kennikat Press, 1978), 37.

9. Ibid., 38.

10. Paul Kellogg, "The Industrial Platform of the New Party," *Survey,* August 24, 1912, 668.

11. Ibid.

12. Ben Lindsey to Jane Addams, July 6, 1912, Ben B. Lindsey Papers, Manuscript Division, Library of Congress, Washington, D.C.

13. "Labor of Women and Children," December 3, 1906, and "Regulation of Women and Child Labor," December 3, 1907, in William Griffith, ed., *The Roosevelt Policy* (New York: Current Literature Publishing, 1919), 454–455, 684–687.

14. Theodore Roosevelt, "A Charter for Democracy," address before the Ohio Constitutional Convention at Columbus, Ohio, February 21, 1912, Roosevelt Collection.

15. Theodore Roosevelt, "What Is a Progressive?" *Outlook,* April 13, 1912, 809.

16. Ibid., 810.

17. Editorial, "The Christ Answer to the Cry of the City," *Survey,* May 4, 1912, 184.

18. Reverend W. B. Norton, "Praises Growth of Progressives," *Chicago Daily Tribune,* August 27, 1912.

19. La Follette cited in "The New Party Gets Itself Born," *Current Literature,* September 1912, 252.

20. Ray Stannard Baker, "Our Next President—and Some Others," *American Magazine,* June 1912, 137–138.

21. "The Old-Fashioned Presidential Candidate, and the New," *McClure's Magazine,* April 1912.

22. "The New Party," *Outlook,* August 17, 1912.

23. Herbert Croly, "A Test of Faith in Democracy," *American Magazine,* November 1912, 22.

24. "Renomination of Mr. Taft, Birth of a New Party," *Times* (London), June 24, 1012.

25. Samuel G. Blythe, "How the Big Split Came: The Story of the Political Revolution in America," *McClure's Magazine,* June 1912. Blythe's story ended with the Progressives nominating TR, with Wilson as his running mate, and the Conservatives selecting Taft, who ran with the conservative Democratic governor of Ohio, Judson Harmon.

26. James J. Montague, "Morgan, Belmont, and Ryan Ordered to Keep Hands Off Convention," *San Francisco Chronicle,* June 28, 1912.

27. "Convention in All-Night Session: Now Hearing Nominating Speeches, Bryan Pledge against 'The Interests,'" *New York Times,* June 28, 1912.

28. Editorial, "Probably Wilson and Underwood," *New York Times,* June 28, 1912.

29. Woodrow Wilson quoted in John Milton Cooper, *The Warrior and the Priest: Woodrow Wilson and Theodore Roosevelt* (Cambridge, MA: Harvard University Press, 1983), 181.

30. On the contest between Clark and Wilson, see ibid., 183.

31. Estal E. Sparlin, "Bryan and the 1912 Democratic Convention," *Mississippi Valley Historical Review* 22, 4 (March 1936): 537–546.

32. "Bryan Threatens to Bolt the Ticket If Named by Aid of Tammany Votes," *New York Times,* June 30, 1912.

33. Cooper, *The Warrior and the Priest,* 183.

34. Editorial, "The Plain Duty of the Democratic Convention," *New York Times,* June 24, 1912.

35. Stephen Skowronek, "The Reassociation of Ideas and Purposes: Racism, Liberalism, and the American Political Tradition," *American Political Science Review* 100, 3 (August 2006): 385–401.

36. Ronald J. Pestritto, *Woodrow Wilson and the Roots of Modern Liberalism* (Lanham, MD: Rowman & Littlefield, 2005).

37. Eldon J. Eisenach, *The Lost Promise of Progressivism* (Lawrence: University Press of Kansas, 1994), 122–129.

38. Editorial, "Which Path," *New York Times,* June 25, 1912.

39. Burton J. Hendrick, "Woodrow Wilson: Political Leader," *McClure's Magazine* 38 (December 1911): 217–231.

40. Woodrow Wilson, "A Political Address at Indianapolis," April 13, 1911, in Arthur S. Link, ed., *The Papers of Woodrow Wilson* (Princeton, NJ: Princeton University Press, 1976), vol. 22, 559; see also Cooper, *The Warrior and the Priest,* 180.

41. "A New Report on a Campaign Address in Boston: Wilson Cheered by a Great Throng," April 27, 1912, in Link, *The Papers of Woodrow Wilson,* vol. 24, 365; and "A News Report of a Political Address in Buffalo, New York," April 10, 1912, in Link, *The Papers of Woodrow Wilson,* vol. 24, 314; see also Cooper, *The Warrior and the Priest,* 185.

42. John Dewey, "The Future of Liberalism," *Journal of Philosophy* 32, 9 (April 25, 1935): 228.

43. "After the Conventions: Mr. Roosevelt and the Old Parties," *Times* (London), July 4, 1912.

44. Editorial, "How the Primaries Worked," *New York Times,* July 3, 1912.

45. Link, *The Papers of Woodrow Wilson,* vol. 21, 376.

46. Hendrick, "Woodrow Wilson: Political Leader," 231.

47. Link, *The Papers of Woodrow Wilson,* vol. 24, 362, 364.

48. "Wilson Refuses to Attend Convention," *San Francisco Examiner,* June 30, 1912.

49. "Clark Says He Will Regain Lost Votes," *New York Times,* July 1, 1912.

50. Editorial, "The Democratic Platform and the Opinion of the Nation," *San Francisco Examiner,* August 5, 1912; and Woodrow Wilson, A Speech Accepting the Democratic Nomination in Sea Girt, New Jersey, August 7, 1912, in Link, *The Papers of Woodrow Wilson,* vol. 25, 11–12.

51. Cited in Cooper, *The Warrior and the Priest,* 186.

52. Louis Brandeis to Charles F. Amidon, July 3, 1912, Microfilm Reel 37, Louis Brandeis Papers, University of Louisville, Louisville, Kentucky.

53. "After the Conventions: Mr. Roosevelt and the Old Parties," *Times* (London), July 4, 1912.

54. Herbert Croly, *Progressive Democracy* (New York: Macmillan, 1914), 345–346.

55. George Kibbe Turner, "Manufacturing Public Opinion," *McClure's Magazine,* July 1912.

56. "The Old Fashioned Presidential Candidate, and the New," *McClure's Magazine,* April 1912.

57. "Governor Notified He's Party Choice to Guide Ship of State," *San Francisco Examiner,* August 8, 1912.

58. Wilson, A Speech Accepting the Democratic Nomination in Sea Girt, 5.

59. Croly, *Progressive Democracy,* 346.

60. "'Quit? No' Says TR after Perkins Talk," *San Francisco Chronicle,* July 4, 1912.

61. Everett Colby to TR, July 3, 1912, cited in Gable, *The Bull Moose Years,* 24.

62. "Many Deserting Roosevelt Ranks," *New York Times,* July 4, 1912.

63. Chase Osborn to TR, July 6, 1912, cited in Gable, *The Bull Moose Years,* 24.

64. TR to Chase Salmon Osborn, July 5, 1912, in Elting Morison, ed., *The Letters of Theodore Roosevelt* (Cambridge, MA: Harvard University Press, 1952), vol. 5, 569–570.

65. Learned Hand to Felix Frankfurter, July 25, 1912, Learned Hand Papers, Harvard University Law School, Cambridge, Massachusetts.

66. Amos Pinchot, Notes for a Letter to TR, February 13, 1912, Amos Pinchot Papers, Manuscript Division, Library of Congress, Washington, D.C. (hereafter, Pinchot Papers).

67. Amos Pinchot to Medill McCormick, July 3, 1912, Pinchot Papers.

68. Ibid.

69. Roosevelt to Paul A. Ewert, July 5, 1912, Morison, in *The Letters of Theodore Roosevelt,* vol. 7, 572.

70. Quoted by Jane Addams, *The Second Twenty Years at Hull House: September 1909–September 1929* (New York: Macmillan, 1930), 27.

71. Kellogg, "The Industrial Platform of the New Party," 669.

72. Hand to Frankfurter, July 25, 1912, Hand Papers.

73. Hiram Johnson to Roosevelt, July 8, 1912, Hiram Johnson Papers, Bancroft Library, University of California, Berkeley, California.

74. Roosevelt to Henry Rider Haggard, June 28, 1912, in Morison, *The Letters of Theodore Roosevelt,* vol. 7, 567.

75. Ibid.

76. Learned Hand to Felix Frankfurter, July 25, 1912, Hand Papers.

77. Roosevelt to Haggard, June 28, 1912, in Morison, *The Letters of Theodore Roosevelt,* vol. 7, 568.

78. "The New Progressive Party," *Independent,* August 15, 1912.

79. "Roosevelt and Johnson Named," *Chicago Daily Tribune,* August 8, 1912.

80. "A Confession of Faith," address before the national convention of the Progressive Party, Chicago, Illinois, August 6, 1912, in Roosevelt, *The Works of Theodore Roosevelt,* 26 vols. (New York: Charles Scribner's, 1926), vol. 17, 258, 260.

81. Both quotations come from "The Progressive Party," *Literary Digest,* August 17, 1912, 244.

82. "Roosevelt Sole Convention Star," *New York Times,* August 7, 1912.

83. "Hail New Party in Fervent Song," *New York Times,* August 6, 1912.

84. Roosevelt, *Works,* vol. 17, 230.

85. See, for example, "The Bible and the Life of the People," *Outlook,* May 27, 1911, 220–224.

86. "The New Party Gets Itself Born," 251.

87. Cited in ibid.

88. "The New Party," *Outlook,* August 17, 1912.

89. Cited in "The Progressive Party," 246.

90. Cited in Gable, *The Bull Moose Years,* 39.

91. Ibid., 44.

92. "Outlook Editors Called Heretics," *Chicago Daily Tribune,* August 26, 1912.

93. George P. Fletcher, *Our Secret Constitution: How Lincoln Redefined American Democracy* (London: Oxford University Press, 2001).

94. "Roosevelt Sole Convention Star."

95. Eugene V. Debs, "The Greatest Political Campaign in American History," St. Louis Campaign Opening Speech, July 6, 1912, Eugene V. Debs Papers, Indiana State University, Terre Haute, Indiana.

96. The program for the convention jarringly displayed the middle-class character of the Progressive Party delegates. It contained hallowed quotations from Jefferson and Lincoln, and importunities for those in attendance to sing reverential hymns. At the same time, the program's back cover prominently featured an advertisement for a company urging delegates to invest in Chicago Business Property, with the lead banner, "Real Estate the Basis of All Security." National Progressive Convention Program, found in James R. Garfield Papers, Manuscript Division, Library of Congress, Washington, D.C. (hereafter, Garfield Papers).

97. Herbert Croly, *The Promise of American Life* (New York: Macmillan, 1909; reprint, New York: Dutton, 1963), 278.

98. Theodore Roosevelt, "The Bible and the Life of the People," 221.

99. Gable, *The Bull Moose Years,* 97.

100. "Church Planks Like Bull Moose," *Chicago Daily Tribune,* December 9, 1912.

101. Croly, *Progressive Democracy,* 210.

102. Norton, "Praises Growth of Progressives."

103. Ibid.

104. "The Progressive Party," 244.

105. Jane Addams, Speech Seconding the Nomination of Theodore Roosevelt, Proceedings of the National Progressive Party, Chicago, Illinois, August 5–7, 1912, 194.

106. William Kent to Jane Addams, August 14, 1912, Jane Addams Papers, Swarthmore College, Swarthmore, Pennsylvania (hereafter, Addams Papers).

107. Arthur Ruhl, "The Bull Moose Call," *Collier's,* August 24, 1912, 20.

108. John Dewey, "Theodore Roosevelt," in Jo Ann Boydston, ed., *John Dewey: The Middle Works, 1899–1924* (Carbondale: Southern Illinois University Press, 1982), vol. 2, 147.

109. *Progressive Bulletin,* vol. 1, September 1912, 1, located in the Roosevelt Collection.

110. Theodore Roosevelt to Jane Addams, August 16, 1912, Addams Papers.

111. Jane Addams, "The New Party," *American Magazine,* November 1912, 14.

112. Roosevelt, *Works*, vol. 17, 254.

113. Draft platform with handwritten changes by TR; and "A Contract with the People," Platform of the Progressive Party, adopted at its First National Convention, August 7, 1912, Progressive Party Publications, 1912–1916; both in Roosevelt Collection.

114. "Beveridge Opens the Convention, Sounds War Cry," *Chicago Daily Tribune,* August 6, 1912.

115. Jane Addams, "Speech Seconding the Nomination of Theodore Roosevelt," 194–195.

116. Draft platform with handwritten changes by TR.

117. Roosevelt, *Works*, vol. 17, 268. Roosevelt first gave expression to this view during his 1910 tour of Europe, when he spoke at the University of Berlin (see Chapter 2).

118. Florence C. Potter to Jane Addams, August 16, 1912, Addams Papers.

119. Julius Rosenwald to Jane Addams, August 12, 1912, Addams Papers.

120. Jean Gordon to Jane Addams, August 10, 1912, Addams Papers.

121. Eugene Lies to Jane Addams, August 8, 1912, Addams Papers.

122. Lillian Wald to Jane Addams, August 12, 1912, Addams Papers.

123. Kellogg, "The Industrial Platform of the New Party," 669.

124. Robins is quoted in Davis, "Social Workers and the Progressive Party," 677.

125. Kellogg, "The Industrial Platform of the New Party," 669.

126. Theodore Roosevelt, "Citizenship in a Republic," address delivered at the Sorbonne, Paris, France, April 23, 1910, Roosevelt Collection, 5, 7.

127. Theodore Roosevelt, "Civic Duty and Social Justice," *Outlook,* August 24, 1912, 296.

128. Editorial, "Mr. Roosevelt's Programme," *New York Times,* August 7, 1912.

129. Roosevelt, *Works,* vol. 17, 299.

130. Theodore Roosevelt, "Women's Rights; and the Duties of Both Men and Women," *Outlook,* February 3, 1912, 262–268. As president, Roosevelt struck a similar tone in an address to the National Congress of Mothers: "The primary duty of the woman is to be the helpmate, the housewife, and mother. . . . Above all, [men's] sympathy and regard are due to the struggling wives among those whom Abraham Lincoln called the plain people, and whom he loved and trusted; for the lives of these women are often led on the lonely heights of quiet, self-sacrificing heroism." Roosevelt, "Address by President Roosevelt before the National Congress of Mothers," March 15, 1905 (Washington, DC: Government Printing Office, 1905), 7, 11.

131. Platform of the Progressive Party, 12.

132. Telegram, Theodore Roosevelt to Jane Addams, August 9, 1912, Addams Papers.

133. Ibid., August 8, 1912.

134. Theodore Roosevelt, "Speech on Suffrage," delivered at St. Johnsbury, Vermont, August 30, 1912, Roosevelt Collection.

135. Jo Freeman, "The Rise of Political Women in the Election of 1912," http://www.jofreeman.com (accessed July 2008).

136. Roosevelt's telegram to Addams of August 8 (see note 133) expressed his commitment to involve women fully in staffing the Progressive Party's national, state, and county committees.

137. Francis Kellor, "What Women Can Do for the Progressive Cause — Why They

Should Do It," *Progressive Bulletin,* September 1912, 7. On the Progressive Party's important contribution to the entrance of women into politics, see Freeman, "The Rise of Political Women in the Election of 1912."

138. Theda Skocpol, *Protecting Soldiers and Mothers: The Political Origins of Social Policy in the United States* (Cambridge, MA: Harvard University Press, 1992), 340.

139. Addams, *Second Twenty Years at Hull House,* 33.

140. Jane Addams, "What the Progressive Party Means to Women," *Progressive Bulletin,* October 21, 1912, 7.

141. "To the Women Voters of the United States from the Women in Political Bondage: Vote the Progressive Ticket and Make Us Free," Progressive Party Publications, 1912–1916, Roosevelt Collection.

142. Eileen L. McDonagh, "Race, Class, and Gender in the Progressive Era: Restructuring State and Society," in Sidney M. Milkis and Jerome Mileur, eds., *Progressivism and the New Democracy* (Amherst: University of Massachusetts Press, 1999), 167 (emphasis in original).

143. Ibid., 186. In a more recent piece, McDonagh praises Addams for "combining liberal individualism and ascriptive maternalism as a foundation for justifying women's entry into the electorate." McDonagh, "Forging a New Grammar of Equality and Difference," in Stephen Skowronek and Matthew Glassman, eds., *Formative Acts: American Politics in the Making* (Philadelphia: University of Pennsylvania Press, 2007), 186.

144. Arthur S. Link and Richard L. McCormick, *Progressivism* (Arlington Heights, IL: Harlan Davidson, 1983), 72–84.

145. "'The Call Which Brooks No Refusal': The Common Welfare," *Survey,* March 4, 1912, 187.

146. Gifford, Pinchot, "Conservation and the Cost of Living," 167–168; see also Amos Pinchot, "What the Progressive Party Means to Conservation and the Bread Question," *Progressive Bulletin,* October 21, 1912, 12.

147. Raymond Robins to Clarence Barbour, September 16, 1912, Raymond Robins Papers, Wisconsin Historical Society, Madison, Wisconsin.

148. William Allen White, "Birth of Party Marks an Epoch," *Chicago Daily Tribune,* August 5, 1912.

149. Kellogg, "The Industrial Platform of the New Party," 669.

150. "A Contract with the People," platform of the Progressive Party, adopted at the First National Convention, August 7, 1912, Progressive Party Publications, 1912–1916, Roosevelt Collection. On the Progressive movement and immigration, see Daniel J. Tichenor, *Dividing Lines: The Politics of Immigration Control in America* (Princeton, NJ: Princeton University Press, 2002), chapter 5.

151. Walter Weyl, *The New Democracy: An Essay on Certain Political and Economic Tendencies in the United States* (New York: Macmillan, 1912), 342–343.

152. Both the 1900 and 1904 Republican Party platforms called on the federal government to protect the right of franchise as guaranteed by the Fifteenth Amendment to the Constitution.

153. Theodore Roosevelt to Rev. Bradley Gilman, July 24, 1912, Roosevelt Papers.

154. Christine Stansell, "Details, Details," a review of Edmund Morris's *Theodore Rex, New Republic,* December 10, 2001, 29.

155. John Parker to Theodore Roosevelt, July 24, 1912, Roosevelt Papers.

156. Parker to Roosevelt, July 15, 1912, Roosevelt Papers.

157. Ibid., July 24, 1912.

158. National Association for the Advancement of Colored People, First Annual Report, January 1, 1911, in "National Association for the Advancement of Colored People," 1911–1932, Organizational Files, Addams Papers.

159. For insightful accounts of Roosevelt's southern strategy and the race question, see George E. Mowry, "The South and the Progressive Lily White Party of 1912," *Journal of Southern History* 6 (1940): 237–247; Arthur Link, "Theodore Roosevelt and the South in 1912," *North Carolina Historical Review* (July 1946): 313–324; and Gable, *The Bull Moose Years,* 60–74.

160. James Garfield, diary entry, August 3, 1912, Garfield Papers; and "Roosevelt Veto on Negroes a Blunder," *New York Times,* August 3, 1912.

161. "Roosevelt Men Bar Southern Negroes," *New York Times,* July 31, 1912.

162. "Post for Mingo Sanders," *New York Times,* August 4, 1912.

163. "Roosevelt on Way: Sounds a Warning," *New York Times,* August 12, 1912.

164. Patricia O'Toole, *When Trumpets Call: Theodore Roosevelt after the White House* (New York: Simon & Schuster, 2005), 197.

165. Theodore Roosevelt to Julian La Rose Harris, August 1, 1912, in Morison, *The Letters of Theodore Roosevelt,* vol. 7, 587–590.

166. "New Party Hears Negro Contests," *New York Times,* August 4, 1912.

167. Proceedings of the Provisional National Progressive Committee, Progressive Papers, Roosevelt Collection, 11.

168. See Chairman Dixon's statement, ibid., 233.

169. Ibid., 116.

170. Ibid., 51.

171. Ibid., 52, 235.

172. Ibid., 246.

173. Ibid., 213.

174. Ibid., 233.

175. James Garfield, diary entry, August 4, 1912, Garfield Papers.

176. "Along the Color Line," *Crisis,* August 1912, 165.

177. Addams quoted in *New York Tribune,* August 6, 1912.

178. Addams, *The Second Twenty Years at Hull House,* 34.

179. W. M. Trotter to Addams, telegram, August 7, 1912, Addams Papers.

180. Jane Addams, "The Progressive Party and the Negro," *Crisis,* November 1912, 31.

181. "Won't Force Negro Party on the South," *New York Times,* August 7, 1912.

182. Proceedings of the National Progressive Convention, 127–134.

183. Ibid.

184. "Know the Truth!" Statement of the Entire Colored Delegation of the National Progressive Convention, August 7, 1912, Progressive Party Publications, 1912–1916, Roosevelt Collection.

185. "Roosevelt and the Negro," *African-American Ledger* (Baltimore), August 17, 1912.

186. Editorial, "Which Party," *Pittsburgh Courier,* August 9, 1912.

187. "Colonel Theodore Roosevelt and His Hostile Attitude towards the Afro-Americans," *Broad Ax* (Chicago), August 17, 1912.

188. Editorial, "Mr. Roosevelt," *Crisis*, September 1912, 236.

189. Booker T. Washington to Oswald Garrison Villard, August 5, 1912, in Louis R. Harlan, ed., *The Booker T. Washington Papers* (Champaign: University of Illinois Press, 1975), vol. 11, 575.

190. Musical program, National Progressive Convention Program.

191. Gary Gerstle, "Theodore Roosevelt and the Divided Character of American Nationalism," *Journal of American History* (December 1999), 1306.

192. "Roosevelt Severely Criticized by His Enemies," *African-American Ledger* (Baltimore), August 10, 1912.

193. Amos Pinchot to Theodore Roosevelt, December 3, 1912, Roosevelt Papers.

194. Gifford Pinchot, "Conservation and the Cost of Living," 167–168.

195. Perkins is quoted in John Garraty, *Right-Hand Man: The Life of George W. Perkins* (New York: Harper & Bros., 1950), 270 (Perkins's emphasis).

196. Amos Pinchot to Roosevelt, December 23, 1912, Roosevelt Papers.

197. Roosevelt, *Works*, vol. 17, 277–278.

198. Theodore Roosevelt to Amos Pinchot, December 5, 1912, Roosevelt Papers.

199. Draft platform with handwritten changes by TR.

200. Theodore Roosevelt, "The Conservation of Business—Shall We Strangle or Control It?" *Outlook*, March 16, 1912, 574–576.

201. Gable, *The Bull Moose Years*, 102–104.

202. Charles McCarthy to George Roosevelt, August 17, 1912, Charles McCarthy Papers, Box 3, Folder 8, Wisconsin State Historical Society, Madison, Wisconsin (hereafter, McCarthy Papers).

203. Perkins is quoted in Garraty, *Right-Hand Man*, 269.

204. The Charles McCarthy Papers contain a good deal of information about the missing antitrust plank and the view of the Pinchots and McCarthy that Perkins had "stolen" it from the final version of the platform. See especially the transcript from the *Chicago Record Herald*, November 21, 1912, McCarthy Papers, Box 3, Folder 10.

205. Amos Pinchot to Roosevelt, December 3, 1912, Roosevelt Papers.

206. Gable, *The Bull Moose Years*, 106.

207. Croly, *Progressive Democracy*, 350.

208. Charles McCarthy to Norman Hapgood, September 4, 1912, McCarthy Papers, Box 3, Folder 8.

209. McCarthy quoted in transcript, *Chicago Record Herald*.

210. Charles McCarthy to Gifford Pinchot, October 11, 1912, McCarthy Papers, Box 3, Folder 9.

211. Addams, *The Second Twenty Years at Hull House*, 34–38.

212. Learned Hand to Roosevelt, August 11, 1912, Hand Papers.

213. William Howard Taft to Charles D. Hilles, August 7, 1912, Taft Papers.

214. Roosevelt, *Works*, vol. 17, 262.

215. Charles McCarthy to Theodore Roosevelt, August 10, 1912, McCarthy Papers, Box 3, Folder 7.

216. Ibid.

217. George Emlen Roosevelt to Charles McCarthy, August 13, 1912, McCarthy Papers, Box 3, Folder 7.

218. Roosevelt, *Works*, vol. 17, 298.

219. Charles McCarthy to George Emlen Roosevelt, August 17, 1912, McCarthy Papers, Box 3, Folder 8.

220. Gable, *The Bull Moose Years,* 109.

221. Reprinted in the magazine *Judge,* October 12, 1912.

222. Lewis L. Gould, *Four Hats in the Ring* (Lawrence: University Press of Kansas, 2008), 183.

Chapter 5. *"The Constitution Is a Living Thing":*
The Progressive Party and the Great Campaign of 1912

1. John Milton Cooper Jr., *The Warrior and the Priest: Woodrow Wilson and Theodore Roosevelt* (Cambridge: Harvard University Press, 1983), 140–141.

2. William Howard Taft, address at the Republican Club of Essex County, Beverly, Massachusetts, September 28, 1912, William Howard Taft Papers, Manuscript Division, Library of Congress, Washington, D.C. (hereafter, Taft Papers).

3. Theodore Gillman, address delivered at a Progressive rally held at Yonkers Public High School, September 17, 1912, 3–4. Theodore Roosevelt Collection, Houghton Library, Harvard University, Cambridge, Massachusetts (hereafter, Roosevelt Collection).

4. Proceedings of the National Progressive Party, Chicago, Illinois, August 5–7, 1912, 38–39, Roosevelt Collection.

5. National Progressive Convention Program, Coliseum, Chicago, Illinois, August 1912, copy found in James R. Garfield Papers, Manuscript Division, Library of Congress, Washington, D.C.

6. Herbert Croly, *The Promise of American Life* (New York: Macmillan, 1909; reprint, New York: Dutton, 1963), 278–279.

7. Cooper, *The Warrior and the Priest,* 140.

8. Croly, *The Promise of American Life,* 278–279.

9. Theodore Roosevelt, speech at Orchestral Hall, Chicago, June 22, 1912, 1, 3, Roosevelt Collection.

10. Charles McCarthy to John Hansen, Charles McCarthy Papers, August 9, 1912, Box 3, Folder 7, Charles McCarthy Papers, Wisconsin Historical Society, Madison, Wisconsin (hereafter, McCarthy Papers).

11. Theodore Roosevelt, speech at Infantry Hall, August 16, 1912, Providence, Rhode Island, Roosevelt Collection.

12. Ibid.

13. Ibid.

14. Ibid.

15. Ibid.

16. "Tomorrow's Presidential Election," *Manchester Guardian,* November 4, 1912; and "The New American Party," *Times* (London), August 6, 1912.

17. Cooper, *The Warrior and the Priest,* 212.

18. Herbert Croly, *Progressive Democracy* (New York: Macmillan, 1914), 343.

19. "Roosevelt Crowds Worry Republicans," *New York Times,* August 17, 1912.

20. Roosevelt quoted in John A. Gable, *The Bull Moose Years: Theodore Roosevelt and the Progressive Party* (Port Washington, NY: Kennikat Press, 1978), 112.

21. William Howard Taft to Ed Colston, July 14, 1912, Taft Papers.

22. William Howard Taft, address to the Republican Club of Essex County, Beverly, Massachusetts, September 28, 1912, Taft Papers.

23. Gable, *The Bull Moose Years*, 112.

24. William Howard Taft to Weir Mitchell, July 14, 1912, Taft Papers.

25. Wilson quoted in Patricia O'Toole, *When Trumpets Call: Theodore Roosevelt after the White House* (New York: Simon & Schuster, 2005), 206.

26. *Atlanta Journal* editorial as quoted in "Go Home Colonel: Atlanta Journal Tells Him He Cannot Deceive the South," *New York Times*, September 30, 1912; and "Opinion: The Negro in Politics," *Crisis*, November 1912, 18.

27. August Meier, "The Negro and the Democratic Party, 1875–1915," *Phylon* 17 (June 1956): 185. Washington prepared a memorandum on the Republican Party's commitment to racial justice for Taft's acceptance speech. See Charles William Anderson to Booker T. Washington, May 10, 1912; and Booker T. Washington to William Howard Taft, July 20, 1912, in Louis Harlan and Gaymond Smock, eds., *The Booker T. Washington Papers*, vol. 2, 1911–1912 (Chicago: University of Illinois Press), 563–565.

28. Meier, "The Negro and the Democratic Party," 185.

29. W. E. B. Du Bois, "Mr. Roosevelt," *Crisis*, September 1912, 236.

30. W. E. B. Du Bois, "Suffering Suffragists," *Crisis*, June 1912, 76–77.

31. Theodore Roosevelt, *The Works of Theodore Roosevelt* (New York: Charles Scribner's, 1926), vol. 17, 303.

32. Ibid., 302, 304.

33. Excerpt in the *Crisis*, October 1912, 282; also see "The New Party," *Outlook*, August 17, 1912, where the editors celebrated "this passion of humanity which led the Progressive Convention and its leader to take the ground which was taken respecting the admission of Negro delegates."

34. *Crisis,* October 1912, 282.

35. "Why the Negro Should Be a Progressive," advertisement, *Crisis,* November 1912.

36. Du Bois quoted in Meier, "The Negro and the Democratic Party," 187, 188.

37. Alexander Walters, "Make Friends of Thine Enemies," *Crisis,* October 1912, 306–307.

38. "Politics," *Crisis,* August 1912, 181.

39. Wilson Carey McWilliams, "Standing at Armageddon: Morality and Religion in Progressive Thought," in Sidney M. Milkis and Jerome Mileur, eds., *Progressivism and the New Democracy* (Amherst: University of Massachusetts Press, 1999), 118. On Du Bois's struggle to square his commitment to the Progressive movement with his struggle for civil rights, see David Levering Lewis, *W. E. B. Du Bois: Biography of a Race, 1868–1919* (New York: Henry Holt, 1993).

40. James Kloppenberg, "James Pragmatism and American Culture, 1897–2007," unpublished manuscript, in the author's possession (the Du Bois quote comes from this paper).

41. Arthur S. Link, "The Negro as a Factor in the Campaign of 1912," *Journal of Negro History* 32, 1 (January 1947), 88.

42. Diary of Oswald Garrison Villiard, August 14, 1912, in Arthur S. Link, *The Papers of Woodrow Wilson* (Princeton, NJ: Princeton University Press, 1978), vol. 25, 25–26.

43. Link, "The Negro as a Factor in the Campaign of 1912," 90.

44. Woodrow Wilson to Garrison Villard, August 23, 1912, in Link, *The Papers of Woodrow Wilson,* vol. 25, 52–53.

45. Oswald Villard to Woodrow Wilson with draft statement on race relations, August 28, 1912, in Link, *The Papers of Woodrow Wilson,* vol. 25, 60–61.

46. Ibid.; Meier, "The Negro and the Democratic Party," 189.

47. Meier, "The Negro and the Democratic Party," 190.

48. Editorial, *African American Ledger,* October 12, 1912.

49. "Closing Days of Strenuous Campaign," *African-American Ledger,* November 2, 1912.

50. Roosevelt to Arthur Hamilton Lee, August 14, 1912, in Elting E. Morison, *The Letters of Theodore Roosevelt* (Cambridge, MA: Harvard University Press, 1954), vol. 7, 598.

51. David Thelen, "Social Tension and the Origins of Progressivism," *Journal of American History* 56 (1969): 323–341.

52. Samuel Gompers, *Seventy Years of Life and Labor: An Autobiography,* vol. 2 (New York: Dutton, 1925), 543–544.

53. Excerpts of the speech can be found in "Wilson Opposes Labor," *Progressive Bulletin,* October 14, 1912, 12.

54. Wilson quoted in "Theodore Roosevelt's Labor Record," National Progressive Party campaign bulletin, Roosevelt Collection.

55. Samuel Gompers, "Labor's Political Campaign," *American Federationist,* October 1912.

56. Gompers, *Seventy Years of Life and Labor,* 534.

57. Timothy Healy, "What the Progressive Party Means to Labor," *Progressive Bulletin,* October 21, 1912, 5.

58. Gompers, "Labor's Political Campaign."

59. "Which Party Can Labor Trust?" extract from the Report of the Executive Council of the American Federation of Labor, filed among the Progressive Party Publications, 1912–1916, in Roosevelt Collection.

60. For evidence of Brandeis's early connection to the AFL, see Samuel Gompers to Louis Brandeis, February 4, 1905, and Louis Brandeis to Samuel Gompers, February 13, 1905, Papers of Louis Dembitz Brandeis, University of Louisville, Reel 10 (hereafter, Brandeis Papers).

61. "Brandeis to Take Stump for Wilson," *Boston Post,* August 29, 1912.

62. Louis Dembitz Brandeis, "Memorandum Submitted to Woodrow Wilson, Democratic Candidate for President," September 30, 1912, in William M. Goldsmith, ed., *The Growth of Presidential Power* (New York: Chelsea, 1974), vol. 3, 1327.

63. Link, *The Papers of Woodrow Wilson,* vol. 25, 324–325.

64. Cooper, *The Warrior and the Priest,* 194.

65. Philip Sheldon Foner, *History of the Labor Movement in the United States* (New York: International Publishers, 1947), 115.

66. Link, *The Papers of Woodrow Wilson,* vol. 25, 73, 74.

67. Ibid., 263, 264.

68. Louis Brandeis, "Labor and the New Party Trust Program," September 18, 1912, Brandeis Papers, Reel 28.

69. Charles Henry Davis to Louis D. Brandeis, September 12, 1912, and Brandeis to Davis, September 22, 1912, Brandeis Papers, Reel 28.

70. Louis Brandeis, "Letter to the Editor," *Boston Journal,* September 28, 1912, in Brandeis Papers, Reel 28.

71. Ibid.

72. Brandeis, "Labor and the New Party Trust Program."

73. Ibid.

74. "Third Term—Trust: Scheme to Deceive Labor Exposed by Louis D. Brandeis, Noted Republican Lawyer and Supporter of La Follette," Democratic Party Platform, Brandeis Papers.

75. "Brandeis Condemns the Third Party Platform," *Cleveland Press,* October 11, 1912, 8, Brandeis Papers.

76. Gable, *The Bull Moose Years,* 121.

77. Gifford Pinchot to Charles McCarthy, September 5, 1912, McCarthy Papers, Box 3, Folder 8.

78. Amos Pinchot to Louis Brandeis, October 8, 1912, Amos Pinchot Papers, Box 13, Manuscript Division, Library of Congress, Washington, D.C.

79. Charles McCarthy to Norman Hapgood, September 4, 1912, McCarthy Papers, Box 3, Folder 8 (emphasis in original).

80. Cooper, *The Warrior and the Priest,* 195.

81. Link, *The Papers of Woodrow Wilson,* vol. 25, 75, 78.

82. Healy, "What the Progressive Party Means to Labor"; "Theodore Roosevelt's Labor Record"; and "Woodrow Wilson Not a Progressive," Progressive Party Publications, 1912–1916, in Roosevelt Collection.

83. Amos Pinchot, "What the Progressive Party Means to Conservation and the Bread Question," *Progressive Bulletin,* September 30, 1912. Special letters were sent to leaders of the women's suffrage movement, female physicians, social workers, and other professionals. See copies of these form letters in "Progressive Party, 1912–1914," Organizational Files, File 136, Reel 42, Jane Addams Papers, Swarthmore College, Swarthmore, Pennsylvania (hereafter, Addams Papers).

84. Gable, *The Bull Moose Years,* 117.

85. James J. Montague, "Pact of Hate Is Formed to Get TR," *San Francisco Examiner,* August 26, 1912.

86. "Moose Underwritten for $300,000,000 for 1912 Race Penrose Charges," *San Francisco Examiner,* August 22, 1912.

87. Theodore Roosevelt, "Speech in Wilkes-Barre, Pennsylvania, August 22, 1912," in Lewis L. Gould, *Bull Moose on the Stump: The 1912 Campaign Speeches of Theodore Roosevelt* (Lawrence: University Press of Kansas, 2008), 31–33.

88. "George W. Perkins and the Progressive Party," *Progressive Bulletin,* September 1, 1912 (captions are in the original). Roosevelt's defense of Perkins received welcome support from the Hearst papers, which although they did not exonerate the colonel and the "dough moose" of impropriety, published the Boston address in their editorial pages. See editorial, "When Rich Men Go into Politics," *San Francisco Examiner,* August 29, 2008.

89. Link, *The Papers of Woodrow Wilson,* vol. 25, 124.

90. Philip Kinsley, "Cheering Throngs Acclaim Roosevelt," *San Francisco Examiner,* September 15, 1912.

91. Roosevelt, *Works,* vol. 17, 307.

92. Ibid.

93. Ibid., 310.

94. Ibid., 314.

95. Richard Fairchild, "An Interview with Charles McCarthy," *Chicago Record Herald,* November 21, 1912, McCarthy Papers, Box 3, Folder 10.

96. Theodore Roosevelt, "A Confession of Faith," August 6, 1912, Proceedings of the Progressive National Convention, 68–69, in Roosevelt Collection.

97. "Roosevelt Favors Recall of President," *New York Times,* September 20, 1912; and "'Recall President,' TR Urges, 'Even If It Hits Me,'" *San Francisco Examiner,* September 20, 1912.

98. Charles McCarthy to Theodore Roosevelt, August 10, 1912; George Emlen Roosevelt to McCarthy, August 13, 1912; and Gifford Pinchot to Charles McCarthy, August 23, 1912, all in McCarthy Papers.

99. "Roosevelt Favors Recall of President."

100. "Let the People Rule!" *Nation,* September 26, 1912, 277.

101. Editorial, "The French Progressives," *New York Times,* September 27, 1912.

102. Editorial, "What He Would Do," *New York Times,* September 20, 1912.

103. Eltweed Pomeroy, "Needed Political Reforms: Direct Legislation; Or the Initiative and the Referendum, and the Recall," *Arena* 28 (November 1902): 465–466. For a more complete discussion of progressive reformers' connection to and departure from nineteenth-century local self-government, see Sidney M. Milkis, *Political Parties and Constitutional Government: Remaking American Democracy* (Baltimore: Johns Hopkins University Press, 1999), chapters 2 and 3.

104. *Le Figaro,* May 11, 1912.

105. Alexander Hamilton, James Madison, and John Jay, *The Federalist Papers* (New York: New American Library, 1999), No. 49, 282.

106. "The Struggle for the Presidency," *Times* (London), October 31, 1912.

107. Benjamin Lindsey to George P. Perkins, September 23, 1912, Benjamin Lindsey Papers, Box 40, Manuscript Division, Library of Congress, Washington, D.C.

108. "'Recall President,' TR Urges."

109. Judson King, "Demand a Workable Initiative and Referendum," *American Federationist,* October 1912.

110. Gompers, "The Presidency in the Pending Campaign."

111. "Governor Wilson Favors the Initiative," *Newark Advocate,* September 26, 1912.

112. Link, *The Papers of Woodrow Wilson,* vol. 25, 235, 240.

113. Ibid., 237.

114. Ibid., 238–239.

115. Ibid., 239–240.

116. On Hearst's "late" but enthusiastic endorsement of Wilson, see John Temple Graves (editor in chief of Hearst's *New York American*) to Wilson, September 24, 1912, in Link, *The Papers of Woodrow Wilson,* vol. 25, 233.

117. "Wilson's Challenge to the Bosses," *San Francisco Examiner,* September 30, 1912.

118. "An Address in New Haven Opening the Connecticut State Campaign, September 25, 1912," in Link, *The Papers of Woodrow Wilson,* vol. 25, 250.

119. Ibid., 243.

120. Ibid., 244–245.

121. Albert Bushnell Hart, letter to the *New York Times*, September 30, 1912.

122. "The Struggle for the Presidency."

123. Quoted in Nick Salvatore, *Eugene Debs: Citizen and Socialist* (Urbana: University of Illinois Press, 1982), 252; for Salvatore's discussion of the strike, see 251–252.

124. Debs quoted in James Chace, *1912* (New York: Simon & Schuster, 2004), 87.

125. Eugene Debs, "Arouse Ye Hosts of Labor!" *New York Call*, August 22, 1912.

126. "A Study of Debs: Socialist and the Man," *Brooklyn Daily Eagle*, September 27, 1912.

127. Debs, "Arouse Ye Hosts of Labor."

128. Chace, *1912*, 224.

129. Ira Kipnis, *The American Socialist Movement, 1897–1912* (New York: Columbia University Press, 1952), 335.

130. Chace, *1912*; and James Weinstein, *The Decline of Socialism in America: 1912–1925* (New York: Monthly Review Press, 1967), 84–85.

131. "Debs and Seidel Nominated," *New York Times,* May 18, 1912, 7; and "Debs Vote in All States," *New York Times,* June 17, 1912, 4.

132. Haywood quote in Salvatore, *Eugene Debs*, 253.

133. Debs quoted in ibid., 254.

134. Ibid., 255.

135. "A Study of Debs: Socialist and the Man."

136. "Debs, Choice of Socialists for President," *New York Sun*, May 26, 1912.

137. John Pratt, "Third Party Dons Fighting Togs for Battle to Finish," *San Francisco Examiner,* June 24, 1912.

138. Warren quoted in Chace, *1912*, 163.

139. "Colonel's Platform Edited by Socialist," *New York Times*, September 5, 1912; and "Didn't Revise Platform," *New York Times*, September 6, 1912.

140. "Eugene V. Debs Says Moose Party Stole Socialist Planks," *Chicago Evening World*, August 14, 1912.

141. Debs, letter to the editor of the *New York Times*, printed in ibid.

142. Ibid.

143. Letter to the Editor, *Social Democratic Herald*, November 19, 1898, Eugene V. Debs Papers, Indiana State University, Terre Haute, Indiana.

144. Eugene Debs, "Why You Should Vote for Socialism," *Appeal to Reason*, August 31, 1912.

145. Croly, *Progressive Democracy*, 281–282.

146. For example, see Mark E. Kann, "Challenging Lockean Liberalism in America: The Case of Debs and Hillquit," *Political Theory* 8, 2 (May 1980): 203–222.

147. Debs, letter to the *New York Times*.

148. William Allen White, *Woodrow Wilson* (Boston: Houghton Mifflin, 1924), 264.

149. Charles W. Eliot, letter to the *New York Times*, September 24, 1912.

150. Hart, letter to the *New York Times*.

151. "Edison Discovers He's a Bull Mooser," *New York Times*, October 7, 1912. Party records show that Edison also contributed to the party's coffers. Progressive Party's Financial Records, Theodore Roosevelt Collection. Because Edison was so highly regarded, the party dearly prized and widely publicized Edison's support. A mark of his

celebrity was that a 1913 readers' poll conducted by *Independent* magazine rated him the "most useful contemporary American." See Eldon Eisenach, *The Lost Promise of Progressivism* (Lawrence: University Press of Kansas, 1994), n41.

152. Gable, *The Bull Moose Years*, 90.

153. Ibid., 121.

154. "Today's Presidential Election," *Manchester Guardian*, November 4, 1912.

155. Link, *The Papers of Woodrow Wilson*, vol. 25, 499.

156. Editorial, *Nation*, October 10, 1912.

157. Editorial, "A People's President," *New York Sun*, November 5, 1912.

158. Editorial, "Wilson a Leader: Knows the People," *San Francisco Chronicle*, October 15, 1912.

159. Wilson quoted in Cooper, *The Warrior and the Priest*, 203.

160. Lewis L. Gould, *Four Hats in the Ring: The 1912 Election and the Birth of Modern American Politics* (Lawrence: University Press of Kansas, 2008), 152.

161. Michael E. McGerr, *The Decline of Popular Politics: The American North, 1865–1928* (New York: Oxford University Press, 1986), 161–162.

162. "General Film and Publicity and Sales Company Contract for Roosevelt Films," *Moving Picture News,* September 7, 1912, 10.

163. Film available in the Motion Picture, Broadcasting, and Recorded Sound Division, Library of Congress, Washington, D.C.

164. These recording are available at http://memory.loc.gov/ammem/collections/troosevelt_film/trffilm.html.

165. Mark Benbow, "The Old and the New: The Democratic Party Campaign Film of 1912 as an Anti-Roosevelt Propaganda Tool," paper delivered at the Conference on the 1912 Election, Mary Baldwin College, Staunton, Virginia, September 24, 2004.

166. Ibid.; the film is available in the Motion Picture, Broadcasting, and Recorded Sound Division.

167. "Governor Wilson in Universal Films," *Universal Weekly*, October 5, 1912.

168. Advertisement, *Moving Picture World*, located in Motion Picture, Broadcasting, and Recorded Sound Division (emphasis in original).

169. Benbow, "The Old and the New."

170. "Insane Letters Relate How McKinley's 'Shade' Ordered Death of TR," *San Francisco Chronicle*, October 15, 1912.

171. Philip Roosevelt, "Politics of the Year 1912: An Intimate Progressive View," Roosevelt Collection.

172. Transcript of Roosevelt's remarks, Milwaukee, Wisconsin, October 14, 1912, Roosevelt Collection.

173. *San Francisco Examiner*, October 15, 1912.

174. O'Toole, *When Trumpets Call*, 218.

175. Transcript of Roosevelt's remarks, Roosevelt Collection.

176. Ibid.

177. Cooper, *The Warrior and the Priest*, 201.

178. Roosevelt, *Works*, vol. 17, 331.

179. Cooper, *The Warrior and the Priest*, 203.

180. "Attempt on Life of Mr. Roosevelt," *Times* (London), October 16, 1912.

181. *New York Evening Post* quoted in O'Toole, *When Trumpets Call*, 221.

182. "Roosevelt Stills Garden Tumult: Grave in Speech," *New York Times*, October 31, 1912.

183. Roosevelt, *Works*, vol. 17, 336.

184. Ibid., 339–340.

185. Ibid., 337–338.

186. Ibid., 340; O'Toole, *When Trumpets Call*, 206–207.

Chapter Six. Back to the Future: The Progressive Party's Legacy for American Politics

1. Learned Hand to Mrs. Douglas Robinson, October 1, 1912, Learned Hand Papers, Harvard University Law School, Cambridge, Massachusetts. On Hand's reaction to the Madison Square Garden speech, see Gerald Gunther, *Learned Hand* (New York: Alfred A. Knopf, 1994), 232.

2. For a very good analysis of the Progressive Party's support, see John Gable, *The Bull Moose Years: Theodore Roosevelt and the Progressive Party* (Port Washington, NY: Kennikat Press, 1978), 131–156.

3. Ibid., 135.

4. Ibid., 136.

5. Joseph Dixon to Progressive Party Workers, November 6, 1912, *Progressive Bulletin*, November 11, 1912.

6. Roosevelt to Benjamin Bar Lindsey, December 27, 1912, in Elting E. Morison, ed., *The Letters of Theodore Roosevelt* (Cambridge, MA: Harvard University Press, 1954), vol. 7, 679.

7. Progressive National Committee, *First Quarterly Report of the Progressive National Service,* March 31, 1913, Jane Addams Papers, edited by Mary Lynn McCree Bryan, University Microfilm International, University of Chicago, 1984, File 136, Reel 42.

8. Herbert Knox Smith, "The Progressive Party," *Yale Review* 2 (1912–1913): 18–32.

9. William Hinebaugh to Samuel Bethel, May 9, 1914, Correspondence of the Progressive Party, National Committee, Theodore Roosevelt Collection, Houghton Library, Harvard University, Cambridge, Massachusetts (hereafter, Roosevelt Collection).

10. Ralph Goldman, *The National Party Chairman and Committees: Factionalism at the Top* (Armonk, NY: M. E. Sharpe, 1990), 275.

11. Statement dictated by the president for Harry Dunlop, for publication in the *New York World*, November 14, 1912, William Howard Taft Papers, Manuscript Division, Library of Congress, Washington, D.C.

12. Theodore Roosevelt to Alexander Smith Cochran, December 31, 1912, quoted in Gable, *The Bull Moose Years,* 151 (emphasis in original).

13. Theodore Roosevelt to Arthur Hamilton Lee, November 5, 1912, in Morison, *The Letters of Theodore Roosevelt*, vol. 7, 633–634.

14. Roosevelt to Cochran (emphasis in original).

15. Kelly Miller, "The Political Plight of the Negro," *Kelly Miller's Monographic Magazine* 1 (May 1913): 3.

16. The author thanks Walter Dean Burnham of the University of Texas for bringing these figures to his attention.

17. Gable, *The Bull Moose Years*, 139–141.

18. Proceedings of the First National Convention of the Progressive Party, Roosevelt Collection, 188.

19. Jane Addams, "Social Justice through National Action," speech delivered at the Second Annual Lincoln Day Dinner of the Progressive Party, New York City, February 12, 1914, printed manuscript located in Jane Addams Papers, File 136, Reel 42.

20. Roosevelt to Gifford Pinchot, November 13, 1912, in Morison, *The Letters of Theodore Roosevelt*, vol. 7, 640–645.

21. Mark Lawrence Kornbluh, *Why America Stopped Voting: The Decline of Participatory Democracy and the Emergence of Modern American Politics* (New York: New York University Press, 2000), chapter 5.

22. See Charles Hallinan to Amos Pinchot, August 23, 1916, and Crystal Eastman to Amos Pinchot, October 17, 1916; both in Amos Pinchot Papers, Manuscript Division, Library of Congress, Washington, D.C. (hereafter, Pinchot Papers).

23. Theodore Roosevelt to Raymond Robins, June 3, 1915, Raymond Robins Papers, Wisconsin Historical Society, Madison, Wisconsin (hereafter, Robins Papers). In response to Amos Pinchot's concerns about the conscription legislation, Wilson wrote, "You may be sure that I sympathize with the objects you have in view, and that I will do all in my power to safeguard the matter and, if necessary, request its alteration if it should at any time turn out to be dangerous." Woodrow Wilson to Amos Pinchot, August 19, 1916, Pinchot Papers, Folder 5. Wilson stuck to his position of strict neutrality far longer than Roosevelt or some members of his Cabinet thought he should. The president's resistance to implementing a military draft led to the resignation of his secretary of war, Lindsay M. Garrison, on February 10, 1916.

24. Raymond Robins to Theodore Roosevelt, May 3, 1915, Robins Papers.

25. William Allen White, *The Autobiography of William Allen White* (New York: Macmillan, 1946), 526–527.

26. Victor Murdock to George Perkins, March 21, 1914, Correspondence of the Progressive Party National Committee, Roosevelt Collection.

27. Gable, *The Bull Moose Years*, 187–188.

28. Alice Carpenter to Amos Pinchot, September 26, 1914, and Amos Pinchot to Alice Carpenter, October 5, 1914, Pinchot Papers.

29. Alice Carpenter to George Perkins, July 28, 1914, Correspondence of the Progressive Party, National Committee, Roosevelt Collection.

30. Addams, "Social Justice through National Action," 7.

31. Herbert Croly, "The Future of the Two-Party System," *New Republic*, November 14, 1914.

32. Herbert Croly, "A Test of Faith in Democracy," *American Magazine*, November 1912, 22.

33. Victor Berger, "Socialism, the Logical Outcome of Progressivism," *American Magazine*, November 1912, 20, 21.

34. John Dewey, "Theodore Roosevelt," in Jo Ann Boydston, ed., *John Dewey: The Middle Works, 1899–1924* (Carbondale: Southern Illinois University Press, 1982), 142, 147.

35. I am grateful to Walter Dean Burnham for helping me understand the nature of middle-class radicalism in the United States.

36. Samuel Harden Church, letter to the editor, *New York Times*, October 4, 1912.

37. "The Socialist Vote in the United States," *Chautauqua* 69 (January 1913): 135–136.

38. "The Election," *International Socialist Review* 13, 6 (December 1912): 461.

39. Peter G. Filene, "An Obituary of the Progressive Movement," *American Quarterly* 22 (1970): 20–34.

40. Daniel T. Rodgers, "In Search of Progressivism," *Review in American History* (December 1982): 114–123. An important exception to this historiography is Eldon Eisenach's fine book, *The Lost Promise of Progressivism* (Lawrence: University Press of Kansas, 1994). Eisenach, however, makes coherent sense of progressivism only by ruling out Woodrow Wilson's New Freedom. And yet, as has been noted, Wilson's understanding of reform was attractive not only to Louis Brandeis and Robert La Follette but also to many members of the Progressive Party.

41. Arthur S. Link and Richard L. McCormick, *Progressivism* (Wheeling, IL: Harlan Davidson, 1983), 42.

42. Woodrow Wilson, "A Campaign Address at Topeka, Kansas, October 8, 1912," in Arthur Link, ed., *The Papers of Woodrow Wilson* (Princeton, NJ: Princeton University Press, 1974), vol. 25, 384–385.

43. Woodrow Wilson, "A Campaign Speech on New Issues, Hartford, Connecticut," in Link, *The Papers of Woodrow Wilson*, vol. 25, 235.

44. Link and McCormick, *Progressivism*, 42.

45. Alonzo Hamby, "Progressivism: A Century of Change and Rebirth," in Sidney M. Milkis and Jerome Mileur, eds., *Progressivism and the New Democracy* (Amherst: University of Massachusetts Press, 1999), 48.

46. Woodrow Wilson, "A Campaign Address in Burlington, New Jersey," in Link, *The Papers of Woodrow Wilson*, vol. 25, 490–491, 492.

47. Stephen Skowronek, "The Reassociation of Ideas and Purposes: Racism, Liberalism, and the American Political Tradition," *American Political Science Review* 100, 3 (August 2006): 393.

48. Woodrow Wilson to Alexander Mitchell Palmer, February 5, 1913, in Link, *The Papers of Woodrow Wilson*, vol. 27, 98–102.

49. Jeffrey Tulis, *The Rhetorical Presidency* (Princeton, NJ: Princeton University Press, 1987); and James Ceaser, *Presidential Selection: Theory and Development* (Princeton, NJ: Princeton University Press, 1979), especially chapter 4.

50. Elmer Cornwell, *Presidential Leadership of Public Opinion* (Bloomington: Indiana University Press, 1965), 46.

51. Editorial, "The Democrats as Legislators," *New Republic*, September 2, 1916, 103.

52. Herbert Croly, "The Two Parties in 1916," *New Republic*, October 21, 1916, 286.

53. Statement of Amos Pinchot, released for publication on September 18, 1916, Democratic National Committee, Pinchot Papers.

54. Amos Pinchot to Woodrow Wilson, November 11, 1916, Pinchot Papers. Most of those who voted for Roosevelt in 1912 supported Hughes, but a critical mass—20 percent by one estimate—supported Wilson, adding critically to his Democratic base of support. Perhaps most important, with the tacit support of Hiram Johnson, who was

elected to the Senate in 1916, Wilson won California by a narrow margin. Many voters split their tickets between the president and Johnson, who was snubbed by Hughes and the Republican National Committee, just putting the state in Wilson's column. Without California, Wilson would have lost the electoral college vote to Hughes. Irving Fisher, "Wilson's Triumph Greater than Fully Realized," *New York Times,* November 26, 1916; and "Acquits Johnson of Hughes Defeat," *New York Times,* December 11, 1916. Many social reformers, in particular, supported Wilson's reelection. In October 1916, eleven of the original nineteen members of the 1912 Progressive Party platform committee issued a statement endorsing Wilson on the grounds that he had signed into law all or part of the twenty-three planks of the 1912 platform. "Progressive Voice Raised for Wilson," *New York Times,* November 1, 1916.

55. Richard B. Sherman, *The Republican Party and Black America from McKinley to Hoover* (Charlottesville: University Press of Virginia, 1973), 113–144.

56. "President Resents Negro's Criticism," *New York Times,* November 13, 1914.

57. August Meier, "The Negro and the Democratic Party: 1875–1915," *Phylon* 17 (June 1956): 173–191; Sherman, *The Republican Party and Black America,* 121–122; and David Levering Lewis, *W. E. B. Du Bois: Biography of a Race, 1868–1919* (New York: Henry Holt, 1993), 522.

58. Jean Bethke Elshtain, *Jane Addams and the Dream of American Democracy* (New York: Basic Books, 2002), 239.

59. Michael McGerr, *A Fierce Discontent: The Rise and Fall of the Progressive Movement in America, 1870–1920* (New York: Free Press, 2003), 282.

60. Du Bois quoted in Lewis, *W. E .B. Du Bois,* 556.

61. Woodrow Wilson, "War Message to Congress," April 2, 1917, *War Messages,* Sixty-fifth Congress, First Session, Senate Document Number 5, Serial Number 7264, Washington, D.C., 1917, 3–8.

62. Quoted in McGerr, *A Fierce Discontent,* 286.

63. Ibid., 287–288.

64. Eugene Debs, Statement to the Court upon Being Convicted of the Sedition Act, September 18, 1918, http://www.wfu.edu/~zulick/341/Debs1918.html.

65. Marc Stears, *Progressivism, Pluralism, and the Problems of the State* (Oxford: University of Oxford Press, 2002), 133.

66. Ibid., 135–136.

67. Royden quoted in Elshtain, *Jane Addams,* 244.

68. Richberg quoted in McGerr, *A Fierce Discontent,* 308.

69. In characterizing Wilson's moderate reform program, the press used the term *normality,* not *normalcy,* which did not exist. Confusion still exists about how the term *normalcy* originated. The best guess is that Harding meant *normality* but said *normalcy.*

70. "Daugherty's Report on Release of Debs," *New York Times,* December 31, 1912; see also Ernest Freeberg, *Eugene V. Debs, the Great War, and the Right to Dissent* (Cambridge, MA: Harvard University Press, 2008), which argues that in the end it was Debs's popularity, not a legal argument, that compelled politicians, the mainstream media, and eventually federal judges to reconsider the government's power to jail dissidents.

71. Kenneth Campbell, "The Progressive Movement of 1924," Ph.D. dissertation, Columbia University, 1947.

72. Sidney M. Milkis and Michael Nelson, *The American Presidency: Origins and*

Development, 1777–2007, 5th ed. (Washington, DC: Congressional Quarterly, 2008), 267–271.

73. Morton Keller, "Social and Economic Regulation in the Progressive Era," in Milkis and Mileur, *Progressivism and the New Democracy.*

74. Raymond Robins to Theodore Roosevelt, May 3, 1915, Robins Papers.

75. Theodore Roosevelt to Raymond Robins, June 3, 1915, Robins Papers.

76. Arthur S. Link, "What Happened to the Progressive Movement in the 1920s," *American Historical Review* 64, 4 (July 1959): 848.

77. As the political theorist Marc Stears has written, Croly and other New Nationalists were certain that the "war's greatest intellectual legacy should not be the abandonment of progressive ideals but a thoroughgoing 'reconsideration of former assumptions.'" Stears, *Progressives, Pluralists, and the Problems of the State,* 128.

78. Herbert Croly, "The Future of the State," *New Republic,* September 15, 1917, 179–183.

79. John Dewey, *The Public and Its Problems* (New York: Henry Holt, 1927), 109.

80. Ibid., 208, 211.

81. Robert Wiebe, *Self-Rule: A Cultural History of American Democracy* (Chicago: University of Chicago Press, 1995), 176.

82. John Dewey, "Individualism, Old and New," reprinted in Jo Ann Boydston, ed., *John Dewey: The Later Works,* vol. 5 (Carbondale: Southern Illinois University Press, 1984), 41–123.

83. Hoover coined the term "rugged individualism" in a campaign address of October 22, 1928, New York City, available at http://www.h-net.org/~hst203/documents/HOOVER.html.

84. John Dewey, *Liberalism and Social Action* (New York: G. P. Putnam, 1935), 26, 93.

85. H. M. Kallen, "Salvation by Intelligence," review of *Liberalism and Social Action,* by John Dewey, *Saturday Review,* December 14, 1935, 7.

86. Franklin D. Roosevelt, *Public Papers and Addresses,* Samuel I. Rosenman, ed. (New York: Random House, 1938–1950), vol. 7, xxviii–xxxii.

87. For an extensive analysis of the Progressive era, New Deal, and Great Society, see Sidney M. Milkis, *The President and the Parties: The Transformation of the American Party System since the New Deal* (New York: Oxford University Press, 1993).

88. Roosevelt, *Public Papers and Addresses,* vol. 1, 751–752.

89. "Democratic Platform of 1936," in Donald Bruce Johnson, ed., *National Platforms* (Urbana: University of Illinois Press, 1978), 360.

90. Roosevelt, *Public Papers and Addresses,* vol. 13, 40.

91. Ira Katznelson, *When Affirmative Action Was White: An Untold History of Racial Inequality in Twentieth-Century America* (New York: Norton, 2006).

92. Kevin J. McMahon, *Reconsidering Roosevelt on Race: How the Presidency Paved the Road to Brown* (Chicago: University of Chicago Press, 2004).

93. Morton Keller, "The New Deal and Progressivism: A Fresh Look," in Sidney M. Milkis and Jerome Mileur, eds., *The New Deal and the Triumph of Liberalism* (Amherst: University of Massachusetts Press, 2002), 317.

94. Roosevelt, *Public Papers and Addresses,* vol. 6, 357–367.

95. Chester Bowles to Samuel Rosenman, "Outline of a Suggested Home Front Speech by Mr. Roosevelt," Box 1, Bowles, Chester folder, Samuel Rosenman Papers, Franklin D. Roosevelt Library, Hyde Park, New York.

96. Oscar Cox to Hadley Cantril, May 3, 1943; Hadley Cantril to Oscar Cox, April 30, 1943; Memorandum, Hadley Cantril to David Niles, James Barnes, and Oscar Ewing, April 30, 1943; and "Public Opinion: The NRPB Report and Social Security, Office of Public Opinion Research," April 28, 1943. All found in Franklin D. Roosevelt Library, Oscar Cox Papers, Box 100, Lend-Lease Files. On the Roosevelt administration's use of polls, see Robert Eisenger and Jeremy Brown, "Polling as a Means toward Presidential Autonomy: Emil Hurja, Hadley Cantril, and the Roosevelt Administration," *International Journal of Public Opinion Research* 10 (1998): 239–256.

97. Roosevelt, *Public Papers and Addresses,* vol. 9, 671–672.

98. *Report of the President's Committee on Administrative Management* (Washington, DC: Government Printing Office, 1937), 53. The President's Committee on Administrative Management, headed by Louis Brownlow, played a central role in the planning and policies of New Deal institutions. Charles Merriam, an influential advisor to TR in 1912, was an important member of this committee.

99. For a discussion of the Great Society and its effect on the progressive tradition, see Milkis, *Political Parties and Constitutional Government,* chapter 5.

100. David S. Broder, *Democracy Derailed: Initiative Campaigns and the Power of Money* (New York: James H. Silberman, 2000); and Richard Ellis, *Democratic Delusions: The Initiative Process in America* (Lawrence: University Press of Kansas, 2002).

101. Sidney Blumenthal, *The Rise of the Counterestablishment: From Conservative Ideology to Political Power* (New York: Times Books, 1986), 9.

102. On the Reagan "Revolution" and its connection to progressivism, see Milkis, *Political Parties and Constitutional Government,* chapter 6.

103. Paul Starobin, "The Daddy State," *National Journal,* March 28, 1998.

104. George W. Bush, Second Inaugural Address, January 20, 2005, available at http://www.nytimes.com/2005/01/20/politics/20BUSH-TEXT.html?_r=1&oref=slogin.

105. For example, see Bruce Bartlett, *Imposter* (New York: Doubleday, 2006).

106. Harvey C. Mansfield, "Newt, Take Note: Populism Poses Its Own Dangers," *Wall Street Journal,* November 1, 1994.

107. William Kristol, "The Judiciary: Conservatism's Lost Branch," *Harvard Law and Public Policy* 17, 1 (Winter 1994): 131–136.

108. Miles Poindexter, "Why I Am for Roosevelt," *North American Review,* October 1912, 473.

109. Ronald J. Pestritto, "Theodore Roosevelt Was No Conservative," *Wall Street Journal,* December 27–28, 2008.

110. Barack Obama, Announcement for President, February 10, 2007, available at www.barackobama.com.

111. Wolfe and Wilentz quoted in Kate Zernike, "The Charisma Mandate," *New York Times,* February 17, 2008.

112. Wilson Carey McWilliams, "Standing at Armageddon: Morality and Religion in Progressive Thought," in Milkis and Mileur, *Progressivism and the New Democracy,* 116.

Index

The abbreviation TR refers to Theodore Roosevelt.

African Americans, *continued*
  rights not supported by Progressives, 17,
    152, 165, 166, 172–173, 193–194,
    196–197
  support of TR's campaign, 123, 174–176,
    201
  Taft and, 168, 193, 201, 257, 314n41
  TR's appointments to federal jobs, 166
  TR's support of civil rights, 194–195
  votes in 1912 election, 257–258
  voting rights, 288–289, 323n152
  white suffragists and, 194
  Wilson's presidency and, 273–276
  Wilson supporters, 197–201
  See also Race relations; Slavery
Aldrich, Nelson, 29
American Federation of Labor (AFL), 202,
    204, 207, 222–223, 234, 279
American Magazine, 155–156, 159, 265
American Union Against Militarism, 261
Anderson, H. L., 170, 171–172
Anti-Federalists, 25–26, 72, 295
Antitrust policies
  of Brandeis, 16, 41, 64, 208–209
  of Bryan, 178, 179
  centralized administration as issue, 16, 17
  disagreements among Progressives, 16,
    41–42, 177–181, 215–217, 258, 259
  of La Follette, 41, 64, 83, 177, 178
  of Progressive Party, 177–181, 208,
    215–217
  Sherman Act, 17, 177, 178, 179, 209,
    216
  of Taft, 179
  of TR, 42, 178–179, 210, 213
  of Wilson, 16, 177, 179, 205–206, 223
  See also Interstate trade commission;
    Trusts
Appeal to Reason, 231, 233, 235
Archibald, John D., 213
Articles of Confederation, 22
Atlanta Journal, 193

Bagehot, Walter, 224–225
Baker, Ray Stannard, 49–50, 128
Ballinger, Richard Achilles, 30
Barnes, J. Mahlon, 232
Barnes, William, 99–100, 108, 113
Baruch, Bernard, 213, 277
Beck, Paul Allen, 9

Belmont, August, 131
Benson, Allen I., 275
Berger, Victor, 229, 231, 232, 265–266, 267,
    268
Beveridge, Albert J.
  on future of Progressive Party, 263
  gubernatorial candidacy, 256
  keynote address at Progressive Party
    convention, 186
  Progressive Party platform drafting, 177,
    178, 179
  progressive views, 152
  at Republican convention, 82
  on women's rights, 162
Bill of Rights
  Hand on, 58
  second, 287, 289–290, 291
Bird, Charles J., 255
Blythe, Samuel G., 130
Bonaparte, Charles J., 83
Bowles, Chester, 289
Brandeis, Louis
  antitrust policies, 16, 41, 64, 208–209
  critique of Progressive platform, 207–208
  on Democrats, 140
  La Follette and, 41–42, 64, 204
  New Freedom progressivism, 16, 206
  as Wilson advisor, 16, 198, 204–205,
    206, 207–208, 213, 223
Britain
  House of Lords, 189, 221
  Liberal Party reforms, 189–190, 221
  party government, 240–241
  social democratic experiments, 105–106
  TR's Oxford speech, 33–35, 36, 71
Broad Ax, 175
Brooklyn Daily Eagle, 230, 232
Brown, John, 38
Brown, Walter, 101
Brownlow Committee, 290–291, 338n98
Brownsville Affair, 166, 168
Bruere, Robert W., 233
Bryan, William Jennings
  African American support, 196
  antitrust policies, 178, 179
  campaign of 1896, 6, 15
  campaign of 1904, 7
  campaign of 1908, 7–8, 86, 196, 203
  challenges to TR on direct democracy,
    218–219

Communists, 280
Communities, 285
"Confession of Faith" speech (TR)
    appeal to duty and national community,
        160
    audience reaction, 3
    direct democracy focus, 217
    direct democracy proposal, 186
    direct primary proposal, 148–149
    peroration, 183, 244
    on potential recall of presidents, 183, 218
    on Progressive Party platform, 156
    racial issues, 173–174
    recording of, 244
    on regulation of trusts, 178
    religious language, 150
    social reforms endorsed, 157, 158
Congress
    campaign finance investigation, 212–214
    Democratic control, 203, 256
    direct election of senators, 14, 42, 55,
        136, 189, 217, 224, 225
    elections of 1910, 30, 203
    elections of 1914, 260, 262–263
    Progressive members, 2
    relations with presidents, 47
    Republican leaders, 29, 30, 47
    Socialist members, 231
    State of the Union addresses, 272
    tariff debates, 29
    TR's relations with, 47–48
Conscription, 261, 277
Conservation Congress, Men and Religion
    Forward Movement, 163–164
Conservation movement, 41, 163–164,
    211
Conservatism
    fear of socialism, 228
    modern, 292–294
    opposition to Obama, 296–297
    Progressives seen as radical, 267
    Republican stand-patters, 22, 56, 80, 98,
        117
    of Taft, 22, 59, 88–91, 190–191, 292
    veneration for Constitution, 221
Constitution
    amendment process, 14, 157
    Fifteenth Amendment, 39
    Fourteenth Amendment, 39, 57, 59

interpretation by people, 217, 250
modifications to increase direct
    democracy, 91
Nineteenth Amendment, 280
Preamble, 8, 14, 22–23, 239
Progressive views of, 8, 21, 185–186
Taft's support, 120–121
TR's views on interpretation, 59, 217, 250
Twenty-First Amendment, 287–288
Conventions. See Party conventions; and
    individual parties
Coolidge, Calvin, 281–282
Cooper, John Milton, 133, 206
Corporate contributions, 212
Corporate power. See Antitrust policies;
    Trusts
Cortelyou, George B., 214
Courts
    judicial review, 58
    recall of judges, 58, 68
    TR's criticism of, 60
    Wilson's criticism of the, 224
    See also Recall of state court decisions;
        Supreme Court
CPI. See Committee on Public Information
Creel, George, 278
Crisis, 172, 173, 175, 193, 194, 196–197,
    199, 275, 276
Croly, Herbert
    on centralized state, 24, 180
    on civic religion, 153
    on democracy, 15
    on education of citizens, 19
    on election of 1912, 265
    on executive power, 26
    on Hamilton, 23
    on new Declaration of Independence,
        152–153, 186, 250, 267
    at New Republic, 264, 272–273, 277,
        283–284
    on Progressive challenge to old system,
        121
    Progressive Democracy, 236
    Progressive Party platform drafting, 177
    The Promise of American Life, 38–39, 96
    on social democracy, 236, 264
    on TR's leadership, 11, 40, 47, 129
    on Wilson, 140, 272–273
Curran, J. J., 153, 214

Johnson, Hiram
  as California governor, 260
  election to Senate, 335–336n54
  in Progressive Party, 146
  at Republican convention, 109
  support of TR's candidacy, 63, 97
  on TR's leadership, 12
  as TR's running mate, 148, 159, 213, 254
Journalists. *See* Press
Judges, recall of, 58, 68
  See also Courts
Judicial review, 58

Kallen, H. M., 285–286
Kansas
  TR's Osawatomie speech, 38, 40–41, 43–44, 55, 93–94
  Wilson's speech in, 270
Kansas City Star, 122
Karl, Barry, 21
Keller, Morton, 20, 289
Kelley, Florence, 68, 69, 161, 167
Kellogg, Paul, 67–68, 69, 125–126, 129, 145, 158–159, 165, 261
Kellor, Frances, 161, 162, 165, 172, 173, 174, 254
Kent, William, 154
King, Judson, 223
Kingsbury, John, 126, 145
Kipnis, Ira, 231
Kirchway, George, 157, 177
Kloppenberg, James, 24–25

Labor standards, 125–126
  See also Working conditions
Labor unions
  collective bargaining rights, 203, 258, 279, 288
  gains during World War I, 279
  Industrial Workers of the World, 228–229, 231, 279
  in liberal coalition, 288
  organizing rights, 203, 206, 207, 208
  political program, 204
  in Progressive era, 26
  relations with Progressive Party, 152, 165, 202, 211, 263
  repression, 279

strikes, 211, 214, 228–229, 231
support of direct democracy reforms, 203, 222–223
support of social reforms, 127
support of Wilson, 202, 203
Wilson's policies, 202–203, 206–208, 279
See also American Federation of Labor
La Follette, Robert
  antitrust policies, 41, 64, 83, 177, 178
  on contest between Wilson and TR, 139–140
  criticism of TR, 12–13, 78–79, 187
  economic policies, 143–144
  National Progressive Republican League and, 41–42, 45, 48–49
  opposition to expanded national administration, 41–42
  political reform program, 42
  presidential candidacy (1924), 281
  on Progressive Party, 128
  as senator, 48, 52–53, 212–213
  similarities to TR, 28
  speaking style, 52–53
  on TR's campaign organization, 78
  as Wisconsin governor, 48
La Follette, Robert, campaign of 1912
  announcement of candidacy, 45
  delegates to Republican convention, 113–114
  differences from TR, 42
  direct democracy ideas, 42, 44
  nomination campaign, 48–53
  primary elections, 48, 83, 84, 97, 103, 106, 204
  Republican Party convention, 113–114
  speech to Periodical Publishers' Association, 51–53
  struggle with TR for leadership of Progressive movement, 28, 48, 49–53, 63–65, 69–70, 72, 78–79, 83, 114
  supporters, 45, 49–51, 64
League of Nations, 280–281
Lewis, William Draper, 157, 177, 179
Liberalism
  coalition, 288
  Dewey on new, 285–286
  Great Society, 286, 289, 291
  rights issues, 165

Minnesota primary elections, 76, 85
Mississippi Freedom Party, 176
Mitchell, John, 127
Mixon, W. H., 123, 169
Modern presidency, 26, 210, 280, 292–293, 295
Monopolies. *See* Antitrust policies; Trusts
Moore, Alexander P., 239
Morgan, J. Pierpont, 131, 177, 180, 214
Morone, James, 72
Moskowitz, Henry, 145, 167, 173, 174
Motion Pictures Patents Company, 244
Movies. *See* Films
Mowry, George, 17, 21–22, 56, 61, 77
Muckraking journalists, 87–88, 106, 121
Munsey, Frank, 78, 119, 142, 144, 178
Murdock, Victor, 262
Murphy, Charles, 133
Murphy, Frank, 288

NAACP (National Association for the Advancement of Colored People), 66, 167, 172, 193–194, 198
Nation, 54, 85, 219, 241
National administration
    accountability, 210, 270
    ambivalence about, 259, 291
    of antitrust policy, 16, 17, 64–65, 178–179
    concentration of power feared, 41, 143–144, 179, 180, 263
    conflict with individual rights, 202, 259, 284
    debates during campaign, 209–210
    debates over Progressive platform, 180–181
    direct democracy and, 14–16, 143–144, 182
    expansion, 64–65, 209–211, 270
    expansion in New Deal, 291
    La Follette's opposition to expansion, 41–42
    paternalism, 211
    reconciling with mass democracy, 190
    socialist opposition to expansion, 236
    TR's views on expanding, 35, 41, 189, 214–215
    Wilson's opposition to expansion, 16, 25, 270
National American Woman Suffrage

Association (NAWSA), 66, 126, 162, 194
National Colored Democratic League, 196, 197
National Conference of Charities and Correction (NCCC), 65, 67–69, 71, 125–126, 127, 145, 157
National democracy, Populist concept, 14–15
    See also Direct democracy
National Independent Political League (NIPL), 172, 173, 193, 194, 196, 199
Nationalism, Hamiltonian, 23, 39, 272
National Negro Business League, 193
National Progressive Republican League, 41–42, 45, 48–49
National Referendum League, 223
Natural rights tradition
    conflict with progressive ideas, 73, 211–212, 237
    expansion by FDR, 287
    Lincoln on, 93, 94–95, 202
    Reagan and, 292
    Socialist Party support, 267–268, 278–279
    TR's view of, 45, 215–216
    Wilson's support, 226
    See also Civil rights; Rights
NAWSA. *See* National American Woman Suffrage Association
NCCC. *See* National Conference of Charities and Correction
Nebraska primary elections, 76, 85
Negro Suffrage League, 196
New Deal
    differences from progressivism of 1912, 286–291
    expanded government role, 291
    as extension of Progressive movement, 5
    political realignment, 196, 286, 290–291
    See also Roosevelt, Franklin D.
New England
    town meetings, 220, 225–226
    TR's campaign tour, 187–189, 207
New Freedom (Wilson campaign), 134
    antitrust measures, 16, 179
    Brandeis's influence, 205, 206
    differences from New Nationalism, 16–17, 25, 209–210, 211, 215, 216, 227
    direct democracy, 19

New Freedom (Wilson campaign), *continued*
  opposition to expansion of national
    administrative power, 16, 25, 270
  principles, 205–209
  rights emphasized, 210
  similarities to New Nationalism, 227,
    237–238
  social centers movement, 17–18, 19
  TR's criticism of, 215–216
New Jersey
  primary election, 76, 103, 135
  results of 1912 election, 258
  Wilson as governor, 76, 128, 134–135,
    137–138
New Liberalism, 285–286
New Nationalism
  compared to British Liberal Party
    program, 189–190
  compared to New Deal liberalism,
    286–291
  constitutional implications, 44, 62
  differences from New Freedom, 16–17,
    25, 209–210, 211, 215, 216, 227
  direct democracy, 19, 20
  rejection of interest group, racial, and
    ethnic identities, 166, 176, 214, 258,
    267
  Republican critics of, 115–116
  similarities to New Freedom, 227,
    237–238
  TR's Osawatomie speech, 38, 40–41,
    43–44, 93–94
  See also Roosevelt, Theodore, campaign
    of 1912
New Republic, 264, 272–273, 277, 283–284
Newspapers. *See* Press
New York City
  Tammany Hall, 133
  TR's speech at Madison Square Garden,
    248–251, 252–253
New York Evening Post, 248
New York state
  direct primary bill, 37–38
  Ives v. South Buffalo Ry. Co., 57, 59
  primary election, 83
  Progressive gubernatorial candidate, 153
  state Republican convention, 83
  workmen's compensation law, 57
New York State Socialist Party, 232
New York Sun, 150, 233

New York Times
  coverage of TR's campaign, 218, 219,
    239, 248–249
  criticism of Bryan, 131–132
  criticism of direct primary, 77–78
  on Debs campaign, 234
  editorials, 44, 85, 133–134
  on party conventions, 137
  on Progressive Party convention, 149,
    168
  support of Taft, 103–104
  on TR, 61, 110, 160, 190
  on Wilson, 134
New York Tribune, 277
New York World, 78, 86, 116, 242, 244
Nineteenth Amendment, 280
NIPL. *See* National Independent Political
    League
Normalcy, return to, 4–5, 281, 336n69
Norris, George, 30
North Dakota, primary election, 83

Obama, Barack, 5, 295–298
Occupational Standards Committee,
    National Conference of Charities and
    Correction, 67–68, 69, 157
Ohio
  primary election, 77, 98–103, 112, 115,
    314n41
  Republican convention delegation, 112
  See also "Charter of Democracy" speech
Ohio Progressive League, 50–51
Oklahoma state Republican convention, 82
Old age insurance, 68
The Old Way and the New, 244–245
Organized labor. *See* Labor unions
Osawatomie, Kansas, TR's speech, 38,
    40–41, 43–44, 55, 93–94
Osborn, Chase S., 143
O'Toole, Patricia, 111, 247, 251
Outlook
  on civil rights, 195
  editor, 71
  influence, 87
  on primary elections, 104–105
  on Republican Party, 102–103
  on Taft, 100
  on TR's campaign, 90, 156
  TR's editorials, 71, 153, 160, 194–195, 201
  on Wilson's campaign, 150–151, 156

Presidential power, *continued*
  independence, 3
  populist views of, 15
  socialist opposition to expansion, 236
  wartime expansion, 277–278
Presidents
  direct election of, 234
  evolution of office, 223
  linked to public opinion, 38–39, 182–
    183, 210, 223, 281, 289–290
  modern presidency, 26, 210, 280, 292–
    293, 295
  as party leaders, 3
  recall of, 182–183, 188, 217–219
  relations with Congress, 47
  strong executive, 271–272
  term limits, 136, 271–272
  TR's view of role, 41
  two-term custom, 29
  See also individual presidents
Press
  black newspapers, 174–175, 201
  conservative, 134, 151
  Hearst papers, 4, 132, 226, 242
  La Follette's criticism of, 52
  muckraking journalists, 87–88, 106, 121
  nonpartisan, 4
  power, 88
  progressive, 122, 209
  Progressive Party convention coverage,
    3–4
  Republican, 86, 103–104
  socialist, 229, 231
  supporters of TR, 84, 110
  TR's use of, 4
Primary elections, racial discrimination in,
  288–289
  See also Direct primaries
Primary elections of 1912
  Democratic, 104, 132
  importance, 136–137, 260
  La Follette's campaign, 48, 83, 84, 103,
    106, 204
  Progressive views of, 48
  in Southern states, 167
  Taft's campaigns, 84, 85–86, 87, 96, 97–
    105, 106–107, 115, 138, 314n41
  TR's campaigns, 82–87, 96, 97–105,
    106–107, 138, 212
  TR's campaign workers, 78

Princeton University
  alumni supporters of Wilson, 140, 241
  blacks barred from attending, 197, 200
  Wilson as president, 197, 200, 202
Progressive Bulletin, 211, 214, 254
Progressive National Committee, 166, 169,
  180, 254
Progressive National Service, 254–255,
  262–263
Progressive Party
  African Americans in, 169–172, 173–176,
    196
  antitrust policies, 177–181, 215–217
  attack on two-party system, 131
  collective mission, 147–148, 149, 164
  comparison to Populists, 14–15
  decline, 8, 255–256
  defections to Wilson, 142–143
  demise, 264
  dependence on TR, 261–262
  diverse groups in, 9–10, 11, 153, 159,
    164, 237
  divisions over policies, 16, 144–145, 187,
    257–259
  effects of World War I, 260–261
  electors, 124
  Executive Committee, 180, 254
  expectations following 1912 election,
    254–255, 257
  formation, 119, 121, 122
  labor policies, 203–204, 208, 209, 258, 263
  labor representatives, 202
  leaders, 125, 145
  legacy, 2–5, 251, 263, 269–276, 295–298
  Lincoln Day dinner (1914), 259
  local organizations, 124
  members of Congress, 2
  middle-class members, 17, 23, 152, 165,
    202, 237, 267, 321n96
  moral creed, 153–154, 155
  organization, 124, 262, 263
  racial and ethnic prejudices, 165–166,
    167, 169–172, 176, 201–202
  racial issues, 16, 152, 165, 176, 181, 193
  religiosity, 127, 149–152, 153–154, 164, 258
  seen as personal vehicle for TR, 8–9,
    147–148
  TR's leadership, 145, 146–148, 150, 159,
    164, 257, 262
  view of Constitution, 185–186

Rauschenbusch, Walter C., 112–113, 127,
153, 163, 258
Reagan, Ronald, 292–293
Recall of state court decisions
opponents, 57–58, 59, 252
in Progressive Party platform, 14, 156
Taft's criticism of, 89–90
TR's support, 55–56, 91–92, 93, 217
Wilson's view, 224
Recall power
of judges, 58, 68
labor union support, 203
of presidents, 182–183, 188, 217–219
Progressive Party support, 217
Republican supporters, 42
social workers supporting, 68
TR's support, 55, 183, 188, 217–219
Wilson's support, 224, 225–226
Reconstruction, failure of, 39, 93, 134, 171,
176
Record, George, 255
Red scare, 280
Referenda
labor union support, 203
Progressive Party support, 217
Republican support, 42
TR's support, 50, 55
Wilson's support, 224, 225–226
See also Recall of state court decisions
Reformers
civil rights supporters, 172–173
criticism of political parties, 66, 70–71
differences among, 11, 158
influence on TR, 159–160
political awakening, 62–69
in Progressive Party, 9–10, 125–128, 129,
145–146, 151, 154–156, 164, 181–182
religious views, 71, 127–128
role in Progressive Party platform, 157
support of Wilson's reelection, 273,
335–336n54
views of TR, 12, 128, 158
See also Addams, Jane; Social Gospel
movement; Social workers
Regulation
of business, 16
of railroads, 22, 47
Wilson's position, 205–206
of working hours, 57, 60, 68
See also Antitrust policies

Religion
Catholics, 153, 282
civic, 152, 153
groups in Progressive Party, 153
Men and Religion Forward Movement,
65, 71, 145, 163–164
in Progressive Party, 127, 149–152,
153–154, 164, 258
Protestants, 282, 287
of reformers, 71, 127–128
separation from state, 282–283
toleration, 282–283
See also Social Gospel movement
Republican National Committee, 82, 110,
113, 214, 243
Republican Party
African Americans in, 167, 168, 169,
174, 175, 193, 196, 201, 275
bosses, 84, 101, 102, 107
convention (1884), 312–313n18
economic policies, 80
first national campaign (1856), 186, 255,
256
founding, 186
Hughes as presidential candidate (1916),
273, 275, 335n54
of Lincoln, 93, 117
moderate progressives, 22, 123
nomination contest (1912), 70, 73–74,
80–81, 138
Old Guard (stand-patters), 22, 29, 30, 36,
40, 47, 56, 70, 80, 98, 107–108, 117
opposition to TR's nomination, 21–22,
56, 107–108, 116
patronage in South, 81–82, 169, 174,
175, 196
platform (1908), 29
pre-Civil War political realignment, 230,
255, 256
of Reagan, 292
in southern states, 168, 169
tariff policy, 29, 243
TR's pledge of loyalty, 80–81
See also Taft, William Howard
Republican Party convention (1912),
107–118
African American delegates, 169, 174
conflict between party regulars and
progressives, 107–112, 117–118,
119–120

Roosevelt, Theodore, campaign of 1912,
  continued
  criticism of decision to run, 90–91
  as crusade, 62, 110–113
  decision to run, 44, 50, 51, 53–54
  differences from Republican
    conservatives, 21–22, 56–57, 102–103
  direct democracy issues, 20, 60–61, 81,
    188–189, 217, 222, 239
  early supporters, 44, 53
  electoral votes, 2, 253
  expenses, 78, 106, 312n10
  factors in defeat, 257–259
  financial supporters, 78, 106, 119, 142,
    144, 180, 211–213, 214
  foreign policy, 181
  formation of new party, 112, 124
  general election campaign, 2, 142, 187–
    189, 192
  goals, 27–28, 38, 61–62
  Johnson as running mate, 148, 159, 213,
    254
  labor issues, 203–204
  as main rival of Wilson, 139–140, 144,
    192, 237–238, 254, 258
  New England tour, 187–189, 207
  opportunity for change, 221–222
  organization, 78, 98
  as personality cult, 78–79, 99–102, 106,
    147–148
  popular support, 79, 222
  popular vote total, 2, 253
  primary elections, 82–87, 96, 97–105,
    106–107, 138, 212
  Progressive Party nomination, 148
  Progressive Party platform drafting,
    156–158
  prospect of defeat, 187, 253, 260
  publicity, 98, 106, 243–244, 245
  public perceptions, 110–111, 266
  racial issues, 166–169, 173–174, 187, 193
  radicalism, 188
  reaction to Wilson's nomination, 142–143
  red bandana symbol, 152, 233, 234, 248
  reformers and, 62–69
  regulatory policies, 64–65
  Republican nomination campaign, 56,
    75–81, 82, 111–112
  seen as demagogic, 13, 57, 94, 99, 100,
    189, 191

  similarities to Obama campaign (2008),
    295–298
  southern strategy, 167, 169, 172, 174,
    193, 257
  speeches, 102–103, 126–127, 160, 161,
    187–190, 217–219, 245–251, 252–253
  states carried, 253, 258, 268
  women's suffrage issue and, 160–162
  See also Progressive Party
Roosevelt, Theodore, presidency
  administrative reforms, 6
  antitrust policies, 213
  decision not to run in 1908, 28–29, 90
  foreign policy, 12
  labor policies, 203, 204, 211, 214
  progressive reforms, 11, 22, 38, 126
  publicity techniques, 78, 239–240
  racial issues, 166, 168, 274
  reelection campaign, 7, 212
  relations with Congress, 47–48
  Square Deal policies, 38, 40–41
Roosevelt, Theodore, speeches
  during campaign, 102–103, 160, 161,
    187–190, 217–219, 245–251,
    252–253
  "Charter of Democracy" (Columbus,
    Ohio), 54–56, 59–60, 61–62, 64, 75,
    79, 81, 88–91, 126
  Chicago Auditorium (June 17, 1912),
    111–112
  "Citizenship in a Republic" (Paris),
    30–33, 71, 96–97, 159–160
  "Civic Duty and Social Justice" (May
    1912), 160
  "The Conservation of Womanhood and
    Childhood," 57
  copies mailed to voters, 79
  on European tour (1910), 27, 30–35,
    37
  "Nationalism and Democracy," 71
  in New Orleans, 126–127
  at Osawatomie, Kansas, 38, 40–41,
    43–44, 55, 93–94
  "The Right of the People to Rule"
    (Carnegie Hall, March, 1912), 59–61,
    64, 75, 76, 79
  Romanes lecture, Oxford University,
    33–35, 36, 71
  at University of Berlin, 37
  See also "Confession of Faith" speech

Southern states, *continued*
Progressive Party campaign, 167, 169, 172, 174, 193, 257
Reconstruction, 39, 134, 171, 176
Republican patronage, 81–82, 169, 174, 175, 196
Spingarn, Joel, 167, 172, 173, 174
Square Deal, 38, 40–41
Standard Oil, 212–214
State and local elections
primaries, 6, 37, 76
Progressive candidates, 2, 124–125, 153, 256
State courts. *See* Recall of state court decisions
Straus, Oscar, 153, 256
Sullivan, Mark, 209
Supreme Court
court-packing plan, 288
Dred Scott v. Sandford, 93, 94
Lochner v. New York, 57
Smith v. Allwright, 288–289
Survey, 67, 68, 125, 127

Taft, William Howard
appointments of blacks, 168
campaign of 1908, 7–8, 86
conservatism, 22, 59, 88–91, 190–191, 292
defense of party system, 101
on Lincoln, 92–93
opposition to TR's new policies, 22
patronage, 75
presidency, 29–30, 87–88, 179, 274
press criticism of, 87–88
on Progressive Party convention, 181
progressive policies, 87–88
racial issues and, 193
relationship with TR, 99
as secretary of war, 168
support of TR's policies as president, 22
support of two-party system, 191–192
TR's disappointment in presidency of, 27, 29–30, 36
Taft, William Howard, campaign of 1912
acceptance of nomination, 120–121
active participation, 86–87, 98, 115, 190–191
African American support, 193, 201, 257, 314n41

antitrust policies, 179
campaign films, 243
criticism of TR's views, 88–91, 93–94, 99, 100–102, 191
expenses, 106
general election campaign, 2, 185, 190–192
humor used, 100–101
lack of charisma, 240
nomination, 115, 117–119, 120
organization, 81–82, 97–98
popular vote total, 253
primary elections, 84, 85–86, 87, 96, 97–105, 106–107, 115, 138, 314n41
prospect of defeat, 192, 237, 260
publicity techniques, 243
reaction to election results, 256–257
Republican nomination campaign, 44, 56, 70, 73–74, 75, 88–91
rivalry with TR, 56
Root's support, 115–116
on socialism, 228
Southern support, 81–82
speeches, 59, 100–102, 190–191
state conventions, 82, 83
states carried, 253
support of Constitution, 120–121, 185, 267
Tammany Hall, 133
Taney, Roger, 93
Tariff policy
Democratic Party platform, 136, 143
Progressive view of, 12
of Republicans, 29, 243
of TR, 12, 83, 144
Wilson on, 139, 143, 227, 272
Taxes, 41
Texas
Brownsville Affair, 166, 168
delegates to Republican convention, 109
Textile workers, 206–207, 228–229, 231
Thelen, David, 202
Theodore Roosevelt; Fighter for Social Justice, 243–244
Thomas, Joseph A., 170
Tillman Act, 212
Times (London), 70, 110–111, 119–120, 129, 136, 140, 221–222
Titanic, 127
Tocqueville, Alexis de, 18, 45–46, 72
Town meetings, 50, 220, 225–226

Trevelyan, George, 29
Trotter, William Monroe, 173, 193–194,
    199–201, 257, 273–275
Troy, Gil, 6, 7
Truman, Harry S., 289
Trusts
    film industry, 244
    Progressive efforts to curb, 1–2, 10
    TR's policies, 64–65
    See also Antitrust policies
Tucker, William Jewitt, 163
Turner, George Kibbe, 106
Twenty-First Amendment, 287–288

Uncle Remus Magazine, 168
Underwood, Oscar W., 132, 133
Unemployment insurance, 68
Unions. *See* Labor unions
Unitarians, 151–152
United Trades and Labor Council (Buffalo,
    New York), 206
Universal Studios, 244–245
Urban counties, votes in 1912 election,
    253–254, 257–258

Vernon, Leroy T., 98
Villard, Oswald Garrison, 175, 198–200,
    274
Voter turnout, 259–260
Voting rights. *See* Civil rights; Women's
    suffrage

Wald, Lillian, 158, 162, 167, 261
Waldron, J. Milton, 194, 199–201
Wall Street Journal, 151
Walters, Alexander, 196–197
War on Terror, 293, 296
Warren, Fred, 233
Washburn, Charles, 62
Washington, Booker T., 166, 175, 193
Washington Evening Star, 78
Welfare state
    Progressive interest in building, 105–106,
        154, 163, 263–264
    Progressive Party platform, 14, 24,
        157–158, 162
    public readiness, 263–264
    TR's support, 154
Weyl, Walter E., 80, 166
Whig Party, 255, 256

White, William Allen
    participation in Progressive campaign, 12
    Perkins and, 180
    on Progressive convention (1916), 262
    on Progressive platform committee,
        13–14, 177
    at Republican convention, 111, 118
    on similarities between Wilson and TR
        campaigns, 237
    on TR's role in Progressive Party, 164
White supremacy, 35, 170, 171, 288–289
Wiebe, Robert, 73, 285
Wilentz, Sean, 297–298
Willard, Charles Dwight, 46
Wilson, Woodrow
    interest in British political system,
        240–241
    on labor unions, 202–203
    on local self-government, 16–17
    as New Jersey governor, 76, 128, 134–
        135, 137–138
    personal qualities, 134, 192, 240, 242
    on political parties, 19–20, 137–138
    pragmatism, 136
    as Princeton president, 197, 200, 202
    progressive policies, 128–129, 134–136,
        208
    public opinion and, 271, 272
    racial views, 134, 197, 199–201
Wilson, Woodrow, campaign of 1912
    acceptance of nomination, 139, 141, 151,
        156, 158
    African American support, 197–201, 257,
        273, 274
    antitrust policies, 16, 177, 179, 205–206,
        223
    Brandeis as advisor, 16, 198, 204–205,
        206, 207–208, 213, 223
    campaign films, 243, 244–245
    campaign style, 140–142
    candidate-centered, 240–243
    constitutional views, 134, 135–136
    criticism of Republican nomination
        contest, 138
    criticism of TR, 187, 211, 213
    direct democracy issues, 223–227
    electoral votes, 253
    financing, 140–141
    general election campaign, 2, 192, 226,
        242–243